THE AGE
OF CLINTON

ALSO BY GIL TROY

THE AGE OF CLINTON

OF CLINTON

····························

AMERICA IN THE 1990s

····························

GIL TROY

THOMAS DUNNE BOOKS ≋ ST. MARTIN'S PRESS NEW YORK

THOMAS DUNNE BOOKS.
An imprint of St. Martin's Press.

THE AGE OF CLINTON. Copyright © 2015 by Gil Troy. All rights reserved. Printed in the United States of America. For information, address St. Martin's Press, 175 Fifth Avenue, New York, N.Y. 10010.

www.thomasdunnebooks.com
www.stmartins.com

Designed by Steven Seighman

The Library of Congress Cataloging-in-Publication Data is available upon request.

ISBN 978-1-250-063724 (hardcover)
ISBN 978-1-4668-6873-1 (e-book)

Our books may be purchased in bulk for promotional, educational, or business use. Please contact your local bookseller or the Macmillan Corporate and Premium Sales Department at (800) 221-7945, extension 5442, or by e-mail at MacmillanSpecialMarkets@macmillan.com.

First Edition: October 2015

10 9 8 7 6 5 4 3 2 1

To Linda and the kids, the best things that happened to me in the Age of Clinton

Contents

Constant revolutionizing of production, uninterrupted disturbance of all social conditions, everlasting uncertainty, and agitation distinguish the bourgeois epoch from all earlier ones. All fixed, fast-frozen relations, with their train of ancient and venerable prejudices and opinions, are swept away, all new-formed ones become antiquated before they can ossify. All that is solid melts into air, all that is holy is profaned.

—KARL MARX AND FRIEDRICH ENGELS, *THE COMMUNIST MANIFESTO*, 1848

A professor named Carroll Quigley . . . said to us that America was the greatest Nation in history because our people had always believed in two things—that tomorrow can be better than today and that every one of us has a personal moral responsibility to make it so.

—BILL CLINTON, NOMINATION ACCEPTANCE SPEECH, JULY 16, 1992, NEW YORK

My own belief is that human beings, particularly the American people, are capable of enduring a lot of difficulty and a lot of tumult and upheaval if they understand it. What makes people insecure is when they feel like they're lost in the funhouse. They're in a room where something can hit them from any direction any time. . . . If you understand what's happening to you, you can make . . . not just changes but necessary psychological adaptations.

—BILL CLINTON, ABOARD *AIR FORCE ONE*, SEPTEMBER 22, 1995

THE AGE
OF CLINTON

"Lost in the Funhouse"

How Bill Clinton Invented the Nineties

There are changes we can make from the outside in; that's the job of the president and the Congress and the governors and the mayors and the social service agencies. And then there's some changes we're going to have to make from the inside out, or the others won't matter.

—BILL CLINTON, MEMPHIS, NOVEMBER 13, 1993

On November 13, 1993, the new president of the United States addressed five thousand African American ministers at the Mason Temple church in Memphis, Tennessee, where Martin Luther King Jr. had delivered his "been to the mountaintop" sermon the night before his assassination. The broad-shouldered forty-seven-year-old Arkansan, just a tad stocky but radiating an attractive celebrity-powered energy, with a ruddy-cheeked baby face topped anomalously by mostly gray hair, looked and sounded more like a snake-charming televangelist than the Leader of the Free World. His Southern accent was surprisingly heavy; his manner delightfully informal; his words disarmingly frank. Junking his prepared text about NAFTA, the controversial free trade agreement, riffing off scribbled notes, he spoke passionately about "the great crisis of the spirit that is gripping America today."

His hosts had introduced him lovingly as "Bishop Clinton." Theatrically wiping away a tear after a second round of hugs, he joked that if he had been a "better boy" he would have become a preacher. Turning serious, President Bill Clinton wondered what Martin Luther King would say if he reappeared now twenty-five years after his death. "You did a good job, he would say," Clinton purred lyrically, repeatedly, cataloging the nation's progress and the African American community's advances, becoming freer, richer, more integrated.

Then, he delivered the bad news. "But," the president imagined King saying,

"I did not live and die to see the American family destroyed." The audience hesitated. Recognizing these words as the loving challenge of a friend, the preachers erupted in applause. "I did not live and die to see thirteen-year-old boys get automatic weapons and gun down nine-year-olds just for the kick of it." More applause. "I did not live and die to see people destroy their own lives with drugs and build drug fortunes destroying the lives of others. That is not what I came here to do." The audience roared.

With the stormy smoothness of a revivalist preacher, the first Democratic president since Jimmy Carter risked sounding like a Reaganite to break the Republican monopoly on values talk. "My fellow Americans," Clinton's resurrected King lamented, "I fought to stop white people from being so filled with hate that they would wreak violence on black people. I did not fight for the right of black people to murder other black people with reckless abandon." Mourning the 18,300 Americans who would die from gunshot wounds in 1993, and the 160,000 children staying home daily fearing neighborhood violence, Clinton wondered: "How could we explain that we gave people the freedom to succeed, and we created conditions in which millions abuse that freedom to destroy the things that make life worth living and life itself?"

The president then made two revolutionary, countercultural statements, which too many Democrats had spent too many years resisting. He linked "the accumulated weight of crime and violence and the breakdown of family and community and the increase in drugs and the decrease in jobs." This was the Great Cultural Train Wreck of post-Sixties' liberalism. Clinton's focus on work echoed the leading sociologist William Julius Wilson. Addressing family, social pathologies, and other cultural problems had for too long been considered Republican territory. Clinton warned we would fail "unless we say some of this cannot be done by Government, because we have to reach deep inside to the values, the spirit, the soul, and the truth of human nature."

Ending three decades of false choices between big government and good values, between fixing politics or culture, with a new synthesis, Clinton discussed "changes we can make from the outside in," meaning with government intervention, combined with the "changes we're going to have to make from the inside out, or the others won't matter." He told his friend Taylor Branch that the speech "just welled up." He considered it his best speech so far, "bar none." Two decades and thousands of addresses later, many agreed.

Bill Clinton: As Ideological As Ronald Reagan

The speech electrified the nation. Blacks' acceptance of this presidential message reflected their community's widespread trust in this son of the New South. Recognizing what Clinton and his British colleague Tony Blair would eventually call the Third Way, *The Washington Post*'s E. J. Dionne wrote that Clinton's attempt to synthesize liberals' notion that "government has a large role to play in fostering social justice," with conservatives' idea that government "is no substitute for nurturing families and strong communities . . . may be a more challenging political project than balancing the budget or creating a new health system." Surprisingly, the civil rights activist Jesse Jackson agreed that the "premier civil rights issue of this day is youth violence in general and black-on-black crime in particular." Jackson also believed "we must look inward in order to go onward."

Bill Clinton ran for the presidency to trigger this kind of conversation. He wanted to make history using the president's bully pulpit. He wanted to preserve traditional values with a liberal, open, pro-government but not big government twist. As a shrewd reader of modern politics, he knew that Democrats would lose if Republicans always trumped them on the three Fs of family, faith, and flag. Clinton's governing philosophy was as comprehensive as Ronald Reagan's. First articulated while addressing the centrist Democratic Leadership Council in the mid-1980s, Clinton's fusion of opportunity, responsibility, and community to revitalize liberalism guided him throughout his presidency.

When Clinton was at his worst, he pandered. When he was at his most popular, he triangulated. But when he was at his best—as he was in Memphis—he synthesized, navigating with his centrist vision. His ability to fuse Reaganite conservatism and Great Society liberalism, the 1950s and the 1960s, traditional anchors and modern freedoms, the opportunities provided by so many rights and the strong communities that emerged from a suitable sense of responsibility, the Hillbillies and the Yalies, Main Street and Wall Street, America's superego and America's id, reflected his and America's dueling legacies, impulses, and beliefs. Balancing it all properly, constructively, he believed, was "the purpose of prosperity," and would, he vowed, help disoriented Americans, many of whom felt "lost in the funhouse" of the 1990s.

It's time to take Bill Clinton, his presidency, and his times seriously. Historians dithered before "getting right with Reagan," letting their political and intellectual disdain discourage thoughtful scholarship for over two decades after his inauguration. The media's obsession with both Clintons' character flaws, fed by Bill and Hillary Clinton's characteristically Baby Boomer self-righteousness masking self-indulgence, have disappointed and distracted too many chroniclers.

Hillary Clinton's ongoing political saga has added more confusion. She simultaneously evades and embraces her husband's tenure, let alone her own complicated track record in the 1990s. Approaching the twenty-fifth anniversary of Clinton's campaign launch, with Hillary Clinton running yet again for president, with illuminating Clinton papers and oral histories now being released, it is time to examine Clinton clearly, seeing through the clouds of his own inconstancy and the constant media barrage, assessing his vision, his policies, his achievements, and his synergy with the 1990s.

Hillary Clinton: Polarizing First Lady in Gossamer Shackles

First Lady Hillary Rodham Clinton was also trying to shape American attitudes, albeit less successfully. The apple-cheeked, unnaturally blonde, forty-five-year-old's blue eyes reflected the fierce intelligence of the overachiever she always was, while her changing hair styles reflected a new insecurity about just what kind of First Lady the American people—and the press—would let her be. Her "politics of meaning" speech in April 1993, similarly advocating "a new ethos of individual responsibility and caring" after the Reagan era's "selfishness and greed," elicited sneers in *The New York Times Magazine* and elsewhere mocking "Saint Hillary."

This polarizing First Lady discovered that Americans were less open to challenges from what Nancy Reagan called the "white glove pulpit" with its silk handcuffs, than from the bully pulpit with its mandate to be America's superman. Hillary Clinton's attempts to share power as "co-president" failed. She was, essentially, fired from her public role as Bill Clinton's sentry—and backbone.

The Whitewater, Travelgate, and presidential pardon and furniture-grabbing scandals in 2001 revealed the thickness of Mr. and Mrs. Clinton's private partnership. Still, her popularity grew when most Americans considered her the victim of her husband's infidelity and when she earned power independently as a senator, rather than hijacking status from her husband. As substantive as Eleanor Roosevelt, as culturally influential as Jackie Kennedy, as controversial as Nancy Reagan, Hillary Clinton would become one of the 1990s' defining icons.

Clinton: A President Who Defined His Decade

Bill Clinton was an extraordinarily talented politician who dominated the 1990s, just as Ronald Reagan dominated the 1980s, and Franklin Roosevelt dominated the 1930s. Not all presidents define their times culturally as well as politically; these three leaders did. And perhaps even more than the 1930s and the 1980s, the 1990s was a time of breathtaking transformation as computers became increasingly networked and portable, taking this revolution viral.

Trying to understand Clinton without studying the politics, culture, technology, and society that shaped him—and which he shaped—is like looking through night-vision goggles, even the enhanced ones sharpened by photocathode technology breakthroughs in the late 1990s. You think you see the subject clearly, but you need daylight and peripheral vision to appreciate the landscape fully. This book's central assumption is that we can best understand Clinton and the 1990s by overlaying the story of his presidency on the broader story of the decade, viewing the two together, to see what stands out.

Particularly sensitive to the changes taking place, Clinton would describe his primary achievement as "He had to make America work in a new world." Characteristically for Clinton and his age, this statement sounded more like a challenge partially unfulfilled than a program fully realized. More concretely, his speechwriter Jeff Shesol says Clinton showed that "Government did not have to be big for it to be a catalyst for positive change in people's lives." Clinton's ideological guru from the moderate Democratic Leadership Council, Al From, says Clinton "saved progressive politics, all over the world, by modernizing it."

Making America work in this new world would not be easy. Internet-powered computers, Everything Machines that seemed accessible everywhere, intensified the modernization processes buffeting America—and the world—since the industrial revolution. Clinton had one foot planted in the solid world of the past and another in the fluid world of the present. He grew up in the sleepy South, amid the artifacts of America's 1950s "Howdy Doody" innocence. Towns often featured rumbling trains and corner grocery stores, where "everybody" knew your name, in real life, not in sitcoms. Homes had squeaky, glossy, linoleum kitchen floors and stiff, overstuffed living rooms. New, clunky hi-fis and wooden television consoles filled many of these parlors, often alongside grainy black-and-white photos in gilded frames of dads who had fought in "W. W. II, The Big One," be they dead or alive. Schools used *Dick and Jane* primers instilling good manners and good morals, reinforcing the conventions of Fifties' family life, while teaching reading fundamentals. A Coke cost 5 cents. A gallon of gas cost 18 cents. A Mr. Potato Head toy kit cost a dollar.

As the Baby Boomer rebels' torchbearer, Clinton embodied the tumult of the 1960s. Access to America's finest schools plunged him into political, cultural, ideological, and moral revolutions. He grew his hair mountain-man-long, along with a beard, encountered the drug culture—whether or not he inhaled—dodged

Vietnam, detested racism, idolized Martin Luther King Jr. and Bobby Kennedy, relished rock 'n' roll, and roamed sexually. He worked on George McGovern's anti-war, pro-choice 1972 presidential campaign, with his girlfriend and eventual wife, Hillary. By the 1980s, as many of his "Big Chill" peers went yuppie, he shaved, cut his hair, and donned a suit, impressing many peers by forgoing New York riches and Washington glory to serve the public at home in gritty Arkansas.

He would then preside over what was now a different America during the rollicking 1990s. Wal-Mart hollowed-out small towns, bankrupting Main Streets as big city anonymity and uniformity spread. Even airports and downtowns started to look like shopping malls, filled with nationally franchised restaurants and stores providing cookie-cutter designs to mass-produce experiences. Homes were larger, sturdier, sleeker, and fancier, filled with electronic gadgets that increasingly defined their owners, with a growing digital divide between the Mac person and the PC person. Bart and Lisa Simpson, Jerry and Elaine from *Seinfeld,* and Monica and Chandler from *Friends* had defeated Dick and Jane, mocking moral uplift, encouraging a "whatever" culture of chaos. A can of Coke—or Diet Coke—now cost a dollar. A gallon of post-energy-crisis gas averaged $1.15. Handheld Nintendo Game Boys debuted at $109.

The Age of Clinton was a time of great wonders and great worries. Defining characters of the time included: Baby Einstein toddlers, Harry Potter fanatics, super-pressured suburban preppies, buff teenage boys, scrunchy-wearing high school girls, couch potatoes who were now mouse potatoes, Goths in black, stoned grungers in flannel, drifting Gen Xers, Seattle latte sippers, menacing gangsta rappers, scandalmongering journalists, Angry White Male voters, fire-and-brimstone evangelists, still-smoldering feminists, indulgent celebrities, Red State conservatives and Red State divorcees, Blue State cosmopolitans and Blue State prigs, married homosexuals, famous lesbians, African American professionals, geeky engineers, billionaire nerds, casually clad Baby Boomers, slick Wall Street titans, flextiming telecommuters, overextended parents, deadbeat dads, single moms, Soccer Moms, Hispanic immigrants, symbolic analysts, Dilbert drones, ever-expanding junk food junkies, ever-better-defined fitness freaks, leisure world retirees, and, in an ever-healthier world with greater longevity, scrawny octogenarians. Each stereotype represents a different piece of America's mosaic, circa 1990s.

The Age of Clinton was the Age of Virtual Prosperity, both because the computer revolution helped fuel the boom, and because debate continues over how real the benefits were and for whom. It was an Age of Indulgence, with the excesses often triggering anxiety and guilt. And, with all the nervousness about the amazing changes, it was an Era of Mixed Feelings, when Americans felt confused morally, ideologically, economically, even amid the unambiguous miracles, technologically, medically, democratically, economically, artistically.

Five Significant Revolutions, One Counterrevolution, and Six Presidencies

Bill Clinton liked calling the 1990s a "bridge" to the twenty-first century, but it was more like a runway, with changes accumulating, building momentum, then taking off. At least five significant revolutions and one counterrevolution occurred in the 1990s, which both shaped and were shaped by Clinton's presidency.

The ongoing Rainbow Revolution made America more diverse demographically and pluralistic ideologically. In a nation long obsessed with race as a black-white dichotomy, the browning of America as Hispanics immigrated en masse, with this broadening spectrum including Asians, had America becoming much less white, but not just black.

With the Digital Revolution accelerating, with technological devices made more powerful, more mobile, and more networked, computers (and many other seemingly miraculous devices) no longer simply extended Americans' reach but transformed their lives. "Hyperlinks subvert hierarchy," creating a new, empowering, human-to-human conversation, Internet enthusiasts insisted. In becoming so connected to technology, some Americans feared disconnecting from tradition and each other.

With desktop computers now ubiquitous, the Internet exploding, finance ever more sophisticated, and manufacturing withering amid global competition, the twenty-first century economy emerged. With this Information Age Reset as the third revolution, the new knowledge-based economy valued special skills, and proved better at generating great wealth than distributing it broadly.

The high-tech revolution also furthered the 1960s' cultural revolution, putting the anything-goes, all-stimulation-all-the-time media into the palms of Americans' hands 24/7. The twentieth century was a centrifugal century, propelling Americans away from communal norms toward their own individualistic paths. Alas, all the leisure, all the disposable income, all the indulgence, did not yield happiness and often created the loneliness and distress of affluenza.

On the flip side was Oprah Winfrey's emergence as America's mother confessor, agent provocateur, icon of diversity, preacher, teacher, and healer. In this I'm-OK-You're-OK Contingency Carnival, the fourth revolution, Americans learned to tolerate different behaviors, not just different looks and backgrounds. Echoing America's evangelical past but in diluted form, Oprah's insurgency in the 1990s, while no Second Great Awakening, was certainly a Well-Marketed Comforting.

Underlying and intensifying these moral and cultural revolutions were revolutions in sex and sexuality. America's mass Gender Bender led to more public and explicit discussions of sex, the proliferation of Internet porn, more acceptance of what had once been deemed deviant, especially regarding homosexuality, more equality between men and women—and more confusion about sex and sexuality.

Such departures inevitably stirred great anxiety and political pushback. The Republican Resistance tried launching a counterrevolution, in politics, culture, and thought. Conservatives triumphed occasionally, especially winning the Congress in 1994 for the first time in almost half a century and working with Clintonized Democrats to reduce crime and discourage divorce. Yet Republicans not only failed to stop America's cultural revolution, many were swept along in it, too.

These wrenching changes help decipher the Clinton conundrum, namely, how could such a talented politician leave so many Americans feeling they achieved so little when he accomplished so much during this time of great potential? The American communal conundrum is how did a society so rich and so free appear so lost and so unhappy? The cultural changes Clinton advanced and surfed undermined his political agenda. The new world he, his wife, and their peers helped spawn was so foreign, he paid an exorbitant political price.

The result was a roller-coaster presidency. So many surprises pop up in the Oval Office, the learning curve is so steep, that every presidency is best understood as a play divided into multiple acts, often with dramatic character changes along the way. The Booms and Busts with this presidency, however, were particularly intense. The Clinton presidency's Act I was Bush League, with amateurish distractions about gays in the military and Cabinet appointments. Clinton found his footing and started forging the First Third Way, Act II, with a balanced budget and NAFTA passing within his first year of office. Act III, the Republican Contract on Clinton, built throughout 1994 as health care reform withered, culminating in the Democrats losing control of the House of Representatives in November and the rise of Newt Gingrich's imperial speakership. With the Oklahoma bombing and the successful reelection campaign, the Nanny Statesman of Act IV emerged, from spring 1995 through the end of 1997, winning welfare reform and reelection. The Lewinsky scandal caused The Lost

Year of 1998, Act V, whereupon, remarkably, Clinton concluded with Act VI, his Second Third Way.

Clinton understood America's confusion and despair. He saw the fallout from the 1960s' changes even as he celebrated many of them. His Memphis speech, among many other efforts, tried recapturing America's lost innocence, rooting Americans in some of their traditions and long-standing assumptions, even while preparing them for the extraordinary changes ahead. In this updated, Arkansas-accented yuppie Greek tragedy, Clinton's great insight, his recognition of these moral challenges and the tangle of pathology linking sexual indulgence, family breakdown, communal decay, and individual distress, could not stop him from making things worse due to his own character flaws. For all his ambition and his triumphs, he also left the nation politically polarized, economically imbalanced, and far too vulnerable to Osama bin Laden's evil.

The most famous song from *Rent,* the edgy opera of an age of few illusions, counts out "five hundred twenty-five thousand six hundred minutes," asking "How do you measure a year in the life?" This is the historian's question, wondering what standards to use and from what perspective. Is it the 86,400 seconds in a day, those now-famous half-million minutes in a year, the ten years in a decade? *The Age of Clinton* examines Bill Clinton's presidency, emphasizing domestic policy more than foreign policy, in the context of the Nineties' five-million-plus American minutes. Each chapter chronicles a different year, often focused on a particular moment, to identify key themes. This approach grounds sweeping trends in that mix of the pedestrian and the spectacular that shapes an epoch, and everybody's life. The intent is neither to demonize nor canonize Clinton but to understand and explain.

A Challenge to Readers

Last year, while writing this book, I turned to a colleague, saying, "I'm frustrated. Bill Clinton made astute statements about family, work, community, responsibility, and freedom. Yet the Monica Lewinsky sex scandal upstages, eliciting snickers when I quote his talks about values." Professor Suzanne Last Stone of Benjamin N. Cardozo School of Law advised: "Challenge your readers. Push them to move beyond their prejudices!" Thus, this challenge. Clinton's behavior was "immoral" and "disgust[ing]." It was "wrong" for him, "wrong" for his "family, and wrong for" Ms. Lewinsky. He "hurt the presidency and the people" by his "misconduct." It "was no one's fault but" his "own."

These words were not taken from the Starr Report, Fox News, or any

Republican's impeachment speech. They are quotations from pages 773, 774, and 776 of Clinton's memoir *My Life*. Richard Nixon spent two decades trying to undo the damage of Watergate, knowing his one-line obituary would be "first American president to resign." Clinton's moral and legal failures were not as spectacular. Still, modern readers must compartmentalize, just as the American people did. Ultimately, the majority of Americans accepted his argument to judge his presidency by his public record. I make no such request beyond challenging us all to move beyond the quick smirk, sneer, or cheer, and see both Clintons in all their dimensionality, in the complicating context of the 1990s.

A shamelessly entertaining Baby Boomer politician who considered becoming a professional musician, Clinton could blow out a tune energetically on the saxophone. He demonstrated his mastery on *The Arsenio Hall Show* in 1992 and at the 1993 Inaugural Ball when he played "Your Mama Don't Dance" with Ben E. King while bopping with Dionne Warwick and Judy Collins—whose 1969 cover of the Joni Mitchell song "Chelsea Morning" gave his only daughter her name. This skill, paralleling his extraordinary political charms, evokes the alluring power of what Walt Whitman called "The Mystic Trumpeter." The poem captures the transcendent power of music—and of a master politician plying his mysterious arts: "What charm thy music works! / . . . O trumpeter, methinks I am myself the instrument thou playest, / Thou melt'st my heart, my brain—thou movest, drawest, changest them at will; / And now thy sullen notes send darkness through me."

For most of the 1990s, many Americans were swept up by Bill Clinton, the "chaotically surging" Mystic Saxophonist. He melted their hearts, changed them at will, and, when he stumbled, sent darkness through them. This is his, and America's, story.

1

1990: Houston
Cowboy Cosmopolitanism
and the End of History?

*For a new breeze is blowing, and a world refreshed by freedom seems
reborn; for in man's heart, if not in fact, the day of the dictator is over.*
—GEORGE H. W. BUSH, INAUGURAL ADDRESS, JANUARY 20, 1989

On Monday morning, January 1, 1990, the president of the United States
and his wife awoke in Suite 271 of the Houstonian, a 22-acre resort in
Houston, Texas, that served as their official voting address. The plush setting,
with 66,000 square feet of athletic facilities in the shadow of Houston's gleaming
office towers, epitomized the city's—and the president's—cowboy cosmo-
politanism, mixing Texas pioneers' traditional, hardscrabble, frontier values with
the glitzy, gilded, boom-time sensibilities of the Eighties. Charging $12,500
in initiation fees, the swanky spa was where God would live "if he'd been rich,"
locals joshed. The president's enemies sneered that between his ancestral
Kennebunkport, Maine, estate and his years in Washington, America's chief
executive was using this $550-a-night hotel address as both tax dodge and
subterfuge, helping this Connecticut Yankee aristocrat impersonate a Texan.

December 31 began for George H. W. Bush with a quick flight to San Antonio, to visit soldiers wounded in the invasion of Panama. He had launched
Operation Just Cause eleven days earlier to depose the drug-running, election-
sabotaging Panamanian dictator Manuel Noriega. That afternoon, the president golfed at the exclusive Houston Country Club. The game ended ominously
with a missed putt.

As the president returned to his hotel suite, Houstonians were planning
splashy celebrations to ring in the 1990s. Nearby, the Yellow Rose Carriage
Company was offering horse-drawn tours around the Houston Galleria Mall,
the gleaming campus of consumption that was one of America's ten largest
malls. Modeled after Milan's glass-domed nineteenth-century Galleria Vittorio

Emanuele II, the mall covered 1.6 million square feet, featuring Neiman Marcus as its luxurious anchor, a skating rink, an office tower, and two hotels.

Across town, the Washington Avenue Showbar was hosting its "New Year's Eve Party of the Decade" a "going-away party for Ronnie, Nancy, Ollie, Jim & Tammy, Oprah & Geraldo . . . and the other crazies of the '80s." Houstonians were finishing a wild decade. Americans were enjoying an eighty-six-month economic expansion as of January 1990 that the Reaganaut economist Martin Anderson called "the greatest economic expansion the world has ever seen." More remarkably, America was winning the Cold War, burying the fundamental assumption that the United States and the USSR would be facing off for centuries. Texan swagger seemed appropriate for the entire country: richer, safer, more confident than anyone would have dared imagine a decade earlier.

Houston We Have Problems

Still, for all the progress, Americans' fantasy that they were free of history and headaches was overblown. The oil glut that helped trigger the Reagan boom nationwide ruined many Texans. Salaries drooped as the crude oil price dropped—from $37.42 per barrel in 1980 to $18.33 in 1989. "The Capital of the Sunbelt" also suffered as Ronald Reagan's budget cuts reduced federal aid to cities by two-thirds, from $37.3 billion in 1980 to $12.1 billion a decade later. With housing prices sagging and jobs disappearing, Houston was troubled.

Desperate and clever, Texans started modernizing. Houston was more than crude cowboys and speculating oilmen. Hosting NASA's Mission Control at the Johnson Space Center, the nation's largest concentration of petrochemical processing plants, and Rice University's sophisticated medical facilities, "Space City" evolved into yet another white-collar urban R and D center. During the decade, Texas grew twice as fast as the rest of the nation.

America's fourth most populous city, with 1.6 million people, Houston was one of its most sprawling, nearly half the size of Rhode Island. Reflecting modern urban America's two great shames, H-Town's poverty rate hit 15 percent in 1990, and crime jumped by as much as 29 percent during the 1980s. The crack epidemic tripled the number of cocaine users nationwide from 1986 to 1989, reinvigorating America's post-1960s crime wave. More than twenty thousand Americans were murdered annually, often in crack-related disputes or frenzies.

President Bush unveiled a $1.2 billion crime package in May 1989. But fear and resignation prowled too many streets. "When people are afraid to walk out of their houses, between sundown and sunup, it's a big problem and to ignore it is a political mistake," recalls Al From, who was challenging fellow Democrats to restore party credibility by fighting crime seriously.

A decade later in 1999, Houston's homicide rate would be down by 63 percent from its peak. Statewide, despite a population that would grow 25 percent, the number of crimes would drop more than 20 percent. Effective policing initiated by Houston's Lee Brown, among others, worked. Brown would become New York's first African American police commissioner in January 1990. Prosperity, an aging population, more police on the streets, more criminals in jail, and, most important, fewer crackheads helped too. More broadly, America's "recivilization" during the 1990s, as the Harvard neuropsychologist Steven Pinker calls it, would reduce the number of violent assaults against the body nationwide, although many feared mounting assaults against the soul.

The wave of Hispanic immigration continued, doubling the number of Hispanics in America from 1990 to 2010, reaching 50 million, 1 in 6 Americans. In absorbing what one demographer would call "an entire Venezuela's worth of Hispanics," America's capacity for diversity expanded exponentially. Jesse Jackson's rainbow rhetoric of the 1980s became a demographic reality of the 1990s nationwide. In 1980, 64 percent of Houston was non-Hispanic white; 19 percent was black; 15 percent was Hispanic. In 1990, only 57 percent was non-Hispanic white, the black percentage was 18 percent while the number of Hispanics grew, now constituting 21 percent of the city's population. Many of those Hispanics also accounted for the 13 percent of Houstonians who were foreign born.

A mass of "illegal" immigrants, ranging from 4.5 million to as high as 13 million people nationwide, posed social, political, and ideological challenges—even if advocates prettified the phenomenon by calling them "undocumented" or "unauthorized." Texas had at least 438,000 illegals in 1990. The number would more than double to over 1 million in 2000.

America in the 1990s would welcome more immigrants than ever. Both the authorized and unauthorized immigrants enriched and enlivened America. Still, a functioning democracy could not have millions of residents living in the shadows. A proud nation could not have the rule of law flouted and its borders violated. Individuals in a democracy could not be marginalized, exploited, abused, and perpetually branded illegal, with the economy addicted to these shadow workers who earned less than citizens for menial jobs.

For all these challenging changes, a charming traditional streak persisted, even in this muggy, traffic-choked, oil refinery–smelly, sprawling, corporate tower–dominated modernist city. Many Houstonians' New Year's Day celebrations would include black-eyed peas, a Southern talisman for good luck, perhaps because the beans swelled when cooked, suggesting expanding horizons for the

New Year, perhaps because the humble dish was the rare food marauding Northern troops did not bother seizing during the Civil War.

The president and First Lady had a more pedestrian takeout Chinese dinner by candlelight. "We were the earliest people in bed in America, I think. Nine o'clock, reading in bed," Barbara Bush reported. She and the president hadn't "seen midnight" in forty New Year's eves. In 1980, this big-boned, no-nonsense, matronly woman's down-to-earth Waspy refusal to dye her hair had prompted mean gibes that the fifty-six-year-old George Bush was campaigning with his mother. Now, her authenticity fed her popularity as the antidote to the imperious, nouveau riche Nancy Reagan.

From Cold War to World Peace?

Mrs. Bush deflected questions about her New Year's resolutions by vowing to "give up desserts . . . until tonight, maybe." Her husband, who had been outed that Saturday crumbling Butterfinger candy bar bits on his oat bran while standing on the resort's breakfast line, took the question more seriously. His New Year's wish, he said, was "Peace. World peace."

Bush's formulaic answer seemed heartfelt—and suddenly attainable—that magical New Year's Day. The nuclear-tinged Cold War conflict between the United States and the Soviet Union itself was ending, smoothly, peacefully, surprisingly quickly. In Prague, 5,450 miles away, the dissident playwright Václav Havel had just been sworn in as Czechoslovakia's ninth president, only eight months after international intervention freed him from prison. Havel ascended following the lightning-fast, student-spurred, forty-one-day "Velvet Revolution." This mustachioed modern prophet promised democratic elections within six months and freed thousands of prisoners, to start the post-Communist healing.

Bush's cautious streak had made him mealy-mouthed throughout 1989. His formidable mother Dorothy Walker Bush had taught him not to gloat. His national security adviser Brent Scowcroft and others doubted the Communist implosion and feared infuriating the Soviets. Scowcroft insisted "The Cold War is not over," two days after Bush's inauguration. The president wanted a "very deliberate" foreign policy: "encouraging, guiding, and managing change without provoking backlash and crackdown." When asked whether the Cold War had ended, the president sputtered: "so I—but if the—in the—I want to try to avoid words like Cold War."

Meteoric progress throughout 1989 compelled a new tone. Bush had interrupted his post-Christmas hunting trip to send a message promising American support for Czechoslovakian democracy. The White House statement said

Havel's "astonishing" December 29 election "marks a fitting end to a year of astonishing change in Eastern Europe."

In Moscow, the general secretary of the Soviet Communist Party and the president of the Supreme Soviet, Mikhail Gorbachev, the man most responsible for this peaceful upheaval, was acknowledging 1989 as "the most difficult year of perestroika," his restructuring and reform program. Stores were empty. Workers were mobilizing. Provinces were restive, with ethnic extremists rioting sporadically. Nevertheless, Gorbachev, who had discussed these changes with Bush in Malta in early December, toasted 1989 as "the year of the ending of the cold war" while predicting: "The 1990's promise to become the most fruitful period in the history of civilization."

The giddy crowds popping champagne bottles and launching streamers on Prague's Wenceslas Square, its cobblestones made slick with spilled spirits, to hail Havel, Czechs' long-sought freedom, and this new, bold Soviet leader, had much more to celebrate. On Christmas Day, Romanian rebels had executed their Communist dictator Nicolae Ceauşescu along with his imperious wife Elena. Two weeks before that, Bulgaria's Communist government had approved multiparty elections. Seven weeks earlier, on November 9, 1989, the people of East and West Germany had together dismantled the Berlin Wall, that despised Cold War symbol Reagan had begged Gorbachev to "tear down."

That July, Bush had traveled to Poland and Hungary. In June, the dissident labor Solidarity movement had swept Poland's free elections. In May, Hungary had inched toward lifting the repressive Iron Curtain dividing the free West from the oppressed Communist East by dismantling its 150-mile-long border fence with Austria. "The world is inspired by what is happening here," Bush, finally animated, had gushed in Warsaw.

And eight months before New Year's 1990, the Soviet Union had held free national legislative elections, for the first time in seven decades. Even then, few imagined those would be the final elections of what Reagan had called "The Evil Empire," which would dissolve in December 1991. Had any of these events occurred in isolation, they would have been considered transformative. Together, the cumulative impact was overwhelming.

Bush Inherits Reagan's Horseshoe

President Bush was finishing a very good rookie year. His call for a "kinder, gentler nation" when accepting the Republican nomination in 1988 kindly, gently, chided his boss. Bush repudiated 1960s permissiveness and 1980s greed.

Liberalism was listing but many Americans had soured on Reaganite materialism. In one poll, majorities perceived that yuppies, stockbrokers, and drug users were "losing favor" among their peers. The paradoxical package gaining favor included "parents spending more time with children," "being concerned about the less fortunate," "putting one's career first," and "having only the best quality things."

More doer than talker or thinker, Bush would deemphasize rhetoric, ideology, and what he dismissed as "the vision thing." One Bush aide lamented that "the movie actor's White House was the one that was hospitable to new ideas. Not the Yalie's." Raised for stewardship more than leadership, Bush knew where he stood, not where America was heading—or where he wanted to take it. Ultimately, the great bipartisan success of Reagan and the other Cold War presidents in helping Soviet Communism collapse propelled him.

Bush got results. While tiptoeing around Eastern Europe's transition, he bravely tackled the Reagan-era Central American impasse. He brokered a bipartisan accord with the Democratic House Speaker Jim Wright to support the Contra insurgents economically, not militarily, while building up to Nicaragua's elections in April 1990. Again cooperating with Congress, he created the Resolution Trust Corporation to manage the huge costs still menacing the federal budget from the 1980s' Savings and Loan banking crisis. Ultimately, the Sandinistas would lose the free elections and the bank bailouts would stabilize the economy.

After watching him govern, Americans liked this more moderate Republican. "Ronald Reagan left his horseshoe under George Bush's pillow," grumbled David Axelrod, a young Chicago-based Democratic political consultant. The short, sweet, successful Panama invasion reinforced this positive new impression of the once-unpopular president. Bush's first year approval rating of 76 percent competed with John Kennedy's 79 percent and Dwight Eisenhower's 70 percent. "He actually achieved his goals," said Roger Stone, a Republican political consultant. While others compared Bush to Theodore Roosevelt, speaking softly while carrying a big stick, Stone noted that Bush's boldness exorcised "the 'wimp' word . . . from the political lexicon forever."

Still, like recurring pains, three problems would haunt the Bush presidency—and the American people throughout the coming decade. The culture wars that began with the youth rebellion of the 1960s and 1970s, then intensified with Reagan's counterrevolution of the 1980s, persisted. Cultural controversies clustered sensitive issues together including race, gender identity, sexual practice, individual morality, and collective confidence in the nation's virtue and future. Similarly, the Reagan-era debate about budget deficits and the welfare state, about tax burdens on the middle class and moral responsibilities to the poor, continued to irritate raw national economic and political nerves. These chronic domestic problems competed with the world's chaos for presidential attention. Ending the Cold War did not eliminate regional conflicts. Some hostile forces once checked by the Soviets now menaced America directly.

A Polluted Public Square?

More cold warrior than culture warrior, George H. W. Bush feared that fights over art, education, sexuality, and ideology would ruin his "kinder, gentler" stewardship. Nevertheless, the tensions persisted. That New Year's Eve 1990, as a twenty-foot lighted Lone Star rose up at midnight alongside Houston's thirty-seven-story Texas Commerce Tower, the soundtrack kids listened to often distressed their parents.

Rap's rise intensified this age-old problem. Perhaps America's most demonized song that New Year's was the lurid, sexually domineering, misogynist "Me So Horny," from 2 Live Crew's album *As Nasty As They Wanna Be*. This monster crossover hit from the rap charts, peaking at 26 on the more staid Billboard 100, was sold on a record album whose cover warned about the explicit lyrics. Still, legislators in at least sixteen states demanded more specific warnings. Prosecutors in Florida and Alabama were preparing cases against record store owners who sold the album to minors. The album's parent-friendly version, *As Clean As They Wanna Be*, only sold 200,000 copies in the four months the dirty version sold 1.3 million.

Anti-porn activists and Christian evangelists increasingly viewed America as Vulgaria, a land with no limits where nothing was sacred. New York senator Daniel Patrick Moynihan would soon lament that Americans were "defining deviancy down." Fears of a Naked Public Square—stripped of religious values to separate church from state—now paled beside fears of a Polluted Public Square—sullied by X-rated lyrics, images, and language. Concerned parents also denounced all-white nihilistic, exhibitionist Heavy Metal acts, especially Guns N' Roses, Metallica, and Ozzy Osbourne.

Free speech absolutists and entertainers counterattacked. "The true winner is mediocrity—saccharin, overproduced garbage like New Kids on the Block, so middle-class, suburban and clean it makes your teeth hurt," Steve Marmel, a comedy writer, warned in *USA Today*. "The losers are diversity and the minority viewpoint, the very things the First Amendment was designed to protect." Less elegantly, when Florida's governor Bob Martinez encouraged 2 Live Crew's prosecution, the band's July 1990 album, *Banned in the U.S.A,* would feature a song with a repeated refrain, "Fuck Martinez."

In March 1990, most record companies agreed to place stickers on "potentially offensive" albums saying "Explicit Lyrics—Parental Advisory." In *The New York Times,* a *Penthouse* editor exposed a more "pernicious" artistic danger circulating unstickered, Richard Wagner's *The Ring of the Nibelung.* Peter Bloch sarcastically warned of the libretto's inclusion of incest, suicide, and other Wagnerian sacrileges.

In Cincinnati, conservatives were advising the Contemporary Arts Center not to run an exhibit displaying Robert Mapplethorpe's photographs of men inserting a finger, a hand, and a whip into other men's private parts. That spring, prosecutors would indict the Center and its director Dennis Barrie. In October, a mostly working-class jury would return a "not guilty" verdict, anticipating 2 Live Crew's Florida acquittals. The ambiguity around definitions of obscenity and the clarity of the First Amendment protection swayed most judges and juries. Still, the museum's legal bills hit $300,000. American sensibilities had changed dramatically, the columnist E. J. Dionne noted. In 1955, a Gallup poll found that 55 percent of men and 73 percent of women disapproved of "women wearing Bermuda shorts on the street." Thirty-five years later, "Gallup wouldn't even think of asking that question . . . most Americans, reluctantly and uneasily, are prepared to let adults be as nasty as they want to be."

Republicans happily exploited what Walter Isaacson of *Time* called this new "age of escapist politics." In 1990, the Supreme Court would invalidate a federal law prohibiting flag burning. Senate Republican leader Bob Dole warned that if any legislator opposed a constitutional amendment to ban flag desecrations, that vote would "make a good 30-second spot" election time. "Values are always important," Democratic representative Dick Durbin of Illinois admitted, remembering Michael Dukakis's 1988 presidential campaign blunders. For Democrats to win post-Reagan, they would have to match the Republicans in the values combat zone.

The Two George Bushes

Bush disliked playing these cultural cards and lacked Ronald Reagan's certainty in managing the nation's economy. Reagan perched his vision of the three Ps, prosperity, patriotism, and peace, on a three-legged stool of cutting taxes, fighting Communism, and boosting defense spending. Bush and the Republicans would stumble with no Cold War to fight and no Republican majority in Congress to fight Democratic demands for tax hikes.

By October 1990, with the economy slowing down and the budget deficit building up, Bush waffled. He felt hog-tied by his "Read my lips: no new taxes" campaign pledge but pressured by government shutdown threats—especially after a three-day taste of it over Columbus Day weekend. During three days of negotiations with the Democratic-dominated Congress, he reversed himself four times. Bush wanted to preserve capital gains tax cuts, which favored America's wealthiest investors. He feared massive automatic cuts imposed by the Gramm-Rudman-Hollings Act. He began negotiating about an income tax surtax, what Reagan had misleadingly, cravenly, labeled a "revenue enhancement."

Reporters interrupted Bush on a Florida jog, and he answered crassly, "Read my hips," while patting his backside. On November 5, when he signed the Omnibus Budget Reconciliation Act of 1990, he signed his presidency's death warrant. One Democratic pollster, Harrison Hickman, rejoiced, that in one day, Bush exposed his "two Achilles' heels—'rich' and 'wimp.'"

Ultimately, this politically self-destructive act was one of great statesmanship. Bush's five-year $482 billion deficit reduction package started taming America's budget deficit, triggering what would be called the Clinton boom. The journalist Jonathan Rauch estimates that Bush's cuts were 27 percent larger than Bill Clinton's. "By breaking his promise," Rauch notes, "Bush put out Reagan's fiscal house fire, and he enabled Clinton and the strong economy to rebuild the house. Bush thus made two presidents' reputations and unmade his own."

Bush also led effectively when Iraqi dictator Saddam Hussein unleashed his army on neighboring Kuwait in August 1990. Saddam's soldiers easily overran the small Arab monarchy, seizing the oil fields, looting the stores, sending truckloads of shiny Mercedes-Benzes and glittering jewels to Baghdad. Margaret Thatcher, Great Britain's Reaganite prime minister, challenged her American colleague: "Remember, George, this is no time to go wobbly."

He didn't. Thanks to sixty-two phone calls to government leaders in the first thirty days after Iraq's aggression, Bush forged an impressive coalition of twenty-eight countries, including Saudi Arabia and Egypt. He prevailed upon Israel to stay out of the coalition—and not retaliate when Saddam bombed the Jewish State with Scud missiles.

Bush's actions that fall would make him look like a foreign policy president uninterested in leading domestically. *Time* would select "the two George Bushes" as 1990's "Men of the Year," a first, for having influenced the world for better *and* worse. Bush's aristocratic, statesmanlike "I'll prevail, or I'll be impeached" foreign policy spine of steel turned rubbery when domestic issues arose. He too candidly admitted at a press conference: "I enjoy trying to put the coalition together and keep it together. . . . I can't say I just rejoice every time I go up and talk to [House Ways and Means chairman Dan] Rostenkowski . . . . about what he's going to do on taxes."

Happy but Pessimistic

Throughout the Christmas season, the focus on Iraq boosted the president's spirits—and poll ratings. Ninety percent of Americans polled felt good about their lives. This "Don't worry be happy" mind-set was remarkable considering the despair that greeted Reagan and Bush when they were inaugurated in 1981. Yet this new Nineties' optimism was brittle. Half of those surveyed feared the nation was on the wrong track. Americans worried about Japan's predominance, the limits of the Reagan boom, crime, the $3 trillion national debt, homelessness, drugs, pollution, and moral drift. "We're not number one anymore," said Barbara Greer, forty-seven, a California real estate agent. "We're so caught up in our yuppie existence, we're letting it slip through our fingers."

The pessimism became acute when pollsters asked what people expected college students to face. "There won't be jobs for them," many feared. This anxiety connected to what two out of three respondents blamed as "a major cause" of America's drug problem, "the breakdown of the family." Here, as the 1990s began, Americans were still struggling with the sexual revolution that launched in the 1960s and went mainstream in the 1970s.

On New Year's Day 1990, George H. W. Bush and the Republicans felt too confident for such worries. They were the party of peace and prosperity, taking credit for delivering 18.7 million new jobs and generating $30 trillion worth of wealth. That day, when an African American became mayor of America's largest city, New York, people celebrated nationwide. An estimated 7,370 blacks were now officeholders. David Dinkins celebrated his personal achievement as reflecting his people's progress. He remembered "when there were no African-Americans in government."

By contrast, eighteen days later, Mayor Marion Barry's cocaine bust in Washington, D.C., exposed the flip side of the African American experience. "King Nightowl" was making the majority-black city a laughingstock even before his arrest. "Know what the mayor's answer is to a paralyzing snowstorm?" one comic joked: "Quick, gimme a straw!"

Foreshadowing Bill Clinton's resurrection, Barry expressed outrage that his outrageous behavior outraged Americans. His mayoral mission was too important to indulge moral or legal trivialities. His defiant chutzpah exploited American moral confusion regarding drug use and adultery as lapses not sins. Many constituents remained loyal as he enrolled in the fashionable Hanley-Hazelden Center in West Palm Beach, Florida. "We love our mayor because he is a human being first before he is the mayor," Gayle M. Petersen wrote to *The Washington Post.*

Playing the race card as O. J. Simpson would do after him, Barry denounced "The Plan," the white establishment's supposed plot to subdue him. Even as two-thirds of African Americans finally prospered economically, millions remained marginalized, ghettoized, consigned to America's underclass, and open to Barry's rhetoric. A court eventually convicted him on one of fourteen counts, fining him $5,000 and sentencing him to six months in jail. Still, Barry's demagoguery further infected America's great, ongoing racial wounds.

Meanwhile, that January 1, 1990, Americans' pop culture remained more saccharine than sadistic. The top song was Chicago's "Look Away," asking an ex-wife who found a new love not to look "if you see me walking by. And the tears are in my eyes." Bette Midler's "Wind Beneath My Wings" asked mawkishly yet compellingly, "Did you ever know that you're my hero?" Robert Fulghum's collection of inspirational essays, *All I Really Need to Know I Learned in Kindergarten,* was starting its sixty-second week as a *New York Times* best seller. On the fiction list, Tom Clancy's escapist adventure, *Clear and Present Danger,* introduced a new post–Cold War set of non-Russian villains, Colombian drug lords.

That television season, ABC's crude, white, working-class feminist comedienne Roseanne Barr competed for primacy against NBC's elegant, African American, upper-middle-class fatherly comedian Bill Cosby—both reflecting modern America's mushrooming mishmash of identities. Along with CBS and ABC, NBC now faced an alphabet soup of cable competitors that emerged in the 1980s, including A&E, CNN, ESPN, HBO, LIFE, MTV, NICK, TBS, TMC, TNT, and USA. For Christmas, home theater systems proved popular, despite costing $3,000 and more. Camcorders also flooded the market, inspiring another top ten TV hit, *America's Funniest Home Videos.*

On the Cusp of a Transformational Decade

There was much to celebrate and much to fear on that 1990 New Year's Day. Many of the men and women who would define the 1990s were living their lives, with most seeming quite ordinary.

Rodney King was serving a two-year sentence for stealing $200 from a Los Angeles convenience store. Clarence Thomas was chairing the Equal Employment Opportunity Commission, awaiting what would be an easy Senate confirmation to the U.S. Court of Appeals for the District of Columbia Circuit. Anita Hill was a freshly tenured professor at the University of Oklahoma law school. Congressman Newt Gingrich was House Minority Whip, dreaming of a Republican takeover of the Congress—run by the Democrats since Dwight Eisenhower's presidency. Rudy Giuliani remained dumbfounded that the mild-mannered David Dinkins beat him in November, in New York City's closest mayoral race in more than eighty years.

In Seattle, Kurt Cobain, a fragile twenty-two-year-old guitarist, was back from an emotionally draining six-week European tour peddling Nirvana's first album, *Bleach*. Howard Schultz, the one-time employee who had purchased Starbucks in 1987, was roasting over 2 million pounds of coffee annually for forty-six stores but had not yet turned a profit. Jeff Bezos, a young computer science major, felt restive working for Bankers Trust Company in New York. He wanted to work with computers more directly and creatively.

Larry Page was a sixteen-year-old high school student in Michigan. His future Google partner, Sergey Brin, five months younger, lived in Maryland. In 1979, Brin and his scientist parents had emigrated from Russia, seeking the freedom that Soviet Communism denied Jews. In the summer of 1990, Brin's father would take Sergey and other students to the Soviet Union on a two-week study tour. Remembering his fear of authority growing up, Sergey would tell his father during the trip: "Thank you for taking us all out of Russia."

O. J. Simpson, the retired NFL running back, was a celebrity pitchman. Despite his Nice Guy persona, O. J. had been arrested a year earlier on New Year's Day, for beating his wife, Nicole Brown Simpson—one of eight times the police were called to the home. Timothy McVeigh was an infantry soldier stationed at Fort Riley, Kansas. Matthew Shepard was a thirteen-year-old junior high school student in Casper, Wyoming. J. K. Rowling, a former English major, was languishing as a secretary, working at Amnesty International, among other offices. A few months later, stuck on the Manchester train line waiting to get into London, she would start imagining a wizard named Harry Potter.

Monica Lewinsky was a student at Beverly Hills High School, living in the soon-to-be-iconic 90210 zip code. Her headmaster would later remember her as a "nice kid and pretty normal young lady."

Al Gore, the forty-one-year-old Democratic senator from Tennessee, was completing the worst year of his life. His six-year-old son had been hit by a car after the Baltimore Orioles' Opening Day game on April 2, 1989, catapulted thirty feet in the air, and landed badly injured but alive. When accepting the Democratic presidential nomination in 2000, Gore would recall that awful moment to humanize his image while emphasizing the seriousness of his mission.

By contrast, George W. Bush, the president's forty-three-year-old eldest son, was finishing a very, very good year. Sober since 1986, in April 1989 Bush finalized a deal that would make him wealthy, satisfied, and famous on his own. His original 1.8 percent ownership stake in the Texas Rangers would grow, eventually yielding nearly $15 million in profits when Thomas O. Hicks bought the team in 1998. Wielding power privately in his father's White House, the younger Bush was considering going public in Texas—and would run successfully for governor in 1994.

Over at Hilton Head Island, South Carolina, the governor of Arkansas, his First Lady, his only child, and hundreds of peers were enjoying yet another Baby Boomer bonding bash grandiosely called Renaissance Weekend. Bill and Hillary Clinton had attended since 1984. Bill Clinton would recall that during these three-day talkfests, "We revealed things about ourselves and learned things about other people that would never have come out under normal circumstances." Many of the resulting friendships would be the basis of FOB, the Friends of Bill network that would campaign tirelessly in 1992, then populate his eventual administration.

Clinton was already planning a presidential run. He had planned a campaign the last election cycle, only to cancel abruptly, fearing "bimbo eruptions." He would explain when he announced in October 1991 that he refused "to be part of a generation that celebrates the death of Communism abroad with the loss of the American Dream at home. . . . Our streets are meaner, our families are broken, our health care is the costliest in the world and we get less for it." A decade into the Reagan revolution, he saw "No vision, no action. Just neglect, selfishness, and division."

And in Saudi Arabia, a thirty-two-year old rising jihadist, Osama bin Laden, heir to a construction fortune, was enjoying a hero's welcome for his supposed valor in defeating the Soviets in Afghanistan.

Liquid Modernity: "All That Is Solid Melts into Air, All That Is Holy Is Profaned"

In 1990, 248.7 million Americans were poised to help make the United States undergo its greatest population growth spurt ever over the next ten years, with a 13.2 percent increase to 281.4 million. Globally, Hong Kong was still British.

Macau was still Portuguese. Yugoslavia, Czechoslovakia, and the Soviet Union were still united; Germany was still divided, East and West. The "European Union" sounded like a powerful labor organization, not the twelve-country political and economic alliance that would form in 1993, and grow to twenty-eight members today. Nelson Mandela was imprisoned. The World Health Organization still listed "homosexuality" as a disease. The most famous Governor Clinton in American history was DeWitt of New York not Bill of Arkansas. And the most famous Hillary in the world was Sir Edmund, who climbed Mount Everest in 1953.

At the start of that transformational, final decade of the twentieth century, Amazon was only a river and a rain forest, Google was only a very big number with lots of zeroes spelled with no "e"s, googol, and "pay, pal" was something you said to someone who owed you money. The World Wide Web sounded like something that might ensnare Spider-Man. People knew about "hi-fi," hi-fidelity stereos, not Wi-Fi.

A PowerBook sounded like something from the comics. When we thought of a cell, we thought biology not telephones—which were never smart—while a PDA was an embarrassing public display of affection not a personal digital assistant. Cookies were something you gobbled but wouldn't disable. Most mail came from the post office not that newfangled Internet.

"Props" were theatrical devices not compliments from "Friends," who were real, not Joey, Chandler, Monica, Phoebe, and Rachel. People knew about sign language—not "Seinlanguage"—"not that there's anything wrong with it." Rent was something you paid not something you saw, while "The View" was something you saw not something you watched. A PlayStation was an area for games in a kindergarten. "Law and Order" was a political slogan not a blockbuster TV franchise. What was mocked as a "girl movie" had not yet been upgraded, slightly, depending on who was saying it, to a "chick flick." When you said "edgy female duo," you thought "Laverne and Shirley" not "Thelma and Louise." TMI sounded liked a multinational corporation not a plea for discretion after hearing too much information.

"Don't ask, don't tell," sounded like a philanderer's recipe for marital harmony not a military policy. A "Drudge Report" sounded boring not scandalous. "Newt" mostly conjured up thoughts of salamanders, not a Republican, while "Tiger" and "Woods" conjured up fears of dangerous animals in the jungle not on the golf course. There had never been a woman secretary of state, a woman national security adviser, a woman attorney general, a woman senator from New York, and no First Lady who had ever used the White House as a launching pad to electoral office. The Dow Jones stock average was at 2753.20, about to quadruple in a decade to over 11,000. America was at peace. And the world seemed to be changing for the better.

What the French expatriate Ted Morgan celebrated as America's "opportunity quotient" and "anxiety quotient" were both spiking. Out of the ensuing collision of impulses, loyalties, commitments, values, and visions, Americans weaved together the latest chapter in their extraordinary nation's collective saga. The winners of the Cold War, that prolonged, often excruciating, rarely bloody, power struggle with the Soviet Union, would become the liberators of Kuwait, the pioneers of the Internet Age, the lost souls of the gay Nineties, and, on that awful September day, the victims of Osama bin Laden's Jihadist delusions.

One of the anomalies of life in 1990s America would be the accelerating pace of change in one of the world's most stable societies. In *The Communist Manifesto*, Karl Marx and Friedrich Engels recognized the destabilizing impact of capitalism's perennial reinvention and renewal. By "constantly revolutionizing" the economy, the "whole relations of society" change, too, creating "everlasting uncertainty and agitation." As a result, Marx and Engels argued, tradition, in all its forms, is perpetually threatened with being "swept away." Anticipating modern America in mid-nineteenth-century Europe, they wrote: "All that is solid melts into air, all that is holy is profaned." Technology and consumerism, both in a state of perpetual update (or obsolescence) and each enveloping in its own way, further accelerated the changes and the disorientation.

Working off that insight, the sociologist Zygmunt Bauman has identified liquidity as modernity's defining characteristic. Flexibility, fluidity, immediacy, impulse, individuality, and consumerism all trump solidity, tradition, patience, responsibility, and communalism. Clintonites themselves would realize the value of the liquid-solid, sacred-profane framing, to explain Bill Clinton, his presidency, and the 1990s. While drafting the 1996 State of the Union address, Clinton's chief speechwriter Michael Waldman, expanding on Clinton's celebration of this "age of possibility" and "of great challenge and change," would describe the 1990s as "An era in which things certain seem to melt into air." In those days when Google was not yet a verb, the speech went through ten drafts before an intern discovered the source. This diligent researcher saved America's Democratic president from quoting *The Communist Manifesto* in his State of the Union.

The "End of History" Euphoria—And Distraction

Back in 1980, few Americans would have predicted how many would begin the 1990s happy or confident, let alone victorious. Despite George H. W. Bush's caution, Houstonians and their fellow Americans were proud of their bloodless Cold War victory. In the great twentieth-century lifestyle war, the Texas-tough Marlboro Man and his domestic-but-chic Martha Stewart wife had defeated Uncle Ivan and his dour Communist spouse. Pumped-up pundits misread the political scientist Francis Fukuyama's spring 1989 essay, "The End of History" as declaring that ending the Cold War eliminated all of America's troubles. Fukuyama emphasized the "universalization of Western liberal democracy as the final form of human government." But, presciently, he saw the "broad unhappiness with the impersonality and spiritual vacuity of liberal consumerist societies" and feared ongoing "terrorism and wars of national liberation" rooted in "ethnic and nationalist violence."

Those concerns, however, were eclipsed by the post–Cold War euphoria, the Texas-size surge in confidence because "we won." There were no victory parades; it was not that kind of war. There was great faith in the "peace dividend" paying off existentially and not just financially at budget time. The Nineties would be fun, with Web surfing, rollerblading, Beanie Babies, Pogs, and the Super Nintendo Entertainment System, among the decade's glorious distractions. Yet on September 12, 2001, with New York and Washington still smoldering, millions of Americans would look back on the gay Nineties and wonder, "What did we do with all that opportunity, why did we fritter away our chances to be great?"

2

1991: Philadelphia
"You Just Don't Get It"

From the "New World Order"
to Domestic Disorder

I refuse to be part of a generation that celebrates the death of Communism abroad with the loss of the American Dream at home.
—BILL CLINTON, ANNOUNCEMENT SPEECH, OCTOBER 3, 1991

On Saturday night February 23, 1991, a passerby called from a pay telephone to report smoke pouring out of the twenty-second floor at One Meridian Plaza in downtown Philadelphia. This thirty-eight-story concrete-and-glass castle of commerce, completed in 1972, broadcast an aura of perfectionism and power. The Meridian Bank building was one of millions of everyday marvels in America the functional. Week after week, from Monday to Friday, masters of the universe and their minions strode inside, clad in sleek power suits. Crossing the expansive lobby toward four banks of elevators, they barreled up toward the heavens at superhuman speeds, rarely contemplating the wondrous device propelling them upward—or the disastrous consequences if the cables conveying this flying metal crate snapped. Working longer and longer days suspended in the clouds, floating above the urban chaos in sanitized, temperature-controlled environments with sealed windows, they bought and sold, analyzed and concluded, hired and fired, debated and gossiped, with machines or subordinates meeting most of their needs.

A center of the old economy and the new, One Meridian Plaza housed Meridian Bancorp's regional headquarters. The bank emerged in 1983, when American Bancorp of Reading merged with Central Penn National Bank of Philadelphia, founded in 1828. Epitomizing the 1990s' merger-mania, Meridian would merge with CoreStates Financial in 1996.

Another tenant was the communications and broadcasting upstart, Comcast, whose name combined both words. This quintessential 1990s entertainment conglomerate was growing into a $200 billion behemoth, offering infrastructure and content. Owning cable television stations, cell phone networks, Internet services, along with stakes in the QVC shopping channel, E! Entertainment Television, the Golf channel, and the Philadelphia Flyers, among others, Comcast would eventually absorb NBC and Universal Studios, too.

On that freezing February night, some rags a contractor sloppily left soaking in linseed oil over the weekend ignited Philadelphia's worst high-rise office building fire. The twelve-alarm blaze raged for nineteen hours. Huge plateglass windows plunged toward the plaza, shattering, scattering shards, severing fire hoses. The 316 firefighters from 51 engine companies, 15 ladder companies, and 11 specialized units, fought heroically—losing 3 of their "brothers" overnight. All were African American, yet most newspapers ignored their race. Blacks' inclusion as civil servants no longer merited headlines. Finally, when the fire reached the thirtieth floor, the ten automatic sprinklers a tenant had installed voluntarily doused the fire.

The blaze showed, a federal investigation later concluded, "what can happen when everything goes wrong." The water pressure system was so weak, one firefighter recalled, the water "squirted like a garden hose." In 1991, George H. W. Bush would also learn "what can happen when everything goes wrong." Although some political fires would burn out by themselves, most would rage, charring his reputation.

A Bratty Perfectionism

For years after, the boarded Meridian Bank building, its top-third charred, would stand untouched, the Cradle of Liberty's carbuncle. Lawyers squabbled over $4 billion in claims, magnifying a $100 million property loss. Every year, lawsuits drained between $30 and $80 billion from the economy nationwide. Manufacturers complained of "tort taxes," the $20 built into the cost of a $100 ladder, the $3,000 built into an $18,000 pacemaker.

This legal dysfunction actually reflected America's smooth functioning. Life in America was no longer nasty, brutish, and short, but cushy, safe, and long. Accustomed to a bratty perfectionism, Americans quickly went legal when things went wrong. Nearly 1 million lawyers and increasingly activist judges encouraged the impulse. In 1991, Richard Overton sued Anheuser-Busch unsuccessfully for emotional distress because drinking Bud Light failed to conjure the "beautiful women and . . . unrestricted merriment" the company's ads promised. In 1992 a seventy-nine-year-old woman would sue McDonald's and collect more than half a million dollars for putting her hot coffee between her legs while in a car and getting burned when the coffee spilled. The litigation mania, escalating fees, and overreliance on the law would so spiral out of control that the next president would be saddled with legal bills as high as $10 million.

After Aetna insurance paid the owners of One Meridian Place $300 million, workers started dismantling the structure. Finally, in 2009, the plush 48-story Residences at the Ritz Carlton would open as a replacement. The 270 condominiums ranging from $550,000 to $12 million would symbolize Philadelphia's downtown revival, especially as a playground for the rich, as other neighborhoods languished.

The day after the Meridian fire, Pennsylvanians absorbed another blow as a military reserve unit from Greensburg, fifty miles southeast of Pittsburgh, lost thirteen soldiers overseas. It would be the deadliest attack on Americans during the Gulf War. An Iraqi Scud missile, possibly fragmented by a defensive American Patriot missile, hit a crowded army barracks in Al Khobar, Saudi Arabia, killing twenty-eight soldiers and wounding ninety-nine.

Forty-three of the injured were from Greensburg and its environs. Recruited as weekend warriors anxious to supplement their incomes as rural Pennsylvania's steel-based economy flagged, many were surprised, most were proud, to be in combat. A year later, a bronze-and-granite monument, facing the vexing Middle East, would honor Greensburg's fallen, two of whom were among America's fifteen female military deaths.

A towering inferno and a desolate rural Pennsylvania field transformed into sacred ground for national martyrs killed by Middle Easterners would be powerful symbols in the next decade. In 1991, the Al Khobar Scud attack was unusual during a remarkably safe Gulf War, for Americans at least. Of more than 670,000 American soldiers deployed, fewer than 400 died. The Greensburg monument reflected the patriotic rush that made George H. W. Bush look politically invincible when the Gulf War ended. The Meridian Bank eyesore reflected the domestic deadlocks that would make Bush politically vulnerable when 1991 ended.

The Gulf War Show: Couch Potato Warriors Unite

For most of Desert Storm's five weeks of war, it looked easy. President George H. W. Bush remained resolute. "What happens if we do nothing?" he kept asking, dismissing fears of another Vietnam quagmire while vowing not to repeat Vietnam-era mistakes of sending in troops "to fight with one hand tied behind their back."

Beneath Bush's calm façade, the tension in the five months since Iraq invaded Kuwait in August 1990 drained him. On New Year's Eve, the president typed a two-page "Dear George, Jeb, Neil, Marvin, Doro," letter to his five children. He wanted to tell them "as a father," that "I have the peace of mind that comes from knowing that we have tried hard for peace." The question so many asked him, "How many lives are you willing to sacrifice?," he confessed, "tears at my heart." "The answer, of course, is none, none at all." But, he explained in words that in 1998, NBC's Tom Brokaw would characterize as typical of the "Greatest Generation" that fought World War II, "How many lives might have been saved if appeasement had given way to force earlier on in the late '30s or earliest '40s? How many Jews might have been spared the gas chambers?. . . . I look at today's crisis as 'good' vs. 'evil.'" Imparting a paternal lesson, he advised: "sometimes in life you have to act as you think best—you can't compromise, you can't give in . . . even if your critics are loud and numerous." He advised: "dear kids—batten down the hatches."

Days before his mid-January deadline for Saddam to leave Kuwait passed, Bush turned to the Congress. Despite lacking a majority in both Houses, he received the first congressional authorization for offensive military action since 1964's Vietnam-era Gulf of Tonkin Resolution. He dismissed hysterics on the left, in the media, and from academe, who warned of mass casualties if the American military engaged Iraq's famed Republican Guard, in what Saddam was calling "the mother of all battles." The African American activist Jesse Jackson testified before Congress that blacks were "scheduled to die first and disproportionately in the war."

The chairman of the Joint Chiefs of Staff, Colin Powell, lashed out at racial demagogues who counted body bags by race. Powell did ROTC at City College, served two army tours in Vietnam, and was Ronald Reagan's national security adviser. In late 1989, he became, at fifty-two, the youngest officer and the first Afro-Caribbean American to head America's joint command. His rise advertised the military as America's least-racist institution. More than one hundred thousand African Americans were serving in the Persian Gulf. A third of all young black men served in the military, twice the rate of young white males. Powell advised: "You cannot have it both ways—favoring opportunity for blacks in the military in peacetime and exemption from risk for them in wartime."

Many of America's leading generals now were Vietnam survivors, including Powell and the commander-in-chief of the U.S. Central Command, or CENTCOM, H. Norman Schwarzkopf. A fifty-six-year-old, six-foot-three,

240-pound tough, gruff, bear of a man, Schwarzkopf would become America's Gulf War hero, an old-fashioned, straight-talking, no-nonsense celebrity soldier in a modern age. The Vietnam catastrophe and Jimmy Carter's Iranian hostage rescue debacle shaped a media narrative about the American military as incompetent. Schwarzkopf resented this contempt for the institution he loved. He remained estranged from his sister Ruth over unhealed Vietnam-era wounds. He—and his peers—had learned from Vietnam's bitter lessons about technology, strategy, discipline, media messaging, and national unity.

At 9:00 p.m., on January 16, 1991, Bush addressed the largest audience in American television history to date. Only John F. Kennedy's funeral in 1963 had attracted a higher percentage of Americans watching television—and the population since had grown by 60 million. Most Americans still watched on the three major networks: CBS, NBC, ABC. But Ted Turner's upstart, CNN, beat CBS in the ratings. "I learn more from CNN than I do from the CIA," Bush told world leaders, ruefully.

CNN's scoreboard journalism shaped perceptions of who was winning, who was losing, and who suffered during the war. America's media-savvy leaders had to manage reporters to win the real war on the ground and the image war on the air. Schwarzkopf refused to answer any questions that might "help the enemy" but also refused to lie. Eighty percent of Americans polled supported the press restrictions contained in a ten-page handbook called Annex Foxtrot.

Many Americans watched obsessively, mastering the Pentagon briefers' obtuse vocabulary. Instant experts, they opined about hard targets and soft targets, about smart bombs and cluster bombs, about "degrading" Saddam's "air cover" and neutralizing his "command and control capacities." These couch potato warriors adopted the Pentagon's antiseptic euphemisms, which turned the two to three thousand civilians killed by America's air onslaught into "collateral damage"—a phrase that entered the general vocabulary.

In Vietnam, reporters cast themselves as dogged crusaders uncovering the uncomfortable truths a manipulative top brass tried to obscure. This time, the Pentagon cast reporters as pushy, whiny, vaguely unpatriotic, preppie hounds risking the war effort. *Saturday Night Live* reversed course from its anti-war origins in the 1970s. In its opening skit on February 9, 1991, reporters hectored military spokespeople, demanding to know the American forces' vulnerabilities, timetables, and passwords. When Colin Powell watched the skit, he recalled, "I knew that we had won the battle for public opinion."

During 1987's Iran-Contra hearings, Lieutenant Colonel Oliver North had exploited these same class tensions, understanding that most Americans sympathized with him as a hardscrabble patriot, harassed by pushy, overeducated lawyers and journalists. In Aaron Sorkin's 1992 movie, *A Few Good Men,* Jack Nicholson's craggy Colonel Nathan R. Jessup would dismiss Tom Cruise's pretty-boy prosecutor, who yells, "I want the truth," by saying, "You can't handle the truth!" In a monologue that instantly became classic, Jessup says, "Son, we live in a world that has walls, and those walls have to be guarded by men with guns. . . . And my existence, while grotesque and incomprehensible to you, saves lives."

Americans had been craving a comeback. The run on American flags and yellow ribbons suggested that in 1991, ten years after his inauguration and two years after his retirement, Ronald Reagan's revolution had peaked. More than exorcising the ghosts of Vietnam, more than bringing "closure" to the Sixties, Americans were championing the Reaganite Eighties. With U.S.A. ascendant, modern technological capitalism and democracy triumphant, traditional values dominant, Americans were jubilant. "If anyone tells you America's best days are behind her, they're looking the wrong way," Bush rejoiced.

Bush carefully combined traditional moralism with a new internationalism. His good versus evil, no appeasement, Saddam-as-Hitler rhetoric expressed his generational anxiety and fortitude. Launching the war, he acknowledged the disappointment that the post–Cold War euphoria had disappeared so quickly. Hoping his UN-sanctioned international coalition and clear actions would inaugurate an era of global cooperation and democratic primacy, he welcomed this "new world order, a world where the rule of the law, not the law of the jungle, governs the conduct of nations."

The coalition's success vindicated the president. On September 23, 1990, weeks after Saddam invaded Kuwait, record-breaking audiences had watched PBS's broadcast of Ken Burns's five-night, nine-episode documentary *The Civil War.* The liberal academic Paul Starr, linking that moment with Operation Desert Storm months later, concluded: "some wars are indeed worth fighting."

When the Gulf War ended after forty-three days on February 27, 1991, Bush looked unstoppable. "This may be the beginning of the second American Century," said Ben Wattenberg, of the American Enterprise Institute, a Washington think tank. "We are the most influential nation in history: We've beaten the totalitarians of the right, then the left and now the bandits, all in a half century's work." General Schwarzkopf appreciated that "something basic had changed since Vietnam." His estranged sister Ruth apologized "for not writing you all those years in Vietnam." Reading her letter, Schwarzkopf "burst into tears."

Bush's poll numbers now reached 90 percent. Reagan's seemingly second-string successor was looking like a master pol. With the president so popular after the war, Vice President Dan Quayle joked: "These days you probably have a better chance to see Elvis than you do a Democratic presidential candidate." The Democratic pollster Stan Greenberg was a rare liberal optimist. "Bush has shown a capacity to stumble in domestic policy before," Greenberg said. "He can stumble again."

Bush indeed faced daunting domestic challenges. More than 70 percent of Americans polled feared that not enough was being done about public schools and education, the state of the country's economy, health care, illegal drugs, crime, poverty, and, the most popular worry of all, the federal budget deficit. Bush's invulnerability proved as fleeting as the post–Cold War euphoria. In one of those overlaps that novelists would fear as too much of a stretch, just four days after Operation Desert Storm ended, an event occurred, far from the White House, far beyond the president's control, which may have sounded the Bush presidency's death knell.

Every Black Man Has a Story: Rodney King

Shortly before 1:00 a.m., on Sunday morning March 3, squealing sirens and buzzing helicopters woke George Holliday, a thirty-one-year-old plumber, living in the San Fernando Valley, within Los Angeles. From his terrace, he saw Los Angeles police officers beating a black man. Grabbing his new Sony camcorder out of its original packaging, he taped the incident. On the video, fifteen officers, three in particular, kicked the man seven times, hitting him with nightsticks between fifty-three and fifty-six times in less than a minute. Monday morning, Holliday submitted to KTLA-TV what became perhaps the most famous amateur footage since Abraham Zapruder filmed John Kennedy's assassination.

Starting with the Nineties, intensifying after September 11, 2001, America would become Surveillance Central, the most photographed nation ever, thanks to proliferating personal devices and institutional security cameras. Now, Rodney King's beating became a national sensation, especially after CNN broadcast it on Tuesday. Holliday was never paid for the videotape. He subsequently lost the camera in a divorce settlement.

The King beating shifted the national conversation abruptly. Explaining African Americans' fury, one twenty-four-year-old told reporters: "Every black man has a story." The "two Americas"—black and white—the post–race riots Kerner Commission saw in 1968, had fragmented further. Three black Americas emerged. A prospering black middle class was freer, wealthier, better educated, better positioned than ever, aided by affirmative action programs in education and employment. Racism persisted but opportunities abounded. A black working class was stagnating, suffering from the loss of good jobs due to America's deindustrialization, even as racism diminished. And at least 1.5 million people constituting the black underclass were chronically impoverished, perpetually on welfare, and broadly illiterate. Many were dropping out of school, failing to hold jobs, rarely using time productively, abusing drugs, committing crimes, and increasingly born to unwed teenage mothers or themselves causing single-mother families—perpetuating the cycle.

Surprisingly, the 1950s' stable black family was disintegrating by the 1970s, as the same openness propelling the civil rights movement weakened traditional community structures and strictures, for blacks and whites. By 1991, the percentage of black children born out of wedlock had more than doubled since 1970 to 64 percent. "Marriage among very young blacks is a disappearing institution," sociologists feared. The child poverty rate was 15 percent for whites, 39 percent for Hispanics, and 45 percent for blacks. Black and white youth unemployment rates, which were roughly equal in 1954, had also diverged. Despite the Reagan boom, 23 percent of young blacks were unemployed.

The University of Chicago sociologist William Julius Wilson developed this analysis in his groundbreaking 1987 book, *The Truly Disadvantaged*. He triggered a debate over whether race or class best explained continuing black poverty and the disproportionate black social breakdown following the civil rights movement. With cities like Philadelphia losing 64 percent of their manufacturing jobs from 1976 to 1987, Wilson blamed economics, not race.

An African American liberal born during the Great Depression in 1935 in white, rural western Pennsylvania, Wilson helped legitimize use of the word "underclass." By 1990, Wilson feared conservatives were using the term to justify political passivity by blaming blacks and treating the problem as intractable. Radicals proposed the term "jobless" to emphasize the economy's failure. Wilson adopted the more descriptive, less insulting term, "ghetto poor."

Just as the question of why some blacks fell behind as civil rights expanded confounded academics, growing black anger amid diminishing white racism confused many older whites. The harsh but popular gangsta rap lyrics were particularly dismaying. In 1991, Ice Cube declared war on America in his album *Death Certificate*: "I wanna kill Sam 'cause he ain't my motherfuckin' Uncle!" In 1992, Ice-T rapped: "I'm a cop killer, better you than me. Cop killer, fuck police brutality!" Eight years later, NBC's *Law & Order: Special Victims Unit* cast this hip-hopping ex-drug dealer and army veteran as Detective Odafin Tutuola.

The rappers refused to take responsibility for their lyrics, insisting they were portraying particular characters. They resented the fury they evoked. They claimed to be reflecting society's violence, not creating it. With young white teens feeding the genre's growth, some experts greeted rap as the heir to the 1960s, the new voice of authentic teenage angst and rebellion. In *The New Republic*, David Samuels rejected this consumerist charade as "cultural tourism," artificially romanticizing black crime.

As many rappers expressed their anger, softer offshoots went mainstream. The sitcom *Fresh Prince of Bel Air* starred the goofy, grinning, endlessly entertaining, and delightfully unthreatening rapper-turned-actor Will Smith as a teenager from West Philadelphia's "hood" living with wealthy Los Angeles relatives. Brothers Keenen Ivory and Damon Wayans's clever, energetic *In Living Color* on Fox, brought a domesticated gangsta sensibility to the variety show format. In America's unwholesome culture, anger stirred the alienated while entertaining the masses.

"Up to the Jew Neighborhood": The Crown Heights Riots

Five months after Rodney King's beating, the often-smoldering Crown Heights neighborhood in Brooklyn, New York, exploded. The triggering incident occurred when an ultra-Orthodox Jewish "Hasid" driving in the motorcade of the Lubavitch "Rebbe," an esteemed rabbi, jumped either a yellow or red light, lost control, and accidentally pinned Gavin Cato, a seven-year-old black child and his cousin against a window grate. Cato died.

Urging each other to go "up to the Jew neighborhood," angry African Americans rioted. Militants would celebrate this "rebellion" or "uprising," as a justified response to white "racism and oppression." During the violence, rioters stabbed Yankel Rosenbaum, a twenty-nine-year-old Hasidic student from Australia. Before he died, Rosenbaum identified one assailant, Lemrick Nelson Jr. Nelson's pants had bloodstains with Rosenbaum's blood type. When a jury acquitted Nelson in 1992, the backlash doomed Mayor David Dinkins's reelection campaign. After two federal trials, Nelson was convicted in 2003 of violating Rosenbaum's civil rights and sentenced to ten years in jail, most of which he had served pretrial.

Newspapers, especially *The New York Times,* described a "Racial Clash" between two equally guilty and violent groups. Twenty year later, a *Times* reporter, Ari Goldman, would confess that his editors refashioned the copy he and his colleagues sent to fit their "frame" of battling bigots in a racial conflict. The *Times* like most of the media suppressed the African American anti-Semitism fueling the riot, while depicting the Jews as equal combatants rather than targeted victims. Goldman "never saw—or heard of—any violence by Jews against blacks." Jimmy Breslin, the feisty *Newsday* columnist, insisted his editors tell the story accurately after black rioters pulled him from a taxi, beat him, and stripped him. Nevertheless, Breslin grumbled, "up in the higher echelons of journalism, some moron starts talking about balanced coverage."

In three days, rioters injured 152 police officers and 38 civilians, looted 6 stores, and torched 27 vehicles. The Hasidim claimed Dinkins responded slowly to allow the community to "vent its rage." Many on the mostly white police force criticized their black mayor and black commissioner for squelching more effective, meaning aggressive, responses.

The Hill-Thomas Showdown: "You Just Don't Get It"

As post-riot recriminations roiled New York, Washington experienced a brutal confirmation hearing. President Bush nominated Judge Clarence Thomas to the Supreme Court. This intelligent, ambitious Catholic kid from rural Georgia had worked in the Senate and the Department of Education, before chairing Reagan's Equal Employment Opportunity Commission (EEOC). A prickly Reaganite, he considered affirmative action demeaning and complained in 1984 that all civil rights activists do is "bitch, bitch, bitch, moan and whine."

Many African Americans, who linked their political and racial identities, considered Thomas's views treasonous. Democrats resented that Bush nominated such a conservative to replace Thurgood Marshall, a civil rights lawyer who became the first African American Supreme Court Justice. Feminists were outraged when Thomas, dodging abortion questions, claimed he never discussed *Roe v. Wade,* even among friends.

Four years earlier, a vicious political and ideological campaign caused the Senate to reject Ronald Reagan's Supreme Court nominee, Judge Robert Bork. Now, the brawl turned personal. Anita Hill, a law professor who, like Thomas, climbed from a humble background to Yale Law School, worked with him at the Department of Education and the EEOC. She claimed that Thomas spoke to her crassly about sex while hounding her for dates. If true, such unwelcome sexual advances created a "hostile working environment," constituting employment discrimination under Title VII of the 1964 Civil Rights Act.

Thomas denied the allegations. Many supporters noted that Hill followed him to the EEOC and solicited recommendations from him previously. Hill, however, had told a friend about the incidents at the time. When asked why she never complained formally, she replied: "Who would I file it with? He was chairman of the EEOC."

Like the civil rights movement, feminism was caught in a bewildering round-about. Both movements revolutionized America. Women's liberation trans-formed women's inner lives, their personal relationships, their social obligations, their political roles. Women were working more, marrying later, doing less housework, begetting fewer children, getting divorced more frequently. But this age of great expectations spawned intense disappointments. Black activists and feminists felt more embattled than empowered as the 1990s began, em-phasizing obstacles remaining not transformations achieved. Seeking traction amid conservative dominance, nurturing grievances to advance their cause made sense. But it poisoned the political atmosphere.

The Senate Judiciary had concluded its hearings when an unknown staffer leaked word of the allegations. On October 8, Democratic representatives Patricia Schroeder and Barbara Boxer led their female colleagues from the House and Senate in a protest march against "the ultimate men's club," the Sen-ate, and demanded a proper investigation. "The times they are a-changin' and the boys here don't get it on this issue," Schroeder complained.

The uncomfortable senators on the Judiciary Committee, all men, agreed to postpone the Senate vote. Professor Hill appeared elegant, demure, steely, and businesslike, busting stereotypes by not being an angry black woman, a flir-tatious sex kitten, or a furious feminist. She claimed Thomas had "spoken of his sexual prowess." He discussed "the size of his private parts." He joked about the pornographic film star, "Long Dong Silver." He once looked at a soda can on his desk and asked: "Who has put pubic hair on my Coke?" Hill's initial reluctance to testify buttressed her credibility. She passed a polygraph test, which Thomas refused to take.

Senator Arlen Specter, a Pennsylvania Republican, doubted Hill, noting, "The lateness of the allegation, the absence of any touching or intimidation and the fact that she moved with him from one agency to another." Trying to "de-molish" Hill's credibility, Specter questioned her "allegations." She snapped: "It's the truth." Flanked by his fellow old white males on the committee—a new prism for most Americans—Specter and his colleagues looked like bullies.

This strange drama, televised live on major networks, transfixed Americans, stimulating a nationwide seminar on sexual harassment. The Hill-Thomas Show-down provided the perfect sequel to The Gulf War Show, revolving around

America's other obsession after violence, sex. Tom Brokaw, who retained his Midwestern reserve despite decades in New York, remarked, "We have never heard that kind of discussion."

Washington became Scandalvania, a town divided into equally unyielding, equally self-righteous camps, demonizing one person and lionizing the other. "They are trying to destroy this decent man," President Bush fumed, appalled by "the smug liberal staffers who leak FBI reports to achieve their ignoble ends." Many women took this fight personally, the Democratic activist Ann Lewis noted, seeing it as linking "their daily lives and political behavior." Representative Nancy Pelosi, a San Francisco Democrat, said, "They are men, they can't possibly know what it's like to receive verbal harassment, harassment that is fleeting to the man and lasting and demeaning to the woman."

Thomas trumped the gender issues by playing the race card. Denying the charges, he said that when he heard these allegations would be aired, "I died." Then, launching a different missile straight into the national psyche, he charged that white liberals opposed to him as a black conservative had engineered this "high-tech lynching for uppity blacks." Americans "still have underlying racial attitudes about black men and their views of sex," he declared. "And once you pin that on me, I can't get it off."

For all his insistence on being judged as an individual, Thomas exploited white guilt and black anger. America's black middle class is "in excruciating pain," crushed by contradictory expectations, Newsweek's Ellis Cose would write in his 1993 best seller, The Rage of a Privileged Class. The conservative academic Shelby Steele would call it "Being black and feeling blue." Middle-class blacks felt rejected as traitors by poor blacks and as outsiders by whites.

Thomas tapped into blacks' anger and stirred whites' "shame," demonstrating what Steele called "the underdog's bite." In September, shortly before the Thomas-Hill clash, ABC's Primetime Live with Diane Sawyer had secretly filmed a black man and a white man of similar ages and backgrounds wandering around St. Louis. Car dealers, shoe salesmen, and store clerks warmly welcomed the white guy. The black guy was ignored, viewed suspiciously, or tailed. In 1984, the comedian Eddie Murphy had masqueraded as white in a Saturday Night Live satire. He "discovered" that when blacks were not around, whites received free loans and danced happily on buses—arrhythmically, of course. Seven years later, ABC's exposé showed the middle-class black's real world of slights and stereotypes.

The Senate confirmed Thomas, 52 to 48, the closest Supreme Court confirmation vote in over a century. Once again, brutal Washington partisanship sapped Americans' faith in politics. The Republicans' manhandling of Hill was so infuriating, many woman credited it with reviving feminism. That fall,

Susan Faludi's lament about the Reagan-era *Backlash* against women became an instant best seller.

A female "buddy movie," *Thelma and Louise,* fed the pro-Anita Hill backlash. Susan Sarandon and Geena Davis played two friends who fight off rape and sexual harassment. The movie ends with the two women driving their 1966 Ford Thunderbird convertible off a cliff into the Grand Canyon.

Some critics griped that the movie embodied the radical feminist slur "every man is a potential rapist." Many women overlooked the violence, nihilism, and anti-male stereotyping to embrace the movie as a liberating "antidote" to the Thomas hearings. Six months after the hearings, when over two thousand women cheered Hill in New York, they sported buttons saying, "Graduate of Thelma and Louise Finishing School," while chanting, "We believe Anita Hill."

Increasingly, the phrase "You just don't get it," became the shorthand telegraphing female frustration with male blockheadedness. "We must never again shy from raising our voices . . . ," said the Arkansas governor's wife, Hillary Rodham. "All women who care about equal opportunity—about integrity and morality . . . are in Professor Anita Hill's debt." With his fledgling presidential campaign already hounded by rumors of his tomcatting, Bill Clinton dodged the fight, saying he never would have nominated Thomas for ideological reasons.

Days after the Thomas confirmation, the Senate passed the Civil Rights Act of 1991 modifying Title VII of the Civil Rights Act of 1964. The new law allowed women to collect damages for sexual discrimination or harassment. "Sex" had been included in the original 1964 law only because Southerners trying to block the legislation added what seemed to them an absurd category even Northerners would reject. Now, reeling from the Thomas hearings, Bush signed the 1991 update. A year earlier, he had vetoed similar legislation, fearing that provisions allowing courts to assess the "disparate-impact" of hiring patterns would impose quotas in hiring. This expansive bill, which would feed America's litigation explosion, along with his 1990 signing of the Americans with Disabilities Act, shaped Bush's legacy as a surprisingly civil-rights-friendly Republican president.

A Kennedy Rape Trial

Throughout the Thomas battle, one senator was particularly uncomfortable, Ted Kennedy. The liberal lion sat beside the Judiciary Chairman Joe Biden, looking red-faced, puff-jawed, dissolute, and defeated. The accusations against Thomas did not compare to Kennedy's criminal behavior in July 1969 when he drove his car off Chappaquiddick Bridge on Martha's Vineyard after a night of partying, leaving a young woman named Mary Jo Kopechne inside the car to drown. On Good Friday, March 30, 1991, after the now fifty-nine-year-old senior statesman had invited his twenty-three-year-old son Patrick and thirty-year-old nephew William Kennedy Smith to go out drinking, the night ended with Will accused of date rape. The woman Patrick picked up that night at the Au Bar in Palm Beach, Florida, later reported seeing the drunken senator "wobbling" around with his shirt on and pants off, possibly without his boxers. Americans did not need that image of Camelot's crown prince embedded in the national psyche. Office jokesters claimed Clarence Thomas muttered that "being called unethical by Ted Kennedy is like being called slimy by a snail."

Two weeks after the Thomas confirmation, Kennedy took responsibility for "the faults in the conduct of my private life" at the Kennedy acolytes' holy of holies, Harvard's John F. Kennedy School of Government. Following this unprecedented apology from a Kennedy, he rediscovered his progressive voice. "Some of the anger of recent days reflects the pain of a new idea still being born," he explained, "the idea of a society where sex discrimination is ended and sexual harassment is unacceptable."

Five weeks later, in December, the William Kennedy Smith rape trial became the next CNN sensation. The three-week trial mingled celebrity, power, sex, class, money, violence, and heartbreak with spring break. Once again, viewers absorbed embarrassing details about sexual mechanics, now set in the Kennedys' fabulous Palm Beach estate. Once again, the defense relied on assumptions of how women acted and rapists looked. The defense attorney Roy E. Black insisted that "Will Smith"—as he was called during the trial—was "articulate, well-spoken, the antithesis of a rapist." It was as if "all rapists looked like another Willie, Willie Horton," Dominick Dunne, *Vanity Fair*'s celebrity chronicler, would write.

The Kennedy attorneys had to approach the victim gingerly, in a culture increasingly averse to trying rape victims instead of rapists. Americans were becoming more aware of "date rape," a phrase first coined in 1973, then popularized by *Ms.* in 1982. Still, unaware of three other allegations against him, jurors acquitted Smith in only seventy-seven minutes.

During the televised trial, the victim had testified with a blue dot obscuring her face. Feeling abused by the jury's quick decision, the media mockery, and the Kennedy counterattack, Patricia Bowman went on national TV to identify herself and empower rape victims. "I'm not a blue blob," she told Diane Sawyer on ABC's *Primetime Live*. "I'm a human being. I have nothing to be ashamed of."

The Great American Victimization Sweepstakes

All the bad vibes made for some cranky November election campaigns. David Duke, a former Ku Klux Klan Grand Wizard and Nazi sympathizer, had come in second in Louisiana's October 19 gubernatorial election, winning 32 percent of the vote to force a runoff. He enjoyed outsized media attention until the November 16 election. "In David Duke, we have seen the face of American decline," the normally sober commentator Michael Kinsley feared, suggesting that Duke's scapegoating of blacks, Jews, feminists, and immigrants for America's "economic stagnation" worked because "When the pie isn't growing, people become more obsessed with their slice." Virginia governor L. Douglas Wilder linked Duke's placement on the Republican ticket to President Bush's previous civil rights veto. The normally soft-spoken governor accused Bush of becoming "the promoter of prejudice" and a "lap dog of the far right" rather "than an eternal guardian of what is right."

Most Americans knew what was right. Duke lost the runoff. The announcement days earlier that the basketball great Magic Johnson was suffering from AIDS led to a nationwide group hug for this African American celebrity—when it could have led to condemnations of the modern black superstar's sexual promiscuity and seigneurial prerogatives. That fall, the Emmy Awards honored the black actors James Earl Jones and Ruby Dee, along with television specials about the school desegregation case, the Watts Riot, and the first African American to star in a movie, Josephine Baker. Even so, America's racial wounds remained infected.

In this year of backlash, white males counterpunched, too. By 1991, with the genteel culture's stiff upper lip replaced by the therapeutic culture's quivering self-pity, with identity politics promoting collective senses of mass injury, groups competed to win The Great American Victimization Sweepstakes. In an age of affirmative action, multiculturalism, sexual harassment charges, *Thelma and Louise,* and gangsta rap, some white males started feeling oppressed. In 1990, the poet Robert Bly's precious, uplifting New Age book *Iron John: A Book about Men* tried liberating the new "soft male." While "more thoughtful, more gentle," than the "aggressive," patriotic, macho "Fifties man," modern men had become too flaccid and were miserable. Bly's call for "the Nineties male" to get in touch with his inner "large, primitive . . . hairy . . . Wild Man," spent sixty-two weeks on *The New York Times* best-seller list.

On campus, fights over curricula, teaching techniques, professorial statements, even students' "misdirected laughter," divided departments, ruined friendships, besmirched student records, and derailed academic careers. The values of "PC" and "multiculturalism" also affected newsrooms, elementary school classrooms, museums, and corporations, where diversity officers increasingly implemented diversity training programs. From forty articles mentioning "multiculturalism" in 1981, two thousand articles would discuss it in 1992.

A thirty-year-old Indian American, Dinesh D'Souza, led this backlash against multiculturalism and political correctness. A Dartmouth graduate and former Reagan staffer, his 1991 blockbuster, *Illiberal Education: The Politics of Race and Sex on Campus,* collected the most outrageous examples of academic doublethink in the service of identity politics. Listed together, they made universities look particularly oppressive, narrow-minded, propagandistic, and foolish. A University of Pennsylvania professor dismissed "reading and writing" as "merely technologies of control," while celebrating rap's oral tradition encouraging anti-white hooliganism. A CCNY department chairman claimed whites became violent because the Ice Age deformed white genes. Disapproval was unidirectional. One manual for race and gender education explained, "It is not open to debate whether a white student is racist or a male student is sexist. He/she simply is." The PC police made it clear: Afrocentrism, wimmin, gays, multiculturalism, and postmodernism were in; white males, patriotism, tradition, the establishment, were out.

Many traditional liberals shared the conservatives' frustrations with these New Left radicals and their identity politics. A June 1991 New York State report, *One Nation, Many Peoples: A Declaration of Cultural Interdependence,* proposed a new social studies curriculum respecting "distinctiveness." One committee member, the Kennedy liberal, Arthur M. Schlesinger Jr., dissented. He then published *The Disuniting of America,* rejecting this "attack on the common American identity," using "history as therapy" to make immigrants and minorities feel good. "The point of America was not to preserve old cultures, but to forge a new *American* culture," Schlesinger insisted. The political philosopher Michael Walzer responded by endorsing "a singular citizenship and a radically pluralist civil society," preserving particular traditions while nurturing common political values in this "nation of nationalities."

In 1994, *New York Times* reporter Richard Bernstein would warn that this new *Dictatorship of Virtue* "threatened" America with "a narrow orthodoxy—and the occasional outright intellectual atrocity—imposed, or committed, in the name of the very values that are supposed to define a pluralist society." The Sixties' activist and academic Todd Gitlin feared these cultural obsessions were balkanizing Americans when minorities needed to ally with whites to reduce "the inequality of wealth and income." Rather than seeking real political power, he lamented, radicals were "Marching on the English Department while the

Right took the White House." The New Left, which began with the Berkeley's Free Speech movement in 1964, had morphed into the PC Left, so obsessed with identity politics and cultural control it proposed speech codes on campus.

Beyond the idiocy and zealotry, American institutions needed to be more welcoming. Certain traditions perpetuated racism, sexism, and homophobia. Medical school professors who once made funny but lecherous anatomical jokes had to stop. Men who patted colleagues on the fanny and called them "dear" had to adjust. More subtly, African Americans detected racial insensitivities even on progressive campuses: the woman crossing to the other side of the street at night when a fellow law student who happened to be a black male approached from out of the shadows; the pursed lips when discussing affirmative action; the "black tables" in college cafeterias nationwide, four decades after *Brown v. Board of Education*.

The Metropolitan Trainwreck

All this bile accumulated as the economy stagnated during 1991. The unemployment rate rose from 6.2 percent in January to 7.1 percent by December. Median income dipped. The proportion of poor Americans rose from 12.8 percent to 14.2 percent. In late October, for the first time, less than half of those surveyed wanted Bush reelected. Seventy percent believed he "spends too much time on foreign problems and not enough on problems in this country."

Many of the internal problems Bush ignored caused Philadelphia's Metropolitan Trainwreck. Deindustrialization and suburbanization stripped the city of rewarding jobs and taxpaying citizens, spawning more crime, homelessness, and debt. "Brownfields" sprouted citywide, ugly, dangerous, deserted lots and decayed buildings that had once been thriving factories. Philadelphia's unemployment rate of 6.2 percent in 1990 was 8.5 percent by 1991.

Forty percent of Pennsylvania's welfare recipients lived in Philadelphia. With fewer taxpaying citizens, finances ebbed while taxes spiked. City dwellers were paying three times the tax rate of suburbanites. "If we raised taxes any more than we did, we would have had to expand the highways to the suburbs for all the moving vans," City Councilman John F. Street warned. With money tight, schools deteriorated and crime jumped 15.7 percent in 1990 alone. The City of Brotherly Love now produced more than half of Pennsylvania's prisoners.

The winner in the 1991 mayoral race, Ed Rendell, a Democrat, vowed to restore civic pride and revive downtown. Rendell would begin by inviting volunteers to spruce up City Hall, whose deterioration reflected the city's general depression. More than 1,500 people would show up for five hours one Saturday afternoon to help Rendell fulfill his campaign promise that within ninety days he would have the corrupt, crony-dominated City Hall "smelling if not like roses, at least like Lysol."

Statewide, on Election Day, Bush's former attorney general Dick Thornburgh lost a Senate race despite starting with a forty-point lead in the polls, two previous terms as governor, and the president's blessing. In April, Pennsylvania's senator John Heinz, the heir to the ketchup fortune, had died in a plane crash. Harris Wofford, his replacement, was a former John Kennedy aide who had never run for office before.

Wofford endorsed national health insurance and excoriated Bush for abandoning Americans to recession. Playing the outsider, he rejected an unpopular $23,200 Senate raise, donating the money instead to a Gulf War veterans' charity. Wofford's "middle-class populism" triumphed, panicking the Bush White House and encouraging the two campaign consultants behind Wofford's landslide upset, James Carville and Paul Begala. Voters in this critical, representative state were mad at Bush, at Reagan, at Thomas—and intrigued by national health reform. Mocking Bush's foreign policy jet-setting, when he attended a NATO summit in Italy, Democrats distributed T-shirts saying, "GEORGE BUSH WENT TO ROME AND ALL I GOT WAS THIS LOUSY RECESSION!"

Developing Clinton's New Covenant

All this bad Bush news encouraged one recently announced Democratic presidential candidate, Bill Clinton. The Democrats' loss in the Thomas confirmation vote reminded many operatives of their 1988 frustrations, when Michael Dukakis absorbed Bush's snarls against liberalism. "They have an instinct for the jugular," said David Axelrod, the Chicago Democratic consultant, "and we have an instinct for the capillary."

Clinton promised to campaign aggressively. Shortly after Wofford's win, he hired Carville and Begala for his presidential campaign. "In the 1980s, Washington failed us," Clinton charged, running against Reagan, Bush, and their era. Articulating "a new covenant," he tried moving beyond 1991's crankiness to a renewed optimism: "Together we can make America great again, and build a community of hope that will inspire the world."

Clinton's New Covenant emerged from Democrats' debate about why they had lost five of the last six presidential elections. Democrats were still reeling from Reagan. Their New Left coalition of "militant blacks, feminists, civil rights leaders, gay activists and labor unions" was too easily typed as a radical cabal of special interest groups. The American people repudiated that kind of party with Walter Mondale's sweeping loss in 1984.

On February 28, 1985, moderate Democrats launched the Democratic Leadership Council, led by Al From, formerly of the House Democratic Caucus. The Reverend Jesse Jackson mocked the DLC as the "Democrats for the Leisure Class." Others, noting the prominence of Virginia governor Chuck Robb and Georgia senator Sam Nunn, dismissed this "Southern white boys' caucus."

Dukakis's loss in 1988 vindicated the moderates. "No matter how popular your programs may be, you must be considered in the mainstream on the shared values of the American people, the ability to defend the nation and the strength to enforce its laws," Clinton concluded. William Galston, a political scientist, argued that the Democratic Party had to find a 1992 nominee, viable in every region, who could also "offer a progressive economic message, based on the values of social opportunity and individual effort." The party had to place itself "squarely in the mainstream, on the side of average families," with "a multiracial coalition based on shared values and common interests." Most important was addressing what Galston, Walter Mondale's 1984 issues director, called "the central social issue of our time—violent crime."

From offered Clinton the DLC chairmanship, promising "a national platform" which would make him president. In March 1990, Clinton agreed. The DLC issued its "New Orleans Declaration," proclaiming "the Democratic Party's fundamental mission is to expand opportunity, not government" while promising to replace the "politics of entitlement with a new politics of reciprocal responsibility." From would recall that emphasizing "equal opportunity, not equal outcomes," in what emerged as Clinton's "philosophical bible," reconnected DLC Democrats to American liberalism rather than European social democracy.

Clinton had learned from George McGovern's losing campaign the political costs of being "out of touch with the demands and desires of the American people," especially the middle class. Seeking to save liberalism from itself, From rooted this DLC rebellion in the Democratic mainstream. The DLC was continuing Thomas Jefferson's faith in individual liberty, Andrew Jackson's fight for equal opportunity, Franklin Roosevelt's "thirst for innovation," Harry Truman's "tough-minded internationalism," and John Kennedy's "ethic of civic responsibility."

Two weeks into his fledgling campaign, on October 23, 1991, at Georgetown University, Clinton promised to "end welfare as we know it," with a time limit of "two years" for recipients. As a governor who loved talking to constituents,

Clinton learned how much welfare recipients detested the system. He often told the story that when he asked a woman what was the best thing about being off welfare, she said, "When someone asks my son what does your mama do for a living, he can give an answer." To the DLC's Bruce Reed, "welfare reform was the best opportunity to outline the new social bargain that Clinton and the New Democrats had been working on. It was the ultimate combination of opportunity and responsibility."

Frustrated liberals and recovering conservatives encouraged the DLC's muscular moderation. In 1990, the former Nixonite Kevin Phillips's *The Politics of Rich and Poor* claimed the Reaganomics-induced gap between rich and poor gave Democrats a chance to appear populist. Thomas Edsall and Mary Edsall warned, however, in *Chain Reaction: The Impact of Race, Rights, and Taxes on American Politics* (1991), that Democrats first had to reassure whites. Republicans were stirring white indignation that despite the high taxes resulting from government attempts to aid blacks, the problems only worsened. In *Why Americans Hate Politics* (1991) E. J. Dionne claimed the constant squabbling over cultural and social issues helped Republicans win elections but alienated everyone from politics.

These analyses and his DLC work shaped Clinton's campaign, and what *The New Republic*'s Sidney Blumenthal called "The Conversation." Clinton emphasized all Americans' economic woes. He distanced himself from racial special interests. He insisted that Democrats had mainstream values, too. And, Blumenthal wrote, Clinton's detailed plans for "leaner, activist government" showed that he was not only talking about how to get elected, but what to do once elected.

Backlash: Identity Threatens Community in a Borderline Nation

As America sank into recession and recrimination, as movies like Oliver Stone's *JFK* fed American cynicism about conspiracies afoot, and as recession-time fairy tales like *The Commitments* celebrated simple, working-class pleasures, the year ended with a surge of imported hope. In March, the Warsaw Pact, the Soviet bloc's backbone, ended Eastern Europe's military alliance. In July, Bush and Mikhail Gorbachev signed the START treaty limiting long-range nuclear weapons, followed by more unilateral nuclear cutbacks in the fall. In August, Boris Yeltsin scrambled atop a tank to confront Communists and defend Gorbachev's reforms. In September, Nelson Mandela, newly freed from prison, signed a peace accord with South Africa's president Frederik Willem de Klerk. On October 31, Israelis negotiated with Arabs in Madrid, including Palestinians and Syrians. On December 16, the Soviet Union voted with the newly independent Eastern bloc states to repeal the resolution it pushed through the UN's General Assembly in 1975, labeling Zionism a form of racism. Most miraculously, on December 26, 1991, the Soviet Union dissolved peacefully, voluntarily. The Commonwealth of Independent States replaced it.

These were mind-boggling changes. Yet, by the end of this backlash year, many Americans felt frustrated by the Cold War victory's limited payoffs and by a Republican president now seen as lacking Ronald Reagan's charisma, vision, or luck. Driving north to Philadelphia's lush suburbs from its airport southwest of downtown, visitors often passed acres of urban moonscape, illustrating America's crumbling infrastructure physically, socially, culturally, ideologically. The year's ugly gender and race wars, over Rodney King and Clarence Thomas, from Los Angeles to Crown Heights, suggested America needed healing at home.

Since 1945, the Cold War had provided Americans with an organizing ideological framework. Now, many Americans debunked traditional narratives and abandoned collective visions and ties. Warning of a massive retreat from the communal, with all its artifices, to a narrow, flattened obsession with the self, the sociologist Jock Young would observe, "Just as community collapses, identity is invented." "Identity" was a diffuse form of belonging often without really joining. Identity encouraged rhetorical commitments without responsibilities. Identity clashes, all these flamboyant assertions of self or one's subgroup, would often distract from the important business of governing.

This more open, forgiving, creative America was also more unsure, unsettled, and unhappy. The "culture of narcissism" the historian Christopher Lasch diagnosed in the 1970s, had spawned a Borderline Nation, a culture exhibiting the collective traits of Borderline Personality Disorder. Borderline traits included: impulsivity, reactivity, anger, identity confusion, feelings of emptiness, severe mood shifts between elation and despair, with resulting relationship volatility, fears of abandonment, and self-destructive behaviors including substance abuse, sexual promiscuity, shoplifting, reckless driving, binge eating, self-mutilating, and even suicide. These pathologies became epidemic in Borderline societies.

Experts call Borderline Personality Disorder "emotional hemophilia." A nation engulfed by constant media-fueled controversies, especially the Anita Hill–Clarence Thomas hearings, to be followed by the O. J. Simpson trial marathon, the Whitewater and Lewinsky scandals, and other spectacles, repeatedly suffered from collective whiplash. America's Borderline culture staggered from fad to fad, from mass impulse to mass impulse—America as Vulgaria. America's

Borderline politics lurched from one moral panic to the next—Scandalvania. America's Borderline economics oscillated between boom and bust, between the abandon of the Wall Street high rollers and the despair of the workers, the un-employed, and the no-longer-even-bothering-to-seek employment, as the gap between the big winners at the top and everyone else grew in Boomville. In Id-land, a highly mobile, overly sexualized, quicksilver society emerged, amid widespread family breakdown, distanced from the past and fearing the future. With the most basic identity and values questions up for grabs, surges of emo-tional distress followed.

The sexual revolution's unresolved issues fueled many of these cultural bat-tles and identity conflicts, demonstrated by the 1990s' rap wars, the Hill-Thomas hearings, the Kennedy rape trial, and the cult of Thelma and Louise. When Florida governor Martinez tried banning 2 Live Crew, seventeen-year-old Adrienne McCartney challenged him—and the conservative establishment by extension. "Are you living in a fantasy world?" she asked. "You don't like abor-tion. You don't like sex education. You don't like curse words. Everything having to do with sex, you go and have a fit. Are you married?"

It often did seem to be "all about sex" in many Nineties' squabbles, making for contentious and colorful times. Those unresolved issues, awkwardly juxta-posed with a yearning to be redeemed as demonstrated by Harris Wofford's un-likely Pennsylvania win, would shape the 1992 elections. Millions of Americans would learn to hope again, thanks to a charismatic Baby Boomer from the tiny town of Hope, Arkansas.

3

1992: Little Rock
"Don't Stop Thinking About Tomorrow"

Bubba, Billary, and the Rise of the Adversarials

We offer our people a new choice based on old values. We offer opportunity. We demand responsibility. We will build an American community again.

—BILL CLINTON, NOMINATION ACCEPTANCE SPEECH,
JULY 16, 1992, NEW YORK

The steady rain and the November chill could not douse the crowd's enthusiasm. They had done it. They had unseated an incumbent. They had deposed the staid, moralistic, *Father Knows Best,* World War II veterans' generation. The "War Room" strategy, counterattacking and focusing on "the economy, stupid," worked. The "opportunity, responsibility, community" mantra, distancing this Democrat from the stale liberalism of the Sixties, convinced. And the seductive riffs of this generation's greatest political talent inspired. The Baby Boomers would boogie into the White House to the beat of Fleetwood Mac's "Don't Stop (Thinking About Tomorrow)," led by the honey-smooth, supersmart, perpetual adolescent, Governor Bill Clinton of Arkansas, and his more disciplined yet more polarizing wife, Hillary Rodham Clinton.

During this searing campaign, Clinton endured accusations of adultery, draft dodging, and smoking pot. Guilty as charged, he surgically refuted particular inaccuracies while chiding reporters for scrutinizing his personal life not his political record. Insisting "character is a journey," he injected a New Age, post-Sixties' sensibility into American politics. The 1992 election became a true generational culture clash.

Clinton was an unlikely winner. George Bush's popularity had discouraged the Democrats' best candidates. The Democrats were drifting ideologically, demoralized by the Great Society's failure, white middle-class anger at perceived black prerogatives, and epidemics of crime, poverty, social instability, and family breakdown. Clinton was suppressing more "bimbo eruptions" than Gary Hart, whose 1988 campaign collapsed in this new Victorian Age—at least regarding presidential politics. Hillary Rodham Clinton's edgy contrast with the matronly, popular First Lady Barbara Bush further upped the cultural stakes.

Nevertheless, Clinton understood that Reaganism was fading in a changing America. He won the cultural skirmishes that year, not just the political battle. Every presidential election invites Americans to analyze yesterday, assess today, and shape tomorrow. Clinton made Bush look like a prisoner of the repressed, monochromatic past, while exploiting Americans' fears in the recession-afflicted present, and empowering a modernizing America to embrace its diverse, free future.

Little Rock was a city of 175,795 people in a poor, marginal state with only 2.3 million residents. In this city of faded glory, its state flag evoked the defeated Confederacy. Its downtown had massive patches of economic bald spots—empty lots. Its governor's mansion, meaning Bill Clinton's home, was in an iffy neighborhood with weathered "Crime Watch" signs. In this laggard state, whereas 75 percent of Americans had graduated from high school, and 20 percent had graduated from college, only 66 percent of Arkansans were high school graduates, with only 13 percent college graduates. The national poverty rate was 13 percent; Arkansas's was 19 percent. Having endured Northern condescension for so long, one Arkansan would rejoice when Clinton won, "The best thing about this is that the rest of the world gets to see we wear shoes and have indoor plumbing." To outsiders, this Ozark outpost was a ridiculous base for the first Baby Boomer president. But to Friends of Bill who knew Clinton and his Southern-inflected, values-oriented middle way, it made sense.

Wal-Mart Populism and Ivy League Progressivism

Arkansas's most important export was Wal-Mart, with Sam Walton as its most famous citizen—until the Clintons' rise. Designated by *The New York Times* as "the most successful merchant of his time," Mr. Sam, as his loyal employees called him, opened the first Wal-Mart Discount City in 1962 in Rogers, Arkansas. By 1992, with 1,735 stores in 42 states, the chain had passed Sears to become the nation's largest retailer.

Wal-Mart grew as Americans earned more disposable income and gained more leisure time, making shopping the new national pastime. America's car culture and consumer culture enfeebled traditional community culture. Abandoning Main Street, Wal-Marts sprouted in strip malls on large tracts of land frequently just outside of town.

A Southern populist turned patrician, Mr. Sam understood how to stay charming—and popular—while becoming America's richest man, worth $23 billion by 1992. He spread his gospel of good service from store to store, cheering his nonunionized workers. "We've got the best group of people ever assembled in retailing," he would shout. "*Yes, we can,*" his workers bellowed in response. "Who's number one?" Sam asked. The staffers replied: "*The customer! Always.*"

Wal-Mart's integrated staff and shoppers reflected the post–Civil Rights South. Wal-Mart's army of 40 percent part-time workers also reflected America's postindustrial economy, lacking the solid base of middle-class workers. Multiple studies found that each new Wal-Mart lowered area pay rates, shrank the job market by an average of 150 jobs, and cost local governments more money by straining welfare services, health care needs, and infrastructure. Critics challenged: Could Americans sustain their thriving consumer culture on $5 to $9 an hour?

Arkansas's intimate political culture was populist in style, and usually kind to patricians in result. Many secrets and much gossip bound the interlocking political and business classes. Both Arkansas Bubba and Ivy League Overachiever, Clinton combined the infectious, common-sense populism of Mr. Sam, the deal-making savvy of a bloviating Southern politico, and the intellectualism of a Rhodes Scholar.

A secular preacher-priest in an age of doubt, Clinton built a bridge to the twenty-first century and to voters mixing progressive expertise with populist homilies. Raised in the South, he empathized with lower-class and middle-class voters flailing about amid chaotic lives. Educated in the Northeast, he was one of the self-selected American Brahmans seeking a new order. The mass middle-class consumer revolution of the 1940s and 1950s, the political and cultural revolutions of the 1960s and 1970s, had dissolved fundamental American assumptions, values, institutions, ways of life. Clinton would preside over a growing information-age revolution, which further accelerated those changes—while trying to help Americans get oriented in the new identity-demolishing, vertigo-inducing, perplexing, exhilarating, ever-more wired (in both senses of the word) modern American "funhouse."

Clinton's family was a real-life Faulknerian Southern Gothic tale. Bill's mother Virginia Dell Cassidy Blythe Clinton Dwire Kelley would marry five times, twice to the same man. Bill's biological father, William Jefferson Blythe Jr., died in an auto accident three months before Virginia gave birth on August 19,

1946, to their only child. The young boy eventually took the name of Virginia's second husband, Roger Clinton. Roger was such a mean drunk that Bill would soften his own image by recalling being fourteen and finally tall enough to confront his abusive stepfather.

Raised by his brassy but loving mother, and doting but demanding grandparents, in the small town of Hope before moving to the bigger burlesque of Hot Springs, Clinton mixed the neglected son's need to please with the poor kid's zeal to succeed. In July 1963, this smart, charming, already ambitious seventeen-year-old was one of two Arkansas "senators" to Boy's Nation, a national convention in Maryland. At a White House reception, Clinton positioned himself at the front of the line to shake President John Kennedy's hand. Three decades later, when Clinton's aides premiered the photograph during the 1992 Democratic National Convention's biopic, the crowd erupted at this passing of the generational torch. "If it is possible to gasp and shout at once, that's what we did," recalls Thomas Dunne, a prominent New York publisher.

Clinton went out-of-state to college, attending Georgetown University's School of Foreign Service, undergraduate class of 1968. In Washington, D.C., he interned with his state's senator J. William Fulbright. Clinton parlayed those experiences into a Rhodes Scholarship at Oxford University.

The curse of the Vietnam War followed him to England. Clinton first used educational deferments and a feigned interest in ROTC to avoid getting drafted. In late 1969, after a high lottery number of 311 freed him from fears of being called, he withdrew from ROTC. Writing to the University of Arkansas ROTC director, Colonel Eugene Holmes, Clinton admitted that he hated the Vietnam War as much as he abhorred American racism. He confessed to accepting the draft "to maintain my political viability within the system." He sought "to prepare myself for a political life characterized by both practical political ability and concern for rapid social progress." This brazen, mature letter reflected his signature mix of idealism and opportunism.

The Adversarial Supercouple:
"Elvis" and "Sister Frigidaire"

Clinton advanced to Yale Law School, graduating in 1973. In New Haven, he was already openly campaigning for president, keeping lists of everyone he met. He befriended many peers who as Friends of Bill would help shape his future, especially the ultimate FOB, the brainy, ambitious feminist who became his wife, Hillary Rodham.

A fellow go-getting Baby Boomer, Rodham was born on October 26, 1947, in Chicago, Illinois. A graduate of Wellesley, class of 1969, she famously approached Clinton first, at the Yale Law Library in 1971, saying: "If you're going to keep looking at me and I'm going to keep looking back, we might as well be introduced. I'm Hillary Rodham." Thus began a tumultuous, decades-long love affair and political partnership between the man nicknamed "Elvis" and the woman nicknamed "Sister Frigidaire" in high school. Hillary admired Bill's people smarts and buoyancy. Bill admired Hillary's intellect and discipline.

Both Clintons resented outsiders who dismissed their operatic marriage as an arrangement. Both would admit, using various euphemisms, that fidelity in marriage was not one of his virtues. At one mortifying strategy session in 1992, regarding what the pollster Stan Greenberg calls "this subject," Mrs. Clinton said, "Obviously, if I could say 'no' to this question, we would say 'no,' and therefore, there is an issue." Their marriage, which began on October 11, 1975, would be surprisingly old-fashioned in its mutual devotion to the head of the household. "Hillary loves Bill, and Bill loves Bill," the Clintons' political swami Dick Morris would explain.

Life in Wellesley and Georgetown, at Oxford and Yale, had steeped both Bill and Hillary in the social, cultural, and political revolutions they eventually would personify. Inspired by civil rights and feminism, infuriated by Vietnam, horrified by the assassinations of Martin Luther King Jr. and Bobby Kennedy, terrified by the urban riots, they were radicalized. With their characteristic arrogance, they and their allies would universalize their assault on tradition as generational. Actually, they were an elite minority. Even in 1992, polls would show Baby Boomers split regarding the Clintons.

These high-achieving revolutionaries have been labeled "The Countercul-ture," "The New Class," "The Movement," "The Yuppies." Perhaps most accurate would be to call them "The Adversarial Insiders." When the literary critic Lionel Trilling described the "adversary culture" in 1965 as the "legitimization of the subversive," these Guerilla Careerists did not seem destined to become America's new establishment. By conquering the academy, the media, the courts, and the Democratic Party, these modernists transformed America. Building on the 1960s' rebellions, the 1970s' implosions, and the 1980s' recalibrations, these Adversarial Insiders made American democracy more horizontal—more accessible, less hierarchical, more informal, less bigoted. Their opponents, Provincial Outsiders, more rooted in their local contexts, preferred America's solid provincial past to its quicksilver cosmopolitan present.

The Clintons believed, Hillary explained, "that the system could be changed from within." Both sought "to practice politics as the art of making what appears to be impossible, possible." Bill's Huey Long–Lyndon Johnson South combined grand political gestures with special political deliveries. Hillary's Chicagoland accepted Mayor Richard Daley's beneficent but controlling boss rule. Both idolized Martin Luther King Jr. They understood politics as a noble calling tempered by pragmatism and pettiness.

Bill Clinton was too good a politician to be very ideological. He and his centrist DLC peers were tired of losing elections. They disliked what modern liberalism had become. Clinton emphasized "equal opportunity, not equal outcomes," middle-class dreams not special interests. He defended those who "work hard and play by the rules." This fusion of Southern populism and Northeast Ivy League progressivism made him "another Bobby Kennedy who could put together working-class whites and blacks," his DLC ally Al From recalled. From respected Clinton's willingness to "battle" for his "deep beliefs," understanding that "You need some grease, a little hocus pocus sometimes, to move things forward." Like the Kennedys, Clinton impressed Americans with a dexterous toughness needed to win and govern.

The Post-Watergate Campaign: "They're All Guilty of Something"

Although Bill Clinton's campaign began in 1991 with expressions of idealism and Kennedyesque generational hopes, by January 1992, it was stalling badly. Rumors of marital infidelity risked making the candidate the ridiculed not the redeemer. Headlines proclaimed, "Wild Bill" and "I'm No Gary Hart." David Letterman snickered that Clinton would outspend other candidates "by at least 2 to 1 . . . on Valentine's Day Gifts."

The Anita Hill–Clarence Thomas fight accelerated the post-Watergate presidential expose-a-thon. In late 1975 the Church Committee publicized revelations about CIA assassination attempts and John Kennedy's presidential frolics, just as Betty Ford candidly discussed once-private matters such as her breast cancer and her daughter's sex life. This presidential primal scene, peeping at various presidents' sex lives, injected sleaze, cynicism, and self-righteousness into political coverage. The feminist notion that the personal is political justified scrutinizing the president's private life. The rise of investigative reporting encouraged snooping. The frank discussion of sexual acts connected to the AIDS crisis made reporters' vulgarity appear noble. By 1987, when Gary Hart's adultery scandal killed his presidential dreams, reporters had become the new national vice squad, holding politicians to Puritanical standards many Americans, including those reporters, were abandoning.

Many seemed eager to gossip and to forgive. More and more reasoned that if Kennedy, and even Franklin Roosevelt cheated, but Richard Nixon and Jimmy Carter didn't, better competent adulterers than loyal duds. "I think presidents are people," Clinton would say, "and I think there are lots of different flaws and shortcomings people have." A voter told *Newsweek,* "We're voting for president not pope."

During the crucial New Hampshire primary battle, America's tabloids brought to life the rumors about Clinton with a big-blonde-haired, fire-engine-red-lipsticked cabaret singer turned Arkansas government employee, Gennifer Flowers. Most Americans first met the Clintons in an extraordinary *60 Minutes* interview run after the Super Bowl, denying reports of the twelve-year affair Clinton actually had with Flowers. Steve Kroft probed: "What do you mean . . . that your marriage has had problems?" Clinton cryptically replied: "I think the American people . . . know what it means." Clinton challenged Kroft and his colleagues to stop playing "gotcha." "This will test the character of the press," Clinton mischievously stated.

Hillary Clinton refused to play the silent, long-suffering wife, like Pat Nixon and Lee Hart during their husbands' ordeals. "You know, I'm not sitting here [like] some little woman standing by my man like Tammy Wynette," Hillary said. Her glib reference to a legendary country star's ode to fidelity offended millions of country fans. These infringements on the Clintons' zone of privacy "offended" Hillary and put tremendous pressure on her, Stan Greenberg recalls. If she was "at odds with him, or hurt, a victim rather than a supportive spouse," his candidacy would crash.

Clinton gambled his future on the cynicism of the celebrity culture while attacking it. Americans became inured to the sins of the rich and famous, thanks to the weekly scandals in the *National Enquirer* and the spectacle on exhibitionist talk shows like *Jerry Springer* with one guest who married his horse, another who married his mother.

This mass celebrity gossip-fest taught Americans "they're all guilty of something." In 1992, the boxer Mike Tyson was convicted of rape. The filmmaker Woody Allen was charged with abusing his adopted seven-year-old daughter after running off with his longtime lover Mia Farrow's twenty-one-year-old adopted daughter. Even the Royal Family began what Queen Elizabeth would call its "*annus horribilis*" of affairs and divorces.

Spectacular acts of violence continued making unknowns famous. Seventeen-year-old Amy Fisher, the "Long Island Lolita," shot her older lover's wife in the face, making her lover, Joey Buttafuoco, famous, too. The necrophiliac gay cannibal, Jeffrey Dahmer, killed seventeen young men and became notorious.

Still, when Pentagon sources leaked Clinton's letter about the draft as the sexual gossiping continued, his campaign looked doomed. Voters who had dismissed the sex stories took this draft evasion charge seriously. A generational changeover could work; refighting every battle from the 1960s wouldn't.

The battle-scarred vassals of Clinton's formidable War Room mobilized to save the great seducer from himself. The manic Cajun consultant James Carville, his Jesuitical partner Paul Begala, the congressional insider George Stephanopoulos, the numbers-cruncher Stan Greenberg, and the advertising whiz Mandy Grunwald improvised political jujitsu techniques they would perfect over the next nine years—one of Clinton's mixed gifts to American politics. With the hair-splitting skill of Talmudists, the brutality of Huns, the mutability of Bolsheviks, Clinton's political virtuosos answered every attack, frequently turning accusations onto the enemy. They seized on the smallest discrepancy to obscure the most obvious truth.

During the nineteenth-century's "Dark Ages of Partisan Journalism," partisans only believed the smears they read about their rivals. Clinton triggered a similar polarization. Whatever his flaws, the lies about him and his wife were even more spectacular. Richard Behar, *Time*'s investigative reporter, conclusively debunked tales that charged Clinton with murder, corruption, and CIA-related drug smuggling for Contra forces in Arkansan airfields. Nevertheless, the story persisted, appearing in well-reviewed, best-selling books. "We entered into this bizarre era when certain stories had legs—even when you cut them off," Behar recalls.

While his minions wallowed in the muck, Clinton shamed any questioners who dared interrupt his lofty discourse by questioning his base behaviors. "You know, Ted, the only times you've invited me on your show it was to talk about a woman I never slept with and a draft I never dodged," Clinton chided *Nightline*'s host Ted Koppel. In fact, the governor had slept with that woman and had slithered past the draft. By the time Clinton and his people finished spinning, parsing, browbeating, blackmailing, blast-faxing, defaming, denigrating, scolding, preaching, and pontificating, reporters were chastened, Clinton's poll numbers were rising, and Gennifer Flowers's reputation was mud.

Impaled on a White Picket Fence
in a Sex-Drenched Culture

In America's increasingly sex-drenched culture, with a "maturing Baby Boom generation" proud of advancing the sexual revolution, many "see affairs as not necessarily such a huge deal," explained Alan Grieco, a Florida sex therapist. In October, Time Warner launched Madonna's coffee-table book, *Sex*. The book was part of a $60 million deal with Time Warner, a corporation whose flagship *Time* once safeguarded family values. Now, this 128-page stack of dirty pictures tried normalizing the profane. Madonna was annihilating boundaries, publicizing her privates, taking private acts public. One photograph depicted her hitchhiking naked in Miami, others showed her doing once-unmentionable things in once-unmentionable places with her rainbow entourage of rock stars, models, and dancers, who were black, white, and Hispanic, gay and straight. More than 1.5 million people spent $49.95 in the first three days to buy *Sex*. Millions of others bought her album *Erotica*. For this "Material Girl," her revolution paid off handsomely.

Clinton's sexual potency and moral messiness helped humanize him, too. "Saturday Night Bill's" prowess reassured many meritocrats, many of whom saw themselves, and Rhodes Scholars like him, as more Woody Allen or Steve Urkel nerdy than James Dean or Tom Cruise cool. His sloppiness humanized him to many at the other end of the class spectrum, mired in the unruliness of their own lives. "To be a modernist," the radical sociologist Marshall Berman explained, "is to make oneself somehow at home in the maelstrom" of modern life; Clinton mastered this surfing skill.

Hillary Rodham Clinton's dissimilarities to Barbara Bush also reinforced the campaign's Adversarial identity. Many of Rodham's Yalie friends had expected her to run for president or join the Supreme Court. After years of feeling caged in Arkansas, she now hoped to flourish on a national stage. Alas, her Washington experience was confined to chairing the Legal Services Corporation and other safe, elite contexts. The media proved hostile, and voters ambivalent about a headstrong modernist First Lady-to-Be.

Hillary Clinton's two biggest moments during the campaign backfired. Her "Tammy Wynette" line sounded haughty. Two months later, she insulted millions of homemakers by boasting, "I suppose I could have stayed home and baked cookies and had teas. But what I decided to do was pursue my profession." Her sharp tongue confirmed anti-feminist stereotypes of career women disdaining American homemakers.

The growing gender wars shaped popular culture. Feminists protested the misogynistic violence of the 1992 hit *Basic Instinct,* which starred Sharon Stone as a psychotic bisexual killer, especially following the 1991 hit *The Silence of the Lambs,* depicting a demented serial killer who skins women. In 1992, *The Hand That Rocks the Cradle* earned $88 million illustrating every working mother's nightmare, the Nanny from Hell inserting herself between the mother and her family. "When your baby's hungry, it's *my* breast that feeds him," the psycho nanny cries. Ultimately, the working mom pushes the killer out the window. The evil nanny is impaled, ever so subtly, on a white picket fence. Sales of "nanny cams" soared.

Hillary's second metaphoric impaling, pillorying her cookies-and-teas crack, occurred in March with tension growing around new charges implicating both Clintons. On March 8, *The New York Times* uncovered the Clintons' money-losing stake in a land deal called Whitewater connected to a failed savings and loan bank. The article asked "whether a governor should be involved in a business deal with the owner of a business regulated by the state" and whether "the governor's wife . . . should be receiving legal fees for work done for the business." Aides feared another scandal would be a campaign-ending "third strike." Desperate, Hillary Clinton wanted to stonewall. She and her cronies at the Rose Law Firm began obscuring the paper trail linking the Clintons with James McDougal, who arranged the Whitewater deal, and his bankrupt Madison Guaranty Savings and Loan.

At the next candidates' debate, former California governor Jerry Brown attacked Bill Clinton's "electability problem" and his "conflict[s] of interest," including "funneling money to his wife's law firm." "I don't care what you say about me," Clinton exploded, his Southern accent thickening, "but you should be ashamed of yourself for jumpin' on ma wife." Clinton was also furious that *The New York Times* columnist William Safire, writing about "The Hillary Problem," called her a "political bumbler" suffering from "foot-in-mouth disease." Bill's defense of his wife made him look chivalrous; Hillary's comments about choosing a profession made her look arrogant. Journalists cruelly branded her "the overbearing Yuppie Wife from Hell."

Hillary lacked Bill's chameleonlike range, charming Bubbas and blue-bloods alike. The years in Arkansas were frequently painful, spawning an irritability rooted in insecurity the public also perceived. To celebrate Chelsea Clinton's birth in 1980, Bill's old friend, Carolyn Yeldell Staley, composed a song depicting parents marveling at their new creation. "We may not be worthy, but we'll try to be wise," she sang, articulating the Baby Boomer humility toward parenting their own parents' generation lacked. "That's a nice song," Hillary snapped afterward. "But who's not worthy? You and your tape recorder?"

In her 1991 book *Silencing the Self: Women and Depression*, the feminist psychologist Dana Crowley Jack found many women frustrated by their marriages and their soft, selfless, "feminine identity," without even being a reluctant Southern political spouse with an unfaithful husband. Age and success eventually rounded Hillary Clinton's edges, but the scrutiny in 1992 sometimes sharpened them. When pollsters presented data showing her unpopularity, Bill Clinton loyally dismissed it saying, "You know, they just hated the way she was doing her hair then."

Hillary was struggling to fulfill her role while being true to herself. "I have compromised, I gave up my name, got contact lenses, but I'm not going to try to pretend to be somebody that I'm not," she would later tell her friend Diane Blair, talking about her reluctant makeover to look traditional in Arkansas. FOBs, shocked by the gap between the Hillary Clinton they knew and the one they saw on TV, begged for a "reorganization of Hillary's vital role in the campaign."

Part of the awkwardness stemmed from Hillary Rodham Clinton's zealous defense of her wayward husband. "Sex always sells," she sighed, dismissing the feminist arguments that the personal was political and that sexual power games were indeed sexual power games. Refusing to play the victim, she often helped victimize other women. Suspected paramours were humiliated in public and harassed by reporters or private investigators. Her insistence in 1998 that even her husband's White House affair with a young intern "was not a power relationship" because it was "consensual," would contradict the central feminist teaching from the Clarence Thomas hearings repudiating flirtations between bosses and their subordinates, which helped create the political context conducive to Clinton's candidacy. After three terms of Reagan-Bush conservatism, the Clintons and the Democrats were playing to win.

Bush's Weakness, Clinton's Callowness, America's Crankiness

In this latest round of the post-Sixties' culture wars, the Clintons were blessed, as usual, with heavy-handed enemies who overreached. President Bush had a tough year. In early January, during a twelve-day 26,000-mile Pacific tour, at a state dinner in Japan, the president vomited on his host, Prime Minister Kiichi Miyazawa, before fainting in front of 135 guests. Back home, Bush felt besieged from left and right. Clinton was blasting him for neglecting domestic policy, demanding "a president who cares more about Littleton, New Hampshire, than about Liechtenstein."

Bush's chief Republican rival, Pat Buchanan, echoed this charge with his "America First" campaign. A right-wing columnist and former White House aide, Buchanan became famous as *Crossfire*'s combative host "from the Right," mounting nightly arguments on CNN pitting liberals against conservatives. Infuriated by Bush's tax hike, foreign adventures, and centrism, Buchanan ran to save the Reaganite Republican Party from its moderate, patrician, business-oriented pragmatic wing.

Clinton plunged into the New Hampshire primary fight. On February 12, the night his ROTC letter was leaked, he spoke in Dover. Fighting laryngitis and despair, he said, "This is the work of my life." He defined the "character issue" as the question: "How can you have the power of the presidency and never use it to help people improve their lives until your life needs saving in an election? I won't be like George Bush," he vowed. "I'll never forget who gave me a second chance, and I'll be there for you until the last dog dies."

Meanwhile, Clinton was on notice to behave. Susan Thomases, a prickly New York lawyer protective of her old friend, Hillary Clinton, recalls telling the candidate: "You're stupid enough to blow this whole Presidential thing over your dick. And if that turns out to be true, buddy, I'm going home, and I'm taking people with me."

February 18 was a strange New Hampshire primary night. The press treated both victors like losers. Buchanan's impressive second-place, 38 percent vote highlighted Bush's weakness. Forty-two percent of Buchanan's voters surveyed admitted they supported him as a protest vote; most did not even like him. On the Democratic side, former Massachusetts senator Paul Tsongas won 33.2 percent of the votes, but reporters decided that Clinton's 24.8 percent gave him the bragging rights.

Clinton labeled himself "The Comeback Kid" and plunged ahead toward winning the Democratic nomination. Economic weakness could cause many to forgive him his character weakness. Clinton, the candidate of sex, drugs, rock 'n' roll, and draft dodging, would convince Democratic voters he was also the candidate of change, compassion, and hope.

Even as Clinton's momentum built, the excessive carping about Clinton's personal flaws soured most Americans, especially as the economy tanked. Pollsters kept finding "none of the above" more popular than anyone running. Once again, vicious partisanship demeaned all politicians and government itself.

Much as Clinton considered himself the candidate of constructive change, his slipperiness kept making him look like just another pol. In late March, at a candidates' forum on WCBS-TV, he answered questions about past marijuana use by saying he "never" broke a state law because he tried it in England but "didn't inhale" and didn't like it. Half of Americans under forty-five and 60 percent of American males his age had tried marijuana. Clinton's "I didn't inhale" line instantly joined the growing playlist of Slick Willie's sleaziest dodges.

Congressional scandals further dispirited America. In 1989, talk radio–stoked grassroots fury had derailed a 50 percent congressional pay raise. In September 1991, an internal audit uncovered 8,300 overdrafts at the House of Representatives' bank for members. Members could write checks that were not covered for months at a time, essentially receiving interest-free loans. Newt Gingrich, working with the "Gang of Seven," freshmen Republican firebrands including Rick Santorum and John Boehner, wanted to expose all House members who benefited. The grandiose Gingrich saw himself as fighting the Democratic politburo, despite his own twenty-two overdrawn checks. Anticipating the 1994 midterm campaign, he called the Democratic Party "a reactionary liberal system made up of a coalition of bankrupt big-city machines, out-of-touch union bosses, trial lawyers, left-wing activists and professional politicians." Johnny Carson, the soft-spoken, sharp-tongued voice of Middle America who hosted *The Tonight Show,* joked: "Folks, you've got to hand it to our House of Representatives. They finally passed something: 5,000 bad checks."

The House bank was sloppy, not criminal. Since Watergate, investigative reporters kept politicians more honest. Many members had no idea their accounts were overdrawn. But populists found it easy to embarrass House members for enjoying prerogatives ordinary citizens lacked. Twenty-four members had abused the system, with related crimes concerning the House post office sending some members to jail, including the powerful Chicago pol Dan Rostenkowski. Americans were having trouble calibrating. Just as many tolerated Clinton's trespasses, they overreacted to congressional stumbles.

Bush's weakness, Clinton's callowness, and Americans' grouchiness encouraged the mercurial Texan billionaire, Ross Perot, to enter the race. Perot opposed the Persian Gulf War, was passionately protectionist, and feared huge federal budget deficits would doom America. In another salute to CNN, Perot announced his intentions to run on *Larry King Live.*

King had become the king of America's Talk Show Nation by being calm, apolitical, and not too personal. He lacked Rush Limbaugh's conservative roar, Howard Stern's potty mouth, Jerry Springer's manic mayhem, or Don Imus's satirical bite. He also lacked Oprah Winfrey's and Phil Donahue's New Age nosiness and sanctimony. With his gravelly voice, horn-rimmed glasses, pronounced overbite, and snazzy suspenders, King had been lobbing softball questions to grateful guests since 1985 on CNN. King's pseudo-intimate celebrity happy talk suited a TV network trying not to offend worldwide. Suddenly, King was playing political kingmaker.

Perot, born in 1930, King, born in 1933, and Buchanan, born in 1938, belonged to American politics' Lost Generation. Too young to have served in World War II as Bush did, too old to have been swept up in the Sixties' shenanigans, the three now seemed like refugees from an older, more traditional era, without Bush's cluelessness. Buchanan embraced America's old-fashioned values, consensus, and conformity, with a bracing harshness. King evoked America's old-school, easy-listening popular culture, with a reassuring tameness. And Perot championed America's time-honored thriftiness with an entertaining Texan bluntness, tempered by his peppery quirkiness.

These men's solidity despite their idiosyncrasies appealed to a confused country, just as 1992's runaway best seller would. *The Bridges of Madison County* was a middle-aged, Middle American love story. Written by Robert James Waller, born in Rockford, Iowa, in 1939, the book sold over 50 million copies. The narrator tells "this remarkable tale" in "a world where personal commitment in all of its forms seems to be shattering and love has become a matter of convenience."

Country hits like Billy Ray Cyrus's breakout hit "Achy Breaky Heart," reinforced the mass feelings of longing shaping the political atmosphere, too. In 1991, with more accurate weekly sales data by SoundScan, country proved itself as radio's second most popular music format, behind adult contemporary music. Garth Brooks sold 12 million albums that year. By 1992, TNN, The Nashville Network, was more popular than MTV. Democrats believed the country music revival reflected political populism fueled by economic frustration, a return to "basic values," rejecting 1980s' excess.

Los Angeles: Riots, Rebellion, or Perdu-Event?

A harsher, less lyrical break with the 1980s came on April 29, 1992, as America's fantasy capital, Los Angeles, exploded. That Wednesday, at approximately 3:15 p.m., the Rodney King case continued disrupting Bush's presidency. The acquittal of three police officers after a televised trial triggered three days of violence.

The verdict shocked millions, especially African Americans. First, came the anguish: "And I didn't just see Rodney King being brutalized. I saw the King of Kings being brutalized! . . . I saw you and me being brutalized," exclaimed the Reverend Cecil L. Murray, pastor of the First African Methodist Episcopal Church (AME). "Don't do it in our community," one speaker pleaded at the

AME, ostensibly calling for peace. Meanwhile, outside, protesters shouting, "BLACK REVOLUTION!" threatened Beverly Hills and Parker Center—LAPD headquarters.

Next, came the violence—heavily televised. Protesters cried: "LAPD ARE REDNECKS! LAPD ARE RACISTS!" Three and a half hours after the verdict, rioters at the intersection of Florence and Normandie pulled Reginald O. Denny from his truck and beat him with a five-pound piece of medical equipment, a claw hammer, a concrete cinder block, their legs, and their fists—fracturing his skull in ninety-one places. Denny survived thanks to four locals who ran to help after seeing the rampage on TV filmed by a news helicopter hovering overhead.

The graphic footage of Denny's beating offered a heartbreaking companion to the Rodney King video. First, white cops beat a black man. Then, black thugs beat a white man—all recorded and replayed endlessly. "I can't believe the cops are looking at this and not doing something," one Los Angeles anchorwoman declared as the rioting intensified. When violence erupted elsewhere in the United States, strong countermeasures kept the peace. Atlanta police arrested three hundred rioters.

America's deadliest modern riot killed fifty-three people. Many more people indulged in arson and looting rather than beating and shooting. They cried: "BLACK POWER," "THIS IS FOR RODNEY," "BURN BABY BURN!" Plumes of smoke darkened Los Angeles's sunlit skyline. Others waved placards or scribbled graffiti crying: "It's a White Man's World," "No Justice No Peace," "*La Revolución Es La Solución!*" Latinos would constitute about half the arrests. Sometimes children looted with their parents, often emitting "war whoops and cheers," reporters glumly observed. One black woman stood watching the looters, sobbing. She couldn't understand how parents could bring their children along to steal. "I'm ashamed of my own people," she cried.

On the streets, angry rioters ran toward buildings to destroy them, as gleeful plunderers ran away, their arms or shopping carts filled with groceries and toiletries, Snickers bars and Kool cigarettes, Clorox bleach bottles and Budweiser six packs, Air Jordan sneakers and Bugle Boy Parachute pants, RCA television sets and La-Z-Boy sofas. Empty shoeboxes littered the parking lot of a Payless shoe store. Spilled milk, crushed vegetables, and broken glass bottles clogged supermarket aisles. Appalled by the nihilistic destruction, the Democratic socialist activist, Harold Meyerson, grumbled in *The New Republic,* "Even on the wacko nether-reaches of what remains of the American left, this will be a hard riot to romanticize."

The nation's second largest city shut down. Rioters targeted Korean-owned businesses, enraged that a Korean shopkeeper had only received probation after shooting an unarmed fifteen-year-old black girl. Korean Americans waved placards demanding "Justice for *All* Minorities" and "We All Can Get Along." Photographs of Korean American snipers, lying in wait on the rooftop of a store, with improvised white headbands, conjured fears of civil war.

Eventually, 13,000 military personnel helped police arrest more than 6,700 rioters. Five thousand buildings were damaged or destroyed. At least 1,600 businesses were ravaged. Another 3,100 businesses suffered. Damages exceeded $1 billion. On Saturday, day four, President Bush declared Los Angeles a disaster area.

Most of the Los Angeles metropolitan area's 11.3 million residents were terrified. Their paradise was lost, menaced by earthquakes, wildfires, now this. At one canyon passing in the Hollywood Hills, an enclave populated by artists, actors, and writers, residents were surprised by how many guns and baseball bats emerged from homes. Meyerson reported, "An uneasy coalition of '60s liberals and survivalists . . . stood guard" for three nights. "I always assumed that if I was going to be on the barricades," one scared, dispirited California liberal confessed, "I'd be on the other side."

Many African Americans politicized these riots as a "rebellion." Ice-T, still smarting from the "Cop Killer" controversy, said: "Black people look at the cops as the Gestapo." The King verdict proved that "justice is a myth if you're black. Of course people will riot." Two weeks after the riots, a twenty-eight-year-old rapper named Sister Souljah wondered: "if black people kill black people every day, why not have a week and kill white people?"

Remarkably, expressions of love followed this explosion of hate. "I especially wanted to help the Koreans," one African American volunteer, Elmore Dingle, said. "I don't want them to think so negatively about blacks." Church leaders urged congregants to return their booty.

The Mexican American actor Edward James Olmos grabbed a broom on Friday morning, May 1, and started sweeping the streets. More than four hundred people joined him, filling up dumpsters they dragged along. The city "looked like Beirut, like an all-out war going on," Olmos recalled, but he felt compelled to respond. He assumed no one would shoot people wielding brooms. At 11 a.m. on Saturday May 2, approximately thirty thousand Angelenos marched into Koreatown for peace and healing.

Noting the good deeds proliferating, the R&B singer Jody Watley complained, "as much as the media was here when everybody was looting and they were calling everybody savages and thugs, there's no media right now." In a media-centered democracy, if pseudo-events were manufactured moments staged for reporters, perdu-events were genuine moments the media missed. *Perdu,*

French for lost or concealed, also could mean a lost sentry, just as an important moment ignored left audiences vulnerable to misinterpretation.

Leaving a state dinner, a tuxedo-clad George Bush entered the "Let them eat cake" imperious insensitivity sweepstakes by responding to the King verdict with maddening clichés: "The court system has worked, and what's needed now is calm and respect for the law until the appeals process takes place." Demonstrating more effective leadership than the president, Rodney King asked, amid the rioting, "People, I just want to say . . . can we all get along?"

Bush's approval rating cratered. Desert Storm's hero now looked like the supplier of riot and recession. Eighty percent surveyed feared America was on the wrong track. Ross Perot denounced Bush's "Government in gridlock," despite Bush's demand that Congress pass his urban initiative to create inner city enterprise zones. The hip talk show host Arsenio Hall would denounce "George Herbert irregular-heart-beating, read-my-lying-lipping, slipping-in-the-polls, do-nothing, deficit-raising, make-less-money-than-Millie-the-White-House-dog-last-year, Quayle-loving, sushi-puking Bush!"

Remembering Napoleon's directive never to interrupt when your enemy is committing suicide, Clinton reacted cautiously as LA burned. He lamented this "reflection of more than a decade of denial of responsibility and of manipulation of political symbols" by Republicans. And he visited the still-smoldering city that weekend, preaching at the First Baptist Church: "we are drifting apart when we ought to be coming together."

The riots boosted Clinton's standing with crucial constituents. African Americans appreciated him for empathizing without patronizing. Many applauded his economic ideas, particularly his calls for welfare reform, demonstrating that blacks did not just respond to what William Julius Wilson called "race-specific issues and programs." Blaming the riots on Reaganism, liberals started trusting Clinton to end the Reagan-Bush regime. As with the shift of Eleanor Roosevelt's good government types from Adlai Stevenson to John Kennedy in 1960, liberals now appreciated Clinton's shape-shifting as necessary pragmatism not moral weakness. Clinton also invited Reagan Democrats back to the party of Franklin Roosevelt. More voters now trusted Clinton than Bush to address America's racial problems, help the poor, and protect the middle class.

The Manhattan Project: Reframing the Clintons

Still, as Clinton clinched the Democratic nomination, 40 percent of voters viewed him as a "fast-talking," "wishy-washy" pol, and his wife as "being in the race for herself" and "going for the power." Voters perceived the two of them as a childless couple of privilege, born with silver spoons in their mouths. Clinton was considered less trustworthy than Bush by 24 percentage points.

To address these "nuclear issues" threatening to obliterate Clinton's candidacy, consultants launched the "Manhattan Project," a secret program reintroducing the Clintons to the American public. Staffers highlighted Clinton's biography as a poor kid made good, his populist commitment to putting people first, and both Clintons' family values. In a kind of systematic desensitization, the scandals had come out early enough to become old news. Now, Bill Clinton continued with his issues crusade while also telling his personal story. Hillary Clinton toned down her approach. Both Clintons began referring to their thirteen-year-old daughter Chelsea to lighten their image. In July the three would pose for a *People* cover shoot.

As part of this charm offensive, Clinton pulled out his saxophone, put on sunglasses, and played Elvis Presley's "Heartbreak Hotel" at the beginning of Arsenio Hall's talk show on June 3. Hall's drummer advised Clinton: "If this music thing doesn't work out for you, you can always run for president." When Hall noted that many young people don't vote because all politicians are "the same," Clinton insisted: "I'm talking about things in this election that I've been working on for years that I really care about." He said he had visited "South Central LA three years before the riot occurred" and had seen "how terrible it was and how things could get out of hand."

The conservative columnist George Will claimed Clinton's undignified appearance "coarsened" American democracy. David Zurawik, *The Baltimore Sun*'s TV critic, would later dismiss Will's argument as opposing "anything that isn't white, male and borrowed from ancient Rome or Greece." These new tactics reflect "a larger movement: the change from white-male hegemony to a multicultural America." Indeed, Bush refused to dish with Oprah or any of them, saying, "I'm the President." His rigidity ignored Calvin Coolidge's awkward Indian headdress photos, Dwight Eisenhower's television ads, and Richard Nixon's appearances on *The Jack Paar Tonight Show* and *Laugh-In*.

Arsenio Hall celebrated this new, populist, television-centered, talk show campaign. "If you break down the [demographics] and look at who watches my show, it sure beats standing on a caboose," Hall said, suggesting that "young viewers" did not respond to traditional whistle-stop campaigning. Politicians had to mimic the corporate marketers' demographic segmentation games.

A week after his Arsenio Hall triumph, Clinton wooed Reagan Democrats by denouncing Sister Souljah's offensive comments about the riots at Jesse Jackson's Rainbow Coalition conference. Clinton said, "If you took the words 'white' and 'black,' and you reversed them, you might think David Duke was giving that speech." Jackson's fury with Clinton delighted reporters. Ever the seducer, Clinton felt so badly, that, Stan Greenberg recalls, staffers had a forty-eight-hour "vigil" staying by his side "to make sure he didn't call" Jackson and apologize. Clinton's innovation, the Sister Souljah Moment, encouraged politicians to demonstrate their audacity to nationwide TV audiences by occasionally telling live audiences what they didn't want to hear. Clinton also showed he was tough enough to govern.

A good DLC member, Clinton distrusted special interest groups. He emphasized his all-American, middle-class character and approach. A "Democrat talking about budget cuts, talking about middle-class tax cuts, talking about welfare reform" was "bold," his campaign chief Eli Segal would recall. And a Democrat emphasizing responsibilities not just rights was "brand new." Urging America's youth to take responsibility, Clinton found that the reform he proposed that generated the greatest applause was national service. The reform that best defined Clinton as a New Democrat was his 1991 promise "to end welfare as we know it," vowing "two years and you're off." Al From would call this Clinton's "most important idea," telling voters "you vote for this guy, you're voting for somebody who is different from the Democrats you've been voting against." With such principled, out-of-the-box stands, Clinton changed the character issue from his personal lapses to Bush's leadership failures.

The economy also hurt Bush. Iconic firms such as Macy's, TWA, and Wang Laboratories went bankrupt. Unemployment hit 7.8 percent in July. The leading sitcom *Roseanne,* with its sharp working-class sensibility, broadcast recession-oriented plot lines during the campaign depicting lost jobs, cut-off electricity, and four hundred applicants for six openings. In the mid-September season opener, eleven-year-old D.J. says, "Mom, if you want, I still have some birthday money left in my closet." Roseanne responds, "Oh no you don't, D. J., but thanks anyway." Years later, the modest Barr insisted: "I am definitely responsible for getting Bill Clinton elected."

Many Americans wanted a change. When Nirvana's grunge album *Nevermind* supplanted Michael Jackson's *Dangerous* on the Billboard Top 200 seller list, it symbolized a gritty, authentic, 1990s' sound eclipsing a slick, glitzy, overdone 1980s' relic. When Johnny Carson, "The King of Late Night TV" since 1962 and a World War II navy veteran one year younger than the sixty-seven-year-old Bush, had a tearful finale on May 22, 1992, the older generation seemed ready for retirement not rehiring.

The Values Standoff

On May 19, trying to explain the riots, Vice President Dan Quayle triggered a clash about single parenting. Quayle claimed that the popular television character Murphy Brown's decision to have a child out of wedlock reflected America's values crisis. In the 1960s, when the liberal intellectual Daniel Patrick Moynihan warned that single motherhood damaged the black family, many liberals lambasted him. In 1992 such talk was even less acceptable, especially from a conservative widely caricatured as a fool. Ignoring all the evidence that single mothers giving birth to 30 percent of America's babies annually threatened society, critics accused Quayle of demonizing unconventional families. "Families come in all shapes and sizes," Murphy Brown, played by Candice Bergen would say when the show ran an episode responding to Quayle.

Talk radio phone lines jammed. "Murphy Has a Baby . . . Quayle Has a Cow," the *Philadelphia Daily News* jeered. Quayle attacked what he called "the media elite and Hollywood." "I don't know who the cultural elite are," Diane English, *Murphy Brown's* creator, responded, disingenuously. "The Vice President is a man who lives in a big house and has lots of money and wears very expensive suits, drives around in a limousine and comes from a family of newspaper heirs." By 1992, Sunset Boulevard enjoyed more cultural power than Main Street or Wall Street. English mischievously added that if Quayle thinks "it's disgraceful" for an unmarried woman to have a child, "he'd better make sure abortion remains safe and legal."

English and her pro-choice allies were nervously awaiting a decision in *Planned Parenthood v. Casey.* This challenge to Pennsylvania's restrictive abortion laws was the eighteenth abortion case to reach the Supreme Court since *Roe v. Wade* legalized abortion in 1973. Fearing that a Reaganized court would outlaw abortion, over 500,000 pro-choice activists had marched in Washington on April 5. Kate Michelman of the National Abortion Rights Action League called Bush "the most anti-choice, anti-woman candidate in American history." Bill Clinton paraded with more than 150 supporters chanting "Pro-Clinton, Pro-Choice," when they passed the White House.

On June 29, the mostly Republican court, unhappily respecting precedent, narrowly affirmed *Roe v. Wade.* The dissenting minority, led by Justice Antonin Scalia, complained that "the imperial judiciary" was deciding issues judicially and constitutionally not legislatively and democratically. By making rights into what Professor Ronald Dworkin called "trumps," public debate became absolutist, polarized, and impervious to compromise.

Rather than celebrating the majority's affirmation of the "essence" of the right, Democrats denounced the decision for allowing state limits such as mandating parental consent for teenagers. Clinton called preserving a woman's right to choose "one of the things this presidential election is about." Anti-abortion activists denounced the court's reaffirmation that abortion was legal. A moderate Democrat, Representative Les AuCoin of Oregon, noted "an amazing transformation. . . . Only a few years ago, the easy vote in Washington on abortion was to vote" against it. "Today, the easy vote is to vote pro-choice."

The Clintons' indiscretions, the LA riots, Sister Souljah, Murphy Brown, Larry King, and *Planned Parenthood v. Casey* jumbled popular culture with politics, exacerbating the culture wars. The conservative pastor Richard John Neuhaus, writing in *The Wall Street Journal,* feared that America was becoming "two nations: one concentrated on rights and laws, the other on rights and wrongs; one radically individualistic and dedicated to fulfillment of the self, the other communal and invoking the common good; . . . one typically secular, the other typically religious; one elitist, the other populist."

Neuhaus overstated this divide. Americans had developed a rough consensus on abortion. Dan Quayle was anti-abortion but insisted he would never foreclose any options if his daughter were pregnant. Clinton, and his eventual running mate Al Gore, Quayle's generational peers, carefully said they supported "choice" not abortion and would not want their daughters exercising that right. Even as the notion of Red and Blue America was emerging, Americans were often more internally torn than externally combative. Clinton's call for abortion to be safe, legal, and rare captured most Americans' ambivalence, and invited them to hear his nuanced positions on other tough issues.

Ross Perot appealed to voters fed up with the Democrat-Republican values standoff, Clinton's political slickness, and Bush's governmental gridlock. Clinton's people resented how Perot, without formally announcing his candidacy, was stealing Clinton's position as the courageous candidate of change. CBS News anchor Dan Rather asked Perot: "Can I quote you as saying, 'Read my lips: no new taxes'?" "No," Perot responded, "you can't ever quote me as saying anything that stupid." Many Americans loved Perot's common sense by sound bite.

The Clinton Makeover

Perot's challenge made a Clinton repackaging even more necessary. Both Clintons' clever makeover culminated in July with the most significant Democratic convention in decades. Since 1968, with more voters choosing delegates through primaries or caucuses, conventions were empty coronations. But Clinton's image-makers understood that millions of Americans would be watching, wanting to abandon Bush for a new hero.

Clinton broke tradition in choosing a running mate. Rather than "balancing the ticket," he selected a moderate Baby Boomer Southerner, Al Gore. This political twinning, the Double Bubba ticket, reinforced the Clintons' changing-of-the-guard message.

At the Madison Square Garden convention, the frequently divided Democrats mounted a love-in. The convention culminated with a short, slick, heart-warming video, produced by the Clintons' friends, Harry Thomason and Linda Bloodworth-Thomason, the producers of the Southern-accented sitcoms *Designing Women* and *Evening Shade*. The video cast Bill Clinton as the American dream personified, a man who still believed in a place called Hope.

During the convention, the mercurial Perot abruptly quit the race. Muttering about Bush-based conspiracies, Perot praised the "revitalized" Democrats. Perot's surprise gave Clinton an unprecedentedly large post-convention public approval bounce.

By contrast, the Republican convention hurt Bush. Snarling, declaring "a religious war going on in our country for the soul of America," Pat Buchanan repudiated the "agenda Clinton & Clinton would impose on America—abortion on demand, a litmus test for the Supreme Court, homosexual rights, discrimination against religious schools, women in combat." Buchanan had forgotten Ronald Reagan's light touch and consensus-building impulse, instead channeling Barry Goldwater's 1964 vintage venom.

Buchanan was right. America was changing. A popular Hollywood biopic starring Denzel Washington now glorified the black radical Malcolm X. Baseball caps with an X became fashionable. The film began with images of the Rodney King beating crosscut with a burning American flag that becomes an X. Even the five-hundredth anniversary of Christopher Columbus's voyage to America would have Latinos, Native Americans, and academics protesting that "Saying that Columbus 'discovered' America is like saying it was an empty land and that the people who were there before weren't worth living." This new, pluralist America had little patience for Buchanan's ugly rhetoric.

Such attacks helped Clinton make the election a referendum on Bush, his listless leadership, the social fallout from the Reagan years, Republican narrow-mindedness, and the recession that was making the Reagan boom a Republican bust. Clinton emphasized the same centrist liberal issues he had run on since 1991, to transcend the mudslinging and dismiss the character questions. Many campaign commercials had captions with facts and statistics, telegraphing his seriousness.

Campaign headquarters in the old *Arkansas Gazette* building in Little Rock illustrated Clinton's outsider status and America's economic challenges. Built in 1908, the structure was abandoned in 1991 when the newspaper closed, idling 726 full-time employees and 1,200 part-timers. Clinton's campaign strategist James Carville hung a sign in headquarters reading:

1. Change vs. More of the same
2. The economy, stupid
3. Don't forget health care.

Victory: The Genie of American Politics

Bill Clinton's victorious election campaign fused the old politics with the new. Watching him work a crowd, making eye contact, shaking hands, slapping backs, glistening with sweat, glorying in "the people," evoked memories of great from-the-gut populists like William Jennings Bryan and Huey Long. His Southern identity reinforced his impression of rawness, of passion, of personal politicking. His run culminated with a fifty-hour, four-thousand-mile cross-country campaigning marathon. A fan urged him: "Take your vitamins." Ever the populist energized by adoring masses, he replied, "You're my vitamins."

Seeing Clinton peddle his plans, mobilize his networks, and fight like hell to win, evoked memories of ideologically principled but politically ruthless progressives like Franklin Roosevelt and John Kennedy. The campaign's best-selling manifesto, *Putting People First,* detailed the Clinton-Gore plans to rebuild infrastructure, reform welfare, universalize health care coverage, cut taxes for the middle class, raise taxes on the upper class and on foreign corporations. The meticulous blueprints reflected the Clinton-Gore progressive faith in planning, seeking personal and national salvation through their smarts and their systems.

This old-fashioned Democratic demagogue was also a carefully packaged commodity fluent in the visually driven patois of television and a fluid exemplar of postmodern mores. He was a celebrity coached by consultants, stage-managed by advertising executives, advised by the Ivy League aristocracy, blessed by the Hollywood royalty, loved by the working class. A son of the television age, a product of the consumer culture, the first president raised on *Howdy Doody* and Brylcreem "a little dab will do ya" TV jingles, he understood that modern politics required mastering pop culture, from *60 Minutes* to Arsenio Hall.

At the same time, a son of the Sixties, a product of the sexual revolution, the first president maturing amid *Jerry Springer* and the Pill, he realized that modern politics required managing the confessional culture. This thoroughly modern man viewed character as a journey, trusted Americans to tolerate some of his faults, and held up his decades-long marriage, despite occasionally lapses, as exemplary. His skills as an old pol and a slippery New Ager earned him the nickname "Slick Willie"; his identity as a yuppie prince in a complex old-yet-new partnership with his wife earned the sobriquet "Billary" for them both.

Ross Perot's unexpected return to the race kept the conversation focused on the deficit, and put reporters further on the defensive, given Perot's distaste for their scandalmongering and horse-race coverage. His 19 percent of the vote would deprive Clinton of a popular vote majority, but siphoned more votes from Bush.

Although Clinton only won 43 percent of the vote, clever Democrats, echoing Reagan's spin after his marginal 1980 victory, celebrated Clinton's "mandate." The continuing fallout from the Clarence Thomas hearings had produced "The Year of the Woman," boosted by fury at the Navy's Tailhook scandal, belatedly punishing drunken "Top Gun" aviators for molesting at least eighty-three women with a "gantlet" of groping hands at the Las Vegas Hilton. One hundred and six women ran for Congress, forty-seven won. The Senate would now have six female senators, including its first African American woman, Carol Moseley Braun of Illinois.

Congress's entering class of 121 constituted its largest since 1948's big postwar election. Half of the rookies were under forty-five, reducing the average age of all 535 senators and representatives to fifty-three. Many newcomers were typical Adversarials. Less than one-fifth had served in the military and almost two-thirds had advanced degrees. Five newcomers were Yale Law School alumni, like the Clintons. The Senate's partisan division remained unchanged. In one ominous sign for Clinton, Republicans gained nine House seats, thanks to 1990's redistricting and Southern Republicans' growing success. Democrats still controlled both houses of Congress but with a weakened majority.

Ultimately James Carville was right, but often misinterpreted. Commentators usually emphasized his "economy, stupid" line while forgetting his first point emphasizing "change." Clinton tapped into cultural trends and political frustrations to help shift mainstream American attitudes about what they wanted and could reasonably expect in a president. Voters occasionally booed when reporters started asking "gotcha" questions about personal foibles. "No one cares!" they shouted in New Hampshire. The majority of voters who considered the economy or change the most important issue voted for Clinton.

Clinton had successfully run against the media as well as against his political rivals. Reagan had shaken the assumption of journalistic objectivity by crusading against "liberal bias." With the spread of advocacy journalism, and the proliferation of media outlets, fewer newspapers and television stations tried to be dispassionate, and even fewer succeeded. Conservative critics treated the news media as "a tremendous advocacy" group, in the words of Van Gordon Sauter, who charged that the liberalism of *The New York Times*, *The Boston Globe*, and *The Washington Post* "manifests itself in their news columns, not just on their editorial pages."

Liberals denied that the mainstream media favored their views, pointing to the harsh coverage the Clintons endured. This media polarization would increase over the decade as the Internet often linked readers from one like-minded source to another, further polarizing American politics.

The victory vindicated the Clintons personally, generationally, ideologically, culturally, even geographically. Skeptics had underestimated Bill Clinton and his native region. His Southernness contributed to his success. The Southern sins of slavery and segregation, the misery in states not-yet-recovered from the Civil War whupping, exempted Clinton's home region from the all-American sense of innocence, steadiness, and confidence. The resulting humility protected him from conveying that Northeastern Ivy League Adversarial arrogance voters disliked. As he matured in an America struggling on a national level with racism, sexism, and imperialism, it became easier for him to feel the pain of marginalized Americans and accept the humble warnings of the skeptical theologian Reinhold Niebuhr, who rejected America's "messianic consciousness" and accepted life's messiness. As he crisscrossed an America undergoing sweeping changes, his native region's values helped him broadcast a reassuring patriotism, traditionalism, and optimism promising change without revolution.

Bill Clinton was a phenomenon. He was "first in his class," as his biographer David Maraniss claimed, the Baby Boomer trailblazer, the poor boy made great who benefited from America's post–World War II meritocracy and delighted his peers with his victory. He certainly was a "natural," as the journalist Joe Klein described him, a political pied piper emitting powerful political pheromones that seduced crowds, who even had middle-aged, twice-married heterosexual political science professors like Benjamin Barber speaking about their attraction toward him in raw, sexual terms as "an affair." And he was the ultimate Comeback Kid, a "survivor," in *The Washington Post* reporter John Harris's apt title, a tough Rocky-like combatant who could absorb tremendous blows, telling Newt Gingrich, "I'm the big rubber clown doll you had as a kid. . . . That's me. The harder you hit me, the faster I come back."

As Arkansas's Boy Wonder prepared to move to Washington, many of the youth-obsessed Adversarial Baby Boomers felt they were playacting in the role of adults, as they "processed" the meaning of a peer becoming the nation's top authority figure. In this year of inversions, many of 1992's biggest movies depicted masqueraders and shape-shifters. *A League of Their Own* had women playing professional baseball in the 1940s as the men fought in World War II; *Basic Instinct* had Sharon Stone shifting sexual identities and Michael Douglas shifting loyalties, as a detective turned suspect's lover. The unlikely gender-bending hit *The Crying Game* had such a surprising twist its advertising centered around asking moviegoers to keep the secret.

It was a year of masking and unmasking. *Dracula* took a seductive human form. *Alien 3* starred a human-alien hybrid clone. *Batman Returns* featured the legendary playboy turned crime fighter. Robin Williams, a fellow Baby Boomer, lent his voice to Aladdin's ductile, endlessly entertaining Genie of many voices and personae. Clinton won by being as artful an improviser as Williams, emerging as the Genie of American politics, the exuberant, expansive, fluid, creative, identity juggler who pulled off a miracle.

Amid the scandalmongering and the scoffing, Bill Clinton inspired Democrats in ways few had experienced since John Kennedy's 1960 run. Clinton's connection with supporters was primal—as was critics' rage. Many Democratic women admitted to having crushes on him. Voter turnout surged by 20 percent. MTV attributed the increase to its edgy, hip Rock the Vote campaign, with Madonna purring, "If you don't vote, you're going to get a spanking."

Clinton stoked the euphoria. He helped Americans distinguish between their Reagan-Bush exhaustion and their still-strong faith in America. By November, his supporters expected his presidency to be redemptive. "I'm almost crying," said Yancy Prosser, thirty, of Little Rock on Election Night. "I've got my hero now. I haven't had one. I was born in 1962 and [John] Kennedy was killed in 1963."

From the right, the reaction was apoplectic, with warnings that were apocalyptic. Conservatives' sense of Clinton as usurper, of his victory as "a cultural coup d'état" and threat to the republic, would feed an opposition that would grow in intensity until his impeachment nearly ruined both the Republican Party and the Clinton presidency.

Just as some from the Greatest Generation were mourning the loss of the White House to this upstart, cynical marketers at DC Comics, frustrated by flat sales, temporarily killed off the once-invincible Superman, after fifty-four years of crime-fighting. The Cold War's ending was trashing useful parts of the Cold War script that had guided Americans for decades.

Crises abroad dulled the excitement at home as Clinton started assembling his leadership team. The former Yugoslavia was spawning new European killing fields. The phrase "ethnic cleansing" entered the language to describe the brutal Serbian rapes, massacres, and displacements launched against the Muslims in Bosnia. In Somalia, the starvation worsened by warlords hijacking food shipments became so heartbreaking that on December 4 President Bush sent in 28,000 Marines to help distribute aid to the suffering. Assessing these and other hot spots in the Soviet Union, Liberia, and Haiti, Clinton explained: "We are seeing the flip side of the wonder of the end of the cold war. The bipolar world gave the U.S. and the Soviet Union a limited capacity to contain some of what we are now witnessing in Bosnia" and elsewhere.

More pointedly, poignantly, the Nobel Peace Prize winner and Holocaust survivor Elie Wiesel asked: "What has become of the rising hope shared by so many?" These world events reminded America's next president that coming from a place called Hope and generating good feelings was only a start. The hard work of actually delivering on promises would follow. It was time for Clinton's Nineties to begin.

4

1993: Washington, D.C.
"We Must Care for One Another"

Clinton's Learning Curve

That's what democracy is about. Read the United States Constitution.
It's about honorable compromise. And that is not weakness if you're mak-
ing progress.

—Bill Clinton, interview with the Wisconsin media,
July 20, 1993

On January 20, 1993, more than 250,000 people crowded around the U.S. Capitol to welcome Bill Clinton's presidency. "You know that feeling that you get when you're a little kid on Christmas and you wake up and see all those presents under the tree?" one female reveler asked. "Well, that's the feeling I get watching this guy." That night, the comedian Dennis Miller, emceeing the MTV Ball at Washington's Convention Center, gushed, "finally, one of our guys is drivin' the car."

As a Georgetown student, Bill Clinton had wandered Washington's glowering streets the night Martin Luther King Jr. was assassinated, in April 1968, fearing King's racial progress was doomed. Now, Clinton returned to a city headed by America's first black woman mayor, Sharon Pratt Kelly. Kelly had unseated the corrupt Marion Barry in 1991 by promising to fix Washington "Not with a Broom, but a Shovel." Headlines emphasized the poverty, crime, and despair afflicting African Americans in this city of 606,900 that was two-thirds black and often designated America's murder capital. Kelly, a lawyer whose father was a judge, represented Washington's large black middle class and upper class; one-third of the Washingtonians earning $50,000 or more were black. In New York City, only 7 percent of those earning such middle-class salaries were black. Her administrative inexperience and her opponents' obstructionism would sabotage her reforming crusade. Barry's cronies labeled City Hall

"Menopause Manor." Such blatant sexism would not last; but neither would Kelly as mayor.

On Inauguration Day, Bill Clinton's sunny vision eclipsed such worries in Washington's municipality, and in his already wobbly administration. The inauguration-fest became a happening for many Baby Boomer celebrities, with appearances by Bob Dylan, Elton John, Bill Cosby, Chevy Chase, Diana Ross, Kermit the Frog, and a reconstituted Fleetwood Mac singing Clinton's campaign song. Mike Myers and Dana Carvey, playing heavy metal morons watching this parade of Sixties' and Seventies' icons on *Saturday Night Live*'s "Wayne's World," felt compelled to inform the new president: "It's the 90s."

In his inaugural address, shaping a mandate he never received, Clinton said: "The American people have summoned the change we celebrate today. . . . There is nothing wrong with America that cannot be cured by what is right with America." His overreach was forgiven that day, but not for much longer. He celebrated "this season of service" as one of renewal, responsibility, idealism, and activism. He reaffirmed "a simple but powerful truth: We need each other, and we must care for one another." He had wanted to say "we must love one another," but both Chelsea and Hillary feared it would sound too "flaky," too Jimmy Carter.

Clinton challenged his fellow politicians to transcend the usual "intrigue and calculation," saying, "Let us give this Capitol back to the people to whom it belongs." The maneuvering he warned against would prove particularly toxic for a politician like Clinton who excelled in creating his own messes, then fixing them.

Clinton's alluring idealism, passion for people, and atomic smarts mixed unstably with a hard-edged will to power, a puppy-dog neediness, and a superhuman buoyancy—during a time of cultural, technological, and economic upheaval. His Yale-Bubba dualisms would propel him, his wife, Hillary Rodham Clinton, and the American people on an emotional roller coaster.

First Hundred Days of Technological, Diplomatic, and Cultural Change, Too

Franklin D. Roosevelt's action-packed debut in 1933 during the Great Depression made the First Hundred Days a benchmark for judging a new administration. The FDR superhero model emphasized the president's mastery of his own destiny. Sixty years later, in his First Hundred Days, Clinton would learn the humbling modern lesson that while mastery is essential, luck helps, too: great inventions and economic upturns can make a presidency look blessed; global headaches and domestic squabbles beyond any leader's control can make it look cursed.

On January 23, Marc Andreessen, an undergraduate at the University of Illinois at Urbana-Champaign, announced the launching of the Mosaic Browser, "the first window into cyberspace." This system for navigating the World Wide Web was easily installed, user-friendly, and image-based not just text-based. Celebrating this "first 'killer app' of network computing," insiders promised: "A Click of the Mouse, a World of Information." Few fathomed just how big and enveloping that world would be. Computers, which wowed in the 1980s as machines that could practically do anything, would become in the 1990s machines that could do everything, everywhere. "Technology is almost magical," Clinton gushed in his inaugural. American euphoria about living in this wondrous age would boost his presidency.

More sobering, five weeks later, on February 26, 1993, a yellow Ford van rented from Ryder and parked in the garage beneath New York's World Trade Center detonated 1,310 pounds of fertilizer. The force blasted a 180-foot hole in the wall of the adjoining train station, igniting fires that burned for two hours. It took over five hours to evacuate the 100,000 people who worked every day in the two 110-story towers. In those days before cell phones were ubiquitous, long before flashlight apps, everyone navigated through dark, smoke-filled stairways. "It was almost like walking through hell," reported Port Authority police sergeant Dan Carbonaro. "We were making our way on hands and knees over rubble." Six people died and more than 1,000 people needed medical treatment, mostly for smoke inhalation.

The attack, by Islamist terrorists whom the FBI caught quickly because one of them returned to Ryder for his $400 security deposit, confirmed Clinton's inaugural warning that in a globalizing world, "There is no longer a clear division between what is foreign and what is domestic." All presidents are held hostage to external events. America's global responsibilities and vulnerabilities in the 1990s quickly debunked the post–Cold War "end of history" illusions. Officials downplayed just how unnerved they were by this lethal illustration of America's vulnerability to global terrorism. The mass denial of this reality would prove costly eight and a half years later.

During this transition, the Whitney Museum's biennial helped set America's cultural agenda, for better and worse, as it had been doing since 1932. While Clinton believed "our Nation can summon from its myriad diversity the deepest measure of unity," many artists and intellectuals, empowered by recognition of "diversity," expressed rage, otherness, and victimhood. The biennial showcased an angry, edgy, grotesque burlesque of eighty-two artists, with gays and minorities heavily represented, asserting difference, assailing sensibilities, flaunting their bodies and body parts, reveling in their emissions and secretions. Works included a puddle of plasticized vomit, a chewed-over piece of lard, and feminist branding irons with sexual messages in the secretive squiggles of Gregg shorthand. Each visitor randomly wore one of five buttons, with one or two words, which together spelled "I Can't . . . Imagine . . . Ever Wanting . . . To Be . . . White."

This biennial became an art show watershed, privileging women, gays, minorities, and their sensibilities. *New York* magazine's art critic Kay Larson, abandoning the "in your face arrogance" of the Eighties, welcomed "the social anguish of the nineties, which erupts here in a rumble of rage and despair." *Time*'s critic Robert Hughes, however, dismissed this "Fiesta of Whining. . . . No sodden cant, no cliché of therapeutic culture goes unused," he moaned. Michael Kimmelman's *New York Times* review proclaimed: "I hate the show."

Leftist disgust with Reagan and Bush initially papered over this growing rift between these multicultural identity radicals and Clinton's now-quite-establishment liberals. Toni Morrison, who could ford the gap, would win the 1993 Nobel Prize in literature, for lyrical novels illustrating America the fragmented. The Clinton Cabinet member most fluent in both argots, America's first African American female surgeon general, Dr. Joycelyn Elders, spoke too frankly about sex and lasted less than two years. In retrospect, the Whitney Museum curator, Elisabeth Sussman, would attribute the controversy to "the ongoing debate over the body and sexuality that has been at the center of our cultural struggles." Issues about the body and sexuality were already at the "center" of the Clinton administration's struggles, too.

Don't Ask, Don't Tell . . . Don't Please Anybody . . .

More crowd-pleaser than tactful statesman, Clinton stumbled two months before his inauguration, and only eight days after his election, on November 11. NBC's Andrea Mitchell asked if he would implement his pledge to allow gays to serve openly in the military. Intoxicated by victory, speaking too truthfully about his progressive views, Clinton said "yes." This candor infuriated military leaders and millions of veterans, many of whom already doubted this draft dodger poised to become the next commander-in-chief. Republicans warned that, with the election over, Clinton liberated his inner liberal.

Every president-elect has trouble shifting so abruptly from wooing to governing, from the campaign trail's promiscuous promising to the Oval Office's impossible choices. Bill Clinton was particularly prone to pander. He was poised to be, at forty-six, the third youngest president and had less national experience than Theodore Roosevelt or John Kennedy did when they moved into the White House.

Waves of ecstatic coverage obscured Clinton's 43 percent popular vote tally. More than 58 million Americans had voted against him. The post-electoral over-excitement and Election Day underperformance created a political vertigo that would disorient the Clinton White House.

The gays-in-the-military dilemma was a gut issue for two powerful groups. Gays were framing equal treatment as a civil rights issue, appealing to an increasingly fluid and tolerant society that worshiped individual rights and abhorred discrimination. The military culture, however, remained hypermasculine and homophobic, with the channeling of male sexual aggression underlying much military discipline. Belonging to a tradition-bound institution, soldiers understood sexual conservatism, gender roles, and conventional family arrangements as society's bedrock.

The resulting "don't ask, don't tell" policy was too slick for liberals and too hippie for conservatives. It encouraged lying in an institution that prized honor. President Clinton and his aides spent more time firefighting early on about gays rather than cultivating the policy initiatives candidate Clinton had pitched. The first time Clinton's new secretary of defense, Les Aspin, met the Joint Chiefs of Staff, the gay issue dominated. "At the end, we spent a few minutes on Iraq, Somalia and Bosnia," one general reported.

This messy policy telegraphed Clinton's guilt at being on the wrong side of history. In 1993, RuPaul's Drag Queen anthem "Supermodel (You Better Work)," conquered dance clubs. Aaron Spelling's made-for-television movie of *And the Band Played On,* detailing the initial denial about AIDS, within the gay community and beyond, won an Emmy Award. The Broadway hit *Angels in America: A Gay Fantasia on National Themes,* a seven-hour meditation about gays, AIDS, and America, won four Tony Awards and a Pulitzer Prize. Perhaps most influential, the Hollywood blockbuster *Philadelphia,* starring Tom Hanks as an AIDS-stricken attorney fighting his wrongful dismissal, won two Oscars.

Hanks was emerging as a modern Jimmy Stewart, a decent, all-American, Everyman. By starring in such easy-watching films as *A League of Their Own* in 1992, and *Sleepless in Seattle* in 1993, he was becoming Hollywood's all-time box office star. Hanks would lose thirty-five pounds while filming *Philadelphia* as makeup magicians covered his body with ugly lesions. That Hanks accepted this role was as monumental in 1993 as was Gregory Peck's portraying a journalist going undercover as a Jew to fight anti-Semitism in *Gentlemen's Agreement* in 1947.

Elite white gay AIDS victims were the shock troops of the gay revolution, more easily embraced than their once-healthy, promiscuous, selves. Americans found it easy to cry along with Beckett's grieving lover, played by the heterosexual hottie Antonio Banderas, especially because the film's final version deleted a sex scene depicting earlier, healthier days. The essayist Daniel Harris resented this "Kitschification of AIDS," reducing "these men into seraphic innocents" to make them palatable. Yet culturally mainstreaming gay soldiers, gay lawyers, gay marriages, gay suffering, even drag queens, advanced one of the post–civil rights era's most revolutionary transformations, despite Clinton's dithering.

A Cabinet That Looks Like America— Or Like Each Other?

Clinton's appointment process also generated controversy. His search for a Cabinet that "looks like America" triggered a special interest lobbying frenzy so crass *The New Republic* feared "the cultural balkanization of our politics." By Christmas Eve, using his E-G-G criteria of ethnicity, gender, and geography, Clinton had nominated seven white men, three white women, three black men, one black woman, and two Hispanic men.

The Cabinet's diversity was skin deep. Clinton's appointees were Xeroxes of one another, mostly Ivy League Adversarials in pinstriped power suits. To James Carville, they were "experts and schoolmarms." To leftist activists, most were corporate shills. To politicos, they were amateurs; Clinton hired few Jimmy Carter or Lyndon Johnson alumni. Drawn from America's secular priesthood, the thirty-two top Clinton appointees had amassed sixty-six university degrees, twelve from Yale or Harvard. Clinton-style diversity entailed welcoming all Americans into America's conformist, careerist cult of success.

The pick for attorney general, Zoe Baird, rated "the most impressive nomination" by *The New York Times,* quickly became the most problematic. Baird and her Yale Law professor husband had employed a husband-wife team of illegal aliens to help with household chores without paying Social Security taxes. These yuppie lapses were meaningless to Clinton, his staffers, and most White House reporters. "Baird's Hiring Disclosure Not Seen as Major Block," *The Washington Post* headlined, in that way newspapers had of trying to shape the news while reporting it.

Talk Radio's Populist Town Hall

"Nannygate" soon had the phone lines ringing and politicians quaking on America's six hundred radio talk shows, now serving as a populist Town Hall. "This is something the people out there just picked up on real fast," said Rush Limbaugh, the king of right-wing radio. "I don't think it's liberal or conservative, it's pure pocketbook."

By "pocketbook" Limbaugh meant class. The scandal unleashed the class antagonisms of millions who resented such imperiousness. Many progressives believed race and gender were the great American divides. Talk radio's political performance artists recognized the power of class. Many right-wing radio hosts caricatured the Clintons and their cronies as meritocratic aristocrats, despite Bill's humble roots, while claiming blacks and immigrants allied with these yuppies against the white middle class. With angry callers saying, "Who does she think she is?" Baird's nomination was doomed.

Baird withdrew. The president looked clumsy, especially after another possible nominee, Kimba Wood, had nanny issues, too. He now needed a female attorney general. White House counsel Bernard Nussbaum recalls that, after he finally found Janet Reno, just before announcing her nomination, the president whispered, "Bernie, this better work, because if it doesn't work, we're going to cut your 'blank' off and we'll nominate you for Attorney General."

These media "feeding frenzies," as the political scientist Larry Sabato dubbed them, fed Republican perceptions of the Clintons as leftist radicals unworthy of the White House and rank amateurs not ready for prime time. "Gotcha" reporters and obstructionist Republicans would keep pounding Clinton, even though people shouted at the Senate Minority Leader Bob Dole as he jogged on Miami Beach, "Give him a chance, give him a chance."

Budget Wars: Responsible Democrats . . .
or Eisenhower Republicans?

As the Clintons settled into their new home and offices, an unexpectedly high budget deficit projection of $300 billion dismayed them. Ronald Reagan's legacy of monster deficits was working, choking government growth. While officials were learning their phone and fax numbers, they faced a complicated, risky mission with a pressing deadline. The "deficit hawks," agitating to save the economy while freeing Democrats from their "tax and spend" identity, pitched good policy as great politics. By 1996, Clinton could become "the courageous leader who truly 'tamed the demon,'" Matt Miller of the Office of Management and Budget advised. Miller's OMB colleague Alice Rivlin agreed, while warning that drastic cuts risked a recession. As the economic team calibrated "how much deficit reduction" to prescribe, the "political folks" were saying, Rivlin recalls, "Hey, wait a minute, we've got to deliver on these promises that we made in the campaign." Clinton approved the cuts. But at one point he exploded: "we're all Eisenhower Republicans. . . . We stand for lower deficits and free trade and the bond market. Isn't that great?"

Through marathon meetings that often degenerated from graduate seminars to bar brawls, Clinton's grasp of the economics and politics wowed subordinates. Franklin Roosevelt and Ronald Reagan wanted dueling advisers to "weave the two together." Clinton loved reconciling conflicting advice. Abandoning campaign promises of a middle-class tax cut, Clinton sought $500 billion in budget reductions over five years with tax increases, spending cuts, and a stimulus package investing in highway and public works projects, summer jobs for young people, and community programs. In March, every congressional Republican opposed this budget despite its fiscal conservatism. Only three Republicans approved the stimulus package.

On February 4, the Senate had passed the Family and Medical Leave Act. Now workers could receive up to twelve weeks of unpaid leave if they or their relatives were afflicted by serious illness or blessed with a baby. Hillary Clinton connected the legislation to her four-month stint at home when Chelsea was born. President Bush's two vetoes of similar legislation validated the Clintons to millions of their supporters.

Hillary Clinton As Chief of Staff-in-Waiting

Bill Clinton boldly, foolishly, chose championing health care reform as a priority, despite the bleak economic news, then, boldly, foolishly, entrusted the project to Hillary, his Bobby Kennedy. Thirty-seven million Americans lacked health care coverage despite health care costs eating up 14 percent of the GNP. The Clintons hoped to control costs while granting health care as a basic right.

Hillary Clinton already functioned as "Chief of Staff-in-Waiting," according to the budget director Leon Panetta. She concluded meandering meetings. She disciplined the president and his staffers. She was more exacting and pricklier than her gregarious husband. Bill Clinton's outbursts were like summer thunderclaps, he "would scream and then within ten seconds he was back, 'How ya doing?'" Panetta recalls. Hillary Clinton's tantrums were Category Three hurricanes, doing extensive, lingering damage. One politico, Joan Baggett, remembers sitting in meetings with the First Lady, thinking, "Please don't let her yell at me."

As conservatives scoffed that Hillary Clinton's health crusade exposed the Clintons' hippie radicalism, the mainstream media applauded. A working First Lady was "more honest" than one lurking offstage, *The New York Times* editorialized. "She will stand *with* her man, or maybe ahead of him." Many professional women agreed that her West Wing office "is not just breaking a glass ceiling but knocking down a thick wall," as Eleanor Clift rejoiced in *Newsweek*.

Hillary Clinton's "co-presidency" triggered fears of women seizing power via their "Mrs. Degrees" not "J.D.s." The administration faced legal challenges about her unofficial, unpaid, unaccountable status. Her consultation process, with multiple working groups then reporting to coordinating committees called toll-gates, seemed Byzantine and Stalinist. First Ladies claimed the job was flexible. In fact, the role came with gossamer shackles discouraging real power and the political equivalent of the Hippocratic Oath: First do no harm.

It was hard to be so ambitious without generating controversy. On April 6, as her father lay dying from a stroke, the First Lady addressed fourteen thousand people at the University of Texas in Austin. With all we have, "we lack at some core level meaning" in our lives, she lamented. Crime in the streets, nihilism on the news, fury in our politics, reflected "alienation and despair and hopelessness."

This push for a "politics of meaning" culminated in a *New York Times Magazine* story Michael Kelly wrote, "Saint Hillary." She appeared on the cover clad in celestial white. Kelly caught her in the act of dreaming, like her husband, about reviving America's soul while reforming the body politic. What Kelly snidely called "a mix of Bible and Bill Moyers, of New Testament and New Age," and what others called "psychobabble," sought a 1950s-style suburban stability tempered by the 1960s' liberating openness. Kelly deemed it moralistic and judgmental, "unintentionally hilarious Big Brotherism." In his memoirs Bill Clinton sweetly, loyally, wrote: "I loved what she said and was proud of her for saying it." Burned, Hillary Clinton ignored the episode in her memoirs, and was more cautious in public thereafter.

A Bruising Benchmark

On April 19, the deaths of seventy-six people, including twenty-five children, at the Branch Davidian compound in Waco, Texas, spread worries about the

Clinton administration's amateurishness. A botched raid that killed four ATF agents and six cult members had prompted a fifty-one-day standoff with David Koresh's disciples. Four hours after the FBI launched tear gas canisters, the Davidians themselves ignited their compound and started shooting their own people. Militia members nationwide now had a rallying cry against U.S. government perfidy.

Reno quickly took responsibility. Clinton's initial silence, urged by his handlers, made him look cowardly. Just as John Kennedy learned self-reliance after stumbling during the Bay of Pigs debacle on April 17, 1961, Clinton would later say: "After Waco, I resolved to go with my gut."

Five days later, dignitaries gathered to dedicate the $200 million U.S. Holocaust Memorial Museum. That November, Steven Spielberg's masterwork *Schindler's List* would reinforce the museum's message that bigotry can turn ordinary people into killers. On the Washington Mall, America's open-air Parthenon, the Nobel Peace Prize winner Elie Wiesel addressed the contemporary European tragedy in the former Yugoslavia. "As a Jew, I am saying that we must do something to stop the bloodshed in that country," he insisted. Clinton also condemned "ethnic cleansing" there and affirmed Wiesel's Never Again teaching. Such sloganeering took "vacuity over the border into obscenity," the author David Rieff later wrote. "His words were literally meaningless." Only two years, 2 million refugees, and 200,000 deaths later did Clinton intervene decisively. Hillary Clinton would write, too uncritically: "We were adjusting to the roller-coaster ride of good and bad news at home and around the world."

Predictably, Clinton failed to deliver a health care proposal in one hundred days. That shortcoming, amplified by the other missteps, made his First Hundred Days a bruising benchmark. A White House pamphlet celebrated this "Season of America's Renewal." Republicans countered with their own pamphlet: "On the Wrong Track." Even Leon Panetta admitted his boss had to do "a better job of picking and choosing" his battles.

The Clinton White House often seemed more factionalized than Versailles. FOB shielded the president. Hillaryland sheltered the First Lady. Conventional Democrats pulled Clinton left, his DLC comrades tried keeping him centered. The campaign kids like George Stephanopoulos kept after the political promises. The professional grown-ups like Panetta kept the government running. The White House staff "was too big and too loose, and there were all these children," cocky wiseacres enjoying their first real jobs, the sixty-two-year-old budget whiz Alice Rivlin remarked. Both empath and energizer bunny, Clinton fed off the generational chaos rather than controlling it. The fifty-six-year-old White House Counsel, Bernard Nussbaum, bristled at the thirtysomethings' addiction to the daily news cycle. Feeding into their boss's need-to-please the most recalcitrant critics, it made for herky-jerky governance.

Clinton As Velcro Not Teflon

Don't "confuse motion with progress," a *New York Times* editorial warned in a wave of demoralizing hundred-day journalistic rebukes. Having ended 1992 with adoring campaign coverage from fellow Adversarials in the press corps, 90 percent of whom voted for Clinton, Clintonites expected continuing journalistic love. "We saw ourselves as smart, and tough, and good," George Stephanopoulos would write, recalling the administration's inaugural arrogance.

Presidents have usually felt persecuted by reporters, especially since the journalistic counterrevolution against the John Kennedy–Lyndon Johnson "credibility gap." Independent sceptics like Bob Woodward and Joe Klein in print and Cokie Roberts and Lesley Stahl on television replaced clubby cheerleaders like Arthur Krock and Walter Lippmann. Vowing they would not be the patsies their predecessors had been when John Kennedy fooled around or Richard Nixon schemed, journalists became hypercritical. The culture became less forgiving and more cynical. Reporters described the presidential candidates in 1960 favorably 75 percent of the time; reporters in 1992 offered favorable coverage 40 percent of the time. The jokes about Jack Kennedy's accent and Jackie's pearls were benign; the jokes about Bill's libido and Hillary's alleged lesbianism were nasty.

The media revolutions moving beyond the three-network universe aggrandized and diminished the president. Clinton's jogging habits, fast food addiction, underwear preferences, and sexual history became public fodder, along with an obsessive dissection of his marriage. As the head of Gossip Nation, the president endured unprecedented attention and abuse. Richard Nixon tolerated the media "microscope, but, boy, when they use a proctoscope, that's going too far." Most reporters' Nixon animus splashed onto Gerald Ford. A newly cheeky popular culture then caricatured this former football star as the national klutz. Jimmy Carter's prissiness annoyed reporters, as did Ronald Reagan's aw-shucks, populist pixie dust masking what many deemed a cruel conservatism. And George H. W. Bush's awkwardness, preppiness, and cluelessness helped journalists cast the Persian Gulf Savior as a recession-triggering incompetent.

Clinton's press war was more baffling. The Clintons and most journalists each felt betrayed by the others' hostility. What Clinton later characterized as a "culture clash" pitted cynical, careerist "gotcha" reporters always seeking an angle against an ambitious, self-righteous White House. Neither personal nor ideological, it was professional and institutional. Many journalists mourned Clinton's artful dodges around the truth; many Clintonites resented reporters' aggressive cynicism which seemed enhanced by Northeastern contempt for Southerners. The generational dynamics also made some journalists feel extra-competitive and critical, jealous of the peer who became president.

"Being responsible and comprehensive doesn't work, because it doesn't sell or create controversy," Clinton would recall self-pityingly. Rookie mistakes exacerbated tensions, including failing to provide "color" about the Clintons' emotions that first day and blocking a hallway passage reporters used. Clinton's passivity surprised his friend Taylor Branch, treating "bad publicity as a scourge to be endured rather than a problem to be dissected, managed, even positively transformed."

Minor botches became major scandals. An indulgent Christophe of Beverly Hills haircut on the tarmac of Los Angeles's busy airport on May 18, helped type Bill Clinton as vain and insensitive to legions of travelers he supposedly delayed. Reporters claimed two runways shut down until *Air Force One* took off. FAA records showed only one delayed air taxi flight—by two minutes. The slur, however, became gospel.

The First Lady's role in firing White House travel office employees that next day, to get the Clintons' "people" in, helped saddle Hillary Clinton with the sexist tag of "Lady Macbeth." The Clintons' blanket denial that the First Lady ordered the firings essentially dared reporters to disprove it. The Clintons' mismanaged Whitewater investment helped type the presidential couple as hypocritical yuppies who publicly deplored materialism while privately gold-grubbing like everybody else. Clinton resented "that the American people were seeing me primarily through the prism of the haircut, the Travel Office and gays in the military."

Bill Clinton and his associates were stuck in Scandalvania, a perpetual hell of gossip, outrage, and inquiries. If Ronald Reagan was the elusive Teflon president, Clinton was Velcro laced with Miracle-Gro, every charge stuck and swelled. The most outlandish lies had nine lives. Libels, even when refuted, became truths believed, soon perpetually recycled in the Web's spin cycle. Just as anti-Semites made Jews ultracapitalists and ultrasocialists, Clintons' enemies typed them as constantly conspiring yet forever fighting, with Hillary a lesbian yet Vince Foster's lover, Bill a wimpy appeasing pacifist yet a drug-running murderer.

The president acknowledged his administration appeared "out of focus." Still, the Clinton administration became the angriest one since Nixon's. The fury clouded the Clintons' judgment during the health care debate, in responding to accusations about Whitewater, and in stiff-arming reporters rather than exploiting their generational affinities.

What's the Point of Getting Here?

Clinton botched another left-leaning nomination in May. Professor Lani Guinier, nominated to be assistant attorney general for civil rights, advocated amplifying minority power with proportional representation and "supermajoritarian decision-making rules." Critics made this sound like affirmative action tokenism threatening American democracy. Her nomination hit the same firewall of American constitutional conservatism that defeated Franklin Roosevelt's 1937 Supreme Court packing plan, and would save Clinton with the Senate in 1999.

Guinier refused to withdraw. Clinton told her: "I'll be the asshole, and you can be the hero." When the guilt-ridden president abandoned his friend—smarmily insisting it was not personal and if she ever needed money he would be the first to lend it—blacks were now as offended as gays had been after the gays-in-the-military retreat. "When these strong winds blow, he tends to back away," Jesse Jackson grumbled.

With his presidency floundering, with his rookie staff punch-drunk from media pummeling, Clinton hired David Gergen as "Counselor to the President," pitching him as a nonpartisan moderate. Appointing this Nixon, Ford, and Reagan veteran brought more professionalism and conventional capital gamesmanship to the West Wing, while confirming impressions of Clinton as a will-o'-the-wisp. A birthday card sold in California showed a photograph of the president smiling with the words "You look positively, absolutely fabulous" on the cover. Inside, the sarcastic punch line read: "Trust me."

At one point, Clinton's temporizing to try dodging criticism so frustrated White House counsel Bernard Nussbaum that he brazenly asked: "Mr. President, what's the point of getting here if we're going to be afraid? . . . This is 1993. In 1996, we'll do whatever is reasonable, whatever has to be done. . . . We've got time to *do* these things. So what's the point? Are we here for the *house*? For the *plane*?" In retrospect, Nussbaum admits "this was a little arrogant," but they were alone, and, unlike many White House staffers, Nussbaum was older and had a lucrative law practice awaiting him. In her autobiography, Clinton's mother, Virginia Clinton Kelley, recalled that she and her boys needed to win over any room they entered—wooing any lone holdouts. Nussbaum said the story illustrated Clinton's greatness as a politician, trying to charm doubters, and his weakness as a leader, needing to placate them, too.

Ronald Reagan did not mind being pegged as a "good time Charlie"; it softened his reputation as a heartless ideologue. Bill Clinton resented the barbs at his fickleness and his addiction to poll-driven popularity, the political equivalent of fast food. In late July, with 47 percent of Americans surveyed saying Clinton was not a strong leader, and only 37 percent approving his leadership, Clinton exclaimed: "Read the United States Constitution. It's about honorable compromise. And that is not weakness if you're making progress."

That fall, when a *Rolling Stone* reporter asked what he would "stand up for and die" for, the president exploded. If "you convince" your readers "I don't have any convictions, that's fine, but it's a damn lie," Clinton snapped, without specifying any principles. Targeting the press for not giving "one damn bit of credit," he claimed "I have fought more damn battles here for more things than any president in the last twenty years." Ronald Reagan understood that fighting the press was futile. Bill and Hillary would only realize that in 1995.

On July 20, a personal tragedy exacerbated the unfolding political tragedy. Vince Foster, the deputy White House counsel, drove to Fort Marcy Park in Virginia, despondent. As the Clintons' confidante and lawyer, he took the scandals personally, especially Whitewater and what Watergate-crazed reporters were calling "Travelgate." Foster had scribbled down in a note to himself that Whitewater was "A can of worms you shouldn't open." Fearing he failed his friends, tortured by working in a town where, he complained in the final note he wrote then tore up, "ruining people is considered sport," Foster shot himself in the head with an antique gun.

On the six-month anniversary of Bill Clinton's inauguration, the latest Clinton comeback ended abruptly, violently. Who could have anticipated when Bill Clinton launched his long-shot campaign in October 1991 that Washington's nastiness would kill one of their dearest friends? In this overly suspicious environment, Foster's suicide encouraged accusations of murder and cover-up, especially after aides removed files from Foster's office before investigators arrived.

The Budget Win Revival: A Focused Presidency

Over the summer, Clinton aides worried about how to "communicate a focused presidency," despite their "overcrowded agenda." The initial chaos taught them "We are better off devoting full weeks to major issues." They wanted to focus on health care, reinventing government, and the NAFTA treaty in the fall, to show "that the President is in touch with the people," that "he keeps his promises," and "that he is a strong leader willing to make tough (even surprisingly tough) decisions." The communication strategists "urgently" requested "guidance," to avoid a programmatic "traffic jam" and manage the "policy, politics and press."

These policy scraps revived the president. On August 10, he signed a bill mandating his five-year economic plan to reduce the budget deficit by $496 billion. The bill balanced $255 billion in spending cuts, especially for Medicare and the military, with $241 billion in tax increases mostly falling on those making more than $100,000, beyond a 4.3 cent a gallon gas tax jump.

Clinton phone-called and horse-traded, bullied and begged. A final holdout, Marjorie Margolies-Mezvinsky, a Pennsylvania Democrat, represented a heavily Republican district. Her "yes" made the House vote 218 to 216. All 175 Republicans voted "no." Republicans sang derisively, "Bye, bye Margie" as she voted. The Congresswoman indeed lost her seat in 1994.

In the Senate, Vice President Al Gore's tie-breaking vote passed the budget, 51 to 50. The last Democratic supporter, Senator Bob Kerrey of Nebraska, wanted higher tax increases, sharper federal bureaucracy reductions, and more middle-class participation. Still, Kerrey told Clinton from the Senate floor: "I could not and should not cast a vote that brings down your presidency."

Although Clinton claimed his budget ended Reagan's revolution, the balance of cuts and taxes reflected a still Reaganized America, with a Democratic twist. Clinton wooed the business community by demonstrating fiscal responsibility, then satisfied Democrats by taxing the wealthy more to balance the budget. Congressman Dick Armey, a Texas Republican, charged: "Democrats believe prosperity comes from bigger Government. Republicans know it comes from ordinary people acting on behalf of themselves and their families."

Clinton's budget win was as momentous as Ronald Reagan's 1981 Air Traffic Controller strike. Finally, the president was leading. Clinton also earned bragging rights as the 1980s' boom continued, and yielded budget surpluses.

Clinton was learning to use the symbolic power of the presidency to face challenges such as the Great Midwestern Flood. The nine-state, four-hundred-thousand-square mile natural disaster overflowing the Mississippi River killed fifty people, destroyed ten thousand homes, and caused $15 billion in damage. Most Midwesterners blamed an "act of God," not "climate change," a still unfamiliar phrase.

Four visits protected the president from the kind of political backlash George W. Bush would experience after Hurricane Katrina. In August, visiting St. Louis, using the flood to drown out the media flow of crime, corruption, and dysfunction, all three Clintons honored nineteen heroes who embodied Clinton's can-do insight that "you can't roll up your sleeves if you're wringing your hands."

That September 7, Vice President Al Gore's Reinventing Government initiative made 384 recommendations proposing 1,250 actions to streamline the federal government. Within five years, REGO would cut 351,000 federal civilian workers, 16,000 pages of regulations, and billions of dollars. Clinton groused that reporters ignored the reforms because they were "neither sensational nor controversial." "REGO" represented Clintonism at its purest. New Democrat ideas synthesized in a 1992 book by David Osborne and Ted Gaebler, *Reinventing Government: How the Entrepreneurial Spirit Is Transforming the Public Sector,* shaped Clinton's thinking, then improved government.

On September 13, the president looked like a miracle worker as he spread his arms and ushered Israeli Prime Minister Yitzhak Rabin into an awkward handshake with the PLO terrorist leader Yasser Arafat at a White House signing ceremony. The negotiations leading to the Oslo Accords began in Norway but soon became a Clinton pet project. Clinton was trying to midwife George H. W. Bush's New World Order while solving long-standing tribal conflicts. South Africa was transitioning peacefully away from apartheid. The new European Union united that once bloodthirsty continent. And the December 15 Downing Street Declaration provided a framework for peace in Northern Ireland.

Eight days later, Clinton signed the National and Community Service Trust Act. Succeeding Franklin Roosevelt's Civilian Conservation Corps and John Kennedy's Peace Corps, Bill Clinton created AmeriCorps. He wanted his signature program to "remind every American that there can be no opportunity without responsibility." In its first twenty years, AmeriCorps would enlist 900,000 volunteers working in schools, nonprofits, and community groups to make their country "a good place for most Americans to live." After signing the bill, Clinton pitched health care to Tabitha Soren on MTV, to 20 pundits over lunch, and to 250 radio talk show hosts. His whirlwind day symbolized the revived spirit of government activism animating the White House—and was fun. Some days, it felt very, very good to be president.

His-and-Her Health Care Reform

The next day, September 22, Clinton premiered his ambitious attempt to reform one-seventh of the economy. Liberal White House staffers had lobbied for this autumn sales pitch. "Surveys indicate that health care remains the second or third priority (behind job creation) for the vast majority of voters, but also that people fear reform is just another promise to be broken," staffers warned. During Clinton's televised address before a joint session of Congress, the teleprompter scrolled the wrong text. He improvised. His eloquence under stress showcased him as a master salesman who did not need Reaganesque scripting.

Deeming the current system "too uncertain and too expensive, too bureaucratic and too wasteful," Clinton vowed to provide "every American" with the "security" of health care as a permanent right, building a simple system based on "choice." He insisted: "in a time of change you have to have miracles." The president honored the miracle worker tasked with implementing the reforms, Hillary Clinton, prompting a standing ovation.

Mrs. Clinton presented health care reform to congressional committees in late September, two months before the 1,300-page bill formally appeared in congressional mailboxes. She had already built up what one White House memo called "a significant amount of trust and confidence" with legislators. By the fall, her steely competence made her more popular than her husband.

The barbs of the 1992 campaign, along with the initial worry about her being too powerful, were fading. The once-awkward feminist intellectual with the horn-rimmed glasses now often appeared as a glamorous cover girl in the nation's trendiest magazines. Yet while reporters marveled that "the emotionless careerist of last year's Republican mythmaking has emerged as a sympathetic First Lady and master of policy detail," the White House remained cautious. "She is not the architect," East Wing staffers insisted, describing her as synthesizer and salesperson. "She is not a health care expert. She will tell you that early on she didn't know the difference between Medicare and Medicaid." Nevertheless, 52 percent believed Hillary had more input into "her" health plan than Bill did; only 4 percent said he had more input. When she testified before Congress, pitching the reform as safe, logical, fair, reporters and legislators swooned.

The president was building momentum in Congress. On November 30, he signed the Brady bill, gun control legislation imposing a five-day waiting period so gun sellers could perform background checks on potential customers. Although proud of defeating the National Rifle Association, the powerful gun lobby, Clinton knew this effort was like locking the door of a house while leaving the windows open. Americans remained remarkably fearful, vulnerable to violence, and menaced by 200 million guns nationwide. Every year, Americans committed 640,000 crimes with handguns. At the same time, the decades-long crime wave encouraged more gun ownership. Gun sales jumped by 45 percent in May 1992 after the Los Angeles riots. The Brady bill itself triggered record gun sales as dealers posted signs warning "Last Chance to Stock Up."

Crime Epidemic As Cultural Malaise

It was one of modern America's great mysteries. The 1960s strengthened so many rights, provided so many freedoms, yet, ultimately, eroded so much of America's quality of life. In this post-Sixties urban hairball, record levels of crime, violence, drug abuse, divorce, suicide, depression, alienation devastated communities, families, individuals. Ronald Reagan had blamed the Great Society, and sought to undo many of its reforms. Bill Clinton revered the Great Society, but sought to undo some of its toxic consequences—while blaming other forces, too.

Just as John Grisham's blockbuster 1991 best seller and 1993 hit movie, *The Firm,* unveiled dark conspiracies behind a law firm's glamorous façade, Clinton's inaugural year was yet another year of terrifying violence lurking behind America's splendid surface. In Florida, eleven murders clouded the Sunshine state tourism industry, including one German woman beaten, robbed, and run over by thugs, as her two children and her mother watched. In Northern California wine country, a repeat felon, paroled just four months earlier, climbed through the window as twelve-year-old Polly Klaas was having a slumber party with two other young girls, abducted Polly, then strangled her. The fear of crime was so widespread that when a Louisiana homeowner killed a costumed Japanese exchange student who showed up at the wrong house while looking for a Halloween party, a jury acquitted the shooter.

Media magnification made the crime wave feel like a tsunami. With the most spectacular crimes from across the nation reported repeatedly around the clock on radio and TV, Americans overgeneralized, even when crime rates started dipping in the 1990s. Watching crime shows like the new hit, *NYPD Blue,* and turning *Law & Order* into a blockbuster TV franchise, made Americans the equivalent of depressives with negativity bias. Primed to expect to see crime everywhere, they did.

The crime epidemic reflected a deeper cultural malaise. On June 24, 1993, a mail bomb sent to the Yale computer scientist David Gelernter mangled his right hand, right eye, and chest. The Unabomber, a Luddite lunatic who started by targeting university professors and airline officials in 1978, wanted to punish computer enthusiasts, but picked the rare computer scientist wary of computers. It would take another three years to arrest Theodore "Ted" Kaczynski, a Sixties' dropout. Disgusted by the media circus glamorizing the Unabomber's crimes, Gelernter concluded: "the twentieth century is the crime scene." Posing a great American riddle: "What made crime get so much worse as life got so much better?" Gelernter blamed what he called the "Intellectualized Elite" that encouraged mass allergies to being judgmental and mass addictions to feeling victimized.

In African American ghettos, fear and crime were so ubiquitous that many horrific crimes rarely made the news. Students shot students at school. An eleven-year-old chose the dress and hymns she wanted for the funeral she expected to have any day. There were 24,526 murders in 1993 overall, amid 1.9 million violent crimes and 12.2 million property crimes. African Americans were six times as likely to be murdered and eight times more likely to murder.

In Washington, D.C., the crime question vexed Mayor Sharon Pratt Kelly's housing policy adviser James G. Banks. The poverty and racism he suffered growing up in the Anacostia section in the 1920s and 1930s did not generate the crime rate of the more prosperous, less racist, 1980s and 1990s. The "social immune system" of "family, neighborhood, and community" had degenerated, triggering insecurity, despair, and crime. He proposed building more mixed-income communities rather than isolating the poor and the troubled together. When he articulated this vision in a Howard University lecture in April 1993, the new secretary of housing Henry Cisneros and Cisneros's boss Bill Clinton noticed.

The Rise of the Imperial Mayors

In New York City, fear of crime shaped the mayoral race that November, even though crime had started dropping since peaking in 1990. New York in the early 1990s was like New York in the 1970s again, another Metropolitan Trainwreck symbolizing America's implosion—although this time without leisure suits, bell-bottoms, long sideburns, or bad hair. The recession had hit hard. A million New Yorkers left, shrinking the tax base. Half the New Yorkers polled contemplated leaving. Race relations were brittle. Homeless people seemed everywhere, enveloping passersby in the stench of body order, hassling them for money.

Rudy Giuliani's comeback campaign against Mayor David Dinkins promised to revive the city by combating crime. Giuliani was a headline-grabbing federal prosecutor during the 1980s who skipped the rebellions of the 1960s, although he was only two years older than Clinton. As a Republican outnumbered in a Democratic city by 5 to 1, Giuliani needed his own centrist synthesis. He supported abortion and gay rights while fighting what New Yorkers were calling "brain-dead liberalism" or "dinosaur liberalism," so concerned with protecting civil rights it failed to protect citizens.

The president knew reporters would interpret a Dinkins loss as a white rejection of blacks and a vote of no confidence in his presidency. Addressing a

$1,000-a-plate fund-raising dinner at the New York Sheraton, Clinton challenged New Yorkers—and their fellow Americans—"to vote for people who are different than we are."

On Election Day, David Dinkins became the first black big-city mayor to lose his first reelection bid. Two-thirds of New Yorkers surveyed believed Giuliani would fight crime better. Giuliani won 77 percent of the white vote; Dinkins won 95 percent of the black vote.

In July 1993, Richard Riordan, a wealthy businessman who ran on the slogan "tough enough to turn L.A. around," was elected mayor of Los Angeles. Together with Philadelphia's mayor Ed Rendell, these three native New Yorkers ushered in what *The New Republic* would call "the age of the imperial mayor," culminating with media billionaire Michael Bloomberg's three-term tenure in New York from 2002 to 2013. Tough-talking, deficit-cutting, coalition-building, "business-friendly, centrist leaders" replaced the pioneering but often ineffectual "Rainbow Mayors," too often held hostage to the identity politics agenda, like Dinkins, Tom Bradley of Los Angeles, Wilson Goode of Philadelphia, and Harold Washington of Chicago.

The shifts in these Democratic strongholds validated Clinton's centrism. As a white Southerner, he appreciated the complexity of the African American experience. Before raising the race issue which David Dinkins so carefully avoided during the 1993 campaign, Clinton boasted: "I'm going to get in a lot of trouble." That same daring shaped one of his most impressive moments as president. His impromptu Memphis speech in November to the five thousand African American ministers, informed by James Banks's analysis, viewed the crime epidemic as a values crisis. His bold challenge to blacks, who were usually condescended to by white politicians, was no Sister Souljah posturing. This challenge came from a friend.

The crime and race problems would persist. One of 1993's most shocking acts of violence occurred that December, when Colin Ferguson shot up a crowded Long Island Rail Road car on the 5:33 p.m. train from Penn Station, killing five and wounding eighteen. A hate-filled psychopath hostile to whites and to "Uncle Tom Negroes," he waited for the train to cross into Long Island before rampaging, "because of my respect for Mayor David Dinkins." When he paused to reload his weapon for a third time, three commuters jumped him and subdued him.

The railroad massacre was at least the eleventh mass shooting of 1993. Others occurred in a Florida office building café, a Mississippi bar, a Wisconsin McDonald's, and a California health club. Early in 1993, Daniel Patrick Moynihan lamented that when gangsters killed seven other gangsters in 1929, the carnage so stood out amid America's expectation of safety in the Twenties, that the St. Valentine's Massacre became notorious. Now, mass murders risked becoming commonplace as Americans tolerated the intolerable. President Clinton insisted Americans had to fight "violence with values."

From Bush League to Textbook Leadership

After his Bush League, amateur hour beginning, Bill Clinton adapted and improved. An energized Clinton confronted big labor with a bipartisan coalition to ratify NAFTA, the North American Free Trade Agreement. In 1992, George H. W. Bush had signed the NAFTA agreement to open commerce with Mexico and Canada. To ensure that Congress ratified the treaty, Clinton had to tweak it and sell it to hostile Democrats. Former secretary of state Henry Kissinger called NAFTA a once in a generation chance to create an important international framework. Union leaders feared Clinton's globalization hastened America's deindustrialization, that America would export jobs to import cheap products, abandoning workers for the sake of markets. Jesse Jackson called NAFTA "SHAFTA."

Ross Perot reemerged, having warned in 1992 that the treaty would make a "giant sucking sound" pulling jobs to Mexico. Perot debated Vice President Al Gore on *Larry King Live* on November 9, days before the House vote. Let's choose "the politics of hope" over "the politics of fear," Gore pleaded. He needled Perot that his family profited from a free trade zone near Fort Worth. Embarrassed, Perot became surly and lost the debate.

Clinton triumphed with what David Gergen called "a textbook case in presidential leadership." Clinton secured more concessions from Mexico to satisfy reluctant Democratic legislators. He coordinated with Republicans. He arm-twisted skeptical Democrats, in an in-your-face Lyndon Johnson way. And he wooed the American people. When Gerald Ford, Jimmy Carter, and George H. W. Bush visited the White House for the Israeli-Palestinian Oslo Accords signing, Clinton convened a pro-NAFTA press conference with the ex-presidents. His note cards scrambled, the president once again improvised, looked unflappable, and made the sale. "Now I understand why he's inside looking out and I'm outside looking in," former president Bush marveled.

Clinton built his across-the-aisle coalition of 234 supporters in the House with 132 Republicans who supported the treaty. The Senate passed NAFTA 61 to 38. Clinton was unapologetic about his aggressive lobbying. "It's not like we were giving them backrubs or whorehouses or money," he later explained. "We were trying to make policy accommodations in exchange for enough votes, and they were trying to look out for the folks back home. That's what the voters hired us to do."

Thanks to a newfound popular buoyancy that fall, the president's poll ratings weathered the downing of a Black Hawk helicopter and the butchering of 18 American soldiers in Somalia on October 3. President Bush had sent 28,000 troops to protect humanitarian efforts in Somalia amid a devastating civil war compounded by severe famine. Somali irregulars dragging the bodies of 2 dead Americans through the streets fueled disgust against the murderers not the commander-in-chief. Still, the slaughter of American troops who had been performing good deeds in Somalia, combined with the beating of American aid workers by hooligans allied with Haiti's government, reinforced a post-Vietnam isolationist instinct. "It was Thugs 2, United States 0," one journalist declared.

After a tumultuous rookie spring and summer, Bill Clinton's more successful fall had him dreaming of a calm Christmas. His 58 percent approval ratings had jumped from a dismal 36 percent in May and 43 percent in late September. Ronald Reagan's end-of-rookie year ratings were only 49 percent, while George Bush enjoyed 71 percent approval in January 1990. America's rising economy reinforced these good feelings about the new president.

America Online: Expanding the Digital Universe

The technological miracles that would define the times also spread good feelings, although 1993's turning point in Internet user-friendliness did not rank in AP's Top Ten News Stories that year. This network of computer networks started connecting mostly university and government supercomputers in the 1960s. The freewheeling academic, public servant, and hippie hackers who developed the Internet kept it open, and until 1992, aggressively nonprofit.

In 1981, News Center 4 in San Francisco reported on this "far-fetched" notion of reading daily newspapers on your home computer. It took over two hours after dialing in to download all that information, without graphics. At $5 an hour, the anchor decided this cumbersome "telepaper" could never compete with the newspaper's "20 cent street edition."

In 1989, the development at Geneva's CERN laboratory of WWW, the World Wide Web, enabled individual users to create their own sites and interact with one another. In 1991, CERN's Tim Berners-Lee publicized this information-retrieval architecture that "allows links to be made to any information anywhere." America's multiple railroad systems had functioned awkwardly for decades until the four-foot nine-inch gauge for all tracks became standard-ized in 1886. This data system began with a Transmission Control Protocol (TCP) and a standard Internet Protocol (IP).

Launching Mosaic's Internet Browser made this once-exclusive digital universe accessible. By 1993, 11,000 interlocking networks in 102 countries con-nected more than 10 million Americans, with 150,000 new users monthly. Companies selling high-powered desktop computers with networking capabilities thrived as the revolution linking millions of personal computers into an envelop-ing, empowering, borderless virtual community began. The Virtual Gold Rush began, too. Now that the Internet was no longer commerce-free, corporations wanted millions of people online spending billions of dollars.

In January 1993, *Wired* magazine premiered, aspiring to be the digital generation's *Rolling Stone,* heralding a cultural cataclysm bigger than rock 'n' roll. The publisher Louis Rossetto envisaged "a revolution without violence that em-braces a new, nonpolitical way to improve the future based on . . . civics beyond government and communities beyond the confines of time and geography."

AOL, ambitiously named America Online, started connecting users to the Internet in September 1993. Customers dialed up, paying $9.95 for five hours a month and $3.50 per hour thereafter. By December, five hundred thousand users had joined AOL's "electronic community." This "new interactive medium can change the way we communicate, inform, educate, work and play," said Steve Case, AOL's president. "A couch potato could summon any movie ever made by pushing a button," *The New York Times* speculated breathlessly.

Until now, even most technologically savvy people predicted a five-hundred-channel universe, imagining television with all its rigidities expanding exponen-tially. Suddenly, a more freewheeling, individualist, malleable universe making every consumer a producer, too, seemed possible. *The New Republic* suggested, wildly, that someone could even "telecast his daughter's cello practice live, to one or ten or fifty people," then she could splice in text and video clips to "produce an interactive multimedia product." The government's strategic document regarding the Internet, equally fanciful, encouraged Americans to "Imagine you had a de-vice that combined a telephone, a TV, a camcorder, and a personal computer. No matter where you went or what time it was," you could see and be seen.

Skeptics remained. The Internet still conveyed data slowly to the few Amer-icans actually online. An item in *The New York Times Magazine* doubted that most users would find "The Internot" that thrilling; all the typing involved would limit the excitement and fun. *Newsweek*'s Robert Samuelson, noting how slowly cars or TVs revolutionized American life, wondered: "Who has time for all the multimedia, interactive mumbo-jumbo?"

Bill Clinton and Al Gore wanted government to perfect and protect the "data superhighway." Since the late 1970s, Gore had championed high-speed telecommunications and an information highway. In his 1991 book, *The Work of Nations: Preparing Ourselves for 21st Century Capitalism*, Clinton's friend and first secretary of labor, Robert Reich, proposed that the government target investments to educate workers and build the fiber-optics network necessary to make America the world headquarters of "symbol manipulation services in a global economy."

As many as two-thirds of employed Americans worked in information-related jobs and almost everyone needed fast, accurate information. Phone companies had already laid 95,000 miles of fiber-optic cable nationwide replacing copper phone wires. Gore wanted government to lay wire for the superhighway's "off-ramps," the switches and cables to homes and institutions, including America's public schools, only 22 percent of which had modems. The phone companies wanted to continue laying the cable, hoping to make private toll roads.

With the Orwellian-sounding National Information Infrastructure (NII) act of 1993, the Clinton-Gore administration sought to facilitate "a nationwide, invisible, seamless, dynamic, web of transmission mechanisms, information, appliances, content, and people." Amending 1991 legislation, the act launched an impressive $3 billion-a-year, interagency effort. The program hoped to "unleash an information revolution that will change forever the way people live, work, and interact with each other."

"One of the biggest changes the human species has ever faced" was imminent, Gore said. He envisioned the government as convener, uniting different sectors of society; as protector, guaranteeing minimum standards; and as equalizer, ensuring access for all, to avoid a country divided into "information haves and have nots."

If Abraham Lincoln was "the godfather of the Pacific railroad," and Dwight Eisenhower the father of the Interstate Highway System, Bill Clinton is the stepfather of the Internet, with the boundless, wireless network fulfilling his mission to modernize America by uniting it virtually. Even if neither Al Gore nor Bill Clinton invented the Internet—scientists did—Gore was its Henry Clay, persistently pushing prophetic legislation that facilitated its growth, just as Clay pushed internal improvements. A tolerant political culture would have forgiven Gore's awkward attempts at self-promotion and prized his visionary contributions.

With profound insight into America's future, proud of what he had accomplished in just one year, Clinton resented the media carping and partisan doubts. November's *Congressional Quarterly* had deemed his first year the most productive presidential rookie year legislatively since Dwight Eisenhower. He believed he had been too modest: "In politics, if you don't toot your own horn, it usually stays untooted." He acknowledged the "constant intrusion of crises like Haiti and Somalia." He blamed Republican partisans' "anti-tax, anti-government rhetoric." And he faulted the press for being too sensationalist, too allergic to "positive stories."

Troopergate As Grinch

Just as the mood lightened that December, scandal hit the Clintons again. On Sunday, December 19, CNN broadcast interviews with two Arkansas state troopers from Governor Clinton's security detail. Violating their code to preserve the confidentiality of those they protect, they described an adulterous governor who slept with Gennifer Flowers and used his guards to tomcat around town. The next day, *The American Spectator* published David Brock's lurid exposé describing a libertine governor with countless conquests including one named "Paula," forever dodging his foul-mouthed, sexually frustrated wife. Some troopers claimed Clinton offered them jobs to buy their silence. The Clintons had "more a business relationship than a marriage," charged Brock, then a right-wing "hit man" journalist.

Meanwhile, *The Washington Times* charged that Clinton aides removed Whitewater files from Vince Foster's office after his suicide. Troopergate, Travelgate, and Whitewatergate fused. The Clintons gamely hosted glittering Christmas parties nightly as these tawdry stories circulated, and aides scrambled to defend their boss. Political consultant Paul Begala told George Stephanopoulos, "I think I'm going to throw up."

The Clintons were caught between two blades of razor-sharp scissors. Right-wing magazines like *The American Spectator* saw the Clintons as the enemy, still resisting his election. Mainstream media reporters, regardless of their politics, were increasingly scandal-hungry and uninhibited. That Christmas season, what the singing superstar Michael Jackson called "the incredible, terrible mass media," toggled back and forth between the Clinton revelations and Jackson's troubles. The same Monday, December 20, of the Troopergate article, Jackson endured a strip search following molestation allegations. That Wednesday, Jackson, teary-eyed, made a live, four-minute statement on CNN, declaring he was innocent of pederasty and describing—in uncomfortable detail—the "dehumanizing and humiliating examination" of his private parts. Before he died in

2009, this oft-accused molester would pay out $35 million to settle two dozen such claims.

The Baby Boomer culture was cannibalizing its icons. To the extent that the Clintons embodied and helped shape the adversarial culture, the sexual revolution, the questioning of authority, these forces now tortured them. Seventy percent of voters thought reporters paid too much attention to Gary Hart's sex life in 1988, then Bill Clinton's sex life in 1992. Yet, somehow, whenever a scandal broke, the numbers of viewers and readers following news from Washington spiked.

As the focal point of an all-consuming media, the star of the national show, the president endured unprecedented attention and abuse. The CNN cable revolution brought 24/7 News. The talk radio revolution filled the airwaves with harsh, opinionated, often explicit chatter. The Internet revolution was just starting to open a world of unfiltered discussions, unsubstantiated rumors, and cascading links that pulled readers further and further into one worldview or another.

Like many Borderline personalities, America's 24/7 media culture collectively had what psychologists called "boundary issues," a lack of limits on behavior and the annihilation of traditional borders in both public and private lives that maintained certain discretions, certain secrets. In what Darrell M. West and John Orman call this "era of politics *as* entertainment and entertainment *as* politics," reporters became Hollywood gossips' D.C. branch, covering politicians, and the First Family, as celebrities.

Louis Sass, a Harvard psychologist, explained that whereas Sigmund Freud's repressive Victorian society mass-produced neurotics, struggling with all the cultural constraints, our modern cultural carnival produced manics and hysterics, struggling without limits. Clinton exhibited some of these telltale Borderline behaviors, with his gargantuan appetites, his temper tantrums, his operatic marriage, his self-destructive sexual addictions, his chameleonlike politics, and his insatiable drive. In this anything-goes culture, a woman, Lorena Bobbitt, could hack off her husband's penis and make both of them celebrities; bankers went from being famous for their rectitude to being infamous for their abandon; teens often ended up giving their divorced parents dating advice, while even innocent priests found themselves perceived as sexual predators rather than sacred protectors.

Bill and Hillary Clinton invited some of this scrutiny. They publicized their private lives when convenient. Both shared a vision of an open, personal, transformational presidency, not only implementing innovative policies but healing

America's soul. As a result, the president would admit he "usually" preferred briefs to boxers. Even the First Lady would share some intimacies, recalling seeing her baby start "to foam at the nose" during an early breast-feeding. Eventually, there would be a presidential paramour who filled out Excel graphs detailing "how far they went" each time she and the Leader of the Free World touched—and preserved clothing soiled by their encounter rather than dry-cleaning it.

Borderline personalities—and societies—are darker than narcissists. The 1990s turn from Reaganite narcissism toward a Borderline society brought out more anxiety, insecurity, anger, and acting out. This was evident in the "politics of personal destruction," the shrillness of discourse, the shock jocks of radio and TV, the hoodlum culture of violent, garbage-mouthed rappers, and the bouts of worry and despair, even as conditions improved objectively.

Presiding over the Republic of Nothing—And Everything

As a rookie, despite moments of brilliance in governance, helping America balance its budget, broaden its trading zone, and start controlling its crime problem, Bill Clinton stumbled frequently, leaving him vulnerable to ridicule, and to the torturous, investigative infrastructure Richard Nixon's Watergate scandal bequeathed to the presidency. At his best, Clinton had Linus's wisdom and eloquence with touches of Snoopy's impishness. But Bill—and Hillary—had these Pig Pen–type clouds of dust and chaos forever hovering around them. Dodging responsibility for any missteps, the Clintons self-righteously attributed every charge to the vicious right and sensational media.

The Clinton Wars, the Whitney Biennial, the Great American Hook-Up on the Internet all reflected America's mass moral confusion, especially its ongoing discomfort with sexuality. Opening up the art world and the political world did not just welcome in rays of redemptive light but first absorbed waves of pent-up anger. Most of the major disruptions to Clinton's first year—gays in the military, the nanny of the first woman nominated as attorney general, the controversial writings of a black woman, and the sexual abandon of the first Baby Boomer president—all derived from America's still unresolved Gender Bender, and the country's awkward entry into a freer, more individualistic, more atomistic state.

With all these changes, America, once a Republic of Something, with shared ideals, for which it stands, even if imperfectly implemented, risked becoming a Republic of Nothing, with everything up for grabs, few core assumptions accepted, and family, responsibility, community, tradition weakened. Nevertheless, on the deepest levels of the American psyche and society—where it takes not only a leader and not only a village but hundreds of millions of prods, both prosaic and profound, in millions of minds to change—Bill Clinton and company helped pioneer a new, more embracing, world a Republic of Everything, a kinder, gentler, welcoming, pluralistic place for people who deviated from what had once been rigidly enforced norms. This new more tolerant world would be apparent under the conservative George W. Bush, whose Cabinet "looked like America" with less effort and self-consciousness than Clinton's, including the widely respected Colin Powell as America's first African American secretary of state. This new world would emerge most dramatically on Election Night 2008, when many Republicans joined Democrats in cheering Barack Obama's election as a redemptive moment for all Americans.

Bill Clinton was trying to reform his own party and his country during a time of great change. In not just mastering many of these changes but embodying them, three decades' worth of cultural and political anxieties stuck to Clinton like gummy sap from an Arkansas Slash Pine evergreen. Other presidents who forged what the Yale political scientist Stephen Skowronek called this "politics of preemption" also attracted harsh attacks, including Woodrow Wilson and Richard Nixon. The "character assassination" resulted when their own party members resented their deviations from party orthodoxy, while rivals feared those very deviations as invasive.

The great successes that stabilized Clinton's presidency in 1993, especially the Budget Bill, AmeriCorps, and NAFTA were more traditional expressions of presidential leadership, forging coalitions, reconciling opposing agendas, mediating conflicts. Clinton succeeded when, rather than being sucked into culture clashes, gender struggles, diversity power plays, and personal fights, he could instead build a stable policy foundation of common values and common purpose with his formidable political skills. Clinton once again showed in 1993 that he could master the learning curve, that he was far more nimble and more substantive than the reporters who covered him.

5

1994: Seattle
The New Nihilism in the Coffee Capital; and Renewed Republicanism in the Nation's Capital

And I think what they were saying is that the Republicans did a good job of defining us as the party of Government, and that's not a good place to be. I think that was a clear message that they were sending in the election.
—BILL CLINTON, THE PRESIDENT'S NEWS CONFERENCE,
NOVEMBER 9, 1994

On April 8, 1994, an electrician named Gary Smith, dispatched to install a security system at a four-bedroom, five-bathroom turn-of-the-century mansion in Seattle, found no one home. Peering through a window, he thought he saw a fallen mannequin. Once he realized it was the corpse of Kurt Cobain, the twenty-seven-year-old lead singer of the grunge band Nirvana, Smith called a local Seattle radio station before calling the police.

Three days earlier, Cobain, fleeing drug treatment, binging on heroin and valium, had shot himself in the head. The troubadour of trauma for the twentysomethings' recently christened "Generation X," Cobain felt crushed between the edginess of his art and the machinery marketing his music. Modern popular culture now specialized in domesticating musical outlaws so they could afford luxuries like the $1.5 million home Cobain and his wife, Courtney Love, had purchased that January. "The worst crime I can think of would be to rip people off by faking it and pretending as if I'm having 100% fun," Cobain wrote in his suicide note.

While suicide rates had steadily averaged thirty thousand annually since the 1950s, teen suicide had tripled and suicide awareness had surged. Discussing once-taboo topics like this one fed demands to legalize assisted suicide for the elderly and the infirm. In 1990, Dr. Jack Kevorkian aided in his first public assisted suicide. He was arrested but acquitted. The practice had not yet been outlawed. In 1991, Kevorkian lost his medical license but continued crusading for this right, as a journalist, Derek Humphry, wrote *Final Exit: The Practicalities of Self-Deliverance and Assisted Suicide for the Dying.* This how-to guide eventually sold more than 1 million copies.

Kurt Loder, the MTV news anchor better suited to reporting on bands premiering than young legends buried, broke into regular programming to announce Cobain's death. MTV's producers pompously compared the following days of round-the-clock coverage to covering John Kennedy's assassination. As millions watched MTV all night, burned Cobain's signature flannel shirts in the park near Seattle's iconic Space Needle, lit candles in memory of their tortured hero, many feared that the voice of the next generation had been stilled. "He was a geek and a god," one fan told *USA Today.* "I really dug him." Bill Clinton asked Eddie Vedder of Pearl Jam whether to address the nation about Cobain's death; Vedder said no, he feared encouraging copycats.

It was not just that Cobain's was another musical Cinderella story, a child of divorce who was bullied in school, recorded his first album for $606.17, and saw his band's second album, *Nevermind,* sell 10 million copies. It was not just that "Smells Like Teen Spirit" and other Nirvana hits mixing depressing lyrics with sometimes surprisingly catchy tunes became anthems of angst for the surprisingly troubled masses. Cobain and his grunge group Nirvana helped make Seattle "the New Liverpool," according to *Rolling Stone.* With equally gloomy bands like Pearl Jam, Mudhoney, and Soundgarden, Nirvana mixed hard rock, punk, and metal to create the "Seattle Sound," expressing this New Nihilism. "I know there was nothing healthy about singing 'Rape Me,'" one Nirvana fan wrote. "Kurt didn't offer any solutions, he just railed against the ugliness and made it his home."

Grunge—a label of disputed origins and elastic meaning—quickly metamorphosed from a musical style originating with young, edgy Seattle-based bands to a lifestyle appealing to America's army of alienated and apathetic Peter Pans. The flannel shirts and leather jackets, ratty sweaters and torn jeans, long hair and layers of clothing, were purposely unglitzy, defiantly un-Eighties. Even the drug of choice switched from upscale cocaine to blue-collar marijuana. The grunge look professed to be carefree, despite its uniformity. It purported to be casual, despite how hard people cultivated it, especially after the budding designer Marc Jacobs's spring/summer 1993 grunge collection. Most practically, it protected against Seattle's cold weather.

Grunge, along with gangsta rap's prison chic, punk's masochism, and heavy metal's exhibitionism, helped mainstream the use of tattoos, body piercing, and even some limited body cutting, as vehicles for self-expression and individuation. Kurt Cobain's left forearm sported the brand of the small independent record label K, "to try and remind me to stay a child," he said. The range of rockers' tattoos, expressing friendship, longing, sentiments, politics, and sheer delight in oneself, illustrated the range of emotions that had as many as 20 million Americans tattooed by 1995. One hip San Franciscan told *Newsweek* these "identity bracelets" kept young people feeling bohemian, even when they sold out. New Agers sold tattoos to "bridge between the physical and the spiritual." "I'm adorning my temple . . . ," said one regular, who added more tattoos week by week, explaining: "It's the only thing you have that can't be taken away from you." A Sunset Strip biker tattooist scoffed: "We're not into that cosmic stuff."

Freethinking child psychiatrists preached tolerance, defining these acts as the Nineties' version of the World War II graffitist's "Kilroy Was Here," affirming the autonomous self in a volatile age. As America individuated, Dr. Andres Martin of Yale suggested, marking the body asserted power and established permanence. To cultural conservatives like John Leo of *U.S. News & World Report,* these "modern primitives" were repositioning "the sadomasochistic instinct . . . to look spiritually high-toned." In the 1830s, Alexis de Tocqueville considered American individualism surprisingly uniform and conformist. In post-1960s' consumerist America, the grunge rebellion, like most others, had been commodified, mass-produced, ritualized, and thus sanitized.

This commercialized, neutralized rebellion celebrating America the contingent, the evanescent, the depressing, imperiled Bill Clinton's sweeping ambitions. This New Nihilism countered Clintonian bonding agents like responsibility and community. This nihilism was kinder, gentler, more indulgent, less harsh, less soulless than the original European version. Nevertheless, there still would be a certain lack of faith in the future, in community, in ideals and big ideas. As individualism and libertinism often made family ties disposable, as big ideas seemed less important with the era of big government ending, Americans— along with many Westerners—seemed to be rejecting many of the basic social and ideological givens that had structured society for so long—and that all humans need. Clinton wanted young activists, not young defeatists. In 1994, the Seattle-style apathy of the young who allied with Clinton culturally combined with the Washington-based antipathy of those who abhorred Clinton culturally and politically to imperil his presidency.

Seattle: *A* Capital of Horizontal America

America's twenty-first largest city, inhabited by 516,259 in 1990, Seattle could lay claim to being the capital—or in Seattle's true progressive spirit—*a* capital of the new horizontal America emerging. Seattle would be hailed as America's grunge capital, America's coffee capital, the headquarters of Gen X, the new hometown of one of America's most popular sitcoms, *Frasier,* and, perhaps, America's funkiest city. Such defining firms as Microsoft, Starbucks, and Amazon would be headquartered in this, America's leading "latte town," or its suburbs.

Cities have their moments. Seattle's combination of intensity, intimacy, angst, and ennui, worked particularly well in the 1990s. The Seattle Sound reflected the city's gritty but wholesome, alienated yet oddly engaged, dynamic. If the World War II veterans were quintessentially Midwestern, wherever they lived, and Baby Boomers fused the Northeast with Southern California, alienated Gen Xers reflected a Northwestern vibe, as loose bolts from around America collected in that corner of the country. In 1993's three-hankie, Oscar-nominated feel-good movie, Tom Hanks plays a widower who moves to the Northwest from Chicago. Before he finds love with the perky Meg Ryan, thanks to his flamboyantly cute if meddlesome son who turns to a talk radio therapist for advice, Hanks, in mourning, is *Sleepless in Seattle.*

Douglas Coupland captured this Seattle Sensibility in his epoch-defining 1991 novel *Generation X.* Coupland lived in Vancouver most of his life, which was like Seattle but with national health care and a tendency to end declarative sentences with "ay" and a question mark. In an increasingly national and homogenized America, popular culture was less about place and more about the collective experiences in the space the mass media shaped. Oozing what he called "Boomer Envy," Coupland described young shiftless people with "McJobs"—enduring "Low pay, low prestige, low benefits, low future"—experiencing "Mid-Twenties' Breakdown," resenting that "Our Parents Had More," as America underwent "Brazilification," with the gap growing between rich and poor. The "Lessness" was economic and cultural. These socially, emotionally, and culturally deprived young people fought consumerism by insisting "I am not a Target Market" while succumbing to it, seeking deeper connections even as their "Divorce Assumption" and their "cult of aloneness" viewed all relationships as disposable, a logical conclusion with half of all marriages dissolving. They were overwhelmed by too much technology (i.e., "cryptotechnophobia"), too much choice (i.e., "option paralysis"), and too much freedom (i.e., "terminal wanderlust").

The Bored and the Shiftless,
in Movies and on TV

By 1994, many critics tired of Coupland's kvetching. His third book *Life After God,* a short story collection, evoked contempt from one reviewer for rehashing the same "self-pitying, small-scale ennui of Generation X." Still, while Coupland showed that Generation X could be an entertaining and lucrative literary subject, the inevitable generational movies mostly failed commercially. *Slacker* (1991), *Singles* (1992), *Reality Bites* (1994), and *Clerks* (1994) were clever, ironic, evocative. In *Reality Bites,* a young Ethan Hawke plays Troy Dyer, a coffeehouse guitarist struggling between subversive idealism and nihilistic cynicism. When a friend wonders "why things just can't go back to normal at the end of the half hour like on *The Brady Bunch* or something," Troy replies: "Well, 'cause Mr. Brady died of AIDS." Robert Reed, who played the all-American 1970s father, died as a closeted gay man with HIV.

Unfortunately, movies about bored, shiftless drifters left viewers bored and restless. Ben Stiller, the twenty-eight-year-old director of *Reality Bites,* wanted to make "a movie about personal relationships," not define a generation that didn't "want to be pigeonholed as Generation X." Stiller's forty-nine-year-old producer, Michael Shamberg, however, admitted he sought a sequel to his defining yuppie movie from 1983, *The Big Chill.*

Bored, shiftless drifters played much better in short bursts on TV. As the 1990s began, *The Cosby Show*'s warm fuzzy family franchise ended, as did *Cheers*'s warm fuzzy community franchise. "There's room on TV for a dysfunctional family you can laugh at," said Matt Groening, the cartoonist who created America's first successful prime-time cartoon since *The Flintstones*. Television publicized the American dystopia with crude, cynical, selfish characters modeling the New Nihilism. *The Simpsons* inverted the Donna Reed–Brady Bunch squareness of Nick at Nite. Instead, the central character Bart, an anagram for Brat, reveled in being an obnoxious, defiant ten-year-old. His sister Lisa would call her brother, "the spawn of every shrieking commercial, every brain-rotting soda pop, every teacher who cares less about young minds than about cashing their big, fat paychecks."

By 1994, the show, which debuted on the new Fox network in December 1989, was already a monster hit, confirming conservative fears that Hollywood hated America. With "Bartmania" unleashed, 1 million T-shirts a day sporting Bart's image and hostile catchphrases like "eat my shorts" were being sold. By 1998, *Time* would designate Bart "one of the 100 most important people of the 20th century," epitomizing this century of "change" more than Mickey Mouse, Superman, or Bugs Bunny.

In March 1993, two teenage Bart-like cartoon characters debuted, Beavis and Butt-head. In their snide, scatological world, Principal McVicker was "McDicker," and the Secret Service was "the secret cervix." While watching a Nirvana video, Butt-head wondered: "Is this, like, 'Grudge' music?" When Beavis then asks where Seattle is, Butt-head replies: "It's this place where, like, stuff is, like, really cool." One critic sighed, "Compared with these Bozos, Bart Simpson is Bill Moyers." During Senate hearings in 1993, Senator Fritz Hollings, a South Carolina Democrat denouncing TV's violence and vulgarity, sputtered about "Buffcoat and Beaver"—which only encouraged Mike Judge and his writer colleagues.

Next, this new American nightmare showcased grown-ups as cases of arrested development. By 1994, *Seinfeld* was emerging as one of the decade's dominant sitcoms. A show about "nothing," whose creators vowed "no hugging, no learning," meaning no Cosbyesque moralistic epiphanies, *Seinfeld* reveled in its nihilistic self-absorption. In one breakthrough episode, the four friends competed to see who could resist pleasuring themselves the longest, popularizing a new phrase, "master of my domain." A few months later, Jerry Seinfeld kept denying rumors he was gay, just "because I'm single, I'm thin and I'm neat." He and George preserved their credentials as hip New Yorkers by injecting another catchphrase into the culture, insisting, "Not that there's anything wrong with it." If "The Contest," by mocking one social taboo, moved America further toward becoming the Republic of Nothing, with no standards, "The Outing," telegraphing tolerance, helped spawn the Republic of Everything. Despite their best efforts, Jerry Seinfeld and his partner Larry David were shaping society, teaching millions how to speak "Seinlanguage."

Although very much the New Yorker starring in this New York–set show filmed in Los Angeles, Seinfeld would call Seattle "my favorite city. It's the first place anyone ever liked me," having had his first sold-out show there in 1983. "I feel like I owe my whole career to Seattle."

Seattle Capitalism As Computer Capitalism

Seattle was sophisticated enough to appreciate Seinfeld's wryness because it comprised more than the disaffected flannel-shirt-and-work-boots crowd. Its mix of progressivism and capitalism appealed to high-tech entrepreneurs like Bill Gates of Microsoft. He was raised in Seattle as an accident of birth; he returned to the large suburb of Bellevue in 1979 on purpose.

In 1986, Microsoft moved to its corporate campus in Redmond, Washington, shortly before its stock went public, and a year before Gates became the world's youngest billionaire. The Microsoft "campus" would soon encompass 8 million square feet, housing most of this computer company's 94,000 employees in Washington State. Seattle capitalism, like Silicon Valley capitalism, was a peculiar form of post-1960s' Baby Boomer computer capitalism. In-your-face, elbow-your-competitors-to-the-side energy came wrapped in down vests, free lunches, snacks galore, and a worship of the great outdoors when not sleeping off another all-nighter.

Beyond its high-tech appeal, Seattle was America's dominant coffee town, what David Brooks would call a "latte town," as obsessive about downscale alternative status symbols as Wasps were about classic signs of success. Some attributed the city's coffee obsession to the perpetually gray weather that left people craving caffeine. Soon, the whole country would be speaking about macchiatos and mochaccinos, dolce lattes, and frappucinos, served by baristas tall, grande, or venti, thanks to Starbucks, the coffeehouse behemoth.

In 1971, the first Starbucks store opened in Seattle's Pike Place Market. In 1982, a Brooklyn-born kid named Howard Schultz joined the company's small marketing department. By 1987, Schultz had raised $3.8 million to buy out the founders, having divined in Milan that a more robust coffeehouse culture could build community. The coffee bar could become a third haven in a new, individuated, secularized America, beyond home and office, replacing churches, general stores, and community centers. More Ben and Jerry than Rockefeller or Carnegie, Schultz pitched "the Starbucks Experience" as "an affordable necessity" not an "affordable luxury," claiming: "We are all hungry for community." Typically, this "community" was as virtual as "friends" would be on Facebook, reflecting parallel play not personal engagement.

Combining McDonald's-type standardization and accessibility with Chivas Regal quality and indulgence worked. Customizing as many as 87,000 different drink combinations also appealed to Americans' urge to individuate. By 1994, two years after a successful IPO, there were 425 stores. Two years later, there were 1,000 stores, with openings in Japan and Singapore. By 2012, 200,000 "partners," meaning baristas enjoying stock options and health benefits, worked in 17,651 stores in 60 countries serving over 60 million visitors weekly.

Entrepreneurs loved this mix of creative energy, well-educated employees, a growing stock of Microsoft alumni, and Washington State's small population size, limiting the number of sales-tax-vulnerable customers for an Internet shopping company. Another virtual pioneer lured west, Jeff Bezos, was a Texas-born wunderkind working in finance in New York who noticed that the World Wide Web increased its activity by an astounding factor of 2,300 from January

1993 to January 1994. He analyzed twenty different products, speculating how selling via the Internet could boost their sales. Bezos realized that offering titles without carrying inventory could outdo any bookstore. He arrived in Seattle in July 1994 and soon started calling his site "Amazon," hoping that the Earth's "biggest river" would inspire the launching of "Earth's biggest bookstore." Eventually, the king of Internet retailing would start planning "the everything store."

Voluntary Simplicity or Stuck in Second Gear?

As Baby Boomers like Bill Gates, Howard Schultz, and Jeff Bezos helped the nation's economy boom, many of their peers felt overwhelmed by America's ever-growing thirst for money. In 1994, the economy soared with gross domestic product growth of 4.1 percent creating 3.3 million new jobs, the most since 1984. In 1992 Joe Dominguez and Vicki Robin coauthored a book that became a blockbuster, *Your Money or Your Life*. The authors advised finding meaningful work while reducing consumption. Robin began running workshops showing people how to manage money amid everyone's overspending. Cecile Andrews's workshops on "Voluntary Simplicity" emphasized managing time better amid everyone's over-programming. And Janet Luhrs, a recovering lawyer and single mother, started *Simple Living: The Journal of Voluntary Simplicity* in 1992, offering fifty ways to date, cook, vacation, and enjoy life without spending money. With 15 percent of America's 77 million Baby Boomers supposedly ready to join their movement, the three made Seattle the center of American simplicity. They combined the growing self-help ethos with a New Age sensibility and some good old-fashioned Social Gospel to heal from corporate burnout, overconsumption, and undersatisfaction.

Echoing the Puritans, the Quakers, the Transcendentalists, and the Hippies, the Seattle Simplifiers helped publicize Mathis Wackernagel's and William Rees's 1995 book *Our Ecological Footprint: Reducing Human Impact on the Earth*. Noting that Americans consumed at least three times more than citizens in other countries, this work influenced Al Gore, who warned of America's outsized and toxic "carbon footprint."

The Seattle Sensibility Popularized and Nationalized

Even with this ambivalence, Seattle was starting to smell of new money, not just teen spirit. The instinct of *Frasier*'s producers to move the snooty psychiatrist of *Cheers* from his fictional perch in Boston to Seattle in 1993 proved correct. Wanting distance from *Cheers,* they first chose Denver, but disliked Colorado conservatives' attacks against gays. Instead, Seattle "seemed like this wonderful, tolerant, idiosyncratic place full of smart people."

Dr. Frasier Crane and his equally pompous brother, Niles, occupied a rarefied Seattle of high culture and haute cuisine, with the requisite coffee hangout, Café Nervosa. When Niles doubted a neighborhood's safety, the Cranes' tough retired cop father snapped, "Oh, Niles, to you a sketchy neighborhood is when the cheese shop doesn't have valet parking." The kooky class dynamics delighted audiences. On September 11, 1994, the writer-producers David Angell, Peter Casey, and David Lee won an Emmy for their writing and Kelsey Grammer won for his acting as the show was honored as Outstanding Comedy Series.

Seattle became, in the words of the *Seattle Times* TV critic, "condo by condo . . . a lot like *Frasier.*" "Microsofties," flush with cash, told brokers "they wanted that cosmopolitan feel of '*Frasier.*'" The city became slicker, with million-dollar condominiums popping up on Queen Anne Hill and fancy fashion shops next to fine wine stores on Sixth Avenue.

While *Frasier* glamorized Seattle, another television phenomenon, *Friends,* which debuted in September 1994 and ran for ten seasons, tamed, popularized, and nationalized the Seattle sensibility, this time in a New York City setting. The six slackers, bossy Monica, flaky Phoebe, spoiled Rachel, geeky Ross, goofy Chandler, and dumb but sexy Joey, are better dressed, cleaner-cut, and live in fancier apartments than their Seattle grunge peers, despite only having McJobs. They hang out endlessly at their coffee shop, Central Perk. In TV-land, all this twentysomething shiftlessness became clean and lovable.

Friends was a cultural phenomenon, affecting Americans' speech patterns and attitudes: Joey's leering "How *you* doin'?"; Ross's plaintive "We were on a break"; Janice's—Chandler's first girlfriend's—nasal "Oh my gawd"; and Phoebe's unmelodic, "Smelly Cat." *Friends'* world was youth-centered and self-centered, pampered by prosperity. As childish as they were—"always stuck in second gear," the theme song suggested—their spoiled, self-indulgent Baby Boomer parents were more immature, especially the dads, a situation paralleled in other shows including *Beverly Hills, 90210, Home Improvement,* and *The Simpsons.* If *Seinfeld* still had Baby Boomer baggage, with that gang's selfishness edgier and guiltier, *Friends* offered a Gen X selfishness with fewer boundaries, without even the veneer of angst.

The Chase: America's Dark Side

Friends was harmless, part of the broader soporific celebrity culture shaping America. As the summer of 1994 began, Americans confronted celebrity amorality when the football legend and celebrity actor O. J. Simpson murdered his ex-wife Nicole Brown Simpson and her young friend Ronald Goldman, just outside her home on June 12, as the Simpsons' children lay sleeping inside.

Simpson was not just another celebrity living in celebrity-land. He had been famous since he was a twenty-year-old superstar running back for University of South California in 1967, then became a Hall of Famer for the Buffalo Bills. Acting, broadcasting football, and his oft-mimicked airport run as a pitchman for Hertz introduced him to new generations of adoring fans. O. J. was O. J., with the most famous set of initials in America since JFK, RFK, and LBJ. With his soft smile and easy, on-camera demeanor, "everyone" just "knew" he remained an all-American nice guy.

As a result, many Americans initially doubted O. J.'s guilt. That Friday, the day after attending his ex-wife's funeral, Simpson tried evading arrest, only to be chased by police in his white Ford Bronco, driven by his friend A. C. Cowlings. The "chase," which was a slow crawl recorded by TV cameras mounted on helicopters, became another big 1994 moment that many in America's celebrity-addled culture compared to Kennedy's assassination. Onlookers shouted, "Go OJ Go!" An estimated 95 million watched on television. The spectacle was sickening, "terrible to watch and impossible not to," *Time* wrote. Radio callers suggested that this otherwise good man had one minor flaw. Jonathan Alter of *Newsweek* denounced the "false intimacy of TV" as "truly damaging to public life," saying "we didn't really know him at all. We just thought we did."

Gradually, most Americans saw O. J.'s dark underside. He had beaten his wife repeatedly. As radio callers debated whether police spoiled him because of his celebrity, one caller suggested: "It can't be favoritism, because they don't send any of them [wife beaters] to jail."

By 1994, Americans were more sensitive to the violence many women endured, including wife beating. Rates of spousal abuse were dropping, by almost 50 percent over the decade. Rates of reporting were rising, although victims called police barely half the time. Too much such violence remained overlooked or excused, although the criminal justice system no longer indulged husbands. Now, abusive spouses averaged higher conviction rates than strangers and received longer sentences. It would take another twenty years and videotapes of Ray Rice beating his fiancée unconscious in a Las Vegas elevator before authorities in sports began addressing domestic abuse among coddled athletes.

The Clintons' Harsh Winter

The O. J. Simpson debacle's timing was particularly problematic for Bill Clinton, who in early May had been slapped with a $700,000 sexual harassment suit in federal court. Paula Corbin Jones, a former Arkansas state employee, accused Clinton of "reckless . . . persistent and continuous" advances when he allegedly dropped his pants while propositioning her in a hotel room in 1991. Paula Jones was the "Paula" from David Brock's Troopergate article. Rather than suing Brock and *The American Spectator* for libel, Jones targeted Clinton. Robert Bennett, Clinton's lawyer, called the suit "tabloid trash with a legal caption on it." Paula Jones now absorbed a barrage of sexist and class-based bigotry, as *Time* would call her "this year's bimbo-with-an-agenda."

Jones was applying new laws governing sexual harassment that Bill and Hillary Clinton had championed. In November 1993, in *Harris v. Forklift Systems,* the Supreme Court ruled that a hostile work environment of persistent sexual innuendo could be damaging without having to prove "tangible psychological injury." The court, including Clarence Thomas, ruled unanimously against Forklift Systems of Nashville and its crude president, who for two years repeatedly propositioned and demeaned Teresa Harris.

Nevertheless, Clinton's supporters now dismissed accusations against their hero with the kind of sexist dismissals that enraged them when echoed by Republican predators like Senator Bob Packwood. Packwood foolishly kept a diary detailing the many times women rejected his awkward advances. Betty Roberts, a Democratic opponent in Oregon, insisted, "It's not an issue of sexual harassment. It's about abuse of power." In Washington, Packwood's status as a rare pro-choice Republican made the charges particularly disappointing to feminists. Packwood would resign in 1995.

Paula Jones was only one of Bill Clinton's many headaches. Throughout the winter of 1994, embarrassing revelations oozed out, his popularity softened, and his health care initiative sputtered. On January 20, clouding his first anniversary in office, President Clinton watched his attorney general, Janet Reno, swear in a special prosecutor, Robert Fiske, to investigate Whitewater and related transactions, including Vince Foster's actions in the White House counsel's office, his suicide, and the White House's mishandling of his office documents. The White House counsel Bernard Nussbaum begged Clinton not to authorize a special prosecutor. There was no "credible evidence of wrongdoing," the legal standard, just a political firestorm demanding extinguishing.

Nussbaum argued that the politicos pushing the idea were "clueless about the dangers of putting into place institutions that, yes, may calm down the press for the next 24, 48 hours, but would act as a knife in your heart for the next eight years." Nussbaum understood that special prosecutors keep on searching to justify their mandates. "The main thing I want to do is have this turned over to him so that we can get back to work," Clinton said, reprising his all-business refrain from 1992. Instead, this decision doomed the Clinton presidency to seven more years of relentless investigations. A decade later, Clinton would call authorizing the special prosecutor "the worst presidential decision I ever made, wrong on the facts, wrong on the law, wrong on the politics, wrong for the presidency and the Constitution."

Harry and Louise Beat Hillary and Bill

Hillary Clinton was suffering, too. Her health care plan was losing momentum. In what in other circumstances would have been a romantic symbol of the Clintons' partnership, the First Lady, not the president, seemed most implicated in Travelgate, the missing Foster files, Whitewater, and the decision to resist subpoenas.

A professional politician, Bill Clinton was tougher than his crinkly eyes, warm demeanor, and pasty face suggested. Still, the obsessive focus on an old, money-losing proposition amazed him, even though it epitomized Arkansas's mutual back-scratching, sweetheart-deal-making political and business culture. Diane Blair, Hillary Clinton's close friend, would note that Bill Clinton was "furious about what has been done to Ark., how they've taken all the joy and happiness out of BC's victory, turned the state into a killing field."

The president detested his critics for targeting his wife, the Clinton family's disciplined straight arrow. Bill had long struggled with his passion for skirt-chasing. Following Southern tradition, his wife and daughter were the virtuous ones.

Throughout the health care debate, David Gergen would notice the guilt-ridden president's judgment impaired, with Hillary Clinton unduly empowered. The most powerful man in the world often looked to Gergen like "a golden retriever that has pooped on the rug." Just when the Clintons needed to be focused, effective, and lucky, they were instead dazed, defensive, and distracted.

Both Republicans and Democrats mobilized intensively for the health care reform fight. Comparing the sales job ahead to a presidential campaign, the Democratic National Committee mobilized field organizers in twenty-three states and allocated $3 million to the effort in 1993 alone. The Health Insurance Association of America's opposing television commercials pitted Bill and Hillary

Clinton's reforms against the homespun wisdom and fears of a fictional couple, "Harry and Louise," often pictured sitting at their kitchen table anxious about paying their bills.

Most political advertising campaigns follow a thunderstorm strategy, saturating an area with a particular message. But some ads were like cloud seeding, notably "Daisy" in 1964 caricaturing Barry Goldwater Republicans as counting down toward nuclear destruction and "Willie Horton" in 1988 caricaturing Michael Dukakis as soft on crime. With just a few showings, these ads triggered gales of conversations and news reports repeating the ads. With the "Harry and Louise" ads targeting the Washington, D.C., New York, and Los Angeles media markets, local news shows ran them repeatedly for free. Lawmakers assumed the ads were as ubiquitous at home as they were in the nation's capital.

With Harry and Louise warning, "If we let the government choose we lose," the Republican assault combined Americans' traditional fears of big government with frustrations over the Great Society's failures. Newt Gingrich and Dick Armey, the leading House Republicans, snapped: "If you like the way the Federal Government runs public housing and the state government runs the Department of Motor Vehicles, you'll love health care under the Clinton Plan." Continuing the class wars of the 1960s, and 1992, Republicans claimed that lawyers and Rhodes Scholars were condescendingly deciding for the supposedly "Befuddled masses." Gingrich and Armey sneered: "The New Testament sets forth how people should live in about 180,000 words. The health-care bill does it in 260,000."

These conservative critics found useful allies in the popular culture they and their constituents loved to emulate and bash. The *Seinfeld-Simpsons'* cynicism mixed with a national paranoia about government secrets. A surprise TV hit that premiered in September 1993, *The X-Files,* broadcast messages epitomized by its famous catchphrases: "Trust No One" and "The Truth Is Out There." David Duchovny and Gillian Anderson played two government agents investigating anomalies, which, the creators insisted, were "inspired by actual documented accounts."

The 1,364-page health care bill proved to be incomprehensible as well. Years later, Al From would regret that his DLC policy wonks never had a chance to draft a proper health reform proposal. Even in the fall of 1993, when 59 percent approved Clinton-care, only 17 percent said they knew "a lot" about the plan. Leon Panetta, Clinton's experienced budget director, would remember thinking the scheme was "impossibly complicated" but keeping quiet because the First Lady "acted as if anyone who disagreed with her didn't know what they were talking about."

The 1990s was a time of outsized personalities and colorful events, the era of George H. W. Bush and Bill Gates, of Kurt Cobain and Oprah Winfrey, of the Great American Hook-Up linking computers with the Internet and the booming new economy, creating new riches—and new income gaps. Ultimately, this was the Age of Clinton. While Bill Clinton served as president from 1993 through 2001, he and his wife Hillary Rodham Clinton dominated America's consciousness, shaping the decade. Above, Bill and Hillary Clinton in early November, 1992, days before his remarkable presidential victory. *(William J. Clinton Presidential Library)*

The 1990s began seemingly miraculously. The Cold War ended as Mikhail Gorbachev, pictured at the 1990 Washington summit with George H. W. Bush, dissolved the Soviet Union's "Evil Empire" peacefully by 1991. America's triumph in the first Persian Gulf War of 1991 made Bush look invincible. Bush and General Norman Schwarzkopf, Jr., visiting troops in Saudi Arabia, became heroes. Missteps such as the catastrophic 1992 Los Angeles riots soon made Bush surprisingly vulnerable. *(Top: George Bush Presidential Library and Museum; Center: George Bush Presidential Library and Museum; Bottom: AP Photo Akili-Casundria Ramsess)*

Born after World War II, Bill Clinton and Hillary Rodham became the representative Baby Boomers. Their daughter, Chelsea, was born in 1980. In 1983, when President Ronald Reagan hosted the Clintons, they had just moved back to the Arkansas governor's mansion. This marked Bill Clinton's impressive comeback from his 1980 defeat, which had made him the youngest ex-governor in American history. *(William J. Clinton Presidential Library)*

In 1992, Bill Clinton emerged as an ebullient campaigner. A natural who loved politics and people, he generated great excitement and great controversy, aided by his running mate Al Gore, and his wife Hillary, pictured here enjoying a break from campaigning during a 1950s-style "sock hop" for Bill's forty-sixth birthday. *(William J. Clinton Presidential Library)*

Clinton's inaugural was glamorous although his roller-coaster rookie year was torturous. Fights over a perceived drift left slowed his momentum. By year's end, Hillary's initial health care reform launch and Bill's budget-cutting and values talk, especially in Memphis, impressed many, at least initially. *(William J. Clinton Presidential Library)*

The 1990s' changing, profane, "liquid" modern culture spawned a Borderline Nation, often hysterical, distracted by 24/7 media spectacles. In 1994, Kurt Cobain's suicide triggered mass mourning, especially in Seattle, where he, second from right, and his friends in the surprisingly influential band Nirvana had popularized the grunge look and sound. That year, the racially polarizing O. J. Simpson murder saga also began, with Simpson's lawyers telling jurors that because his hand "did not fit" into a bloody glove found at the crime scene, "you must acquit." *(Top: AP Photo/Mark J. Terril; Bottom: AP Photo/Vince Bucci, Pool, File)*

Newt Gingrich led the Republicans to midterm victory in November, 1994. Speaker Gingrich frequently frustrated the president, as illustrated here during one of many White House negotiations. After the Oklahoma City bombing, Clinton led the mourning, visiting the site on April 23, 1995, along with the First Lady. Gingrich's pettiness, mocked by the *Daily News,* helped Clinton recover. *(Top and center: William J. Clinton Presidential Library; Bottom: AP Photo/*New York Daily News*)*

Bill Clinton loved policy as well as politicking, delighting in crafting his agenda-setting State of the Union addresses annually, as seen above, working closely with his speechwriters. Many dismissed Clinton's Good Father strategy of fixing schools and ending "welfare as we know it" as pandering, but it brought Clinton back to his core centrism. *(William J. Clinton Presidential Library)*

With consultants warning that delay could be lethal, two recurring challenges in the Clinton White House slowed momentum: the "lack of trust" in Clinton's constancy and the "lack of focus," in the fall because of NAFTA and Somalia, and, in the winter of 1994, because of Whitewater. Rather than mollifying Republicans, the First Lady bashed doctors, pharmaceutical companies, insurance executives, and conservatives. Mrs. Clinton mocked those who "drive down highways paid for by government funds" and "love the defense department" but object "when it comes to . . . trying to be a compassionate and caring nation." Pressed by his wife, the president emphasized his bottom line, universal health coverage. Hillary Clinton urged her husband to wave a pen in his 1994 State of the Union address, promising to veto any alternatives. Clinton complied and alienated moderates.

Bill Clinton was defending a byzantine program ill-suited to the small-government era Ronald Reagan introduced. "Health care isn't the talk on the street," said an Illinois pollster Mike McKeon. "It's crime, it's jobs, it's welfare." In July, addressing the National Governors Association, Clinton the compromiser said he would accept "somewhere in the ballpark of 95 percent." Within minutes, Hillary Clinton had her husband on the phone, aided by the White House's dogged telephone operators. "What the fuck are you doing up there?!" she yelled. "You get back here right away."

Perhaps betraying a husbandly ambivalence about following too many wifely marching orders, President Clinton did not throw himself into the fight as intensely or as nimbly as he had with the budget and NAFTA. By February 1994, only 41 percent surveyed approved of the plan, emboldening the business community to abandon the bill. The bill died of congressional neglect. Neither the Senate nor the House voted on it.

Few remembered now how likely prospects for change appeared in 1993. "America's ready for health-care reform and so are we," South Carolina's Republican governor, Carroll Campbell, declared, as Republicans scrambled to offer their own alternatives. Senator Thomas Daschle would recall that the president chose to advance NAFTA in 1993 because it "was in big trouble" as opposed to health care.

That winter and spring of 1994, as Congress and the public soured on the plan, the press was skewering both Clintons about Whitewater and an alleged cover-up. The resulting "breakdown on trust . . . dredged up the campaign period," as Clinton's "poll numbers began to drop pretty sharply," Stan Greenberg explains. White House aides grumbled that "common" business law firm misfires like "billing disputes, shredding of client documents" were "being portrayed in the most sinister imaginable light." Admitting that the White House "mishandled" Whitewater, they sought outside experts insisting "enough is enough," to embarrass reporters into focusing on other matters. Clinton claimed, dismissively, "this is really about a real estate investment I made almost 16 years ago that lost money and sputtered to a not-successful conclusion several years ago." During his European trip in January, when NBC's Jim Miklaszewski asked a second Whitewater question during an interview, Clinton threw off his microphone and stormed off.

Some preachers imagine hell as a place where individuals relive past sins eternally. In Washington's netherworld, incredibly intelligent, cynical, and ruthless people scoured politicians' pasts, seeking something, anything, to justify dispatching leaders to the Fifth Bolgia, or stony ditch of Dante's Eighth Circle of Hell, the tar pit for the corrupt, stuck perpetually in pitch because they had "sticky" hands in life. Such scrutiny uncovered Hillary Clinton's remarkably profitable commodities trades, endless Whitewater complexities, and minor anomalies in Clinton tax returns.

The Era of Limbaugh

The talk radio king, Rush Limbaugh, led the conservative charge against "Billary's paternalistic utopia." This big, blustery radio disc jockey and talk show host since he was sixteen, had a winning smile and a sense of fun that softened his harsh rhetoric. Part clown, part gladiator, he treated politics as both a circus spectacle and a blood sport. His radio show went national in 1988. By 1996, his three-hour show reached 20 million people five times a week via 665 stations. His late-night TV program was syndicated on 225 stations. With his two best sellers, he, typically, egotistically, proclaimed that "historians will someday refer to [these times] as the Era of Limbaugh."

Limbaugh's fears were political. He believed Clinton, the supposed "New Democrat, is actually an unreconstructed New Dealer," that Hillary would impose "nationalized, socialized health care" on Americans, and that he needed to "expose the hypocrisy, fraud and deceit of the liberalism that is holding this nation hostage." His fury was ideological. Defending the "family values" that remained "very important to mainstream America," he maintained that "America is still a God-fearing nation" despite "New Age mumbo-jumbo and liberal psychobabble." And his hatred was visceral. No charge was too extreme in proving "how deceitful, cunning, and disingenuous this president can be"; he called Hillary silly, "sanctimonious, arrogant, condescending," pretentious, and demagogic. This was politics by punch line and innuendo. It stirred millions and it drew blood.

By 1994, unnerved, speaking live to KMOX radio, Clinton complained, "After I get off the radio with you today, Rush Limbaugh will have three hours to say whatever he wants, and I won't have any opportunity to respond, and there's no truth detector." Clinton's tantrum knighted Limbaugh as "the leader of the opposition," the *National Review* snickered. Conservatives hailed Rush as the voice of the people.

Clinton also faced a newly hostile Washington. Paralleling the New Deal Brain Trusters and the New Frontier Ivy Leaguers who arrived in Washington and never left, the Reagan Revolution created permanent colonies of Beltway Reaganauts. During twelve years in power, conservatives had grown an institutional network of think tanks, policy journals, political clubs, publishing houses, radio shows, lobbying firms, law firms, PR firms, government relations departments within major corporations, and media stars that now formed a perpetual opposition. In Congress, Republicans assembled the modern politician's torture chamber of overlapping congressional and criminal investigations. Being an FOB, and especially, a Friend of Hillary, became an expensive proposition as loyalists were hit with six-figure legal bills and threatened with indictment.

The Clinton-bashing industry proved lucrative. Ann Coulter was a lawyer who first clerked for a Reagan-appointed judge. She transitioned from public service to caustic political commentary in the mid-1990s. Her first book *High Crimes and Misdemeanors: The Case Against Bill Clinton* called for Clinton's impeachment. Kenneth Starr first came to Washington from California to work in the Reagan Justice Department in 1981. He would become Clinton's toughest adversary as independent counsel. Barbara Olson was a lawyer who lobbied for Clarence Thomas, would investigate Travelgate as chief investigative counsel for the House Committee on Government Reform and Oversight, and would eventually become a well-known talking head and author, hostile to the Clintons.

Hillary Rodham Clinton became the rare First Lady who was less popular than her husband. From February to March 1994, his approval rating dropped 11 points, to 47 percent approving, 45 percent disapproving. Her unfavorability rating soared from 29 percent in February to a plurality of 42 percent in March. Once again Bill and Hillary bonded in adversity.

Clinton's activist centrist presidency was in shambles. Weakened by the attacks, the jokes, the exposés, he watched helplessly as the health care reform died in committee and the Democrats' prospects for the 1994 congressional midterm election dimmed. America appeared increasingly angry, polarized, adrift, insecure, and suspicious of its president. When Clinton talked to *Sports Illustrated* about his beloved Arkansas Razorbacks surging toward their first NCAA national basketball championship, the reporter wondered if Clinton was trying to distract from Whitewater. Comics joked that when it came to remembering Whitewater details, Clinton appeared as senile as Ronald Reagan, or that both Clintons had trouble hearing each other over the sounds of the paper shredder. Two of the top ten ways David Letterman thought Clinton could improve his popularity were "quit doin' all that weird illegal stuff nobody understands" and "just once, in public, turn to Hillary and yell, 'Pipe down, woman!'"

Jon Katz of *New York* magazine accused his fellow reporters of exhibiting "disingenuous and Cotton Mather-ish obsessions with character and morality." Even Daniel Schorr, CBS's dogged Watergate investigator, called the coverage "overdone." While acknowledging that the sensationalist 24/7 news-world created a "journalistic hall of mirrors" magnifying peccadilloes into scandals, Michael Wines in *The New York Times* noted that "most backtracking has come from the White House," not reporters. Wines insisted that tales of presidential financial chicanery certainly interested reporters in the past, which, unlike the 1990s, was "an age of innocence."

The Zone of Privacy Rezoned

With his administration blitzed by Whitewater interrogations and revelations, with reporters devoting three times as much attention to Whitewater than to health care, the president insisted at a televised news conference on March 24, "We're changing people's lives. That's what counts." His refusal to be "distracted" was unconvincing when the words "Whitewater" and "tax" were each mentioned twenty-five times during his forty-minute session. Following his note cards to "Defend HRC," leaving "No distance between you and HRC regarding Whitewater," Clinton praised his wife, who was getting a "bum rap."

The controversial First Lady needed another makeover. That spring, according to her friend Diane Blair, Hillary Rodham Clinton resolved to "work through her anger so she can talk calmly to press." As someone with little tolerance for opposition even from White House loyalists, the First Lady viewed her critics as vicious, irrational partisans. She still could not understand, Blair scribbled, "Why [is] everybody so anxious to destroy them.????"

On April 22, 1994, Hillary donned a pink suit and met reporters in the cozy State Dining Room. She wanted to put this "embarrassing" money-losing affair that "keeps being beaten like the deadest horse there is . . . into a proper perspective." She addressed "the women in this room," reporters, as particularly understanding the challenge "for us as a country maybe to make the transition" toward having such a prominent woman. The friendly yet commanding First Lady joked that her "zone of privacy" was being "rezoned." That lawyer's phrase came from the landmark 1965 *Griswold v. Connecticut* case reading into the Constitution a right of privacy that allowed married people to buy birth control. Both Clintons would free this phrase from its legal ghetto, with five times as many usages in newspaper articles in the 1990s as the 1980s.

Hillary Clinton's Friday afternoon press conference, as the public focused on Richard Nixon's imminent death, was mostly aimed at Washington insiders, especially those "women in this room." The First Lady was retreating. She would respect the 62 percent who thought she should not make policy and become a more traditional First Lady, at least publicly.

Nixon's death that April allowed Clinton to put his own troubles into perspective. Forced by American protocols to eulogize the ex-president elegantly, Clinton used Nixon's lifelong political engagement to drive home the importance of taking responsibility. Feeling targeted unfairly as Nixon did, Clinton also framed Nixon's burial day as a day of balance, "to remember President Nixon's life in totality."

Nixon's passing at eighty-one, followed by Jacqueline Kennedy Onassis's death a month later at sixty-four, provided one more coda to the 1960s. The Sixties had been ending since the Seventies, of course. Now in the Nineties, as many principal players were dead or retired, it seemed the rebellion had worked. The Adversarials were in charge. Countercultural values were mainstreamed. Lyndon Johnson's secretary of defense Robert McNamara was finishing memoirs admitting that regarding Vietnam: "we were wrong, terribly wrong." The era's signature art form was being mummified, as builders installed the last steel beam in Cleveland's Rock and Roll Hall of Fame and Museum in July. In October, Yoko Ono would donate John Lennon's glasses, leather jacket, and a guitar to the museum.

An unexpected two-and-a-half-hour movie hit gave the 1960s a superficial 1990s' makeover. *Forrest Gump* inserted a clueless Zelig, played by Tom Hanks, into many of the decade's defining events. The film eventually grossed $677 million and won the Best Picture Oscar. This sweet, meandering, yet surprisingly compelling movie made the Sixties more kitschy than cranky, more sunny than stormy, more fun than fierce, and kind of random.

That summer of 1994, Clinton pushed his crime bill, following his pollster Stan Greenberg's advice to move to the center, 1992 style. The political debate about crime had turned ridiculous. "Law and order" Republicans, blaming the criminals, demanded more punishment yet no gun control, while "Great Society" Democrats, blaming society, demanded more preventive programs yet lighter sentencing. Synthesizing the Republican and Democratic approaches, Clinton proposed tougher mandatory sentences, funding new prisons, hiring a hundred thousand more police officers, pushing a three-strikes rule against repeat felony offenders, while also investing in crime prevention programs and banning nineteen types of automatic weapons.

When congressional Republicans first opposed his measure, Clinton, seething, claimed this tested America's democratic legitimacy. "The American people have said over and over this is their first concern," he cried. "If we can't meet this concern, there is something badly wrong in Washington."

Clinton agreed to reduce some of the youth job programs connected to crime prevention while cutting costs by about 10 percent. Cynthia McKinney, a Georgia Democrat and disappointed Congressional Black Caucus member, claimed Clinton's compromise "contains an ounce of prevention, a pound of punishment and a ton of politics." Clinton insisted, however, on banning assault weapons, despite moderate Democrats' pleas that voting for the economic plan, the Brady bill, and now this would make them easy targets for Rush Limbaugh–style assaults against them as knee-jerk liberals in November.

When the bill passed, Clinton rejoiced, saying, "This is the way Washington ought to work." But his stubbornness on guns hurt Democrats. "The price of a safer America would be heavy casualties among its defenders," he would recall. And as with the Brady bill, gun merchants reported another sales surge.

The Contract with America

A weakened president led his listless party into the 1994 midterm elections against a galvanized opposition. Clinton now faced a formidable generational peer, Newt Gingrich, born in 1943. Gingrich's PhD in European history proved that not every Baby Boomer, and not even every Baby Boomer intellectual, was liberal. As hyperbolic as Clinton was charismatic, Gingrich labeled Bill and Hillary Clinton spoiled, arrogant hippies, hoping to win the political battle with class and cultural warfare.

On September 27, all the Republicans running for Congress that year gathered on the Capitol steps to endorse Gingrich's Reaganite "Contract with America." This visionary strategy cleverly nationalized the 435 House and 35 Senate races. It dictated to reporters a narrative of a popular tide rejecting Clinton, paradoxically, as both a temporizing, incompetent incumbent and a "tax and spend liberal."

The Republicans vowed to "end politics as usual." Exploiting the House banking scandal, they promised to clean up Congress. Targeting big government, they promised to reduce all congressional committees and staffers by a third. The number of congressional employees since 1900 had increased a hundredfold, from barely three hundred to more than thirty thousand. Revealing Gingrich's Franklin Roosevelt–sized vision, the candidates committed to pass ten bills during their First Hundred Days. They promised to balance the budget, cut taxes, fight crime, and reform welfare. "This is going to be the House that Newt built," former Republican congressman Vin Weber had predicted, impressed that finally a congressional Republican was ready to try winning a "majority."

Washington insiders scoffed. Democrats were accustomed to winning and Republicans, to losing, having been in the minority since the Eisenhower administration. In April, Joe Klein predicted "an aggressive—probably futile, but vastly entertaining—fall campaign" from Gingrich. Although they, too, did not imagine losing the House, White House staffers knew they were in trouble and needed "to stop making mistakes." They tried "affecting the coverage" of Gingrich's campaign rollout. Finding "outrageous quotes and positions taken by GOP leaders," they fed them into op-ed pieces and TV ads. They sought events and issues to enhance Clinton's "stature" as the president, "not commentator-in-chief, parliamentarian or policy wonk," emphasizing his "central mission" of "fighting for the middle class." Clinton kept on insisting that pocket-sized lists of his accomplishments be distributed, sure, his political consultant Joan Baggett recalls, that if voters "only knew" what he did, "then they would like him."

Many other factors shaped the election, including a slew of scandals embarrassing House Democrats, who had grown arrogant, complacent, and corrupt. Too secure in their power, too disdainful toward regular Americans, too blinded by Washington networking, congressional Democrats "mistook the AFL-CIO for labor, the AARP for the elderly, the VFW for veterans, the Children's Defense Fund for children," Newsweek reported.

Americans were as cranky in 1994 as they had been in the spring of 1992, before Clinton's surge, exacerbated by a baseball strike that resulted in the first autumn without a World Series since 1904. Grunge, the Seattle sensibility, and even Friends represented a younger generation's rejection of the Baby Boomers' political engagement and often self-righteous earnestness. Now, this election was the revolt of the peers and the grown-ups against Boomer values and behaviors.

And it was the triumph of the Rush Limbaugh–loving, feminist-hating, affirmative-action-resenting, red-meat-eating, tax-burdened, displaced, demonized, and delegitimized Angry White Males. These mad men were caricatured yet popularized by Michael Douglas's character William "D-Fens" Foster in the 1993 Joel Schumacher movie *Falling Down*. Laid off, divorced, caught in traffic, overcharged for cheap drinks, alienated from the false intimacy of calling adults by their first names, and harassed by gang members, he goes on a shooting rampage before a sympathetic cop kills him.

A President Shell-Shocked

On Election Day, Republicans seized power in the House of Representatives for the first time since Dwight Eisenhower's presidency forty years earlier. Thirty-four House incumbents lost, all Democrats. Not one Republican incumbent lost running for governor, senator, or representative. The largest Republican congressional contingent since 1946 would include seventy-three freshmen. The defeated New York governor Mario Cuomo would denounce these "Republican storm troopers." The congressman about to become the first Democratic Minority Leader since 1954, Richard Gephardt, called them "trickle-down terrorists" advancing a program rooted in "division, exclusion and fear."

Clinton and his aides were "shellshocked," Joan Baggett recalls. Democrats were panicking intellectually, too. The fall's most talked about book broached the taboo questions of intelligence and genetics, claiming that blacks averaged fifteen points lower than whites on intelligence tests. *The New York Times* columnist Bob Herbert called *The Bell Curve* by Richard Herrnstein and Charles Murray a "scabrous piece of racial pornography masquerading as serious scholarship" whose facts and figures were "just a genteel way of calling somebody a nigger." Harvard's leading evolutionary biologist Stephen Jay Gould believed the attention this "manifesto of conservative ideology" masquerading as "an academic treatise" generated, reflected this "historical moment of unprecedented ungenerosity, when a mood for slashing social programs can be powerfully abetted by an argument that beneficiaries cannot be helped, owing to inborn cognitive limits expressed as low IQ scores."

Predictably, conservative intellectuals supported the book equally vehemently. Michael Novak in *National Review* charged that the book threatened the "cognitive elite's" guiding liberal belief in government programs' power to change the environment to achieve salvation, meaning "equality." Unfortunately, in post-Sixties' America, politics often distorted debate, making such questions more a matter of theology and group identity than rational or scientific inquiry.

The 1994 Clinton collapse was as dramatic as Richard Nixon's fall in 1973, Lyndon Johnson's in 1966, and Harry Truman's in 1950. Bill Clinton seemed to symbolize the worst of the Democratic Party: as gluttonous and incompetent as big government; as undisciplined and relativistic as America's youth; as elitist and anti-family as all the other draft-dodging aging hippies. Despite being a Southerner, Clinton had lost the South. The 1994 midterm elections marked the culmination of the process that began thirty years earlier when President Lyndon Johnson muscled the Civil Rights Act through Congress, knowing it would turn the South Republican. A cynical alliance of African Americans, liberals, and Republicans had gerrymandered districts after the 1980 and 1990 censuses, creating pockets of black-voting Democrats and white-voting Republicans. *Newsweek* lamented: "Segregated representation seemed a long way from Martin Luther King's dream."

There was a cultural dimension to this sea change, too. Pundits half-joked that Barbra Streisand, tax and spend, National Public Radio, Ralph Nader, Volvos, Jesse Jackson, safe sex, soaking the rich, condoms in school, *Heather Has Two Mommies*, reinventing government, Doc Martens, and Harvard were out. In came Pat Sajak, gays in the closet, Rush Limbaugh, Chevy Suburbans, electric chairs, *The Washington Times* not *The Washington Post*, Jesse Helms, midnight curfews, NRA, bashing the poor, term limits, prayer in school, no sex, wing tips, West Georgia College, and dismantling government.

Having underestimated Gingrich's chances to win, pundits now overestimated his chances to succeed. *Newsweek*'s "Revolution of 1994" story began: "It took about 60 years to erect the modern welfare state. Newt Gingrich wants to dismantle it in a hundred days." Laments about the end of the New Deal and the end of the welfare state were premature.

Every election triggers a second struggle to interpret the results. In 1994, White House moderates and Clinton's DLC allies blamed Clinton's reversion to old Democrat big government policies. Moderate senators, including Connecticut's Joe Lieberman and Louisiana's John Breaux, urged the president to remember the centrist approach that elected him and reflected Americans' post-Reagan consensus.

Trying to continue his anti-Washington line from 1992, Clinton attributed the Republican victory to a backlash against Democrats who were now in charge of Washington, and all its problems. He credited the Republicans with cleverly "defining us as the party of Government." He acknowledged the people's skepticism as to whether the administration had delivered safer streets, more stable jobs, and a better economy. Foreshadowing his 1996 comeback, Clinton believed he heard the public saying: "We don't think the government can solve all the problems."

Clinton was a shrewd enough reader of the American political scene to know he had been repudiated. Most Americans questioned his integrity and found him erratic. Nevertheless, Stan Greenberg found that only 22 percent of independent voters concluded that Clinton's was a failed presidency; 68 percent hoped "Clinton would get his act together." Facing low expectations, freed from the Democrats' imperial congressional barons, and with an indomitable will to win, Clinton had not yet surrendered.

Still, he was hurting and not trying to hide it. Looking left, he felt the sting of the Seattle Slackers' rejection, ideologically, politically, stylistically. Looking right, he felt the sting of conservatives' and centrists' rejections. Clinton's reversals, failures, and scandals, combined with congressional Democrats' arrogance, made it easy to characterize the vote as the Angry White Males' rebellion.

Adding to the Democrats' humiliation, many young Americans voted Republican or stayed at home. Exit polls showed that eighteen- to twenty-nine-year-olds, 21 percent of 1992's electorate, only constituted 14 percent of the electorate two years later. A *Seattle Times* reporter discovered that Generation Xers saw "the Reagan era as a time of opportunity, the Clinton years a time when a college degree often leads to little more than a clerical job." Tabitha Soren, dubbed the voice of her generation thanks to MTV's "Choose or Lose" voter mobilization campaign in 1992, concluded, "The excitement and hopefulness about a revolution in Washington, D.C., are gone." In an MTV poll, 37 percent said the negative campaign ads alienated them and 32 percent felt politics was too corrupt to bother voting.

Clinton wanted to mobilize Americans in bursts of communal activism fueled by idealism. Unfortunately, the acrimony in Washington, the cynicism in the press, and Clinton's own incompetence alienated the young. After nearly two years in office, he had failed to make involvement in politics or community service appear as compelling as getting swept up in Seattle capitalism, or wallowing in grunge alienation. Clinton recognized Gingrich's Contract with America as a sleight of hand, making a series of local elections feel like a national movement; young people's abandonment, however, was a slap in the face. Clinton's project to rally Americans around opportunity, responsibility, community, could not compete with American culture's defeatism, cynicism, and selfishness.

Meanwhile, as Clinton and Americans indulged and fretted, Rwanda bled. On April 6, Hutu extremists shot down the airplane carrying Rwandan president Habyarimana and the Burundian president. The Rwandan Armed Forces and Hutu militias started slaughtering Tutsis and moderate Hutu politicians. Through mid-July, the frenzied butchery would continue, until French military intervention and the Tutsi-dominated Rwanda Patriotic Front (RPF) ended the mass murder. As more than eight hundred thousand people died, constituting three-quarters of the Tutsi population, with countless others raped, brutalized, tortured, Bill Clinton dithered. His spokespeople bickered with reporters, acknowledging "acts of genocide" were occurring while refusing to condemn the mass murders as "genocide." Legally, the formal designation would have compelled intervention.

Four years later, Bill Clinton apologized, biting his lip to telegraph sincerity and taking "responsibility." Fear of more American casualties after the Somalia debacle, his political problems, and America's distraction paralyzed Clinton for those critical three and a half months. The annual Associated Press survey of American news executives would find O. J. Simpson's impending murder trial the top U.S. news story of 1994, relegating the Rwandan genocide to ninth place. During this year when *Dumb and Dumber* would be the big Christmas box office hit, many wondered whether the president and his country were too distracted to do good and ensure effective, responsible governance. It would have required great political daring to defy the neo-isolationist status quo, the navel gazing, and the post-Vietnam post-traumatic stress and take risks for foreign tribesmen of a different color in a land few could find on their maps. In America's new horizontal, fun, and lurid democracy, was there room for such old-fashioned virtues like courage?

6

1995: Oklahoma City
"Their Legacy Must Be Our Lives"

The Claw-Back Kid Finds Windows of Opportunity

> *There is a group who believe that our problems are primarily personal and cultural. Cultural is a—basically a word that means, in this context, there are a whole lot of persons doing the same bad thing. [Laughter.] And that's what people—and then if everybody would just sort of straighten up and fly right, why, things would be hunky-dory. And why don't they do it?*
>
> —BILL CLINTON, REMARKS AT GEORGETOWN UNIVERSITY,
> JULY 6, 1995

On Wednesday April 19, 1995, a surprising number of Americans were entering the third month of watching what would be O. J. Simpson's nine-month trial. Daily cable TV viewership was up 25 percent to follow this live, multi-episode parallel to *Law & Order,* the hit police procedural series that began in 1990. The day before, one of Simpson's pricey, slippery, stagey "Dream Team" defense lawyers had been shut down midsentence, in a rare display of muscle by Lance Ito, the presiding judge. Barry Scheck was implying that police had framed Simpson by planting some blood. The testimony would resume soon on the Pacific Coast. At 9:04 a.m. Central Standard Time, the media spotlight shifted abruptly when a seven-thousand-pound truck bomb mixing fertilizer and fuel devastated a federal building in Oklahoma City.

The Alfred P. Murrah building, named after an Oklahoma judge, was a squat rectangle with an ugly concrete frame flanked by two "glass curtains" of windows, reflecting the concrete-heavy architectural "Brutalism" in vogue when the building opened in 1977. All those windows brought sunshine to the 550 employees who worked there regularly for the Social Security Administration, the Bureau of Alcohol, Tobacco, and Firearms, the Drug Enforcement Agency, and the Secret Service. All that glass now delivered death and dismemberment in what newspapers then called "the worst terrorist attack ever undertaken on American soil."

The blast ripped open the building's north side, damaging 300 neighboring structures, killing 168 people, and wounding 780 more. Nineteen children who attended a day-care center, America's Kids, died when the building's second floor collapsed. The hulking building's exterior now looked like a burned cake scooped out by boys who forgot their manners and their utensils, with charred debris hanging ghoulishly from every floor. One heartbreaking image showed a firefighter, Chris Fields, cradling a dying infant in his arms. Baylee Almon had celebrated her first birthday a day earlier. Now, her bloody face contrasted with her innocent white socks. "This is why we live in Oklahoma," said Sharon Coyne, who lost her fourteen-month-old daughter Jaci. "Because things like this don't happen here."

The "thing" that happened once again highlighted America's vulnerability to terrorism, one of the post–Cold War world's terrifying, shadowy plagues. But what Bill Clinton called this "awful, awful bombing," helped him reinvigorate his presidency. After the crime "a lot of the meanness went out of America," Clinton would say, hailing Americans for remembering their core values. He restored his popularity by being more presidential, more values-focused, and more centrist, functioning as the Good Father not the Hip Brother. In 1995, another window of opportunity for him as a leader was the growing excitement over the New Economy and the Great American Hook-Up to the Internet, celebrated with the launch of Windows 95. An increasingly nimble leader seeking common ground, Clinton could rally Americans during a crisis like the Oklahoma City bombing while helping them feel good about the technological advances, economic recovery, and heroic citizens around them.

America's Grace

Oklahoma was a traditional state cherishing small-town virtues. "Sure we have crime here—who doesn't," one local admitted. "But in a place where everybody knows everybody it doesn't get out of hand." Three-quarters of the population regularly attended church, as opposed to half of Americans overall. More than half of Oklahoma's disproportionately devout population were evangelical Protestants, twice the national average.

Anita Hill's Sooner origins confirmed her innocence to many. *The Simpsons* telegraphed the virtue of Ned Flanders, Homer Simpson's happy, square, fundamentalist neighbor, by making him a graduate of Oral Roberts University (ORU) in Tulsa. Throughout the 1990s, enrollment in religiously affiliated universities would increase by 12 percent. "I'm at ORU to hook up with God's people," an Arkansas coed told a reporter, probably unaware what "hooking up" now meant on campuses where students did not renounce alcohol, cigarettes, and sex.

America was becoming more polarized religiously. America remained more God-fearing and churchgoing than secularizing Europe. The 1960s' rebellion doubled the number of people identifying as secular while triggering a backlash that galvanized and politicized religious conservatives, explaining ORU's uptick. A second backlash then followed, as young people raised in an open culture rejected religion's growing fusion with the right.

Yet, despite this conservative identity as what soon would be called a Red State, Oklahoma was changing. In 1950, 20 percent of working Oklahomans were farmers. By 1970, 5 percent were farmers. By 2000, less than 1 percent would farm. The federal government became Oklahoma's biggest employer. Its 65.2 percent urbanization rate remained below the 78 percent national average but was unprecedented for Oklahoma.

Despite the polarized culture war discourse, despite electing an ardent conservative, Jim Inhofe, to the Senate in 1994 after he campaigned for God and guns but against gays, Oklahomans were modernizing in sync with other Americans. Even as commentators spoke of Republicans' Red America versus Democrats' Blue America, rates of divorce, abortion, drug use, alcohol abuse, and births-to-single mothers did not break along those political or geographic lines, and remained high throughout the land. America's divorce rate was 4.7 per 1,000 people, with Nevada's 11.4 rate the highest and Massachusetts' 2.8 the lowest; Oklahoma's was 7.7. The 30.1 percent of children born to unwed mothers came close to the 32.4 percent national rate—twice Mormon Utah's rate and half of Washington, D.C.'s 62.3 percent rate. The state's gay underground was becoming visible, with a gay monthly, *The Gayly Oklahoman,* an Oklahoma Gay and Lesbian Political Caucus, and an Oklahoma Gay Rodeo Association. The abortion rate did deviate from national trends, with 10.1 abortions per 1,000 Oklahoma women of reproductive age, half the national rate of 21.3, reflecting a systematic pro-life legal and educational campaign.

Along with their fellow Americans, Oklahomans flocked to *Mrs. Doubtfire* and other modernist entertainments trumpeting Hollywood values. The 1993 movie starring Robin Williams as a divorced father who masquerades as an aging female nanny to be close to his children, was still resonating. The happy ending reunites the dad with his kids but not his wife. Mrs. Doubtfire preaches:

"some parents, when they're angry, they get along much better when they don't live together. . . . There are all sorts of different families. . . . But if there's love, dear . . . those are the ties that bind, and you'll have a family in your heart, forever." This spreading gospel of divorcity, validating divorce and "different families," made this period of religious polarization one of growing tolerance, too. These conflicting impulses and "interlocking personal relationships among people of many different faiths," the demographers Robert Putnam and David Campbell explained, were "America's grace."

Oklahoma, like the rest of America, had also gone online. The many websites featuring bomb-making "recipes" were upsetting, while the many chat rooms offering solace were soothing. After the bombing, over 2 million Americans on America Online, CompuServe, and Prodigy, participated in what one reporter anachronistically called "the largest water-cooler conversation in America."

McVeigh and the Militia's Smorgasbord of Hate

Only seventy-five minutes after the bombing, an Oklahoma state trooper on Interstate 35 stopped a car without a license plate. After noticing a bulge in the driver's belt awkwardly hiding a pistol, the trooper detained Timothy McVeigh. Within two days the FBI identified him as the Oklahoma Bomber.

FBI profilers had predicted the bomber would be a young, angry, lonely, white veteran seeking to avenge the Waco inferno on its second anniversary, April 19. McVeigh symbolized America the disconnected, living in the Republic of Nothing. The child of divorce, a Gulf War veteran, expert at computers but awkward around women, a gun nut and conspiracy buff, his life provided a canvas upon which political ideologues projected their agendas. Conservatives emphasized the family breakdown and alienation; liberals highlighted the militant politics and guns.

McVeigh was executed. Two of his army buddies and co-conspirators, Terry Nichols and Michael Fortier, were imprisoned. When asked about co-conspirators, McVeigh echoed Jack Nicholson's Marine colonel in *A Few Good Men*, yelling: "You can't handle the truth . . . isn't it kind of scary that one man could wreak this kind of hell?"

Actually, McVeigh and Nichols were tied to the militia movement, a web of far-right, anti-government extremist groups with names like United States Militia Association, Constitution Defense, and Patriots Alert. Enraged by big government, hating gun control, whipping each other into conspiracy-fearing frenzies online, an estimated one hundred thousand angry Americans joined the militias.

In 1978, the white supremacist William Luther Pierce wrote what became their modern Bible, eventually purchased by over half a million people. *The Turner Diaries* imagined an eight-year race war to free America, triggered when Jewish human rights groups dispatch black gangs to invade white homes, searching for guns banned by the "Cohen Act." Pierce's war begins with a bombing of the FBI building in Washington a few minutes after 9:00 a.m., using a bomb placed in a rental truck. FBI agents found pages from *The Turner Diaries* describing that crime in McVeigh's car.

These renegades magnified the racism, nativism, and anti-Semitism of the Ku Klux Klan and other professional haters by riding American ideological currents with respectable pedigrees. Their populism echoed traditional suspicions of big government, sharpened by periodic bouts of mass anger dating back to Andrew Jackson's conversion of popular indignation into political reform. Their conspiracy theories paralleled American fears of democracy's vulnerability to dictators dating back to 1776. Greater law enforcement scrutiny and public disgust would reduce these fanatic gangs from an estimated 858 at their peak in 1996 to 194 in 2000.

Newt Gingrich, Imperial Speaker

That McVeigh came from the right was a lucky break for Bill Clinton. He began 1995 feeling lost. Newt Gingrich launched an imperial speakership, seeing himself as America's new leader. Clinton sat glumly on the sidelines as Gingrich sought to enact his Contract with America.

Newt Gingrich and Bill Clinton were beefy, needy, sons of the New South, scarred by complex family lives, frequently perpetuating that messiness in their own relationships. Both Baby Boomers' Peter Pan refusal to grow up drove their Pied Piper–like charm. Each was brilliant, intellectual, visionary, and flawed. Together, they represented a new breed of leaders, lacking George H. W. Bush's Waspish reserve or Ronald Reagan's genial distancing, let alone Dwight Eisenhower's quiet authority or Franklin Roosevelt's patrician power. Their neediness created a frankness that appealed to supporters in America's new, more fluid, political culture.

Gingrich was pragmatic enough to support civil rights and try soft-pedaling Republicans' social agenda, just as Clinton was pragmatic enough to distrust too much big government and acknowledge America's values crisis. Both these larger-than-life professorial politicians sought big ideas to tame the big changes vexing Americans. While their similarities and shared passion for policy could keep them kibitzing, they also found each other ideologically repugnant. Gingrich had been fighting people like Clinton, representing the loudest if not most representative strain in his age group, for decades. Gingrich also had a mean streak that Clinton lacked. In 1994, he branded Democrats "enemies of normal people" and called the Clintons "countercultural McGoverniks."

Acknowledging that he and Hillary supported George McGovern for president in 1972, the president denounced Gingrich for embodying "the self-righteous, condemning, Absolute-truth claiming dark side of white southern conservatism." In "Newt Gingrich Declares War on 'McGovernik Counterculture,'" the Beatnik poet Allen Ginsberg wondered: "Does that mean war on every boy with more than one earring on the same ear? Will there be laws against Punk, Generation X, the Voidoids, Slackers, Grunge?" Getting more political, Ginsberg asked, "What about African-Americans? That's a terrific Counterculture."

Ginsberg, modern America's obscene, howling gay prophet, who would live until 1997, had won. Post-Sixties' America reflected his sensibilities and Clinton's more than Gingrich's, although the twice-married-and-soon-to-be-divorced-again-because-he-had-a-mistress Speaker lived a more modern life than he admitted. The political analysts Jack Germond and Jules Witcover suggested Republicans might consider a "muzzle" for Gingrich's "recklessly" distracting rhetoric.

Gingrich treated his maiden speech as Speaker like an inaugural address, promising "the busiest early months since 1933," and proclaiming grandiosely: "This is a moral crisis equal to segregation, equal to slavery." He promised to push for every provision of the Contract with America during the first hundred days. Not since Woodrow Wilson moved into the White House in 1913 had an academic altered Washington's power structures so dramatically. Wilson expanded the presidency by making the chief executive more prime ministerial, addressing Congress directly, shepherding legislation more intensely. Gingrich contracted the presidency by making the Speaker more prime ministerial, addressing the people directly, and trying to make his office the center of American politics.

Even when trying to be statesmanlike, Gingrich stumbled into controversy. He called Connie Chung of CBS "despicable" for reporting that his mother heard Newt frequently calling Hillary Clinton "a bitch." Congressman Barney Frank of Massachusetts said, "He is the most partisan and destructive guy we have ever seen."

As Gingrich strutted and Clinton moped, liberals despaired. Anthony Lewis of *The New York Times* called Clinton "The Lost Leader" listlessly failing to fight Republicans' "radical legislation" threatening the Constitution. Robert Healy of *The Boston Globe* pronounced "The Problem with [the] Clinton Presidency is Clinton."

Tempers on both sides flared easily. In late January, Dick Armey, the House Majority Leader, defending Gingrich from corruption charges for a $4.5 million book deal from HarperCollins, owned by the conservative Rupert Murdoch, called his Democratic colleague from Massachusetts, "Barney Fag." Barney Frank indeed was gay and out of the closet since 1987. Denouncing the Republicans' "climate of meanness and intolerance," Frank snapped: "I don't think it was on the tip of his tongue, but I do believe it was in the back of his mind." When Gingrich returned the book advance to still the controversy, he echoed Clinton's disconnect, observing the acrimony as if he never fed it. Ours is an "age of extraordinarily cynical, adversarial press," Gingrich said, "an age of a White House press corps that devoured Carter, tried to devour Reagan and lost, devoured Bush and are now working on devouring Clinton."

The ferocity flared when the Congress debated welfare reform or any potential subsidy cutbacks. President Clinton said Republicans want to "make war on the kids of this country." The Missouri Democrat William Clay dismissed conservative arguments as Hitler's "big lie." "More children will be killed," the Child Welfare League of America warned in an anti-Gingrich ad. "More children will be raped."

Gingrich excelled at starting arguments, not changing America. Public discourse became more Reaganesque than Clintonesque but the Constitution's checks and balances checked and balanced him. With a slim majority of 53 to 47, Republican senators, subject to filibusters, were more cautious. Gingrich stumbled by acting as if Ronald Reagan had never governed and Bill Clinton had never been elected. Just as centrist Democrats were correcting the Great Society failure to realize that culture counted, many Americans were realizing that Reagan's supply side economics went too far as well. Gingrich's targeting of successful initiatives like the school lunch program made it easy for Democrats to blast him as the Grinch. Gingrich's call to balance the budget while cutting taxes seemed like dieting by binging on sweets.

In the first hundred days, Gingrich only passed two bills that originated with his Contract. One held Congress to the same laws corporations followed. The second limited the federal government's ability to mandate state actions without financing them.

Contact with Clinton often subdued Gingrich, infuriating his Republican colleagues. "We both own Mustangs, we both love policy, we both eat too much, and we both feel very irritated at the Washington press corps," Gingrich exulted. Occasionally, this connection brought out the best in each of them. *Newsweek*'s April 10, 1995 cover asked "What Good Is Government?," promoting thoughtful vision statements *by Bill Clinton* and *by Newt Gingrich*. Characteristically, each of these narcissistic intellectuals rooted their ideologies in autobiography. Clinton's faith in government stemmed from Dwight Eisenhower's integration of Little Rock public schools in 1957. From there, and thanks to "my grandfather" who "taught me about Franklin Roosevelt and the New Deal," he grew up believing "the national government had to affirmatively step in to make sure everybody had a fair chance." Gingrich, affirming that culture counts, contrasted the "orderly, structured" post–World War II world he was born into, versus "the chaos of the 1960s."

Clinton realized "that big government is not the solution to every big problem." Gingrich moderated his doubts about government by saluting the civil rights movement, the military, even the "Treasury and the Federal Reserve," as "federal agencies that stay in touch with reality every day." He graciously noted that Clinton "gets it . . . I don't know any politician in America who has a better intuitive sense of reengineering government and society, of the world market, and of information technologies." The problem, Gingrich concluded, was Democratic Party pressure arousing the president's inner "Mondale or Dukakis," resulting in "the same old Big Government nonsense."

Despite such occasional warmth, Gingrich's anniversary antics approaching the hundred-day mark diminished the president. The Speaker and the House Republicans reenacted the signing of the Contract with America, as if it were the signing of the Declaration of Independence itself. Gingrich cheekily demanded the three major networks and CNN broadcast his thirty-minute evening address, as if he were president. CBS, CNN, CNBC, and C-SPAN agreed. Demonstrating his broad ambition, echoing Clinton, he preached, "no civilization can survive with 12-year-olds having babies, with 15-year-olds killing each other, with 17-year-olds dying of AIDS, with 18-year-olds getting diplomas they can't even read."

While Gingrich generated excitement in Washington, only 38 percent of Americans surveyed had heard of his Contract. Most Americans seemed more concerned with O. J. Simpson's trial and baseball's return after its disastrously long strike, albeit for an abbreviated 144-game season. The judge trying Simpson, Lance Ito, had better name recognition than Gingrich or Al Gore. Gingrich's job approval rating of 39 percent approximated Clinton's ratings, hovering in the low 40s.

Clinton: The Shape-Shifter Debates His Next Incarnation

Clinton bristled when reporters suggested that Gingrich was running domestic policy, leaving foreign policy to the beaten president. Gingrich's bombast, Clinton's drift, and dramatic foreign events reinforced the impression. In late January, the Mexican economy nearly collapsed. Labeling it "the first crisis of the twenty-first century," Gingrich patriotically supported the president. Clinton approved a bold $20 billion bailout. Thomas Friedman of *The New York Times* would praise this "least popular, least understood, but most important foreign policy decision of the Clinton presidency." By July, Mexico's economy had stabilized.

As Gingrich peddled his Contract, Clinton confronted violence in Bosnia, instability in Haiti, unrest in the new Russia, which was planning on selling nuclear reactors to Iran, tensions between Israelis and Palestinians, and surprising strides toward peace in Northern Ireland.

Drafting the State of the Union address, Clinton and his aides debated this shape-shifter's next incarnation. Michael Waldman, special assistant to the president for policy coordination, bluntly noted that Americans were wondering whether their president was a "pander bear" or a "visionary." Deputy assistant for domestic policy Bill Galston sought "to enlarge the President so that he is seen once again as large enough to occupy his office." Championing the middle class was not enough; it is "like being for oxygen," Waldman feared.

A quirky, brainy, savvy pollster, Dick Morris, lured Bill Clinton back to midcourt. Morris advocated "bite size" initiatives that could succeed rather than splashy programs like health care reform that would fail. Fearing Democratic outrage and media ridicule for using a consultant with many Republican clients, Clinton concealed Morris's involvement, speaking to "Charlie" by telephone.

Morris challenged Clinton to redefine the presidency "by compromise, reconciliation, values, and healing," abandoning the "traditional class-warfare language." Morris knew his client well. The values talk appealed to Clinton's deeper mission to reform America from the "inside out" while satisfying his need to seduce the one holdout in a room full of fans. Clinton believed triangulating was noble not sleazy. "I had always tried to synthesize new ideas and traditional values, and to change government policies as conditions changed," he would recall. Morris convinced him to commandeer four popular Republican positions: "to eliminate the deficit, require work for welfare, cut taxes, and reduce the federal bureaucracy." Morris helped Clinton be Clinton, someone who believed that the right move could be popular, too, and who since 1985 with the DLC had sought that consensus-building, golden path.

Delivering the State of the Union, Clinton was humble but not servile. He admitted: "I have made my mistakes." In words that would prove prescient after the Oklahoma bombing three months later, Clinton asked Congress to avoid "partisanship and pettiness and pride." He sought $60 billion in tax cuts over five years. He championed a Middle Class Bill of Rights to seize the center and outmaneuver Gingrich. He said it "should properly be called the bill of rights and responsibilities because its provisions only benefit those who are working to educate and raise their children and to educate themselves." This framing reflected his shadowy consultant's insight that most voters "didn't care who got the tax cut as much as they cared about what they had done to deserve it."

Clinton's shift divided his White House staff. Most of his aides preferred a liberal, confrontational approach, not what a *Philadelphia Daily News* editorial called "Gingrich lite." These advisers did not want to follow the Republicans back to Reaganomics. They advocated updating Harry Truman's 1948 partisan attack on the "Do Nothing" Republican Congress. To George Stephanopoulos, " 'triangulation' was just a fancy word for betrayal." Secretary of Labor Robert Reich called Morris's approach "all I detest in American politics" and "the antithesis of leadership," which entailed courageously confronting tough questions. Others, simply warning of Clinton's zeal for policy details, mocked his Middle Class Bill of Rights as "McBOR."

Clinton delivered a tough noontime address to the American Society of Newspaper Editors in Dallas on April 7, the same day as Gingrich's unprecedented televised address. The president now cast legendary reformers like Theodore Roosevelt, Woodrow Wilson, and Franklin Roosevelt as taming more radical impulses, saying they "incorporated what was good, smoothed out what was rough, and discarded what would hurt. . . . And that is my job." Ready to veto, if "necessary," Clinton said his "test" of all initiatives would be: "Does an idea expand middle class incomes and opportunities? Does it promote values like family, work, responsibility, and community? Does it strengthen the hand of America's working families in a global economy?"

Still, Clinton remained subdued. On April 10, the Senate Majority Leader, Robert Dole, a Kansas Republican, announced his candidacy for the presidency. Four days later, Clinton "quietly filed for re-election." His fragility was apparent April 18, during a forty-minute prime-time press conference, which only CBS of the major networks broadcast. Pushed to explain his stance in a changed Washington, Clinton insisted plaintively, "The president is relevant," with each repetition of the word "relevant" reinforcing his marginality.

Tragically, less than one day and one deadly bombing later, Bill Clinton was very relevant. A red-eyed Clinton fought tears in his initial remarks. The nation's civic high priest and chief law enforcement officer, he offered the victims sympathy and vowed to catch the culprits.

That Sunday, the president and First Lady addressed a nationally televised memorial service from the Oklahoma State Fairgrounds. Clinton appeared presidential, authoritative, sensitive, as America's mourner-in-chief. "Those who are lost now belong to God," he said. "Someday we will be with them. But until that happens, their legacy must be our lives."

"Every once in a while you need a reminder that maybe the country is going too far one way or the other," Clinton's DLC partner Al From recalls. "Oklahoma City was that reminder" not to go too far with the anti-government rhetoric. Clinton vowed never to use the term "federal bureaucrat" again. It diminished the good people who served their fellow Americans. Emphasizing the mass murderers' militia links, the president began spinning the tragedy as a warning against the dangers from one particular end of the American political spectrum, the right, even as he crafted an appeal to woo the right.

America the Cranky

Clinton sincerely feared the incitement of the "right-wing radio talk-show hosts, whose venomous rhetoric pervaded the airwaves daily," and "Web sites encouraging people to rise up against the government." Limbaugh had warned of a pending "second violent American revolution" because "people are sick and tired of a bunch of bureaucrats in Washington driving into town and telling them what they can and can't do with their land." Clinton also sensed the political advantage. Sounding centrist and soothing, he condemned the "promoters of paranoia" for spreading hate and fomenting discord. "They leave the impression that, by their very words, that [sic] violence is acceptable." One cartoonist would draw the by now-iconic photo of Baby Baylee in Firefighter Fields' arms, adding the caption: "Damn Rightwing Radio."

Limbaugh said it would be "irresponsible and vacuous" to connect talk radio with the McVeigh outrage. White House aides insisted Clinton was speaking generally not specifically. Most hosts, such as G. Gordon Liddy, refused to take responsibility for the tone in the country. The convicted Watergate felon had advised on his radio show in August that if agents from the Bureau of Alcohol, Tobacco, and Firearms come "to disarm you and they are bearing arms, resist them with arms. . . . Kill the sons of bitches."

On the television show *Inside Washington,* the liberal columnist Carl Rowan went further than Clinton, claiming "the harsh rhetoric of the Gingriches and the Doles . . . creates a climate of violence in America." Rowan blamed the bombing on the "angriest of the angry White men," inflamed by the line that "affirmative action means Blacks have stolen everything from White guys." A Democratic congressional campaign committee's mailing said Gingrich "promotes the policies of a terrorist." When the Unabomber killed again on April 24, perhaps resenting the shifted spotlight to Oklahoma, his radical environmental rants did not trigger an anti-leftist backlash. "It is grotesque to suggest that anybody in this country who raises legitimate questions about the size and scope of the federal government has any implication in this," Gingrich fumed.

The mass tenderness the Oklahoma bombing first evoked vanished in clouds of recriminations. American politics has long had a streak of populist anger running like a gusher of underground oil that clever demagogues tapped occasionally. In the 1980s, Ronald Reagan tamed the conservative anger building since the 1950s, intensified by the 1960s and 1970s. His "aw shucks" approach suited a have-a-nice-day culture wherein, psychiatrists like Carol Stearns lamented, Americans increasingly frowned on anger. Perhaps, Stearns and her historian husband, Peter Stearns, wondered, the violence in the media and in the street provided some outlets for so much repressed emotion.

By 1995, *New York Times* columnist Russell Baker feared the opposite. He grumbled that "America is angry at Washington, angry at the press, angry at immigrants, angry at television, angry at traffic, angry at people who are well off and angry at people who are poor, angry at blacks and angry at whites." Why did life's inevitable twists evoke such fury amid peace and prosperity?

In fairness, the economic uptick was only beginning. Average household wealth started rising again with overall indebtedness dropping in 1995. People living their lives in real time not academic retrospect did not rejoice immediately, especially because median wealth fell 17 percent from 1989 to 1995. Anxiety lingered, even as more Americans found work, saw their salaries rise, and joined the half of U.S. households that by 2001 would own stock directly or indirectly. The media often focused on the African American underclass or the disaffected Gen Xers. But they were not the only Americans who feared falling behind the glamorous millionaires and billionaires enjoying increasingly fawning coverage. "The locus of poverty," the historian Jacqueline Jones observed, was "not black, Northern, or urban."

The perpetual poor of rural America remained largely invisible. Reporters were more likely to write about America's most violent and visible poor, the black underclass, or publicize the anguished voices of America's unexpected poor, those tumbling out of the middle class. In North Canton, Ohio, most major companies had "downsized," many after mergers, infuriating a fifty-four-year-old former bank employee, Lucy Smith. Most people on the unemployment line "are like me, not poor people in raggedy clothes." Generation Xers and their older siblings, seeing the median hourly wage for those twenty-six to thirty-five drop by 18.7 percent since 1979, became "boomerangs," landing right back home after going away to college.

Increasingly, poverty skewed younger rather than older, in a country that helped reduce elderly poverty by nearly 50 percent from 1970 to 1995 while tolerating a 37 percent rise in childhood poverty. Globalization, deindustrialization, the limited remuneration for McJobs, and excessive benefits for their bosses, had benefited Wall Street while hurting Main Street. The rich enjoyed more of the nation's wealth. Despite Clinton's rhetoric, more Americans could not make ends meet.

The Nineties' boom remained as anomalous as the Eighties' boom. Despite macro indicators rising, many individuals' micro-standing sank. Professor Joseph E. Stiglitz, the chairman of Clinton's Council of Economic Advisers, would observe, "We knew that the idea of a lifetime job was a thing of the past," and explain that Clintonites spoke about "lifetime employability" and "lifetime learning" to familiarize Americans with the idea of perpetual re-careering. This clinical assessment discounted workers' anxiety. The newly fired usually feared, "*This* layoff is forever," especially with the ease of exporting jobs or eliminating them.

Still, the shrill attacks on Clinton, the daily left-right yelling on CNN's *Crossfire,* Smashing Pumpkins singing "Despite all my rage I am still just a rat in a cage," the continuing violence on screen and in the streets, suggested the crisis was existential, not just economic. Media manipulators stoked anger. As Russell Baker lamented, "Good news . . . does not sell papers or keep millions glued to radios and TV screens."

America's soul hurt. Young people were often falling into the perpetual poverty set by traps of excessive drug use, teen pregnancy, and dropping out of school. Their parents were often distracted by daily deficits in time, monthly deficits in money, and overall deficits in satisfaction and security. "I hold the fecklessness and self-absorption of my generation substantially responsible for the darkening fearsome world that younger Americans face today," William Finnegan, born in 1952, would write. In *Cold New World: Growing Up in a Harder Country,* the *New Yorker* writer condemned "a hapless abdication of parental roles and family obligations by adults who themselves never grew up." In 1995's best-selling "prequel" to the *Wizard of Oz, Wicked: The Life and Times of the Wicked Witch of the West,* the heroine, who is deemed "wicked" because of Oz's intolerance, identified the nasty edge to a growing "clueless" culture of "whatever," "chillout," "so is your face," and "eat my shorts." The witch-to-be Elphaba ponders the links: "Evil and boredom. Evil and ennui. Evil and the lack of stimulation."

Sometimes, Americans remembered to laugh at life's twists and turns, including "ray-ay-ay-ayn on your weddin' day," along with the energetic, whimsical Alanis Morissette, whose song "Ironic" was a big hit in 1995. But more fans connected to her harsh, explicit, breakthrough hit, "You Oughta Know," incensed by "the mess you left when you went away . . . the cross I bear that you gave to me." Assessing the angst, both personal and collective, in America and the world, Czech president Václav Havel would urge Harvard's graduates that spring: "we must recollect our original spiritual and moral substance."

The collective addiction to artificial stimulants revealed the depth of the abyss. As with poverty, America's drug problem often was given a black face. Blacks were disproportionately poorer than whites, but blacks used drugs at the same rates as whites. African Americans were 12 percent of the American population and an estimated 13 percent of the nation's drug users. Blacks accounted for 35 percent of all arrests for drug possession, 74 percent of all drug-related prison sentences, and much of the focus of the war on drugs, partially because of racism and partially because many more blacks were in the violent drug trade, with more blacks than whites abusing drugs rather than using them casually.

Experts debated why getting high and binge drinking were such popular activities. Anthropologists' "social-control theory" blamed modernity, shrinking attachments to family, community, society, and tradition. Psychologists' "self-control theory" observed America as a Borderline nation, with often inadequate parents raising many impulsive, reckless, shortsighted people. Sociologists' "social learning theory" highlighted this Age of Indulgence's "social environment," with peers and popular culture glamorizing drug use. Political scientists emphasized the poverty, powerlessness, and despair making drugs an escape, an oasis of pleasure in a lifetime of anguish. And economists emphasized environmental factors creating opportunities for use and abuse, including disposable income, spare time, and the international drug trade's national distribution network. Together, all these elements fed a craving for drugs, but also a yearning for leadership out of this existential swamp.

Bill Clinton, the Claw-Back Kid

With America reeling after Oklahoma City, Clinton began clawing his way back. He had grown as a leader. His calls for healing resonated. As in 1992, his down-home recipe for redemption mixed self-criticism, self-flagellation, and self-promotion, spiced with dollops of luck. Now, he added a more grounding values orientation answering a profound public emptiness. With his approval ratings jumping from 42 percent to 51 percent after the bombing, the public response boosted his confidence, which made him more effective with the public, then more popular.

Clinton endured criticism masterfully, apologizing sincerely then internalizing the most relevant lessons. He apologized to a DLC meeting for disappointing "the folks the Democratic Party ought to be championing," those in "the struggling middle class," by coddling minorities and the poor. Republicans "had a two-word message: 'less government.' Our message took an hour to recite," Clinton later admitted.

Clinton continued tapping the presidency's pageantry to enhance his power, visiting Moscow in May to mark the fiftieth anniversary of World War II's conclusion. That June, when visiting Montana, the calculating Clinton took time off to go horseback riding, "to show that I wasn't a cultural alien rural Americans couldn't support." One farmer remarked: "he ain't anything like they make him out to be." Clinton wondered how he could convince the rest of the country.

That month Clinton launched a National Homeownership Strategy with housing secretary Henry Cisneros. The Clintonesque, encyclopedic initiative listed "one hundred things we were going to do to increase home ownership to two-thirds of the population," Clinton recalled. "This is a big deal," he insisted, linking widespread homeownership to his mission "to reinforce family values in America, encourage two-parent households," and fulfill "the American Dream." Urging all players to get "creative" to "lower barriers," to overcome the "major impediment[s]" of a "lack of cash" for down payments or monthly payments, the Clinton administration encouraged easy mortgages, easy refinancing, and easy access for lenders to financial markets. Borrowers with spotted credit histories ineligible for low-interest "prime loans" were encouraged to take expensive, higher risk "subprime loans."

By judging institutions on how many mortgages they approved, especially for minority buyers, HUD bullied banks and other lenders into lowering their standards. The policy, aiming "to achieve all-time-high levels of homeownership by the end of the century," increased the percentage of Americans owning their own homes marginally, from 64 percent to 67.4 percent by 2000, although blacks and Hispanics did benefit. Alas, easy credit inflated housing prices. Easily obtained mortgages were sometimes impossible to maintain. Others refinanced their homes, shopped the money away, and ended up in debt. Unscrupulous lenders with shoddy business practices made things worse.

Thirteen years later, during a Republican's tenure, these first and second mortgages, bundled into vulnerable mortgage-backed securities, would help crash the economy, making the 2008 recession a bipartisan achievement. In retrospect, Cisneros would admit that "people came to homeownership who should not have been homeowners." While blaming "unscrupulous participants—bankers, brokers, secondary market people," he confessed: "families are hurt because we as a society did not draw a line. . . . We were trying to be creative."

Seeking to heal the country, on June 11, Clinton and Newt Gingrich appeared together at a senior citizens picnic in New Hampshire. Despite competing signs outside saying: "Welcome to *Newt* Hampshire" and "Kick Newt's Butt," the two vowed to cooperate. Both endorsed a nonpolitical commission to reform lobbying laws and limit special interest influence. One Secret Service agent made the rare, and much appreciated, gesture of congratulating the president for the healing event.

Windows 95 and the Internet Tidal Wave

As the battling often babyish Baby Boomers acted grown up, one of the most established Baby Boomers, despite being ten years' their junior, was preparing his big summer launch. Bill Gates, born in 1955, was working toward the late August premiere of Windows 95, his latest operating system. When Gates and his business partners introduced the Microsoft Disk Operating System in 1981, MS-DOS, millions of Americans started learning how to type "Ctrl" along with another letter for various commands. In December 1987, Windows 2.0 opened the world of desktop icons and the Control Panel, competing with Apple's user-friendly interface. Windows 3.0 and 3.1 followed in 1990 and 1992, addicting Americans to PCs at home that were faster, flashier, and more fun. Games like Solitaire, Hearts, and Minesweeper upgraded the computer from a work tool to the Ultimate Everything Machine.

In January 1994, Bryant Gumbel of NBC's *Today* asked, off air, "What is Internet anyway? What do you write to it, like mail?" He and Katie Couric debated whether you called the @ sign "at" or an "'a' with a circle around it." Having mentioned an Internet report about violence, Gumbel said he "felt stupid" reading violence@nbc.ge.com as "Violence *at* NBC."

By 1995, millions were madly surfing what Gates called "The Internet Tidal Wave." He christened mass access to this network of networks "the most important development since the advent of the PC." With the personal computer revolution linking with the computer networking revolution, Gates and his colleagues were creating "the world's new digital nervous system." The rush for the perfect Web browser, then the ultimate search engine, began, as two young Stanford students, Larry Page and Sergey Brin, were first bonding.

Eighty percent of the world's computers used Microsoft operating systems. Windows 95 would have a Taskbar, Minimize, Maximize, and Close buttons on each Window, an improved Start button, and easier built-in access online. Most Windows 95 packages came with the first version of Internet Explorer and the Microsoft Network, its new online service. All this overlapping interactivity excited consumers and offended antitrust prosecutors in Washington and Europe.

Shortly before the Microsoft launch, Netscape Communications, formerly Mosaic, an Internet server and Web browser that would rival Internet Explorer, went public with an IPO. Frenzied bidding drove the price of 5 million shares of the fifteen-month-old company to $71 a share at one point. It ended the day at $58.25.

One Netscape founder, Marc Andreessen, soon appeared on *Time*'s cover as one of America's "Golden Geeks." America was embracing the Internet, *Time* explained that summer, "that boomtown of the wired world." The competitive Gates vowed to beat Netscape, triggering The Browser Wars.

By October, at least 24 million North Americans had surfed within the past three months. Approximately 2.5 million had already shopped on the Web. They tended to be upscale, educated, and earning more than $80,000 a year. Meanwhile, Steve Jobs's Pixar produced *Toy Story*, its first computer-animated feature film, with Tom Hanks the voice of Woody, the old reliable cowboy doll, and Tim Allen the voice of the new robot, Buzz Lightyear. With corporations investing millions to develop websites, the humorist Dave Barry would joke amid this "frantic scramble. . . . nobody has told the corporations that 93 percent of these users are in sixth grade."

Some worried about computers distorting human beings, human interactions, and human society. The Unabomber was an extreme expression of this anxiety, perverting traditionally benign Western fantasies of escaping machinery and returning to nature. MIT's Sherry Turkle noted that in the 1980s, Americans established direct, often intense, relationships with their PCs. Now, "the computer had become a portal that enabled people to lead parallel lives in virtual worlds." Some had "RL" real life, and their screen life—or lives. "Views of self became less unitary, more protean," as people became integrated into their networks, like *Star Trek*'s Borgs.

The August 24, 1995 release of Windows 95 became a major cultural event starring Bill Gates. A best seller and multiple talk show appearances further brightened his celebrity orb as his net worth hit an estimated $15 billion, making him the world's richest self-made man. Microsoft's twenty-year-old "vision for a computer on every desk and in every home is slowly coming true," Gates said. Introducing Jay Leno at the promotional kickoff, Gates joked: "Windows 95 is so easy, even a talk-show host can figure it out." A "computer virgin," Leno found Windows 95 so impressive, "it's now able to keep track of O. J. Simpson's alibis all at once." An estimated 40 million users would buy Windows 95 its first year.

Microsoft spent millions to run television commercials with the Rolling Stones singing "Start Me Up," to bathe the Empire State Building in its company colors, and to produce "the world's first cyber-sitcom." This lame but informative thirty-minute introduction to the new product's features starred Matthew Perry and Jennifer Aniston. The "Friends" embarrassed themselves by approaching Bill Gates's office chanting, "taskbars and email and shortcuts oh my." Aniston asked if the "task bar" was "anything like a snack bar." Perry called the Recycle Bin "an enabler for the indecisive."

Perry and Aniston's goofy video captured many Americans' gee-whiz wonder as they downloaded Windows 95, logged onto the expansive Internet with Netscape, and started using e-mail, "you just hit the send icon and away it goes." These miraculous novelties became necessities. This growing euphoria, fed also by the soaring stock market, lightened America's mood and Bill Clinton's prospects.

The growing ease of downloading not just words, not just images, but videos on computer, would doom one of the 1990s' great success stories, Blockbuster Video, and the entire home video industry. Founded in 1985, Blockbuster Video became ubiquitous in the 1990s. David Cook, its founder, applied sophisticated data-tracking technology to monitor distribution and tailor inventory to each neighborhood's demographics. By 1993, 3,400 stores offered between 7,000 and 13,000 titles. Starting the night at the video store, including the inevitable, longer-than-expected search, became a new ritual and a $21 billion business. For millions raised on the rigid rationing of television and movies at particular times, roaming Blockbuster's aisles to choose your entertainment felt liberating. By 1999, the entertainment flowed digitally via the computer through Netflix and other websites, not the videotape or DVD. Blockbuster soon went bust.

Manifestos: Technology = Culture and Culture = Technology

These visions of freedom would inspire politicians and ideologues, not just America's growing legions of technology addicts. In *To Renew America,* Gingrich, echoing Clinton, envisioned the Internet's freedom, openness, decentralization, and accessibility as handmaidens of his "opportunity society," eliminating poverty, bureaucracy, hierarchy, centralization, and oppression. From across the political spectrum, the editors of *Wired* would issue a 1996 manifesto celebrating "the digital revolution" as "a communications revolution which is transforming society." Explaining that "Technology=Culture" and "Culture=Technology," the utopian technologists trusted the Internet's openness to create "a new civic society in which the technological possibility for everyone to speak, to connect, becomes the basis of all political action." Instead, they mourned, politicians "treat us like idiots while campaigning for office . . . then ignore us."

The columnist Charles Krauthammer opposed such technological determinism. Sensitive to technology's centrifugal forces as well as its liberating impact, Krauthammer warned about the harm to community when everyone can spend all their time "cocooned in front of the wide-screened 'home entertainment center.'" Even worse, "Those who do go out move zombie-like through the streets, hard-wired to Walkmans, as oblivious and unavailable to society as the voice-plagued schizophrenic." Besides, "The cultural onanism of movies-on-demand-by-fiber-optic-wire may be personally satisfying, but it does nothing for community."

The Verdict: Black or White Riots?

That fall, the president feared another racial booby trap as the O. J. Simpson trial ended after 126 witnesses and 153 days of testimony. Defense lawyers exploited the racist statements of one investigator, Mark Fuhrman, to dismiss DNA evidence showing the defendant's blood mixed with the victims. Suddenly, the police and the justice system were on trial. Simpson pretended his hand could not fit into the expensive, blood-soaked leather glove found at his home. His charismatic attorney, Johnnie Cochran, pronounced: "If it doesn't fit, you must acquit."

Clinton joked before the verdict was announced: "are we going to have black or white riots today?" He feared black riots upon an O. J. conviction and angry white male backlash at the polls if O. J. went free. One hundred mounted police officers stood by the courthouse.

On October 3, as many as 150 million people watched the verdict announced on television. This communal experience of gathering to watch a big moment on the small screen would become increasingly rare with growing Internet use and, later, smartphone penetration. When Simpson was acquitted, millions of blacks shouted and high-fived; most whites moaned and sulked. Clinton blurted out, "Shit."

Once again, apparent winners and losers both walked away disillusioned. Most whites saw Nicole Brown Simpson as the victim of domestic abuse and most blacks saw Simpson—and themselves—as victims of racism. One juror, a former Black Panther, gave Simpson a black power salute. "Were we watching the same trial?" *Newsweek* wondered.

Black wariness was pervasive. Eighty percent of African Americans mistrusted the criminal justice system. Many blacks believed rumors about Church's Fried Chicken being a KKK front, the CIA spreading AIDS as a "conspiracy to kill black folk," and the government encouraging drug abuse to subdue black youth. In 1992, Snapple, a new natural juice and ice tea company, denied that the ship on its label was a slave ship or that the "k" on the label signifying it was kosher really honored Klan owners. The company's founders, Hyman Golden, Leonard Marsh, and Arnold Greenberg, responded: "How could three Jewish boys from Brooklyn support the Ku Klux Klan?"

The ongoing fights about affirmative action, welfare reform, and the middle-class inability to make ends meet intensified the white backlash against what appeared to be another expression of minority entitlement. One white Midwestern liberal grumbled, "Why is the problem always the job or the schools or the police? Why is the problem never because 'one of us' did something wrong?" Wags asked: "Would it have been funny if O. J. was convicted?" The response: "Yeah, it would have been a riot!" This white resentment offended many blacks.

As Americans raided the thesaurus to emphasize just how divided, polarized, and disconnected they were, millions were dreaming of a black man as what *The New York Times Book Review* called the "great white (or, even better, black) hope. . . . Eisenhower reborn," the nonpartisan dream candidate to unite America. That autumn, Colin Powell's up-by-your-bootstraps memoir, *My American Journey,* became a best seller amid a triumphal book tour. Dropping bromides more rapidly than his subordinates launched cruise missiles on Saddam's Iraq, Powell pronounced: "We have to start thinking of America as a family. We have to stop screeching at each other."

Crime and the African American Values Revolution

Equally surprising, the crime debate was shifting. Many blacks and liberals still believed economic distress and racism triggered criminal behavior. "Broke niggas make the best crooks," the hot hip-hop duo Luniz rapped on their 1995 debut album, reflecting Great Society assumptions, liberal white guilt, and the civil rights establishment's politically correct line. In 1994, Cornel West wrote in *Race Matters* that black conservatives unfairly overlooked black youths' being "isolated from the labor market, marginalized by decrepit urban schools, devalued by alienating ideals of Euro-American beauty, and targeted by an unprecedented drug invasion."

Gradually, community activists were heeding Clinton's advice to be self-critical. Jesse Jackson called fighting gang violence "the new frontier of the civil rights struggle." A liberal African American columnist, Cynthia Tucker, detested the 1990s' ghettos more than the 1950s' color lines. She wrote: "stereotypes don't kill. They don't present nearly the threat to black Americans that black criminals do."

Blacks suffered most from black criminals. More than half of minority children felt unsafe in their own neighborhoods after dark, only 16 percent of white children did. Racism and economic privation alone did not explain this scourge; family breakdown and moral anarchy, with kids raising kids, fathers abandoning children, and rampant drug abuse fueled a new, violent nihilism. "America is losing the family," Princeton professor John J. Dilulio Jr. warned.

Young, poor, undereducated, underparented black men intertwined criminality with masculinity, mocking middle-class values and education as weak, servile, and effeminate. University of Pennsylvania professor Elijah Anderson repudiated this "oppositional culture" expressed in the "Code of the Streets." Stanley Crouch, winner of a 1993 MacArthur Foundation "genius" award, endorsed a war on gangs with lengthy prison sentences to break the "criminal occupation of our cities." In his 1995 book, *The All-American Skin Game, or, The Decoy of Race,* Crouch denounced "the black media" and "irresponsible intellectuals," for "rabble rousing" while defending "Afro-fascist rap groups" whose "Thug rappers chant out the most trivial reasons imaginable for committing acts of violence in order to 'get some respect.'" Crouch's prescription was Western civ: "The values of civilized behavior must be reestablished and defined as fundamentals beyond race."

This growing African American values revolution—changes to make from the inside out—fused with the traditional rage toward America—changes required from the outside in—during the "Million Man March" on Washington, D.C. Coincidentally, it occurred two weeks after the Simpson verdict. Louis Farrakhan, the Nation of Islam's demagogic preacher, wanted to prove that African American men were not "criminals and druggies and dropouts." He would honor them as "men with jobs and families and communities" while challenging them to meet "their responsibilities."

Hundreds of thousands marched. Farrakhan thundered, "every time we drive by shoot, every time we carjack, every time we use foul, filthy language, every time we produce culturally degenerate films and tapes, putting a string in our women's backside and parading them before the world, every time we do things like this we are feeding the degenerate mind of white supremacy." Farrakhan sent the men home to start implementing the program. "This is powerful, black men together, and I love it," said one marcher.

Clinton's Big Picture Presidency

President Clinton was on his own journey in 1995, taking responsibility after wallowing. The painful repudiation of November 1994, followed by the partial eclipse in January, had sent the bookish president to the library shelves, scouring presidential biographies. He concluded that his most successful predecessors concentrated on the "big picture" and "underlying values." He had neglected to help voters see the larger framework. Abraham Lincoln "was always explaining the times people were living in and putting the big issues in terms of choices that had to be made," Clinton explained. Clinton also felt betrayed by the far left and the far right; the decadent, violent, nihilistic rappers; and the depraved, violent, nihilistic militias. The harshness of both extremes reinforced his faith in himself and his reasonableness.

In late July, Clinton displayed his growing boldness by endorsing affirmative action after a five-month-long review process. Many liberals had feared that the triangulating president would abandon the controversial program to woo the center and the Angry White Male. Instead, Clinton coyly pronounced "Mend it, don't end it" and kept the status quo. He claimed to have found the "middle ground," by opposing quotas, reverse discrimination, hiring the blatantly unqualified, and keeping programs in perpetuity. But beyond those tweaks, he situated his support for the program as the search for "common ground as we move toward the twenty-first century." His vision of modern America ensured equality, celebrated diversity, reaffirmed values, reinforced community, and tackled the real economic source of middle-class anxiety. He refused to be distracted by incendiary, race-oriented sideshows.

In September, Clinton auditioned his new sweeping, centrist approach nationwide. In Denver, he compared this "period of change" with the "profound" upheavals of "one hundred years ago when we became an industrial and urbanized society, moving out of a rural agricultural society." Globalization, the information-technology nexus, the post–Cold War chaos, raised fundamental questions:

"How can we change and do what we need to do and be true to our basic values: freedom and responsibility, work and family and community, the obligation to find common ground and to work together . . . ?"

Clinton sought "to get people to get out of their funk" about all the changes. "What makes people insecure is when they feel like they're lost in the funhouse," fearful of losing their "footing at any time." Steadiness would come from a growing economy and a vibrant community developing a web of obligations and reciprocal benefits. Although Clinton frequently filled out the cultural scorecard, boasting about adoptions going up or teen pregnancies going down, his cultural vision went beyond "a whole lot of persons doing the same bad thing" (or good thing). He wanted to shore up the foundations of American ideology and identity.

Clinton would continue invoking "Oklahoma City" to attack Republican divisiveness while appearing nonpartisan and statesmanlike. He celebrated American values embodied by the heroism of Captain Scott O'Grady, an air force pilot shot down while enforcing NATO's no-fly zone over Bosnia. O'Grady survived in hostile territory thanks to his wits, his twenty-nine-pound survival kit, and helpings of trees, plants, and ants. Clinton preached that Oklahoma City softened Americans. Then, when "Captain O'Grady survived those six days in Bosnia and came home, it gave a little lift back to our country, and it made us think about all the things we're proud of about America."

An emboldened Clinton addressed America's race problems following the O. J. Simpson acquittal. As Farrakhan's "million men" marched on October 16, Clinton confronted the "simple truth" that "White Americans and black Americans often see the same world in drastically different ways." Now the Lincolnesque truth-teller, he warned, "something is terribly wrong . . . when there are more African American men in our correction system than in our colleges." Acknowledging white racism and black poverty, he addressed "white fear," too. Clinton hoped that blacks and whites together could tackle their common challenges of "Crime, drugs, domestic abuse and teen pregnancy." Trying to co-opt Farrakhan's march, the president said it proved that "our entire country is reasserting our commitment to the bedrock values that made our country great and that make life worth living." Similarly, Clinton approached the budget showdown more holistically. He insisted: "this is not about money; it's about values."

Political Magazines: Glitzy Democrats
and Wonky Republicans

That September two political magazines debuted that would further shape the discussion. *George* and *The Weekly Standard* each followed different aspects of Reaganism, seeking to cure what ailed their respective parties. *George* tried sprinkling some of the magic celebrity pixie dust Reagan generated so naturally over the earnest, sourpuss Democrats—despite being avowedly nonpartisan. The *Standard* continued Reagan's projects of mainstreaming conservative discourse and institutionalizing a right-wing infrastructure.

Named after the first president and founded by the son of another, John Kennedy Jr., *George* lamented politics' commodification, while—Nineties' style—exploiting it, too. After *People* labeled him "The Sexiest Man Alive," after *The New York Post* publicized his bar exam travails with the headline "The Hunk Flunks," Kennedy was finally embracing his celebrity. Infuriated by the spectacle of Madonna offering political commentary and the supermodel Cindy Crawford posing for the first cover dressed like George Washington but with an exposed belly, Judith Shulevitz in *The New Republic* declared the magazine "an affront to everybody who wants to believe that politics, no matter how empty, no matter how corrupt, can still change the way we live our lives."

The Weekly Standard was more wonky, less glitzy. "We're somewhat self-consciously trying to be the voice of the new conservative era," said Fred Barnes, one of the trio of founders along with John Podhoretz and Bill Kristol. The *Standard*'s advertising declared: "Just when the liberals thought things couldn't get any worse . . . now it's our turn!" Lighter, hipper, and suppler than *National Review,* the *Standard* offered the expected focus on Gingrich, then added unexpected touches. Kristol dreamed of "President Powell." Christopher Caldwell skewered *Sports Illustrated* for being politically correct. David Brooks mocked PC sex manuals and left-wing magazine ads offering "exhaustive advice on performing sex acts in high-minded ways." The cultural critiques reinforced Gingrich's drive to "reassert and renew American civilization."

Bankrolled by the conservative media magnate Rupert Murdoch, *The Weekly Standard* was part of a broader effort to expand on the impressive conservative infrastructure the Reagan Revolution had pioneered. Conservative think tanks, lobbying groups, foundations, 501 (c) (3) organizations—named for their tax status allowing them to champion ideas without endorsing specific candidates—proliferated. Conservative publishers like Regnery and corporate giants like Murdoch's HarperCollins published big books aspiring to be the Revolution's Bible, including Dick Armey's exhaustively titled *The Freedom*

Revolution: The New Republican House Majority Leader Tells Why Big Government Failed, Why Freedom Works, and How We Will Rebuild America and Newt Gingrich's *To Renew America,* with its first printing of 750,000 copies. The new revolving door of print and television journalism helped people like Barnes, a regular on television's weekly, peppery panel, *The McLaughlin Group,* reach millions of people and earn millions of dollars. And, starting in October 1996, Murdoch would boost conservatives and polarize the television news world with the advent of the Fox News Channel. Ultimately, however, while dreaming of Reagan, modern Republicans were stuck with Gingrich.

November 1995: *Shalom Chaver*—And a Budget Showdown

All this set the scene for November 1995, one of those action-packed months that culminated the transformation that began with the Oklahoma City bombing. Once again, Clinton found himself reacting to events—but boosting his standing by acting effectively and with more gravitas. In early November, a young Israeli assassinated Prime Minister Yitzhak Rabin. Clinton, the young draft-evading Baby Boomer, and Rabin, the flinty Israeli war veteran, had become close. Clinton's heartfelt eulogy with the phrase "*Shalom Chaver,*" literally "Good-bye friend," but also "Peace my comrade," moved millions.

A little more than two weeks after the Rabin trauma, Clinton's emissary to the troubled lands of the former Yugoslavia, Richard Holbrooke, achieved the seemingly impossible. Holbrooke brokered the Dayton Accords ending the Bosnian War. When Clinton ended the month visiting a Northern Ireland emerging from the troubles, he seemed a miracle man.

Clinton's success abroad drove Newt Gingrich to distraction at home. With Clinton insisting on more limited budget cuts, the Republicans went nuclear. The result was a government shutdown and the furloughing of eight hundred thousand workers. Liberal Democrats like Secretary of Labor Robert Reich felt "Bill already gave the store away last June when he agreed to balance the budget." But Chief of Staff Leon Panetta and other staffers were thrilled when, in yet another mid-October marathon session with the Republicans demanding more and more budget cuts, the president finally said, "I just can't do this." Clinton admitted: "I know it may cost me the election. But I'm not going to do this." Panetta, thought, "He *does* get it! There is a point at which that line has to be drawn." Clinton told the Republicans: "If you want your budget, you'll have to get someone else to sit in this chair."

Assuming the people would blame Clinton, Gingrich overshot. Shortly after the Rabin funeral, Gingrich suggested the government shutdown resulted because the president refused to negotiate during the long flights on *Air Force One* to and from Israel. Moreover, Gingrich resented sitting in the back of the plane, and disembarking out the back door. "This is petty, but I think it is human," Gingrich said, being far too candid.

The White House released photos showing the president interacting warmly with the Speaker and Gingrich's wife, Marianne. Clinton's aides explained they all returned from Israel exhausted after 4:00 a.m. and thought Gingrich would be happier walking down the steps closer to his own vehicle. *The New York Daily News* ran one of those devastating headlines that derails political careers. The tabloid's entire front cover pictured a crying, fat Newt under the bold headline "Cry Baby" followed by "Newt's Tantrum: He Closed Down the Government Because Clinton Made Him Sit at Back of Plane."

The resulting backlash, Republican retreat, and Democratic resurgence boosted Clinton, placing him in a surprisingly stable position while contemplating his reelection campaign in 1996. By the end of 1995, more than half of Americans polled approved of Clinton's performance, the highest since February 1994. Only 29 percent supported Gingrich. The public now trusted—or distrusted—Republicans and Democrats about roughly equally to balance the budget, while Congress's reputation had dropped again to about one quarter of the nation satisfied.

In 1995, Americans were looking for leadership. Hollywood conjured up a perfect president, Michael Douglas, starring in Aaron Sorkin's *The American President*. Mel Gibson offered a grittier, bloodier hero in *Braveheart,* while Tom Hanks celebrated clean-cut, all-American ingenuity in the gripping astronaut rescue movie, *Apollo 13*. The best-selling, enthusiastically reviewed *Lincoln,* by the Harvard historian David Herbert Donald, introduced a liquid Lincoln, pragmatic, political, with a surprising fatalism avowing "my policy is to have no policy." Clinton—who called *Lincoln* one of his favorite books—frequently demonstrated a passivity and fluidity that were more frustrating than Lincolnesque. He never effectively managed the O. J. Simpson spectacle, despite his aspirations to transform race relations. But when attacked, a different, sharper Clinton emerged, demonstrating the kind of grit and "enormous capacity for growth" Donald's Lincoln had, too. When targeting militiamen, Rush Limbaugh, and Newt Gingrich, Clinton was focused, shrewd, passionate, effective. He fed off conflict and his enemies, seeking to seduce, ready to conquer. Unfortunately, such sharp-elbowed leadership caused collateral damage, disillusionment with politics and politicians.

Bill Clinton was now ready for a revival. This intellectual president was using his Emotional Intelligence, a concept popularized in Daniel Goleman's best seller of the same name that year. And as Dick Morris poll-tested values propositions and Band-Aid solutions, Clinton returned to his DLC past and his core mission—renewing Americans' faith in themselves and their country. At Georgetown, Clinton's Western Civilization professor Carroll Quigley taught that the West's "future preference," the belief that "the future can be better than the past, and each individual has a personal, moral obligation to make it so," was a perpetually renewable source of American energy, inspiration, and focus. At his best, his core values, his sense of mission, a common ground pitched to the middle class, rooted the president, making him successful and popular, especially against foils like Newt Gingrich and Bob Dole.

7

1996: Alphabet City, New York
"Take Me or Leave Me"

Cultural Salvoes from Blue America

*The era of big government is over. But we cannot go back to the time
when our citizens were left to fend for themselves.*
          —BILL CLINTON, STATE OF THE UNION ADDRESS,
                                    JANUARY 23, 1996

Shortly after three o'clock in the morning of January 25, 1996, Jonathan
Larson, a thirty-five-year-old composer excited that previews were beginning for his first big New York musical that night, walked into his bite-sized,
unheated, West Village walk-up. Even with a roommate, he could barely afford the
rent. Born in White Plains, distinctive-looking with a Kramer-from-*Seinfeld*
Brillo-head of hair but the deep-set, soulful eyes of a creative Einstein, Larson
had bounced around the New York art scene since 1982. He had enough successes to keep dreaming but not enough to stop waiting tables until recently.

Larson started boiling water for tea and collapsed. His roommate found him,
moments later, dead of an aortic aneurysm. That night, the New York Theatre
Workshop canceled the preview. Instead, cast members sang through the show
for Larson's friends and relatives. By the second act, the actors had returned to
their usual places and were mounting the full production, through their tears.
When they finished, with everyone crying and cheering and shouting and hugging, someone called out "Thank you, Jonathan Larson." The resulting volcanic
roar embodied Larson's one-line summary of his modern opera. "*Rent*," he said,
"is about a community celebrating life, in the face of death and AIDS, at the
turn of the century."

Set in Alphabet City, *Rent*'s New York was not the Big Apple of Rudy
Giuliani's conservative, corporate, and working-class voters. It was a New York
of abandoned tenements not gleaming office towers, of seekers and losers not

Masters of the Universe. Larson's *La Bohème* update, what *Time* punnily called "Lower East Side Story," was a Gen X artist's manifesto. It had to be set in the horizontal, chaotic, edgy New York of poverty and crime, of AIDS and drug abuse, of gays and transvestites, of greedy landlords and grifting tenants, of premature death and thwarted creativity, of talented young people adrift, unmoored, deeply dissatisfied, destabilized by freedom.

Rent turned their anger, alienation, otherness, and dread into an exuberant celebration of freedom, iconoclasm, indulgence, bohemia, with nothing wholesome in sight. As Marx and Engels predicted, all that is holy seemed to have been profaned, yet somehow consecrated by Larson. Glamorizing phenomena traditional Americans often abhorred, Larson turned the bearded, tattooed, pierced, hedonistic, promiscuous, troubled, sometimes diseased and sometimes dying but always marginal losers of the darker, nontouristy New York into noble warriors fighting for art and authenticity in a cynical, consumerist society.

The S&M dancers, drag queens, performance artists, and the simulated sex onstage contrasted with the Disneyfied Broadway of tired reruns and spectacles with massive helicopters re-creating the American evacuation in *Miss Saigon* or chandeliers plummeting from the ceiling in *The Phantom of the Opera*. Larson's "La Vie Bohème" became the national anthem of the Republic of Everything, as the cast sang: "To loving tension, no pension. . . . To starving for attention, hating convention." In its twelve-year, 5,123-performance run, *Rent* attracted Americans from all regions and all ideologies. It became one of many salvoes from Blue America that through popular culture helped mainstream behaviors and ideas America's "silent majority" once rejected.

Rent's cast sang "Seasons of Love" at the 1996 Democratic National Convention, as the song became a generational anthem and a commencement ceremony standard. In America's increasingly borderless popular culture, this led to the anomaly of angelic elementary and junior high school children nationwide, surrounded and videotaped by their loving parents and grandparents at a critical rite of passage, belting out a song originally sung by characters playing gays, transvestites, heroin addicts, and AIDS patients. Just as the mass embrace of the Oklahoma City bombing victims brought a bastion of Red America into every American heart, popular cultural phenomena like "Seasons of Love" and *Rent* itself brought heralds of Blue America into every American home. This cultural convergence helped Bill Clinton function as a national leader, not just as chairman of Blue America Inc.

Implicit in Clinton's reelection narrative was a story of change, of rediscovering the center. In truth, his redemption paralleled *Jerry Maguire*'s. In that 1996

Hollywood morality tale of a wayward sports agent, Tom Cruise's character wins by remembering his original, idealistic mission, although on some levels he remains the same callow charmer he always was. Bill Clinton won reelection by returning to his initial vision of finding a post-1960s', post-1980s' synthesis. This presidential mission entailed simultaneously embracing yet resisting the new cultural chaos Larson captured, perpetuated, and validated in *Rent*. Clinton as Good Father was not just Republicanism-lite. His paternalistic maternalism was more profound yet also an awkward fit for him personally as he remained the same magical, mercurial, master of disaster he always was, as adept at stumbling into jams as he was at escaping from them.

The Three Ps Reduce Crime

New Yorkers could laugh during *Rent* in 1996 because the grittiness it romanticized was becoming detoxified. Since Rudy Giuliani's mayoral election, the job rolls had grown by 110,000. The welfare rolls had dropped by 220,000. Tourists were returning, as was the World Series crown. The Yankees won the world championship in 1996, for the first time since 1978, then three times in a row from 1998 to 2000, led by 1996's classy Rookie of the Year, "Captain Clutch," Derek Jeter.

Miraculously, major crimes dropped 39 percent in three years, thanks to Mayor Giuliani and his police commissioner Bill Bratton's three Ps of partnership, problem-solving, and prevention. In 1982, the criminologists James Q. Wilson and George Kelling had popularized the "broken windows" theory, warning that minor vandalism encouraged major disorder. New York's once overwhelmed cops began targeting "quality of life" gateway offenses such as subway turnstile jumping and graffiting. With "community policing" as pioneered by Charleston police chief Reuben Greenberg in South Carolina, police partnered with locals to solve underlying problems like drug abuse and school truancy. The computerized statistics system, CompStat, helped pinpoint criminal outbreaks while holding police commanders accountable in monthly, three-hour sessions.

Most academics, who blamed crime on society's ills, scoffed. "The police do not prevent crime," leading criminologists insisted. Others feared a cowboy mentality, as inquiries to New York's Civilian Complaint Review Board jumped 30 percent. Yet more than a third of major police departments adopted CompStat's entrepreneurial, proactive approach, with resulting crime drops.

Since the 1980s, living as he did in a crime-infested Little Rock, Bill Clinton had recognized the Great American Crime Wave as endangering national mo-rale and liberal credibility. Championing the crime bill, decentralizing govern-ment, emphasizing community, responsibility, and quality of life, all reinforced New York's crime-fighting strategy. The drop in teen drug use and the rise in the prison population helped, too. Accepting the 1996 nomination, Clinton vowed, "We cannot rest until crime is a shocking exception to our daily lives, not news as usual."

A Culture of Kitsch and Irony

Despite the media attention gays and other edgier groups commanded, main-stream culture was kitschier, sappier, and safer than *Rent*'s success suggested. In August, more than fifty thousand gyrating fans in Yankee Stadium set a world record for mass dancing to the top dance craze—and 1996's number one song—the "Macarena." The year's number two song teamed the popular diva Mariah Carey with the edgy black R&B group "Boyz II Men" in "One Sweet Day," mourning loved ones lost to AIDS. The number three song, "Because You Loved Me," became an instant classic, as Céline Dion belted out: "You were my strength when I was weak . . . You saw the best there was in me."

Goofy antics, saccharine odes, even MasterCard's clever, conflicted slogan, "There are some things money can't buy; for everything else there's MasterCard," offered fleeting escapes from Americans' constant stress. Harvard's Juliet Schor noted that since the 1970s, Americans were working more—an additional month annually—spending more, but enjoying less with less free time. The comic strip *Dilbert* satirized the silly rituals many American workers took for granted, as they and their "cow-orkers" sacrificed their "induhviduality," indig-nity by indignity. Dilbert's Pointy Haired Boss—PHB—was nameless, inten-sifying Dilbert's terror, and heightening PHB's universality.

Despite Scott Adams's delightfully subversive approach to American corpo-rate culture, the very managers the strip targeted often tamed *Dilbert*. In an ironic culture happy to laugh at itself, the strip served as a self-satirizing safety valve for office tensions. And in a consumerist culture that commodified com-pulsively, Dilbert coffee cups, calendars, hats, key chains, T-shirts followed, as did the "Dilberito," a vegan microwave burrito in three flavors.

As a software engineer, the fictional Dilbert witnessed the real changes sweeping the business world. The Steve Jobs–Bill Gates PC revolution freed many Americans from lumbering dinosaur corporations. With the 1920s' prom-ise of a chicken in every pot updated to a computer on every desktop and Internet access in every home, with flextime the rage, many individuals could start working at home, customizing work hours, or start up independently.

Soccer Moms, Smothering Parenting, and the Broken Windows Theory of Politicking

This greater autonomy particularly benefited many American women, more than 70 percent of whom now worked outside the home. These "Soccer Moms," as Clinton's people called them, still managed most of the child-rearing, domestic work, and kid-chauffeuring duties. Applying his own Broken Windows Theory of Politicking, Clinton used small-scale, values-filled initiatives they appreciated to recapture the middle. His communications adviser Don Baer said, "V-chips, computers in classrooms, school uniforms. They are all about giving her control over the lives of her children." Dick Morris explained that "with each of these proposals, Clinton delivered a message of relevance to the lives of the people that had not really been offered in more than a decade."

Clinton's paternalistic maternalism proved popular because, despite Americans' historic distrust of big government, many modern parents needed support, even from the Nanny State. More parents were spending more time working. Nearly 1 million couples divorced annually. Yet experts continued to confirm that "parents matter," that as Cornell's Urie Bronfenbrenner taught, the family is the "most powerful, the most humane, and by far the most economical system known for building competence and character." Politically, interest in children was the highest pollsters had seen in two decades, with "family" topping the list of the most important issue in people's lives.

Often mistrusting their instincts, used to being trained, millions devoured all kinds of parenting guidebooks. The "pregnancy bible," *What to Expect When You're Expecting*, sold 34 million copies. *Parents* magazine sold 2.2 million copies a month; its rival *Parenting* sold 2.1 million.

In this egotistical age, many parents, seeing themselves and their families as the center of the universe, monumentalized every step in their children's lives. The hype began with the first ultrasound that became so fashionable to wave around. In 1991, rather than hiding Demi Moore's advanced pregnancy, as *Vanity Fair*'s assignment editors advised, Annie Leibovitz photographed the actress, naked, discretely obscuring her breasts, for what became a sensational cover. All this "love for the ones we bring to term," surprised the feminist writer Naomi Wolf. "Mozart for your belly; framed sonogram photos; home fetal-heartbeat stethoscopes" contradicted years of justifying abortions by insisting "the fetus isn't a person." Wolf infuriated many pro-choice comrades by proposing more humility regarding pro-life arguments.

Once born, many children experienced a befuddling mix of smothering mothering and permissive parenting. A new intimate yet indulgent generation arose, that knew not the enforced distance and rigid discipline of Dr. Spock. These helicopter parents-to-be drove the kids around in cars proclaiming "Baby on Board." They played Baby Einstein videos to fast-track their kids to Harvard—before the company had to offer customer refunds to compensate for its sweeping, unsubstantiated educational claims. And many followed the advice of "attachment parenting" champ William Sears, who encouraged "baby wearing," "marsupial mothering," prolonged breast-feeding, and "family beds," saying "welcoming your baby into your bed is just another part of a parenting style of trust and openness."

Obsessive about health and safety issues, these parents applauded like-minded leaders. On December 26, 1995, Maine became the forty-ninth state to mandate seat belt use, at least in the front seat—New Hampshire resisted. Clinton made sure to "urge all Americans" to buckle "every child in an approved restraint," while supporting the federal law going into effect in 1997, requiring air bags in all cars. "Bill Clinton is a master at playing to people's fear of losing control," *Time* marveled.

As kids matured, their parents spent hours chauffeuring them to playdates and tightly scheduled, carefully selected, skill-building activities. In adolescence, elite parents put tremendous pressure on children to perform and get admitted to college, countering sagging scores nationwide. As cell phones proliferated, these "electronic umbilical cords" kept youngsters feeling protected yet scrutinized.

The culture of indulgence clashed with the culture of discipline, as parents often lacked the backbone to give their children the necessary behavioral constraints. Many Baby Boomer parents, moralistic about helmets, seat belts, and peanut butter in classrooms (fearing allergies), were surprisingly lax about drinking, drug use, and premarital sex in adolescence. Protective of their children's self-esteem, conflict-averse, confused about the lines between right and wrong, uncomfortable with authority, these early smotherers often ended up being parental pushovers.

The Single Parent/Stable Home Divide

The chaos of parents' lives often also swept up the kids. The number of children living in single-parent homes would go from 15.9 million in 1990 to 19.2

million in 2000, constituting 28 percent of American children—11 percent with never-married parents, 15.6 percent with divorced parents, 1.2 percent with widowed ones. No particular family constellation guaranteed any particular outcome. Yet the new line dividing successful from unsuccessful Americans was not race but being born into a tight-knit, values-centered, two-parent family or into underparented bedlam. Intact families were starting to correlate with class, education, and income. Poor families were twice as likely to break up. Children of single parents were two to three times as likely to experience emotional or behavioral problems. The divorce rate for college graduates was dropping to 16 percent for those who married between 1990 and 1994.

A poor white class emerged that was as embedded in dysfunction as the black underclass—and whose young admired that nihilistic culture through rap music. In 1999, 22 percent of white births would be to single women. More than two-thirds of single mothers earned less than $20,000 annually. Of white children born in 1980, less than a third would live with both parents by the time they were 18; by contrast, 81 percent of kids in the 1950s lived with both parents. "Unless these exploding social pathologies are reversed," the former Reagan administration official and best-selling author of cultural jeremiads, William J. Bennett, warned, "they will lead to the decline and perhaps even the fall of the American republic."

While Bill Clinton overcame fatherlessness, with some surviving scars, Marshall Mathers built his career by wallowing in the resulting anguish, alienation, and dysfunction. In 1996, the rapper released his first album, *Infinite,* under his stage name Eminem. Limited sales and a resulting suicide attempt led him to develop his angry, abusive, violent, pill-popping, foul-mouthed, itinerant, and extraordinarily popular Slim Shady persona. Eminem would voice the frustrations of America's white, fatherless, walking wounded. His breakthrough *Slim Shady EP* debuted a song about a father telling his infant daughter he murdered his wife: "There goes Mama, splashing in the water / No more fighting with Dad, no more restraining order." By 1999, Eminem would be his generation's hot white rapper.

Opposing this cultural pollution, the National Fatherhood Initiative began in 1994 to fight the record number of "father-absent" homes that produce disproportionate rates of social and psychological disruption. It also targeted pop culture's "Doofus Dad" stereotype, epitomized by Homer Simpson, Tim Allen's character in *Home Improvement,* and Ray Romano's in *Everybody Loves Raymond.* By 1996, academics like Alan J. Hawkins and David C. Dollahite, tentatively, bravely, started proving that fathers were important emotionally, morally, and ideologically, not just economically. This caring "Generative Fathering" transcended "the imposed identification of fathers as primarily absent, abusive, deadbeat, deficient, or unnecessary." This fatherhood revival reflected what Tom Wolfe called "the great relearning," the rediscovery of America's once-common sense.

Girl Power: What I Really, Really Want

Meanwhile, many mothers and wives sought to preserve the equality feminism helped them achieve, without accepting the sameness some feminists sought to impose. John Gray's *Men Are from Mars, Women Are from Venus* (1992), sold more than 50 million copies by affirming the kinds of gender differences that placed Deborah Tannen's 1990 book *You Just Don't Understand: Women and Men in Conversation,* on *The New York Times* best-seller list for four years. *Reviving Ophelia: Saving the Selves of Adolescent Girls,* Mary Pipher's 1994 book about raising adolescent girls in a lookist, "girl-poisoning culture" to retain their preteen "courage, competency, and irreverence," started a three-year run on best-seller lists in 1996. That year, Michael Gurian's *The Wonder of Boys: What Parents, Mentors and Educators Can Do to Shape Boys into Exceptional Men* sold robustly, warning about "enmeshing male development with a female culture in transition."

Modern American women felt pulled in multiple directions. One of the decade's blockbuster books, selling fifty thousand copies a month in 1996, *The Rules: Time-Tested Secrets for Capturing the Heart of Mr. Right,* infuriated feminists but thrilled many young, single women with its traditional message. Ellen Fein and Sherrie Schneider offered thirty-five very coquettish rules, 1950s style, including, "Don't Talk to a Man First (and Don't Ask Him to Dance)."

A British novel that year, *Bridget Jones's Diary,* would ultimately sell 15 million copies worldwide by encouraging the seductive aggressiveness *The Rules* discouraged. The fictional diary, released in America in 1998, tracked a single woman who understands that "romance does not work anyway. Look at [the] royal family. Look at Mum and Dad." No one's reliable, Jones feared. "It's the three-minute culture. It's a global attention-span deficit."

In 1997, a sleeker, sexier, neurotic woman would start captivating as many as 18 million TV viewers weekly, for the next five years. Calista Flockhart played Ally McBeal, a Boston lawyer singing the song of the self-absorbed. When her romantic rival asks, "Ally, what makes your problems so much bigger than everybody else's," McBeal answers simply, grandiosely, deliciously, "They're mine."

Eve Ensler's conversation-stopping, taboo-breaking *Vagina Monologues* debuted in New York in 1996 raging against many of these culturally imposed neuroses. The show recruited celebrities from Yoko Ono to Angelina Jolie for blunt, intimate riffs about the traditional slap at first menstruation, an OB/GYN exam's unnecessary indignities, embarrassment about body parts and functions. Less nobly, but more popularly, the British pop group Spice Girls echoed this "Girl Power" call. The music video of their breakthrough hit had them overrunning a stuffy hotel and shaking up the establishment. They—and millions worldwide—half sang, half chanted, "Yo, I'll tell you what I want, what I really, really want."

It Takes a Village to Reframe Hillary

In the White House, Hillary Clinton questioned what she, the American people, and reporters really, really wanted of her position. Following 1994's "Angry White Man's" revolt, Mrs. Clinton concluded: "I'm the projection for many of those wounded men. I'm the boss they never wanted to have." Fourteen years later, Fox News would confirm her fears with an ugly "expert's" report claiming that when male voters hear Hillary Clinton's "nagging voice," they hear "Take out the garbage." She resented reporters as fellow Adversarials who lived modern lifestyles yet tortured her for living hers authentically. "It's the honesty of their partnership that's driving them nuts and making her a target," the political scientist Diane Blair noted after chatting with her friend. But, Blair noted, "On her deathbed she wants to be able to say she was true to herself and is not going to do phoney makeovers to please others."

Hillary Clinton was not just what Blair called "a pioneer in an anachronistic role." She also was the failed health care czarina who essentially had been fired by her husband. She was the working lawyer enmeshed in Whitewater scandals. And she was the intimidating White House enforcer. During the White House travel office debacle, the presidential aide David Watkins wrote there would be "hell to pay" if he "failed to take swift and decisive action in conformity with the First Lady's wishes." By August 1995, with a favorability rating of only 31 percent making her the most unpopular First Lady in modern history, she needed another makeover, despite her denials.

Following the 1994 election debacle, Hillary and Bill Clinton hosted New Age gurus at Camp David, seeking solace. New Agers encouraged inner healing by mixing a Sixties' sensibility with earlier American fusions of positive thinking, pragmatism, individualism, and spirituality. These celebrity shamans served spiritual fast food promising success, happiness, and meaning. Books like

James Redfield's *The Celestine Prophecy,* inviting individuals to embrace cosmic coincidences in their lives, sold 20 million copies. Healers like Deepak Chopra, boosting heightened consciousness and alternative medicine, became famous. And with 93 percent of Americans believing in angels, *Touched by an Angel* attracted 15 to 20 million TV viewers weekly, feeding mass fantasies of strangers approaching, saying, "I am an angel sent by God to tell you that He loves you."

Although the Clintons consulted with conventional religious advisers, they were sufficiently fluent in the therapeutic culture to accept New Age coaches. After Roger Clinton's drug arrest in 1984, the family had undergone counseling. Bill Clinton said it helped them understand the underlying pathologies triggering the addiction.

The Clintons' advisers included Anthony Robbins, a flamboyant "peak performance coach" who developed tips for success from his celebrity buddies, and Stephen Covey, whose 1989 book 7 *Habits of Highly Effective People,* fusing business literature with self-help, was on its way to selling more than 25 million copies. Hillary Clinton clicked with Jean Houston, who paired clients with mythical or historical role models through imagined interactions, and Mary Catherine Bateson, whose 1989 book *Composing a Life* viewed life as an improvisational art.

Houston saw Hillary Clinton as an epoch-making transition figure. Hillary-the-braniac, suddenly facing failure, appreciated Houston's analysis that the backlash reflected "fear of the 'rising feminine.'" Houston explained: "Everything is in dissolution, traveling from no longer thereness to not yet hereness." Realizing her potential as a change agent, the First Lady nevertheless disliked being a "full-time surrogate" with only "derivative" power, saying "that's not what I enjoy doing, what I want to do." She was a policy person.

Hillary Clinton rediscovered and refined her voice. She visited Southeast Asia with Chelsea, to great acclaim. In China she proclaimed: "human rights are women's rights and women's rights are human rights." And she started writing her manifesto, *It Takes a Village.*

Throughout 1995, Clinton threw herself into her writing project with the zeal of an undergraduate overcompensating for a dormant love life. By January 1996, she felt more settled. She planned an eleven-city launch for her book.

This notion that "It takes a village to raise a child" illustrated both Clintons' post-Sixties' synthesis. Hillary championed traditional values in a modern multicultural world. Building on her "politics of meaning," this time she earned respect and $1 million in royalties donated to children's charities. She endorsed traditional extended families and affordable day care, the mother-child bond and the Nanny State, while condemning the "mass culture that too often celebrates risky behaviors and distorts values." She wanted a "nation that doesn't just espouse family values but values families and children," sustained by overlapping commitments to the nuclear family, extended family, community, and the nation, with government help when necessary.

The occasionally prickly power-player of 1993 had become 1996's sage mom. This was Hillary the good, the devout Methodist, the faithful wife, the "authoritative" mother and crusader for children, the safest of First Lady projects. *It Takes a Village* marked a milestone in American cultural history as the leaders of the Sixties' elite that repudiated tradition rediscovered it. Hillary Clinton publicized studies showing that divorce harms kids, drugs are destructive, promiscuity is degrading, and "every child" needs an "intact, dependable family." While prescribing a government program for every problem and validating alternative families, she preached: "every society requires a critical mass of families that fit the traditional ideal."

The exhilaration of becoming a best-selling, sweaty-palms-and-elevated-heart-rate-inducing, known-by-your-first name celebrity, tempered the pain as the First Lady endured another public makeover. She had long advised political wives, "Don't ever lose your own identity in this process." In the White House, she said to Diane Blair, defiantly, "I know I should do more to suck up to the press . . . I know I should pretend not to have any opinions—but I'm just not going to. I'm used to winning and I intend to win on my own terms."

The love she received on tour reconfirmed what Hillary Clinton called the "disconnect between Washington and the rest of the nation." Yet Whitewater haunted her. In a cruel twist—or a fumbled manipulation—on January 5, 1996, as the tour began, the Clintons' secretary Carolyn Huber announced she had stumbled onto the Rose Law Firm billing records in the Clintons' "book room." Five investigative bodies had requested the records, which suddenly appeared two days after the statute of limitations expired. Bank regulators now could not sue the Rose Law Firm or any attorneys involved in Madison Guaranty's $60 million bankruptcy. The records showed more involvement in the bank's affairs than Mrs. Clinton remembered, billing sixty hours over fifteen months.

Almost daily, Hillary Clinton's book tour yielded distracting, demoralizing questions. *Newsweek*'s cover story promoting her book excerpts asked: "Saint or Sinner?" *The New York Times*'s conservative columnist William Safire called the First Lady "a congenital liar." Michael McCurry the White House spokesman said, "The President, if he were not the President, would have delivered a more forceful response to that on the bridge of Mr. Safire's nose." Clinton's muscular response was instinctive, touching, and popular. Most distressing, on January 19, the Whitewater special prosecutor Kenneth Starr, convinced that

Hillary Clinton was obstructing justice, issued the first subpoena ever in American history compelling a First Lady to testify in court.

Hillary Clinton started working on controlling her fury. On April 22, 1995, when Starr and his attorneys had deposed the Clintons privately, at the White House, she had greeted them coldly. Her husband had infuriated her by schmoozing them, giving them the usual Executive Mansion tour featuring the Lincoln Bedroom. Eventually, she calmed herself, but lost ten pounds in the week and a half before her testimony, "not a diet I would recommend," she said archly.

As she put on a mask with false bravado, telling reporters: "Cheerio! Off to the firing squad," her husband fumed: "Look what they were doing to Hillary." Clinton often "reacts violently when people criticize Hillary," their old friend Mickey Kantor has observed. "He literally gets red in the face." Clinton considered Whitewater "a perpetual diversion." He bridled under legal advice suggesting the Clintons cooperate and found it excruciating that his wife had to fight alone. "I'm tired of this limp-dick shit," the president cursed. "I want somebody to stand up to these people." Clinton's friend and chronicler, Taylor Branch, warned against this "dark mood," noting "your biggest weakness, is a tendency to lump 'the press' together with your political opponents." Rivals needed to be defeated; reporters had to be charmed.

Preparing the 1996 State of the Union address, one adviser, Paul Begala, urged Clinton to "defend the honor of the First Lady. . . . The Republicans are attacking her without compunction, in part because they know the Democrats are too chickenshit to retaliate. So it's left to the President," who should challenge "Republicans to come after him if they have a problem with his agenda," but "leave his wife alone." At the speech, Clinton, pausing to compose himself, would hail Hillary Clinton as a "wonderful wife, a magnificent mother and a great first lady," prompting a bipartisan standing ovation.

On January 26, 1996, the First Lady entered the court house grandly. The once-mousy hippie in the Clinton wedding photo now exuded a movie-star panache during one of her most humiliating moments. Camille Paglia dubbed Hillary Clinton "the drag queen of modern politics, a bewitching symbol of professional women's sometimes confused search for identity in this era of unlimited options."

When asked to describe Hillary Clinton in one word, the top responses were polarized: "strong," "intelligent," "dishonest," and a sexist term that the Pew survey people delicately said, "rhymes with rich." In 1996 exit polls, 47 percent of voters still disapproved of the First Lady. She no longer sat next to the president in meetings and avoided many strategy sessions. Privately, she still advised him. Publicly, Bill Clinton would run for reelection solo.

Bill Clinton As Good Father

That January, Bill Clinton experienced his own mood swings. As a policy wonk—Nineties-speak for intellectuals who speak bureaucratese fluently—Clinton enjoyed each State of the Union address, his adviser Bruce Reed recalls, as the chance to prepare "his blueprint for governing." On January 9, 1996, amid speech preparations, the Federal Appeals court decreed that President Clinton could not delay Paula Jones's sexual harassment lawsuit until his tenure ended. Yet another round of scandal generated more embarrassing headlines, more marathon legal meetings, more distractions.

The cliché that even paranoids have enemies applied to the Clintons. An intrusive, sensationalist press fed by right-wing partisans certainly harassed them. Neither as pure as they claimed, nor as guilty as their enemies believed, the Clintons were not bad people, just slobs, as Alice Roosevelt Longworth said of Warren G. Harding. Their ethical blind spots amid Arkansas's clubby political culture, their sense of entitlement, some sincere errors, a few minor misdeeds, and an instinct to lie when pressed made them vulnerable. Following the president's massive miscalculation in authorizing a special prosecutor, it all metastasized in the rancorous Nineties' media environment into cascading scandals that almost sank his presidency.

In his State of the Union, Clinton twice evoked America's "common ground" and mentioned "values" when discussing everything from the budget to Bosnia. Mastering his new role as Good Father, he repeatedly used the words "work" and "children" in this new "Age of Possibility." He tweaked Republican proposals and proposed reforms on the cheap, including increasing the minimum wage, modest health insurance adjustments, scholarships, and job training. He denounced teenage smoking, endorsed the V-chip parental control on television, and championed school uniforms. "At times it sounds as though Bill Clinton is running for the PTA, not president of the United States," Ronald Brownstein jibed in *The Los Angeles Times*.

This Democratic president backed Ronald Reagan's counterrevolution by declaring: "the era of big government is over." Positioning government as activist, centrist, and friendly not big, burdensome, and bureaucratic, Clinton added a critical phrase most overlooked: "But we cannot go back to the time when our citizens were left to fend for themselves."

One headline joked, it was a "Terrific Speech by Reagan, I Mean Clinton." "This is not much fun," one White House staffer grumbled as Republican budget cutting eviscerated Democratic programs with Clinton's acquiescence. "This is not what most of us came here to do."

The White House theme now was: "The era of big government is over; the era of taking responsibility to meet our challenges has begun." It was president as parenting-coach. Clinton and his aides wanted "to challenge communities and parents to find more ways to put values back at the core of what children learn in school and at home." Advisers like Bruce Reed and Gene Sperling urged parents: "Don't wait for the V-chip—turn off the TV right now. Help your kids with their homework, and if they don't have any, make sure they get some." They wanted to "Challenge the software industry to develop new educational software so the most exciting video game in America is learning, not Mortal Kombat." They proposed "a national mission to expect more of ourselves and one another."

A poor kid redeemed by education, Clinton was passionate about improving America's schools. In March, he and Gore flew to California to help install 6 million feet of computer cables into 3,000 schools. "Someday, your children will marvel at the idea there ever was a classroom without a computer," the president told students in Concord, California, enjoying this updated "old-fashioned barn-raising." "You can tell them you were a pioneer," he suggested, proclaiming: "We will make the best of this new technology together. Let the future begin."

"He's a much stronger figure than he was a year ago," said Eddie Mahe, a Republican consultant. "He stopped carrying on like some out-of-work hippie. The American people want a president, not a tennis mate." Clinton's favorability ratings were pushing toward 60 percent. The combined rates of unemployment and inflation were the lowest in twenty-seven years, helped by low interest rates. Democrats were awed by Clinton's comeback and appalled by his capitulation.

In this cynical age Clinton built his reputation on the debris of other pols who had preceded him. Like their president, Americans compartmentalized, applauding Clinton's centrism, forgiving his trespasses. The Clintonites' "internal mantra," "public values trump private character," floated on jaded assumptions that "everybody did it." When one June 1996 survey asked respondents to name the best aspect of Bill Clinton's character, the top response was that he did not have one. A Pew Research Center poll found that people described the president's personal image as: "Good, wishy-washy, okay, dishonest, liar, fair, trying, intelligent, slick, great, honest, crooked, leader, two-faced."

Clinton sensed Americans' ambivalence. Those concerns, combined with the lingering Whitewater–Paula Jones headaches and his self-righteous fury against Republicans, fed a desperation in his fund-raising. Clinton's people developed "Plan B" to use "soft money" the Democratic National Committee raised to run commercials in the spring, highlighting the president's stand on issues without explicitly appealing for his reelection.

In 1996, Clinton would attend more than 230 fund-raising events, which raised $119 million. What Senate investigators later called the Clinton "thirst for money" overrode traditional sensibilities, as the Clintons dangled the White House as a lure for the rich and generous. Beyond what the Senate report would call "this merchandising of the Presidency," the Democrats cast their fund-raising net so far it included suspicious Indonesian, Chinese, and Lebanese donors, leading to more character questions.

Ending Welfare As We Know It

Throughout the spring of 1996, Clinton struggled over welfare reform, an issue critical to Morris's poll-driven centrism and Clinton's political identity. The director of the domestic policy council, Bruce Reed, had taped a sign saying "End Welfare As We Know It" to his White House office wall. He, Al From, and other moderates feared that facing the voters without welfare reform would sap Clinton's credibility. Most Democratic congressional leaders, however, feared alienating African American voters. The Democrats' senior welfare expert, New York senator Daniel Patrick Moynihan, wanted reform but dismissed Clinton's populist approach as "boob bait for the bubbas."

Clinton made the conversation about America's economy and society more candid. Even liberal activists acknowledged the welfare system was broken, demoralizing recipients and feeding the problem of multigenerational behavioral pathologies. One in seven American children received welfare. Thirty-eight percent of those were black and 33 percent were white in a country that was 12.9 percent African American and 75.1 percent white.

Republicans fashioned a "workfare" bill putting recipients to work after two years in a row on welfare. The bill gave block grants to each state and imposed five-year lifetime limits on welfare recipients. One Urban Institute study estimated—wildly incorrectly—that a million children would suffer.

Clinton vetoed the first two Republican attempts as too Draconian. Intense negotiations began. Republican backbenchers mobilized more than a hundred colleagues to pressure Gingrich to leave out the drastic cuts in Medicaid, daycare support, and food stamps, which Clinton refused to sign. The Republicans were too close to having the Democratic president fulfill one clause of the Contract with America to be so rigid. In Congress, most Republicans supported the bill. House Democrats were split 98 to 98. Senate Democrats voted 25 to 21 in favor.

This third compromise bill now pressured the president. His political people estimated a third veto would cost him 5 percentage points in the polls and hurt his unique identity. Morris screamed, "if he vetoes, he'll lose."

Moynihan dismissed the bill as "welfare repeal." Liberal academics like Harvard's Theda Skocpol branded it the "Shirk Responsibility for the Poor Act of 1996." The "whole purpose of coming to Washington four years ago was to reverse the trend toward widening inequality in wealth and opportunity," Clinton's secretary of labor, Robert Reich, believed, warning that "signing this bill would violate everything we stood for." Hillary Clinton shrank from the debate, calling it "the president's decision."

Compromise came more easily to Bill Clinton. "What good will you do if you lose?" Morris insisted, sounding the Clintonites' ends-justify-the-means trumpet blast. Presiding over a house divided, Clinton called a Cabinet meeting on the eve of the vote. Clinton admitted that even without the Medicaid cuts, "This is a decent welfare bill wrapped in a sack of shit." He calculated that subsequent legislation could undo the two most offensive provisions, cutting food stamps drastically and banning federal benefits to immigrants. The vehement debate was uncharacteristically orderly, with everyone cowed by the high policy and political stakes. Finally, returning to core principles, the president pronounced: "I want to sign it. Let's do it." Morris exulted to a friend: "That's it. The election is over."

Seeking to advance "the basic values of work, responsibility and family," the current system eroded by encouraging long-term dependence on debilitating government handouts, wanting welfare to be "a second chance, not a way of life," Clinton compromised and led. He considered his signing one of his "most important decisions," having "spent most of my career trying to move people from welfare to work." Most blacks hated the status quo and supported the president. At the bill signing, Clinton hosted Lillie Harden, the woman who years ago had told him about anticipating her son's pride that she had a job rather than a handout.

The welfare reform reflected the Reaganizing of liberalism and the illusion of classlessness amid the unhappy reality that there were two, vastly different Americas. Most Americans lived in Middle Classville, epitomized by the lush suburban landscape. In this Democratic Gilded Age, all but the most aristocratic, spendthrift "super rich" called themselves middle class, while many modestly paid Americans spent themselves into debt to maintain a middle-class veneer. A second America, Poorville, epitomized by the barren urban moonscape of abandoned buildings in many inner cities and the windswept, rickety houses of rural America, encompassed America's perma-poor, often in single-parent households, swirling in social, cultural, economic, and moral chaos. Clinton refused to abandon this second, suffering America but he needed to woo Middle Classville to win.

Clinton Defends Marriage, Enrages Gays, Even As Gays Advance

Clinton also enraged his gay allies by signing the Defense of Marriage Act in September 1996, defining marriage as heterosexual, while permitting states to disregard gay marriages from other states. DOMA flouted Democrats' nationalist and civil libertarian values. "If there are people here who don't like it," Clinton snapped, "well, I've created seven and a half million new jobs and maybe it's time for them to go out and take some of them."

Dodging another gays-in-the-military brouhaha, Clinton signed the law at 12:50 a.m., without photographers. He declared that "this legislation should not . . . provide an excuse for discrimination, violence or intimidation against any person on the basis of sexual orientation." He ignored this craven moment in his memoirs, and later endorsed overturning DOMA.

The AIDS trauma mobilized many gays to proclaim their sexuality and demand their rights. The conversation about AIDS transmission also stretched the public's vocabulary and tolerance for once-taboo subjects such as "condoms" and "safe sex." Condom use increased from 21 percent among teenage males in 1979 to 67 percent in 1995—although 3 million teens annually still acquired a sexually transmitted disease. Fear of AIDS also helped level off rates of adolescent sexual activity. Rates of sexual intercourse among high school girls in urban areas jumped from 37 percent in 1971 to 50 percent in 1979, hovering at 48 percent in 1999. Teenage males' rates increased from 66 percent in 1979 to 76 percent in 1988, then dropped to 49 percent in 1999. Jokes conveyed the new anxieties. One teen lover reassured his girlfriend after unprotected sex that he had passed three of his last four AIDS tests.

Greater awareness and miraculous medicine changed the politics and perils of AIDS. In October 1996, 1.2 million people, including Clinton and Gore, visited the AIDS Memorial Quilt covering the Washington Mall with 37,856 memorial panels celebrating 70,000 lives. The Names Project, the world's largest piece of community folk art, helped make fighting AIDS as hip as fighting homelessness, hunger, and pollution. United Colors of Benetton advertisements showed AIDS patients dying, a young hunk sporting a tattoo saying "HIV POSITIVE," and a giant pink condom in Paris.

With AIDS the leading cause of death among twenty-five- to forty-four-year-olds, more money went to AIDS research than to fight heart disease, America's top medical killer. In 1995, with a record 48,979 deaths, "almost a whole Vietnam War's worth of people were dying of AIDS each year," recalls Dr. Julian Adams, a leading AIDS researcher. On June 21, 1996, the FDA approved the first nonnucleoside reverse transcriptase inhibitor NNRTI, Nevirapine, which Adams invented with colleagues. That year, the number of deaths dropped by 23 percent, thanks to therapeutic "cocktails" combining these protease inhibitors with other antiviral drugs, as conceived by Dr. David Da-i Ho. "For helping lift a death sentence," on AIDS sufferers, *Time* declared Ho its 1996 Man of the Year.

The AIDS conversation mainstreamed gays, especially as fears of AIDS subsided. By 1996, most Americans were comfortable associating with people who were HIV positive. In America's celebrity-obsessed culture, each celebrity coming-out story inspired imitators, be it Republican congressman Steve Gunderson in 1994 or the Olympic Gold-medal-winning diver Greg Louganis in 1995. In 1997, the popular TV comedienne Ellen DeGeneres would confirm what many people had already assumed, by coming out to Oprah Winfrey. With art imitating life, Ellen's character "Ellen" on her hit sitcom *Ellen* came out to her therapist, played by Oprah Winfrey. A year later, *Will & Grace* premiered, with Will Truman a straitlaced gay lawyer playing off his friend, Jack McFarland, a flamboyant gay flake.

Many gay activists began presenting themselves as Will Truman normal rather than the edgy sexual revolutionaries who scandalized passersby at gay pride parades. Considering homosexuality "innate," the conservative critic Bruce Bawer wanted to make it "morally neutral and without interest," like left-handedness. Andrew Sullivan, *The New Republic*'s editor from 1991 to 1996, explained: "A need to rebel has quietly ceded to a desire to belong."

Urvashi Vaid, a lesbian activist, opposed these calls for "legitimation," in her 1995 book *Virtual Equality*. She wanted gays and lesbians to remain sexual outlaws until society changed to accommodate them. Another anti-assimilationist, Daniel Harris, feared seeing the "proverbial tasteful gay man basic to the subculture" becoming "a stockbroker."

Lawyers like Evan Wolfson began crusading for gay domestic rights as a matter of equity in law and a reflection of gay normalcy in fact. In 1989, New York's highest court treated gay couples as families in rent-control disputes. By 1993, at least thirty municipalities recognized gay couples as "domestic partners" to secure benefits. That year, the Hawaii Supreme Court agreed in *Baehr v. Lewin* that banning same-sex marriage violated the state constitution's equal protection clause. Shrewdly echoing Clinton's values speak, positioning gays as "pro-marriage" when heterosexuals were abandoning the institution, Wolfson spoke about "love, commitment, self-sacrifice and equality." Despite Clinton's betrayal of gay marriage advocates that year, their long-term strategy of mainstreaming would eventually succeed.

1996 Campaign: Weak Opposition and Fragile Incumbent

The Democrats' values-based campaign boosting one of America's most notorious sinners always seemed half a misstep away from scandal. Staffers believed "Clinton could overcome personal attacks as long as he kept addressing the 'real problems of real people.'" His personal deviations had to seem marginal, not central, to his identity.

Just before the Democratic convention, the broad net tabloid journalists used to troll for scandal caught the architect of the values agenda, Dick Morris. When Deputy Chief of Staff Erskine Bowles asked Morris to resign after *The Star*, a supermarket tabloid, photographed him cavorting with a prostitute, Morris asked, "Why? What the hell did I do that he [the president] wasn't accused of doing in the exact same magazine four years ago?" Confirming the image-driven morality in the age of Clinton, Bowles replied: "You've admitted it's true."

Clinton's aides were furious at Morris, although Bruce Reed was relieved, hoping reporters would stop seeing every Clinton move as poll-tested and calculating. Hillary Clinton forbade public attacks on the disgraced consultant. Hillary's generosity paralleled that of Lady Bird Johnson when Lyndon Johnson's key aide Walter Jenkins was arrested in a men's room for solicitation shortly before the 1964 election. These two First Ladies, both married to raw, impulsive, wandering men, understood the human struggle with sin and demonstrated great capacity to forgive.

The press treated Morris as a perverted egomaniac; Clinton's escapades usually played as frat-boy harmless. His roguishness was part of his rugged appeal, to men and women. In the 1990s, women were not the only ones bewildered by mixed messages. Presidents were supposed to be strong but sensitive, First Ladies, independent but deferential. Most Americans still wanted Clint Eastwood not Jerry Seinfeld leading. Jimmy Carter the farmer and George H. W. Bush the oil wildcatter learned that, despite macho achievements, occasional incertitude in office defined them as wimps. Bill Clinton, the draft evader and policy wonk, learned that Americans prefer tough talk, nostalgic moralizing, resolute action, and even a bad-boy charm, to New Age psychobabble, tidbits about underwear preference, and reasoned moderation that might seem wishy-washy.

Atlanta '96: Everyday Olympians

Like Ronald Reagan in 1984, Clinton was lucky to run for reelection when America was hosting the Olympics. Although a nonpartisan event, the resulting patriotic frenzy boosted faith in the incumbent. The 15,000-mile, 42-state, 84-day torch relay building up to the July Olympics celebrated patriotism, idealism, celebrity, and commercialism. The cross-country relay started on April 27 in Los Angeles, the torch having arrived from Greece. The relay honored Olympians, celebrities, and 5,500 community heroes; Clinton called them "star citizens."

It was a new rainbow America, with a wheelchair-bound "runner" from San Francisco, a Hispanic uncle who adopted six nieces after his sisters contracted AIDS in New York, an African American reverend thrown off Edmund Pettus Bridge in Selma during the "Bloody Sunday" protests, now running with the same mayor of Selma, in 1996 as in 1965, who repented. It was a prosperous and generous America, epitomized by Eugene Lang, a self-made New York businessman who paid college tuition for thousands of disadvantaged students who finished high school. And it was an America still mourning as an Oklahoma City police officer and the brother-in-law of a victim ran hand-in-hand, tears streaming down both faces. When the torch reached the White House, Clinton preached: "The Olympic spirit is the spirit of personal responsibility and best effort, the spirit of community, the spirit of unity."

It was also a commercialized America, with Coca-Cola spending $100 million to impose its brand all over the Olympics. Sponsors covered 80 percent of the Olympics' $1.58 billion budget. The 10,000 runners wore uniforms with the words "Coca-Cola" prominently displayed as well as a big "C" for Champion Sportswear. Americans had become walking billboards, paying extra to advertise corporate brands on hats, shirts, and bags. A trend that began with T-shirts in the 1970s evolved toward fancy polo shirts with the Lacoste alligator and the Ralph Lauren polo sign in the 1980s, became ubiquitous in the 1990s.

More than 2 million visitors streamed into Atlanta for the games, and more than 3.5 billion people watched a record 197 countries compete for "the gold." The 1996 Olympics resonated particularly powerfully thanks to the Internet. Two hundred Olympics-related websites reached 10 to 15 million Americans. The Olympic junkie, now armed, as one reporter noted, with remote TV clicker in one hand and a mouse in the other, could discover more information than ever before—much of it unnecessary. Astonished fans could also organize their Olympic journeys online, buying tickets, making reservations, signing up to volunteer. Alas, the IBM computer network system, "Info '96," crashed or slowed to an excruciating pace as usage soared.

On July 27, a pipe bomb exploded in Olympic Park, the latest blow in a bloody spring and summer. On April 3, Clinton's secretary of commerce Ron Brown and 34 others died when their jet crashed in Croatia. That same day, the FBI finally arrested the Unabomber, Theodore J. Kaczynski, fifty-three, in a hut in Montana, responsible for 16 bombings over 17 years. His brother David Kaczynski had recognized familiar phrasing in the Unabomber's 35,000-word manifesto, which *The Washington Post* and *The New York Times* had been blackmailed into publishing. On May 11, ValuJet Flight 952 crashed in the Florida Everglades, killing all 110 aboard. On June 25, an al-Qaeda truck bomb killed 19 in an American military barracks in Saudi Arabia. On July 17, TWA Flight 800 exploded shortly after taking off from New York, killing 230. And ten days later, the Olympic Park bombing injured 111 and resulted in the deaths of 2 people. Meanwhile, throughout this period, a spate of fires in black churches prompted the federal government to establish the National Church Arson Task Force.

The mysterious TWA crash triggered a huge boost in Internet traffic, then years of wild conspiracy theorizing. With data galore, ease of interaction, and no filters, speculation flourished, often with anti-government, anti-establishment malice. It would take the National Transportation Safety Board four years to blame a short circuit.

While TWA Flight 800 made paranoid folks look foolish, the Olympic Park bombing made the authorities look terrible. An alert security guard, Richard Jewell, saw the lethal backpack and helped clear most of the area, minimizing injuries. The hero was soon wrongly suspected as a cop wannabe who planted the bomb seeking glory. Class bias shaped the harsh coverage. The husky thirty-four-year-old who lived with his mother had Jay Leno calling him the "Unadoofus," the FBI tailing him, and a cloud hanging over him for nearly three agonizing months before being exonerated. In 2003, authorities arrested the right-wing fanatic Eric Rudolph for the bombing, which he detonated as part of his deranged fight against abortionists, gays, and America's turn toward "global socialism."

"Jewell Syndrome," this rush to judgment and aggressive imprisonment of a private citizen in Scandalvania, caused much media breast-beating and expensive civil settlements with Jewell—until reporters did it again. Many Americans disliked the arrogance. During Jewell's eighty-eight-day ordeal, when he visited his ex-girlfriend's family, followed by three unmarked FBI cars, hundreds of white ribbons hanging from trees greeted him, protesting the unfair grilling.

Another classy gesture, as the campaign season intensified, occurred in June when the Christian Coalition Executive Director Ralph Reed promised to raise $1 million from white evangelicals to assist forty black churches that had been burned in the previous eighteen months. This leading evangelist wanted to apologize because white evangelists had been "on the wrong side of the most central struggle for social justice in this century." Ultimately, the federal investigation discovered that more white churches than black churches had been burned during that period. The offenders ranged from bored teenagers to avenging Satanists.

President Plaid Beats Senator Stiff

That summer, Clinton's luck landed him a seventy-three-year-old, listless opponent, Senator Bob Dole. Dole was a war hero and an impressive legislator. But World War II felt like ancient history, and his capacity for elaborate legislative edifices played poorly in a campaign demanding simple presidential planks. "The Internet is a good tool to use to get on the Net," he said, sounding tragically unhip. Asked about Clinton's AmeriCorps volunteer program, Dole said he was taking no position pro or con on this domestic Peace Corps but was confident Congress would fund it. David Nyhan of *The Boston Globe* would call Dole "too cranky, too Washington, too bitter, too negative, too old-timey, too flip-floppy, too shopworn, too weather-beaten." In exit polls, two-thirds of voters would hold Dole's age against him.

Dole suffered from his association with Gingrich and the budget debacle. He and all Republicans were cast as Neanderthals for opposing the mainstream media's push for gay rights, abortion, and gun control. Dick Morris called the Republicans' values agenda "largely negative: it was anti-gay, anti-sex, anti-single mothers, anti-abortion, anti-everything but the nuclear family." Clinton was more positive and nuanced, wanting abortion legal, safe but rare and regulated; seeking welfare reform with humane support; balancing the budget while preserving what Ronald Reagan called the "safety net"; fighting crime with tough sentencing and early intervention focused on prevention. Seeking guidance in the complex values dilemmas they faced in modern life, many Americans were increasingly impatient with Dole's anachronistic, square Ozzie-and-Harriet absolutes.

"I've been tested and tested and tested," Dole liked to say, emphasizing his maturity. "I won't lead you off a cliff." But President Plaid better suited this moment than Senator Stiff. The author of the brilliant fictionalization of Clinton's 1992 campaign, *Primary Colors,* Joe Klein, now wrote in *Newsweek* about 1996: "This race will test whether the certainties of the World War II generation can still resonate in the ambiguous world its children inhabit . . . as the millennium approaches."

A Values Crisis, Left to Right

This ambiguity feeding mass anxiety, which Morris identified and Clinton soothed, alarmed intellectuals, too. Thinkers left, right, and center bemoaned Borderline America's moral disorder. A leading Harvard liberal, the philosopher Michael Sandel, offered a values-based reading of American history justifying communitarianism in *Democracy's Discontent* in 1996. From the right, Gertrude Himmelfarb denounced *The De-Moralization of Society* in 1995, while Judge Robert Bork in 1996 warned that Americans were *Slouching Towards Gomorrah*. Professor Amitai Etzioni's *The New Golden Rule* (1996) sought to nourish "both social virtues and individual rights" by maximizing order and autonomy, voluntarily. His rule: "Respect and uphold society's moral order as you would have society respect and uphold your autonomy." Less elegantly, TV's showboating Geraldo Rivera, ignoring his own culpability, said, "I'm sick of the garbage" on television.

Clinton disappointed liberals by keeping the values talk cultural not economic. Secretary of Labor Robert Reich noted bitterly that "the economic message for the campaign is to be nothing but happy talk." The "darker side of the economy—increasing job insecurity, widening inequality—must not be mentioned. . . . I can't talk about it. I'm locked in the cabinet," Reich complained.

Clinton's Honor Targeted

Republicans tried to win by questioning Clinton's honor. The conservative attack machine relied on two anti-Clinton broadsides in particular. *Unlimited Access: An FBI Agent Inside the Clinton White House* sold a reputed half-million copies peddling allegations of sexual indiscretion, homosexuality, and sheer boorishness. Gary Aldrich, serving as gossipmonger more than author, catalogued dozens of charges to attack the Clintons' "adjustable ethics and moral relativism."

David Brock doubly disappointed conservatives. The author of *The American Spectator*'s Troopergate article and a best-selling attack on Anita Hill, he denied having confirmed the rumor for Aldrich that Clinton was smuggled out of the White House for trysts. Brock's biography of Hillary Clinton also repudiated the anti-Clinton "hate-mongering," pronouncing "Hillary has gotten a bad rap from all sides." Brock would later apologize for his previous work, becoming a liberal partisan who now denounces conservatives for "promoting . . . mean-spirited diatribe[s] filled with every conceivable cultural prejudice from the Stone Age."

More embarrassing revelations came from the Washington insider Bob Woodward. His book *The Choice,* published in June 1996, made Hillary Clinton's relationship with her New Age shamans sound creepy, alleging White House séances to channel Eleanor Roosevelt. The substantive First Lady now seemed as loopy as Nancy Reagan, who consulted an astrologist. Mrs. Clinton joked about consulting Eleanor before every speech, but the attack rankled.

At the Republican National Convention that August, Representative Susan Molinari of New York said Clinton's promises had the shelf life of a Big Mac on *Air Force One.* Bob Dole targeted both members of the presidential couple in his acceptance speech. "With all due respect," he said, with no respect intended, "it does not take a village to raise a child. It takes a family to raise a child." Posing as the avatar of American values, Dole said, "Let me be the bridge to an America that only the unknowing call myth. Let me be the bridge to a time of tranquility, faith and confidence in action."

Bill Clinton incorrectly but conveniently heard Dole say he wanted to build a "bridge to the past." Clinton then emphasized "building a bridge to the 21st century." "Hope is back in America—we are on the right track to the twenty-first century," Clinton proclaimed. "Our strategy is simple but profound: opportunity for all, responsibility for all, a strong American community where everyone has a place and plays a role."

The Fox Gold Rush—Rightward

On October 7, 1996, the twenty-four-hour Fox News Channel premiered. Rupert Murdoch's News Corporation already owned *The Weekly Standard, The New York Post,* HarperCollins, 20th Century Fox Studios, Fox Broadcasting Company, Fox Sports, FX, and dozens of TV and cable stations. Murdoch had the moxie and the money to make Fox broadcasting a "fourth network." Fox

Sports humiliated CBS by outbidding it for National Football League games. Now, Murdoch was ready to fight CNN and MSNBC. One show that debuted that night, *The O'Reilly Report,* would soon displace *Larry King Live* as the most popular cable news show. Fox News would outdraw CNN, feeding an intense rivalry between Murdoch and Ted Turner.

Fox News vowed to be "fair and balanced" in reporting. But Murdoch and Roger Ailes, an old Nixon hand hired as founding chairman, believed that, as Ailes put it, "most of the news tilts to the left." Fox's founding would make the news business more explicitly ideological. It would make Murdoch "this era's influential figure," according to the media critic James Fallows, building his empire with sensationalism, populism, technological sophistication, style, political connections, and the occasional partisan edge. At the same time, Murdoch transformed what Fallows called the "semi-sacred trust" of journalism into the "news business," another corporate activity.

Clinton's reelection would contribute to Fox's growth. Its roster of right-wing pundits would feed off Clinton's missteps, real and imagined, making him the reluctant muse of the 24/7 Washington scandal industry. Similarly, in December, the Christmas Day murder of the six-year-old "Little Miss Colorado," Jon-Benét Ramsey, gave Fox its post–O. J. blockbuster. Fox's less politicized anchors wallowed in sordid stories like the Ramsey murder, reeking of violence, sex, or perversion.

Murdoch's journalism revolution was part of the broader Clinton-era deregulation gold rush. The Telecommunications Act of 1996 opened up the information industry, allowing cross-ownership—and many hardware and software synergies—between phone companies, TV stations, Internet services, and movie studios. The law made it easier to enter into the business, which since the 1930s had been heavily regulated by considering the airwaves and phone lines public assets. The Act had a Clintonesque touch, with the Communications Decency Act banning sending indecent materials to minors on the Internet. But the law emphasized access, facilitated openness, encouraged synergies. Fallows called this "arguably the most important economic event of the Clinton era."

The Good Father, Reelected

Clinton felt vindicated by his reelection triumph, becoming the first two-term Democratic president since Franklin D. Roosevelt. Exit polls showed Clinton making gains from 1992 with liberal Republicans, liberal independents, and moderate independents. Dole appeared to be a captive of the far right without Reagan's charm. Americans were optimistic about the future, most concerned with the economy.

Clinton's comeback since 1994 was impressive. Yet he won only 49.2 percent of the popular vote, and only four of eleven Southern states, with Ross Perot's candidacy and anger about campaign finance in the final weeks depriving him of that long-sought popular majority. The Republicans gained in the Senate and still controlled the House. His wife remained popular with just under half the electorate.

Democrats' Kennedyesque high hopes for him and his own grand ambitions constantly dwarfed Clinton's presidential record. Despite his scaled-down policies, Clinton aspired to be a presidential superhero like Abraham Lincoln and Franklin Roosevelt. He regretted that no major war or economic upheaval would prove his greatness. His backup was Theodore Roosevelt's peaceful but momentous presidency, helping Americans adjust to modernity.

Frustrated Republicans resented this political huckster for stealing their souls, and best lines. "We're the ones who are pro-family, pro-community, pro-spirituality," the Republican pollster Frank Luntz fumed. Beyond the power calculus, the media sensationalism, the conservative fiefdoms, the fraying Capitol Hill relations, the hatred ran deep. Attitudes about sexual discipline alienated Clinton's Adversarial elite from their rivals. His shape-shifting and center-seeking combined with his personal sloppiness kept Americans mired in the post-Sixties' sex wars.

At a time when the national conversation lamented America's "character-starved culture," only 41 percent of the electorate considered the president honest and trustworthy. However, 58 percent of the electorate, and 69 percent of Clinton voters, considered "issues" more important than "character." Just as their behaviors often deviated from the moral standards they endorsed, many Americans distinguished between this president's private life and his public calls for morality, sobriety, and respect for women. Clinton benefited from a renewed appreciation of the culture of appearances in which public morality obscured private indiscretions, and a weariness with a culture of exposure that mixed private libertinism with a lurid, cynical public Victorianism.

Clinton later called the gap between his popularity and his popular vote totals "a sober reminder of the power of cultural issues like guns, gays, and abortion." When Clinton slipped on these radioactive issues, he had trouble governing. He was most successful when engaged in traditional presidential actions such as building coalitions, passing laws, waging war, seeking peace.

Clinton's foibles made it easy to caricature his Good Father cultural Band-

Aids as poll-driven ruses, artful retreats from big issues. But these positions were not just survey-induced, artificially sweetened Dick Morris specials. Clinton had been thinking about opportunity, responsibility, family, community, faith, crime-fighting for years.

Clinton's Republican-sounding cultural crusade had a deeply Democratic twist. In *Rent,* Jonathan Larson played with conventional polarities by evoking the godliness in what first looked like a burlesque of the profane. Theatergoers cried as his AIDS-stricken drag queen, "Angel," became one. Clinton's Blue-tinged synthesis reframed values talk as communal, transcending Republicans' obsession with individual bad behavior. At Georgetown in 1995, he wondered: "Why can't we say to people, look, you've got to behave if you want your life to work, but we have common problems, and we are going to have some common responses." This "Good Father" would not rely on "exhortation alone," leaving citizens "to fend for themselves." He vowed: "It's going to require some common action," including gun control, drug testing, and V-chips on TVs.

Even many supporters missed Clinton's subtleties, especially because of his own struggles to match his behavior to these beliefs. As a result, a song from *Rent,* "Take Me or Leave Me," often applied to Americans accepting Bill Clinton, in all his imperfections. In 1996, this year that "whatever" became a common phrase, as Democrats celebrated Clinton's miraculous resurrection, many independents seemed resigned to their fate, accepting the president who, for a second time, fewer than half of them chose.

8

1997: Silicon Valley
"Think Different"

The Everyday Wizardry of Everything and Everywhere Machines

America demands and deserves big things from us—and nothing big ever came from being small.

—BILL CLINTON, SECOND INAUGURAL ADDRESS,
JANUARY 20, 1997

O n August 6, 1997, at Macworld Expo, the Apple trade show, the grand wizard of user-friendliness, Steve Jobs, was celebrating his return to Apple after a forced but lucrative twelve-year exile. Apple's revenues had dropped by a third in two years. Creative, desperate, Jobs announced a partnership with their archrival Microsoft. Jobs's frenemy, the uber-geek Bill Gates, appeared on a huge video screen. Some of the 1,600 Apple nuts booed. "Apple lives in an ecosystem," Jobs explained, pitching a $150 million deal that would redeem Apple.

The hub of this shared "ecosystem," Silicon Valley, was to computers what Detroit was to cars, Abilene was to cattle, Philadelphia was to Constitutions: national headquarters, source of synergies, state of mind, spiritual center, defining symbol. This region of suburban sprawl thirty miles by ten miles, stretching south of San Francisco through San Jose, was dubbed Silicon Valley in the 1970s, honoring the sand-like material in semiconductor chips. Subsequently, the tomorrow-shapers there produced, perfected, and mass-marketed integrated circuits and microprocessors, personal computers and video games, lasers and cell phones.

Now, in 1997, Silicon Valley was evolving from manufacturing hardware with its roller-coaster business cycles, to developing, financing, and marketing the future in software development, with its New Economy promise of perma-growth. Silicon Valley's new stars were microelectronics, computers, computer networking, and biotechnology. Apple, in Cupertino, California, was charting its comeback by challenging Americans to "Think Different," its new slogan. AuctionWeb, founded in San Jose, would become eBay on September 1, receive a $6.7 million investment from the venture capital firm Benchmark Capital, and in November, start boosting its site as "proven, fun and safe." The growing volume of searches on Google, founded in Stanford University, Silicon Valley's Vatican City, had so clogged the university's website, Google was changing its domain name to google.com.

Approximately 2.3 million people lived in this 3,000-square mile hothouse, cultivating breakthrough technologies and innovative software, millionaires and billionaires, new companies and additional jobs, and, alas, congestion, pollution, and economic polarization. Average salaries of $46,000, although higher than the national average of $29,000, were often insufficient to afford houses. A four-bedroom single-family residence that would cost $207,633 in Minneapolis went for $671,347 in San Mateo. At its best, income distribution in the old manufacturing economy could be diamond-shaped, with a bulging well-paid middle class; the high-tech economy risked creating an inverted asset pyramid as the super rich became super richer, leaving little for most workers servicing them in McJobs. When campaigning for reelection in Silicon Valley, Bill Clinton said he wanted to make sure that when he celebrated all the new jobs created at a banquet, a waiter wouldn't cry out, "and I have three of them," as one cartoonist teased.

Just weeks after Macworld that fall of 1997, in yet another symbol of the shift in gravity, gravitas, and hipness from the Northeast to the Northwest, Clintonville's crown princess, Chelsea Clinton, arrived at Stanford. Other freshmen, laden with new microwaves, laptops, television sets, and, for the trendiest, cell phones, piled out of their parents' or stepparents' minivans, sedans, and SUVs. She arrived in an armored limousine with the president of the United States, the First Lady, an entourage of Secret Service agents, and nearly 250 nosy reporters.

Chelsea Clinton and her classmates would imbibe Silicon Valley's gospel mixing materialism and idealism. We are "creative spirits," Jobs told Macworld. "Not just out to get a job done, but out to change the world." Apple's Think Different campaign, costarring Albert Einstein, Bob Dylan, Martin Luther King Jr., among others, would honor "The rebels. The troublemakers. The ones who see things differently." And conclude: "While some may see them as the crazy ones, we see genius. Because the people who are crazy enough to think they can change the world, are the ones who do."

Bill Clinton could match Steve Jobs and every other Silicon Valley evangelical as a techno-cheerleader. In the fall of 1995 he directed his speechwriter Don Baer to learn more about the innovative thinking and rhetoric about constructive disruptive change in Silicon Valley. "The 21st century will give more people more chances to live out their dreams than any time in human history," Clinton rejoiced when visiting San Jose in 1996, knowing "technology can be the greatest force for good we have ever known." He cautioned, however, that "technology is not inherently good or bad." Clinton worked hard to ensure that the technology the Silicon Valley people developed would be used, as the 1960s TV character Maxwell Smart, Agent 86, advised, "for goodness instead of evil."

Live Different

Increasingly, thanks to Silicon Valley's manufactured miracles, Americans were living different, living fairy tales with writing, speaking, and thinking machines. As Sir Arthur C. Clarke, the British science fiction writer who wrote *2001: A Space Odyssey,* explained: "Any sufficiently advanced technology is indistinguishable from magic." The 1990s were an age of wonder. While big industrial processes and complex machines were being revolutionized, this technological revolution injected many miracle inventions into homes and offices, for individuals and their families.

In 1990, the buzz involved diversions such as Game Boy and Sega Genesis as well as a jump forward in home printing with Hewlett-Packard's HP Laser-Jet III printer. In 1991, it was Super Nintendo, the digital answering machine, the Apple PowerBook 100, and the Panasonic RX-DT707 portable CD stereo system. By 1992, Sony trumped Panasonic with its MiniDisc player and its Trinitron TV, while the Ensoniq ASR-10 computerized keyboard gave schoolkids more musical reach than most philharmonic orchestras. In 1993, the handheld revolution began in earnest with the IBM Simon Personal Communicator, the Psion 3A, and the Hewlett-Packard 100LX. In 1994, computers became faster, lighter, more user-friendly, and more interactive thanks to the Connectix Quick-Cam, the Logitech WingMan Extreme Joystick, the Microsoft Natural Keyboard, the Apple PowerBook 500, and the Apple Newton Message Pad. Information transferred more easily with the SanDisk CompactFlash card. In the Eighties, Americans projected human characteristics onto computers, which had "memory" and could "sleep." All these upgrades, super-powered by what Clinton called the "Everyday miracle of the Internet," propelled computing into the realm of the supernatural, at least metaphorically.

In 1995, improvements not revolutions predominated, with the Sony Discman, the Sony PlayStation, the IBM ThinkPad 701C, and the Iomega Zip 100 Drive—although the Sony Handycam DCR-VX1000 advanced the handheld video revolution, making everyone a roving Cecil B. DeMille or Walter Cronkite. A year later, the Motorola StarTAC, the first clamshell "flip" phone, weighing 3.1 ounces, and costing $1,000, kick-started the cell phone revolution as the PalmPilot 1000 became the dominant handheld device. The digital camera craze began, with the Casio QV-10 digital camera and the Kodak DC25 camera. Meanwhile, the RIM Inter@ctive pager, which sent and received messages wirelessly, heralded the day when most Americans would be tethered to e-mails 24/7. Now, in 1997, the Toshiba SD-3000 DVD player would liberate the act of watching movies and TV shows from movie theaters and homes, while the Garmin GPSCOM 170 would help people wander around with their new mobile toys without getting lost.

The decade ended strong with the Apple PowerBook G3, the Apple iMac G3, the BlackBerry 850 wireless handset, the Iridium satellite phone, the Philips flat TV, the Mustek ScanExpress image scanner, and even Mercedes-Benz SmartKeys for the car of the future in 1998. In 1999 there would be the TiVo HDR110 digital recorder, the Microsoft IntelliMouse Explorer, the Sony VPL-CS1 SuperLite projector, and the Sony AIBO ERS-110, a robot dog.

Time had been designating a "Man of the Year," usually a political leader, since 1927, although in 1960, America's "scientists" were men of the year and in 1982, the computer was "machine of the year." In 1999, reflecting the ongoing Gender Bender, the editors would start honoring a "Person of the Year." In this enchanted decade, in 1996 the Man of the Year was the AIDS researcher David Ho; in 1997 it would be the computer executive Intel's Andrew Grove; in 1999 it would be Amazon's founder Jeff Bezos. The three represented America's overlapping scientific, computer, and Internet revolutions.

Dolly: The Birth Heard 'Round the World

Every day brought new innovations and attendant challenges. In February 1997, Scottish researchers introduced the world to Dolly the sheep, the world's first cloned adult mammal. *Newsweek* called it "the birth heard round the world." Scientists had first imagined this in 1938. This initiative stemmed from a search for more and cheaper milk.

This was no simple birth. Even when asked whether Dolly was seven months old, the time elapsed since her birth, or six years old, the age of her clone, the lead researcher, Dr. Ian Wilmut, faltered. "We just don't know," he said. "There are many things here we will have to find out."

At a time when big science, big money, and big government dominated, the Roslin Institute was partially privately financed, run by a start-up company PPL Therapeutics PLC. As other scientists cashed in on their work by demanding shares, the Roslin scientists still earned modest, mid-five-figure salaries. They refused shares, to keep their science pure and their integrity intact. This altruism fascinated many Clintonites. In planning "Second Term Legacy Projects," staffers considered establishing "Discovery Investments" and "Discovery Partnerships" facilitating public-private alliances to pursue "breakthroughs in cancer and AIDS research treatment."

Amazement at this godlike act of deciphering one of cell biology's biggest mysteries mingled with revulsion at the prospect of human cloning. Journalists wondered: "wherever the lamb went, was Mary sure to follow?" Fears spread of cloning humans for "spare parts," bypassing males in the reproductive process, or cloning replacements for dead children.

The threat here was horizontal. Big, unwieldy, morally problematic projects like nuclear bombs or biological weaponry tapped the capacities of nation-states and could be more easily regulated. Cloning offered a contemporary, democratic challenge. A simpler, cheaper infrastructure made it possible for an unknown scientist somewhere to cross that clear red line into human tinkering.

The administration triangulated. Existing law permitted private initiatives to explore human cloning but banned federal funding. Fearing a backlash against "important genetic research," Clinton's advisers drafted a statement for him to "reassure the public, deter restrictive, ill-advised legislation, and strengthen the nation's resolve to consider ethical questions carefully before advancing human cloning." Clinton urged scientists to "move with caution and care," warning against "trying to play God."

"I am not a fool," Dr. Wilmut the embryologist seethed, resenting the fuss. He mocked the fear of replacement kids, saying: "You could never get that child back . . . People are not genes." His boss Ron James said, "Ethically, we would be wrong not to do research that would benefit mankind because it could be misused."

Many people feared machines trumping humans, in a year when the big movie would be a classic tale of human overreach, *Titanic,* and another cautionary tale, *Jurassic Park,* seemed omnipresent, with comic books, video games, and a movie sequel. "It's the ultimate shopping experience: designing your baby," the biotechnology critic Jeremy Rifkin grumbled. "In a society used to cosmetic surgery and psychopharmacology, this is not a big step." On May 11, the world's chess champion, Garry Kasparov, gave up, in a fit of exasperation, in his duel with Deep Blue, IBM's chess-playing computer. Forgetting that humans programmed the machine, many worried that, four years before 2001, Stanley Kubrick's classic cinematic warning of machines overrunning humans was happening.

Cyber Addiction and Anxiety

Machines were dominant yet useful. Laptops, cell phones, e-mail, and beepers extended the workday, and enhanced expectations that certain workers were available 24/7, the new way of saying "around the clock." Typically, a young ORACLE computers sales representative, Todd Beamer, brought his computer, cell phone, and PalmPilot on vacation. Resenting his distraction, his wife Lisa Beamer teased him about his electronic "security blankets." Americans reported working 160 hours more each year than they had twenty years earlier, adding hours mostly before nine or after five. Psychiatrists reported that the resulting anxiety disorders were more prevalent than depression or substance abuse.

The tech addiction started early. The hot toy of Christmas 1996 was Tickle Me Elmo, a fuzzy infantile toy that laughed when squeezed. More elaborate were virtual pets such as the Tamagotchis, Giga Pets, and Furbys, interactive robots requiring regular TLC or they "died." Sometimes, working parents brought the virtual pets to the office, so their beeps would disturb business meetings rather than classrooms. The robotic pets risked luring children into a technologically sanitized world of safe interactions, making the messiness of real friendships less appealing.

With more Americans entering "cyberspace," worries grew about cyber communication and cybersex. Viewed through the media's distorting lens, marriages seemed to be collapsing as partners flirted online or switched genders or ages or races or looks when describing themselves online. The divorce revolution rooted in the 1970s showed that marriages did not need newfangled machinery to break.

With America's *Pathfinder* spaceship exploring the surface of Mars, sheep being reproduced from their cells, and communication increasingly quick, global, and choreographed, the potentials for good and ill were growing faster than many people's moral capacities. Clinton delivered the commencement address at Morgan State University in Baltimore two months after Dolly's debut and a week after Kasparov's tantrum. He celebrated the miracles abounding, full of promise, molded by science, shaped by technology, powered by knowledge.

Then, affirming "our basic sense of right and wrong," he championed guaranteeing broad access, never using science to discriminate, preserving individual privacy and autonomy, while remembering "that science is not God," so we keep "our deepest truths . . . outside the realm of science." Tradition still counted.

The People's Princess

This yearning for tradition helped explain the mass fascination with Princess Diana. In these democratic times, the British monarchy continued entrancing its former subjects, the Americans, even as the royals endured a nightmarish decade, with Prince Charles and Diana divorcing in 1996. Diana's vulnerability boosted her popularity, making her death on August 31, 1997, in a car accident while racing away from paparazzi, all the more unnerving. She was thirty-six.

Americans joined the British masses in mourning. "Diana—you'll always be queen of America's hearts," one mourner wrote in one of many makeshift memorials, piling up letters, flowers, and candles, in what became the new ritual for communal mourning. British prime minister Tony Blair dubbed her the "people's princess," the overexposed aristocrat who disclosed her bulimia, tension with her in-laws, unhappy marriage, and divorce trauma. The global fascination was addictive, and reinforcing. For days the coverage was all Di, all the time. One commentator noted, "Even in a world of 500 channels, sometimes there is just one thing on."

The global Diana obsession upstaged the death days later of Mother Teresa. Memories of the eighty-seven-year-old saint of Calcutta could not compete with the sudden loss of this young, glamorous do-gooder. While some critics snidely compared the spoiled celebrity princess with the humble humanitarian, most used Mother Teresa's genuine virtue to bolster Diana's legend.

The Disney Renaissance of a Disney World

As gossip continued about the royals' dithering when Diana died, not knowing whether to deify a fallen princess, Americans swarmed Broadway to see an imaginative depiction of power struggles in the animal kingdom. *The Lion King* musical began previews on Broadway in mid-October, shortly after Princess Di's death. Based on the 1994 Disney movie, the show would win six Tony Awards, and become the first Broadway show to gross more than $1 billion.

Audiences often gasped in wonder at the elaborate puppetry and colorful costumes during the opening number. The appealing songs and storyline added a New Agey environmental sensibility to the Shakespearean tale of generational palace intrigue. The young heir, Simba, learns from his father, Mufasa, that "we are all connected in the great Circle of Life." Simba becomes empowered after adding the easy-listening Clintonesque philosophy of Timon the meerkat and Pumbaa the warthog. "Hakuna Matata"—no worries—they sing, one of the Democratic Gilded Age's defining songs and slogans.

Simba, the insecure lion king, joined Ariel, the love-struck little mermaid, and Aladdin's wise-cracking genie as one of the great stars and marketing engines of the Disney renaissance. Founded in 1923, serving as America's premier dream-making company during the Age of Innocence, The Walt Disney Company had stumbled in the 1970s, after Walt died and cynicism spread. The company's revival started in the Eighties with merchandizing and theme parks. By 1990, fifty Disney stores had opened. Its theme parks had more hotel rooms than New York or Los Angeles. Disney opened Euro Disneyland in 1992. The Animal Kingdom and Disney's Magic cruise ship would both launch in 1998. Phase two involved spreading the Disney magic through multiple entertainment outlets, especially its new television and radio stations after purchasing Capital Cities/ABC for $19 billion in 1996.

Returning to its core business of manufacturing stories that defined American childhoods, the company created new "classic" icons like Simba while introducing its traditional heroes to new generations of American children through new ventures and new technologies. In 1994, the company finally released its 1937 hit *Snow White and the Seven Dwarfs* on home video and laser disc, selling 50 million copies overall, making it the world's best-selling video. A year later, in September 1995, the company formed Disney Online, followed in 1996 by the launch of Disney.com.

In this "Disney Decade," the company built Disney's town of Celebration, near Orlando, Florida, "a place that takes you back to that time of innocence." Celebration was "not just a housing development but a community." Everything was planned. Services were privatized. The houses were all within walking distance of the town center. A "Pattern Book" detailed how every structure and garden should look. Residents were limited to one garage sale per year and one political sign posted only 45 days before an election, no bigger than eighteen by twenty-four inches. In October and December, fake leaves and snow wafted down on Market Street in the town's center, generated by machines attached to the streetlamps.

These were the "small complicated rules" the French philosopher Alexis de

Tocqueville feared would create the "soft despotism" of the mildly satisfied and the politically disengaged—a sanitized parallel to many Generation X's grungier withdrawal. Outsiders mocked this 24/7 theme park as "creepy," "Big Brothery," and far too "Stepford Wives." The writer Michael Pollan worried that Disney had "developed a new kind of community for the 90's, one that has been shorn of politics and transformed into a commodity—something people buy and consume rather than produce."

Most residents were happy. "I used to just wave at my neighbors from the car," one newcomer reported. "Now we stop and gossip on the corner." Another dismissed concerns about the heavy-handed control, saying, "This is no democracy, I know that. But, hey," he shrugged, "it's the 90's."

Disney blundered in 1994, when a coalition of historians and environmentalists blocked its proposed $650 million, 3,000-acre American history theme park in Virginia, nearly adjacent to the Manassas Civil War battlefield. "We have so little left that is authentic, that is real, and to replace it with plastic history, mechanized history, is a sacrilege," said David McCullough, president of the Society of American Historians. The notion of Mickey Mouse and Goofy teaching history, of Disney "imagineers" sanitizing the slavery experience or turning Civil War killing fields into amusement park rides, offended public sensibilities.

Despite retreating near Washington, Disney conquered New York. On May 26, 1996, Disney opened its Disney Store on 5th Avenue and 55th Street in midtown Manhattan. The store, which soon grew to 30,000 square feet and 148 employees or "cast members," treated shopping as entertainment. As with the Warner Bros. Studio Store and the NBA store, even when pedestrians left empty-handed, they bonded with the brand. In 1997, Disney recorded $22.5 billion in sales. Media giants like Sumner Redstone's Viacom and Rupert Murdoch's News Corporation each grossed less than 60 percent of that.

Disney's renaissance proved contagious, helping revive America's most infamously blighted street. The "Crossroads of the World," Times Square at 42nd Street, had degenerated into the cesspool of New York, thanks to the Great American Crime Wave, compounded by the drug epidemic and the sexual revolution. The area glamorized by the 1933 Warner Bros. film musical *42nd Street* as "naughty, bawdy, gaudy, sporty," had become grimy, slimy, sleazy, and scary. Carnival barkers and burlesque dancers had given way to pimps, prostitutes, pickpockets, pornographers, muggers, hustlers, drug pushers, drug users, dirty old men, and pimply teens looking for their first cheap thrills. By 1984, 2,300 crimes were recorded on the one block between Times Square and Eighth Avenue, including 460 violent felonies. The city planning commission chairman that year admitted that 42nd "is the one street where the city has lost control."

The Times Square Business Improvement District, one of many such initiatives citywide, spearheaded creative coalitions joining city and state, for-profit and nonprofit, property owners and commercial tenants to fight crime, clean the streets, welcome tourists, police businesses, and develop the neighborhood, as an open-air, neon-drenched, entertainment and shopping mall, helped immeasurably by Disney magic and dollars. A Disney store on 42nd Street near Seventh Avenue heralded the arrival of other shopping and entertainment complexes. In 1997, with low-interest city and state loans, Disney invested $34 million to redevelop the New Amsterdam Theatre as the home for its theatrical spectacles, starting with *The Lion King*. Madame Tussauds wax museum, a Starbucks, a Yankees Clubhouse, and other stores, restaurants, theaters, and hotels, inspired and reassured by Disney, followed.

Broadway denizens and New York intellectuals detested the Disney invasion, longing for Times Square's decadence, now that it was being tamed. "I would like them to leave a little of New York for the old-timers, for New Yorkers," grumbled Fred Hakim, who owned a lunch counter on the strip for fifty-six years. Protesting the invasion of a "mall sensibility" on what had been a "quintessential urban block," *The New York Times* columnist Frank Rich said the shift personified "the essence of Disneyfication." In theme-park America, the country's gritty realities were replaced by "Disney's Main Street, U.S.A.," which preserves "a romanticized vision of our lost towns, clean and crime-free and always jolly. . . . What used to be a civic ideal in America is now a movie set we visit during vacations." Gretchen Dykstra, the president of the Times Square Business Improvement District, sighed, "There is a tendency among some academics to romanticize the gutter."

America was becoming Disneyfied for better and worse. Las Vegas experienced a similar immersion in choreographed urban fantasy. Successes in fighting crime, in redeeming once-unredeemable areas, in stimulating the stock market, boosted social confidence. A euphoric streak emerged in this culture of wonder, eclipsing the angst of Kurt Cobain and his Seattle downers. The big summer bubblegum pop hit of 1997 by a wholesome threesome from Tulsa, Oklahoma, epitomized the mood. "MMMBop, ba duba dop," Hanson sang. "So hold on the ones who really care," this home-schooled, churchgoing boy band, aged seventeen, fourteen, and twelve, preached. "In the end they'll be the only ones there." As sunny as the Beach Boys, as peppy as the Beatles when they first debuted, as desperate to please as rivals like New Kids on the Block and the Backstreet Boys, the boys made no apologies for their frothy music. "I think everybody's tired of being sad," the band's twelve-year-old cutie-pie Zac observed. "Bring on the fun, fun, fun."

Gluttons in Relaxed Fit Jeans and Spartans in Spandex

This all-American sense of fun, fun, fun, mingled with a sense of fear, as American culture wavered between hedonism and Puritanism, between too much indulgence and too much guilt. Americans seemed to be the world's fattest people and the buffest, the most spoiled and the toughest. Fast food was a $110 billion industry, sucking up nearly half the money Americans spent on food. Dieting was a $40 billion industry. Health club memberships jumped during the decade by 48 percent from 20.7 million to 30.6 million members, as Americans rushed to buy healthier, more organic, and fancier foods. *The American Medical Association Family Health Cookbook,* published in 1997, earned an advance of $750,000, guiding Americans toward "good health and great taste," with each recipe analyzed nutritionally.

Even as the percent of overweight Americans nearly doubled from 33 percent in 1960 to 62 percent in 2000, with 27 percent obese, millions of Americans jogged, cycled, pumped iron, and contorted themselves in multiple ways, worshipping in the cult of the sculpted body. Many aging Baby Boomers, led by the jogger-in-chief Bill Clinton, worked out with the zeal of Ponce de León seeking the Fountain of Youth. The pressure on women to be thin intensified. By 1990, the typical fashion model was 23 percent skinnier than the average American woman. In 1965 typical models were only 8 percent thinner.

Particularly surprising was the growing young male obsession with looking "cut," seeking sharply defined muscles and perfect "six-packs." Heterosexual muscle men like Arnold Schwarzenegger and Sylvester Stallone helped mainstream gay sensibilities, now reflected in PR campaigns like Calvin Klein's shirtless Marky Mark ads in 1992 and Klein's infamous 1995 borderline-teen-porn jeans commercials. Suddenly, taking off your shirt in public exhilarated those with the right definition and humiliated the flabby majority.

Even Batman became increasingly buff. George Clooney's armored suit, conveying a sense of a sculpted body for the 1997 flop *Batman & Robin*, weighed ninety pounds. "Now boys can become as psychologically and physically debilitated by body-image concerns as girls have been for decades," the science writer Stephen Hall winced in *The New York Times Magazine*. This quest for the new standard of body perfection and performance led many athletes to use performance-enhancing drugs, inaugurating Major League Baseball's home-run-hitting, mass-cheating, muscle-bound steroids era.

In the 1960s, few young men worked out to get protruding "pecs." Exercise equipment was not found in homes. Gyms were big indoor areas for basketball, not climate-controlled gathering places for strange-looking machines with muscular "trainers." Arugula was too obscure even to be a punch line. Three-quarters of the American food budget was spent on home-cooking. Americans averaged 250 fewer calories daily including 100 fewer calories of sweets. American adults were 24 pounds lighter. The overproduction of food, and the shift, especially when eating out, to more fats and oils, bulked up America.

These disparities in personal behavior, which Americans could control, reflected the country's vastness, its diversity, and its ongoing, often overlooked, class divides. The United States was big enough so that 50.4 million "frequent exercisers" in 1999 could still leave tens of millions flocking to 12,500 McDonald's outlets in the United States alone in 1997—and they were not eating the 91 percent fat-free burger patty, the McLean Deluxe, introduced in 1991, dropped in 1996.

This disparity between the gluttons in Relaxed Fit jeans and the Spartans in spandex reflected three historic strains in American culture that intensified in the 1990s. The pursuit of happiness was more zealous than ever following the 1960s bacchanal and loss of innocence. Enforcing public Puritanism had nevertheless become a mass media specialty. And the utopian drive to achieve a perfect, consequence-free life seemed downright achievable with so much science, technology, and social science data available as insulation against the world's chaos.

The Great American Smoking Showdown

The clash between indulgence and strictness, complicated by questions of corporate culpability when individuals engage in injurious behavior, fueled the Great American Smoking Showdown. On April 14, 1994, seven leading tobacco executives embarrassed themselves when they denied smoking was addictive, although most admitted that they would discourage their children from smoking. The seven distinguished-looking white males in business suits exuded the sense of authority that intimidated Americans in the 1950s. Their botched testimony galvanized smoking abolitionists.

In six hours of questioning before the House Energy and Commerce Subcommittee on Health and the Environment, chaired by the zealous Henry

Waxman and broadcast live on C-SPAN and CNN, the executives admitted fiddling with nicotine levels, only to improve flavor, not cultivate addiction, of course. They claimed the "anti-tobacco industry wants . . . prohibition," a dirty word since the 1920s. James W. Johnston, the CEO of R. J. Reynolds, selectively harvesting from the new Spartanism, said everything people eat, from Coca-Cola to Twinkies, could be harmful. Congressman Waxman retorted: "Yes, but the difference between cigarettes and Twinkies is death."

On January 1, 1995, California became the first state to ban smoking in all enclosed workplaces, including restaurants and bars. Now, smokers smoked outside, as bars lost their signature blue smoke inside. Within two decades, more than 80 percent of Americans would live in states with such bans.

In February 1996, Jeffrey S. Wigand, once a $300,000-a-year vice president of research and development at Brown & Williamson, became the whistleblower of the decade. He claimed his company had sought a more addictive nicotine mix and blocked him from developing a safer cigarette. Interviewed by Mike Wallace on CBS's flagship investigative news show, *60 Minutes*, Wigand branded Big Tobacco "a nicotine delivery business."

CBS lawyers squelched the segment, because Wigand violated his confidentiality agreement. When *The Wall Street Journal* published Wigand's testimony in Mississippi's lawsuit against cigarette makers seeking reimbursement for treating smoking-related illnesses, *60 Minutes* was humiliated but freed to broadcast. Russell Crowe portrayed Wigand in the 1999 film, *The Insider,* promoted with the tagline: "Two men driven to tell the truth . . . whatever the cost." The tobacco pushers were now considered the nation's most brazen liars.

Mississippi's attorney general Mike Moore played the good ole' David confronting the tobacco Goliath. Unlike during the 1960s, Mississippi would be, in Moore's words, America's "safe haven for the truth" in the Smoking Wars. When an Ole Miss law school classmate told him about a secretary's mother who ended up on Medicaid while dying from tobacco-related heart disease, they pioneered a novel legal theory. Product liability lawsuits against cigarette manufacturers always failed because judges and juries held smokers responsible for smoking. Now, Moore claimed the tobacco companies benefited unfairly because the state paid for health damages they caused and should cover.

Recruiting thirty-nine other state attorneys general, Moore and his mostly state-university trained buddies beat teams of Ivy League lawyers with this claim. Moore was fighting the "most corrupt and evil corporate animal that has ever been created in this country." "Tobacco kills four hundred twenty thousand people a year," he noted in 1998. "That's 21 times the number of deaths" from "illegal drugs." "The worst part of this epidemic is that it isn't the product of deadly natural forces raging out of control, but a sophisticated, deliberate marketing campaign, targeted at our children," President Clinton said.

Moore knew that "Nobody had ever beaten the tobacco industry before." But he and his friends believed that "if we won, we might . . . save more lives than most doctors have ever saved in history." By 1997, President Clinton and Big Tobacco's Park Avenue lawyers were advocating settlement negotiations. Fearing public fury and waves of personal injury lawsuits, the leaders of Big Tobacco initially agreed to a $368.5 billion settlement with Moore and his colleagues in June 1997. The details of the settlement changed, but the precedent had been set. Big Tobacco had been defeated. Social disapproval was mainstreamed even as the collective social addiction persisted. "Smoking ain't going to go away," said Richard Kluger, the author of a 1996 book, *Ashes to Ashes,* on "America's hundred-year cigarette war."

Lobbying for tough legislation in 1998 to raise the price of cigarettes and increasing penalties for marketing to children, Clinton said: "Thirty years of deception—now Congress must act to bring it to an end." He called it "an American issue. . . . This is not about politics."

A Truly Golden Moment

In 1997, Clinton was enjoying his role as the Good Father during what he would call "a truly golden moment for America" and becoming more popular as a result. All this technological wizardry, all these attempts at reasserting control, thrilled him—and validated his approach, to use a verb gaining in popularity. Clinton and his aides once again set historic goals, hoping to deliver what one strategy memo called "the most productive first year of a second presidential term in memory."

"At this last presidential inaugural of the 20th century, let us lift our eyes toward the challenges that await us in the next century," Bill Clinton proclaimed on January 20, celebrating his political parallel to Silicon Valley's magic making: "Problems that once seemed destined to deepen now bend to our efforts." Always competing with Franklin Roosevelt, Clinton wanted to be as visionary. The national challenge now was managing the Information Age, not surviving the Great Depression; this inaugural address was the first to mention the words "microchip" and "Internet."

Having sworn his oath on a Bible opened to Isaiah 58:12, "thou shalt be called, the repairer of the breach," Clinton appealed to Republicans. Rejecting "the politics of petty bickering and extreme partisanship," he warned: "nothing big ever came from being small." Clinton wanted to lead a civic renaissance, restoring civility, renewing democracy. He positioned the president as preacher, tending the soul of the nation, not simply head of government and head of state. It was ambitious, and necessary in a country growing increasingly alienated from politics' nastiness.

With more of a technocrat's analysis than a zealot's passion, Clinton again charted a Third Way, triangulating between liberalism and Reaganism. "Government is not the problem, and government is not the solution," he declared. "We—the American people—we are the solution." A techno-pioneer, he sought "a new government for a new century—humble enough not to try to solve all our problems for us, but strong enough to give us the tools to solve our problems for ourselves; a government that is smaller, lives within its means, and does more with less." In concluding his twenty-two-minute speech, before a smaller crowd than 1993's exhilarated masses, Clinton reinforced the rhetorical bridge he had been building to the new century, with foundations of community, responsibility, citizenship, and justice.

Two weeks later, in his State of the Union address, Clinton translated these big ideas into scaled-down Polly Pocket policies, a miniature line of children's toys Mattel started marketing in the early 1990s. He used the words, "child," "children," "young people," "family," or "families," fifty-six times. In America, Clinton proclaimed, "every eight-year-old must be able to read; every twelve-year-old must be able to log on to the Internet; every eighteen-year-old must be able to go to college; and every adult American must be able to keep on learning for a lifetime." Presidents do not always "pay this kind of attention to education," Clinton acknowledged. But remembering the Cold War's bipartisan foreign policy wherein "politics stopped at the water's edge," Clinton appealed for "a new nonpartisan commitment to education, because education is a critical national security issue for our future, and politics must stop at the schoolhouse door."

Clinton used the speech to launch the Welfare to Work Partnership, a model Third Way program. Led by Eli Segal, who started AmeriCorps, this public-private partnership helped Clinton's controversial welfare reform succeed by encouraging corporations to hire welfare recipients. A bigger push, the Welfare to Work Coalition to Sustain Success, recruited religious groups, civil society, and the federal government in the effort, too. From a starting goal of hiring 10,000, the federal government hired nearly 50,000 welfare recipients by 2000. Segal's partnership started with five companies and by 2000 involved 20,000 companies with 1.1 million new hires. This communal, win-win effort reduced the welfare rolls by 60 percent, to 5.8 million. "The percentage of Americans on welfare reached the lowest level since 1963, 2.1 percent," a White House brief-ing book rejoiced.

Craving more such successes, Clinton sought to bury the partisanship of his first term and balance the budget while saving America's children. As he con-cluded his address, the networks split the TV screens, to show a jury convict O. J. Simpson in the civil suit his victims' families brought against him. Clinton hated the "media's limited appetite for policy, compared with breaking scan-dal." In 1912, when Woodrow Wilson was asked to summarize a speech he would deliver later that day because the baseball championship would monop-olize the afternoon wires, the professorial presidential candidate balked. "I have a feeling that the question of who is to be President is equally as impor-tant as who wins the world's series," he sniffed. Eighty-five years later, with a more powerful media and a more frustrated incumbent, many spoke about Clinton's "split-screen presidency," using this coincidence to capture the con-stant manic-depressive toggling between fluff and substance.

The mediums Clinton used to convey his message of unity simultaneously undermined it. The president and the media were two muscle-bound giants, pos-sessing immense power to dominate American thought yet debilitated by Americans' contempt for both. The president as celebrity-in-chief was lionized and pulverized, magnified and trivialized, by reporters.

Prime-time programming, reinforced by Hollywood movies, fed the public contradictory and misleading images. Most celluloid presidents were handsome and heroic—a Michael Douglas in *The American President* (1995), a Harrison Ford in *Air Force One* (1997). Others were devious or sniveling as in *Absolute Power* (1997), starring Clint Eastwood as a cat burglar more virtuous than the president. First Ladies fared even worse. *The American President* made Michael Douglas a widower so he could appear vulnerable and alluring. In the 1996 hit *Independence Day,* the First Lady is a hard-driving careerist who spurns her hus-band's request to return home from a political trip before the alien invasion and pays for her independence with her life.

These blockbuster films and the all-news-all-the-time TV stations kept at-tention focused on the chief executive. Alas, the scrutiny was often "harsh." Clinton needed to show, staffers noted, he was "taking real actions," especially on the "priorities . . . which the press is ready to cover if he acts (e.g. balanced budget, education, campaign finance reform in a proactive way)." They knew the "President has the greatest leverage" in his first year after election. They wanted to position him as being "above politics" and reaching "across party lines." To stop reporters from defining his 1996 victory as "reactions to a weak opponent or the Republican Congress," they wanted to "define" the election's "mandate" as a "clear affirmation" of Clinton, "his record, his vision, and his plans for leading the country."

Clinton and his people were constantly trying to frame "priorities," which they endorsed sincerely in ways that would pass media muster—and avoid media mockery. All this attention redoubled White House efforts to manage the news. "No day went by without the president and his coterie laboring mightily to generate favorable headlines and deflect damaging ones," *Washington Post* media critic Howard Kurtz observed. The elder statesman Dean Acheson once dismissed Richard Nixon by comparing him to a shortstop so concerned about how he looked when fielding, he bobbles the ball; Clinton often made the same error.

The new chief of staff, Erskine Bowles, ended the first term's chaos. With round glasses and an aging choir-boy look exuding competence and rectitude, this North Carolina investment banker headed the Small Business Administration before joining the White House staff. He imposed discipline on the president and his aides, including insisting that Clinton the great seducer stop agreeing with everyone during budget negotiations. With leading liberals like George Stephanopoulos and Robert Reich gone, Bowles helped keep Clinton centered and centrist.

A "New Story Line" of "Multiracial Hope"

Clinton hoped to encourage substantive racial reconciliation during his second term. His Memphis speech challenging African Americans to fight black crime, poverty, and irresponsibility still resonated. With racial relations calm, now was the time to work on "things that are going to be critical to our future before the wheel runs off." Clinton's special counsel and key adviser on race, Christopher Edley Jr., had long lobbied for movement beyond "antidiscrimination," using Clinton's role as "First Preacher and Chief Teacher" to encourage the necessary change in "civic virtues" and "private practices." Delivering the University of California San Diego commencement address on July 14, 1997, Clinton launched a blue ribbon commission as the central vehicle for "the President's Initiative on Race."

Faith in a commission varied with one's faith in the president. Senator Carol Moseley Braun of Illinois noted Clinton's particular "credibility" on the issue, with Father Theodore Hesburgh of Notre Dame citing Clinton's Memphis speech as the right launchpad. Skeptics feared all rhetoric and no action could worsen race relations, while some White House aides feared the initiative was more symbolic than real. Hillary Clinton would play an important role in re-minding more radical White House staffers that the president could only prog-ress if he led from the white, male, middle-class center on this one.

In drafting the address, Clinton's advisers tried but failed to highlight their boss's broader themes of "opportunity" and "responsibility." They did unveil a "new story line" of "multiracial hope," to understand America as "the world's first truly multiracial democracy." He told the graduates, a "half-century from now, when your own grandchildren are in college, there will be no majority race in America." The surge in the Hispanic population, the growing tensions be-tween blacks and Koreans, the phenomenon of native-born Hispanics and Asian-Pacific Americans marrying white spouses, blurred the black-white racial fault lines. Clinton wondered: "Can we define what it means to be an Ameri-can, not just in terms of the hyphen showing our ethnic origins but in terms of our primary allegiance to the values America stands for and values we really live by?" Playing the New Democrat, Clinton rejected multicultural smarmi-ness as well as racist harshness. He acknowledged: "The ideals that bind us to-gether are as old as our Nation, but so are the forces that pull us apart."

This wise speech in mid-June anticipated one of his presidency's most mov-ing moments in late September. Clinton returned home to mark the fortieth anniversary of the day in 1957 when President Dwight Eisenhower deployed the 101st Airborne Division to escort nine young black children to school in Little Rock. It "was here at Central High that we took another giant step closer to the idea of America," Clinton said, thanking the Little Rock Nine for helping "open the doors so we could become the people we say we want to be." Clinton recalled watching as an eleven-year-old fifty miles away in Hot Springs, shocked that protestors were taunting kids for trying to learn. "It was Little Rock that made racial equality a driving obsession in my life," he explained.

After the speech, in a remarkable moment of healing, the Little Rock Nine, now older, grayer, and heavier, walked through the door that racists, including Governor Orval Faubus, had tried blocking. This time, the president of the United States and the governor of Arkansas, Mike Huckabee, held the door open for these everyday heroes. Minnijean Brown Trickey faltered as she crossed the threshold, overcome with emotion. Clinton and Huckabee grasped her hand and comforted her. In an age of Silicon Valley wonders but political cynicism, this miracle represented the titanic redemptive capacity of democratic politics and liberal ideals.

Unfortunately, the president's race initiative lacked such majesty. Chaired by the African American historian John Hope Franklin, the commission seemed too tied to past achievements to shape future ones. Franklin refused to hear opponents of affirmative action. Unlike Clinton, Franklin and most of his colleagues stayed mired in the black versus white paradigm. Within the White House, New Democratic advisers especially feared the initiative was "suffocating in its own pillow of political correctness," as Michael Waldman would put it. Recoiling from much of the White House finger-pointing and breast-beating, the columnist Charles Krauthammer would quote Orlando Patterson, a leading African American academic. Patterson called the United States "the least racist white-majority society in the world," offering more "legal protection of minorities than any other society, white or black" and "more opportunities to a greater number of black persons than any other society, including all those of Africa."

The great opportunities amid 1997's good feelings would dissipate amid 1998's sordid politics. Clinton's great race initiative would seem more like colorful Band-Aids put on legs with multiple fractures. After fifteen months, this temporary council would propose creating . . . a permanent presidential council on race.

Marching Toward Diversity

In retrospect, Clinton's race initiative was a milestone in America's march toward diversity and multiracial inclusion. Having a president "celebrate our diversity" helped align the national conversation with the changing national realities. Clinton preached that "The marvelous blend of cultures and beliefs and races has always enriched America, and it is our meal ticket to the 21st century." Increasingly, university leaders talked about broadening the diversity conversation from one of racial diversity to "diversity in age, gender, religious beliefs, geographical origin, political perspective, physical ability and sexual orientation," as the president of Colorado State University explained. Similarly, corporations began speaking about moving from "valuing differences" to "living diversity," creating "a cultural and social ambiance that is inclusive and empowers all groups in the corporation" so that the "employee population . . . reflects the population overall, as well as specific communities served." The goal, a Deloitte newsletter explained, was "embedding diversity into the DNA of the organization."

With about a quarter of the country now identified as "people of color," the workforce and the marketplace were changing. With, for example, the buying power of the LGBT community estimated at $835 billion, hovering between the $696.5 billion Asian American community and the $1.1 trillion African American market, closer ties with various American subgroups made good business sense. Often, "it is hard to form a brand relationship unless you have people that come from these cultures and ethnicities that can connect," Don Knauss, Clorox's CEO, noted.

The Westminster Clinton

White House squabbling had died down. Newt Gingrich was distracted by his own scandal. Using 501(c)(3) nonprofit status to raise money for political ends ensnared him in dozens of ethical violations that ultimately cost him a $300,000 fine and a humiliating congressional reprimand. Neither party wanted a budgetary showdown. In late July, Democratic and Republican negotiators compromised. Republicans won a $500-per-child tax credit, as desired in Gingrich's Contract with America, lower capital gains tax rates of 18 percent, and a drop in inheritance taxes, including exemptions as high as $1.3 million for family farms. Democrats secured $1,500 tuition offsets for middle-income college students, a $24 billion package for extending children's health care coverage, and a jump in the cigarette tax from 24 cents to 39 cents per pack by 2002. "This historic investment in children's health is a major victory for America's children and working families," said Marian Wright Edelman, president of the Children's Defense Fund, who had fought Clinton's 1996 welfare reform furiously. Thanks to the booming economy, Clinton would sign "the first balanced budget in a generation," and receive credit for finally achieving some bipartisan cooperation.

Clinton received a validating transatlantic hug when the Labor Party's Tony Blair became Great Britain's prime minister in May 1997. Mid-forties, intellectual, charismatic, and hip, with a young, super-smart, charismatic, and hip working wife, this Westminster Clinton also combined a love of politicking with a passion for ideas. Blair was overhauling his party's hidebound leftist ideology to produce a smart, humane, progressive but capitalist Third Way suited for twenty-first-century governance. When Blair met the DLC's Al From, Blair produced a piece of paper with the three magic Clinton words written on it: opportunity, responsibility, and community. Blair's guru, the sociologist Anthony Giddens, added to the conversation about this utopian-realist muscular moderation, championing a "cosmopolitan nationalism" that can facilitate the "democratized family" during this time not of "moral decay," but "moral transition."

As they recruited other leaders, and hosted a series of Third Way conferences, Blair and Clinton would also be joined by France's socialist prime minister,

Lionel Jospin. Jospin wanted to say, "Yes to the market economy; no to the market society." Sometimes these aphorisms were too cutesy. In the Third Way's "elitist" reliance on "spin doctors" and nimble leaders pitching "community" over "liberty," the liberal parliamentarian and sociologist Ralf Dahrendorf detected a "curious authoritarian streak" that was downright Singaporean. For Clinton, Blair's emergence was a blessing. Clinton "appeared no longer as a strange, isolated figure, but as a forerunner, model, and senior partner in a newly reframed transatlantic alliance," his adviser Sidney Blumenthal would write. No longer a "political exception," Bill Clinton was now "the leader of an international movement."

Scandal at Motel 1600

During this very good year for both Clintons, they still spent too much time managing scandals. In April, the White House admitted that some Clinton aides funneled $400,000 in money and easy jobs to their disgraced colleague Webster Hubbell. That same month, the Clintons' Whitewater partner James B. McDougal was sentenced to three years in prison for fraud and conspiracy, while his ex-wife Susan McDougal was jailed on contempt of court charges for refusing to testify against Clinton. Throughout that spring, Kenneth Starr's team fought to see certain notes of White House lawyers. The White House handed them over June 23. In July, Starr's office determined that Vince Foster had committed suicide—although wild rumors still circulated.

Whitewater was like a persistent toothache, providing constant, low-level pain. The post-1996 campaign finance charges were like a series of flus, hitting intensely each time with potentially disastrous consequences, if not cured. In 1996, Clinton's subtle but obvious peddling of nights at "Motel 1600"—as critics rechristened 1600 Pennsylvania Avenue—in exchange for political contributions triggered traditional fears that the republic would decline. In an ironic tribute to the First Lady's central role in this presidency, Hillary Clinton helped sell off access to presidential events.

The quid pro quo was not unprecedented; the Clintonian brazenness and scale were. One hundred and three White House coffees raised $26.4 million, averaging $54,000 per Danish eaten. Lincoln Bedroom sleepovers pulled in at least $100,000 per night. The president, vice president, and First Lady never solicited explicitly or called them "fund-raisers," but all guests knew why they were invited. One discovered document showed Clinton's campaign manager Peter Knight estimating that one coffee for Texans would generate about

$500,000. Other memoranda referring to these "political/fundraising coffees" spoke of "projected revenue" before events and amounts "in hand" after.

The Clintons' fund-raising sins were more moral than legal. The Clintons vetted their activities with lawyers expert in contemporary "ethics" and campaign law. This Clintonesque rationale that the ends justify the means showed how the Adversarials applied their 1960s' guerilla tactics and self-righteousness to serve money and power in this Democratic Gilded Age. Just as they enjoyed catching Hillary Clinton profiteering like a good Reaganite on the 1980s' commodities market, reporters loved watching Sixties' rebels who cut their teeth during the Watergate era indulging in Nixonian fund-raising. The Clintons once again confirmed the media's storyline of dishonest pols, increasing the cynicism.

The Clintonites intensified the disappointment by self-righteously parading as extra-virtuous. "During his first campaign, Mr. Clinton pledged he would be . . . the most ethical president in the history of this country," *The Hartford Courant* editorialized in "Bill Clinton as Motel Manager . . . . In fact, this administration has been one of the most ethically deficient."

Most Americans were inured to it all. Two-thirds of those surveyed considered Clinton's tactics no worse than other presidents. Clinton's approval rating stayed stable around 60 percent. A Herblock cartoon with Bill Clinton saying, "True, I had coffee with those big contributors but I didn't swallow," showed that Clinton lowered the majority's expectations about politicians' behavior while raising the bar by believing a tactic had to be illegal to be unacceptable. Even the president was no longer a paragon of virtue. Clinton was at once defining deviancy down and skirting scandals sideways. In a healthy republic, the law should only be a measure of last resort.

A more serious threat to the democracy's integrity was the money trail from Chinese intelligence operatives into the Executive Mansion. The Democratic National Committee would eventually return $2,825,600 in illegal or improper donations, with 80 percent of those funds coming via Charlie Trie and John Huang. Trie ran a Chinese restaurant in Little Rock in the 1970s but by the mid-1990s had partners with deep pockets and Chinese government connections. Huang was a nine-year employee of the Lippo Group, an Indonesian-based conglomerate controlled by the Riady family. His campaign largesse in 1992 secured a deputy assistant secretary spot in the Commerce Department, then a job as DNC vice chairman in December 1995. Huang remained surprisingly intertwined with his old company. Much of the $3.4 million Huang funneled came either from foreigners or from Lippo-related employees who were then illegally reimbursed. Another mysterious funder, Johnny Chung, gave some of his gifts right in the First Lady's office, and tried using his photos with the Clintons to attract business. "The White House is like a subway," he proclaimed shamelessly, having visited fifty times: "You have to put in coins to open the gates."

These sleazy stories fed fears of "The China Plan" to influence the American elections. As revelations mounted, secretary of state Madeleine Albright would protest to China's leaders in Beijing—who denied it. The theatrical Republican senator Fred Thompson opened Senate hearings claiming investigators from his Governmental Affairs Committee found proof that "high-level Chinese government officials" sought "to pour illegal money into American political campaigns" to "subvert our election process." Nine and a half months, 34 lawyers, 427 subpoenas, 1.5 million documents, and $4.35 million later, Thompson's committee deadlocked over the conclusions in its 1,100-page final report. Thompson looked foolish for producing no authoritative evidence of Chinese manipulation.

Chinese Villainy Doesn't Sell

Even in multiculti America, many had difficulty following the different Chinese names. The Chinese did not scare Americans as the Russians did during the Cold War, or even the Japanese did during the 1980s. Deng Xiaoping's "socialist market reform" made China capitalist enough so it did not appear as totalitarian as it was, despite an estimated 230,000 people undergoing "reeducation" in 280 forced labor camps.

That year, the Hollywood heavyweight Richard Gere discovered that Chinese villainy did not make it in the box office. A Tibetan Buddhist and a follower of the Dalai Lama since 1978, Gere had become Hollywood's leading Free Tibet activist. When presenting during the 1993 Academy Awards, Gere infuriated the Hollywood establishment by ignoring his script and denouncing the "horrendous, horrendous human rights situation there is in China, not only towards their own people but to Tibet as well." In 1997, he costarred in *Red Corner,* a thriller with Gere in his *Pretty Woman* master of the universe mode as a hotshot lawyer framed for murder in China. "In America, he would know his rights, but here, justice does not translate," the trailer warned ominously.

Gere was already banned from China—now, his movie was, too. Gere would be named *People*'s "sexiest man alive" in 1999. Gere-centered movies like *Pretty Woman* in 1990, *Sommersby* in 1993, *Primal Fear* in 1996, *The Jackal* in 1997, and *Runaway Bride* in 1999 all generated more than $50 million in box office. *Pretty Woman* earned $463,407,268. *Red Corner* tanked, earning $22 million.

Characteristically, Bill Clinton was as eloquent in attacking money in politics as he was shameless in collecting funds. Rahm Emanuel, a fierce Clinton loyalist, bluntly advised the president: "We are facing real questions on our sincerity in regards to campaign finance reform." Reporters now believed the administration was just "lip synching our resolve for change rather than leading the effort for political reform." As questions multiplied in 1997, the president offered long-winded explanations that clouded the issues while dispatching shock troops to offer what one of them, Lanny J. Davis, would call "a credible counterpoint message," essentially, the classic Clinton jujitsu of claiming everybody else did it, then attacking the prosecutors for unfairness.

Good Father but Bad Husband?

In March 1997, as embarrassing campaign finance revelations mounted, Clinton starred in a new round of politically calculated public service commercials. Amid stirring portraits of George Washington and Abraham Lincoln, President Clinton declared: "Every day, I try my best to meet the challenges that come with doing the toughest job in the world . . . being a parent." Boosting the Coalition for America's Children, Bill and Hillary Clinton declared: "We're fighting for the children. Whose side are you on?"

In April, on Earth Day, Papa Clinton would expand an "early-warning system" for reporting the release of toxic chemicals into the environment, "to keep . . . children safe from toxic pollution." In July, Professor Clinton would call for a summit of computer industry leaders, educators, and parents to restrict access to indecent material online. And in August, Dr. Clinton would order pharmaceutical companies to test most new drugs for the proper children's doses. A former Reagan speechwriter, Doug Gamble, would scoff that Clinton should have sworn his oath of office "with one hand placed on Dr. Spock's *Baby and Child Care* instead of the Bible."

In the White House, the Good Father's image clashed with the fallout from actions as a bad husband. Insiders reported that the president's biggest worry was Paula Jones's civil action, triggered by the Troopergate article. Jones was both genuinely aggrieved and greedily willing to be used by Clinton's opponents.

A week before the 1996 election, Stuart Taylor reexamined the Jones Case in Steve Brill's magazine *American Lawyer*. Jones had spoken to friends immediately after the incident, enabling them to corroborate many details. Taylor attributed the contrasting responses to Anita Hill and Paula Jones despite Jones's "stronger" case to the "class bias of feminists and liberals." "Drag a hundred dollars through a trailer park and there's no telling what you'll find," James Carville sneered.

Thanks to Taylor, Paula Jones appeared on *Newsweek*'s cover just two weeks before Clinton's second inauguration. The week of the inauguration, the Supreme Court heard Clinton's claim that if the president could be subject to civil lawsuits while in office, he would become a "magnet for litigation." On May 28, the court rejected that argument unanimously, using more elegant language to affirm the court of appeals' blunt language: "the Constitution did not create a monarchy."

Clinton's lawyer Robert Bennett had nearly negotiated a settlement in May 1994, paying off Paula Jones and affirming that she never engaged "in any improper or sexual conduct." At the last minute, aggressive White House spin doctors insulted Jones in the media and she scuttled the deal. As a result, Clinton's extramarital affairs became fair game in the suit that was going forward so that Paula Jones could demonstrate a "pattern of behavior."

In June 1997, Bennett warned Jones he would "put her reputation at issue" if she made broad inquiries into Clinton's private life. But as a liberal president who signed the Violence Against Women Act in 1994, limiting the use of a victim's sexual past in court cases, Clinton could not approve such bullying when a woman was charging sexual harassment. As Bennett backpedaled, the feminist backlash against him broke many women's uncomfortable silence over Clinton's peccadilloes. Many feminists admitted they cared more about "Jones's allies" than Clinton's sins.

Everyone played their part in the by now too-familiar ritual. In Congress, the Republicans hauled presidential aides before committees and subpoenaed truckloads of documents. The Democrats condemned the partisan witch hunt. In the White House, the damage control unit first tried to suppress embarrassing information, then leaked it at the last minute to provide "context." In the newspapers, bold headlines gradually faded into short summaries, as the public stifled yawns. As for Bill Clinton, he kept doing his job, outfoxing Republicans, acting presidential, and shepherding a booming economy.

Even many of the most aggressive reporters "felt ambivalent," as *Newsweek*'s Michael Isikoff did, about tracking down rumors of "a consensual sexual relationship." But Isikoff and others came to believe that Clinton was "far more psychologically disturbed than the public ever imagined." The "scale" of Clinton's "private misbehavior . . . required routine, repetitive, and reflexive lies to conceal itself." This "culture of concealment" had "infected his entire presidency,"

Isikoff believed, with "corrosive effects" on the administration and the body politic. Such widespread wrongdoing justified the most aggressive reporting.

Despite these sporadic bursts of disgrace, Clinton's popularity hovered around 60 percent all year, making 1997 his most popular year in office. In 1996, he had averaged 55 percent approval, after rarely enjoying majority support his first three years. Supporters pointed to the balanced budget, the drop in crime, and the focus on education as proof that their president cared about their concerns. Unemployment, averaging 4.9 percent in 1997, had not been so low since the early 1970s. Without the constant scandals, Clinton's approval ratings could have spiked higher.

Titanic Worries: America Amuck!

The scandalmongering resonated with deeper social anxieties. Underlying the 1990s' peace, prosperity, and partying, Americans were skittish. In 1997, two of America's greatest novelists produced instant classics capturing the sense of loss, the underlying fear, the collective vertigo millions were experiencing. The tablets had been smashed—traditional scripts trashed—frequently replaced with much shopping and mass confusion.

Philip Roth's Pulitzer Prize–winning *American Pastoral,* released in May, caught America in the act of having a nervous breakdown. The country reels amid the New Nihilism, expressed by the implosion of Swede Levov's American Dream, as his suburban daughter becomes a terrorist during the 1960s: "He had learned the worst lesson that life can teach," Roth wrote, "that it makes no sense."

Don DeLillo's *Underworld,* released in October, obsessed about all the waste America generates. One character admits, "Marian and I saw products as garbage even when they sat gleaming on store shelves, yet unbought. We didn't say, What kind of casserole will that make? We said, What kind of garbage will that make?" Waste, DeLillo wrote, is "an interesting word" with "such derivatives as empty, void, vanish and devastate."

Both best sellers missed the innocent world that was lost, despite the Great Depression, the Great War, and yesteryear's many prejudices. Roth was born in Newark to first-generation Jewish immigrants in 1933. DeLillo was born in the Bronx to Italian-Catholics in 1936. *Underworld* begins with a tour de force capturing the excitement of Bobby Thompson's "shot heard round the world" in the 1951 baseball pennant playoff between the New York Giants and the Brooklyn Dodgers. *American Pastoral* has a lovingly exhaustive description of the manufacture and sale of women's gloves, back in the day. "This country is frightening," Swede Levov's brother Jerry laments. "Oh where oh where is that outmoded America, that decorous America where a woman had twenty-five pairs of gloves? . . . America amok! America amuck."

The New York Times listed both novels in 2006 as among the greatest works of American fiction in the last twenty-five years. Both books missed the morally clear, grounded, good old days, while disgusted by the gravity-free and gravitas-free zone America had become. Both novels blamed America's decline on sexual licentiousness without mimicking the false nostalgia of the Christian evangelicals who treated sex as something newly discovered in the 1960s. In 1969, Roth's *Portnoy's Complaint* rejected the old sexual regime's repression and guilt. Still, the new "if it feels good do it" approach appeared even more toxic, dissolving families, friendship, and faith, in one another and the country. These pre-Lewinsky novels anticipated the connection millions of Americans would make between the indiscretions of the representative American and the insecurities of the moment.

The year's biggest movie also mourned America's lost innocence in this high-tech Gilded Age. James Cameron's *Titanic* was as big as its name, as grandiose as its subject, and nearly a disaster, too. Its $200 million budget, covering a 17-million-gallon water tank and a 750-foot-long Titanic replica, made it the most expensive movie ever made as of 1997. The final cut's running time of three hours and fourteen minutes made recouping expenses seem unlikely.

Titanic became the first movie ever to gross $1 billion. It would win eleven Oscars in 1998, including "Best Picture," prompting Cameron to shout the heartthrob Leonardo DiCaprio's now-classic line, "I'm the King of the World!" The film worked as the ultimate "chick flick" (a Nineties' phrase), with star-crossed lovers, a sappy theme song, Céline Dion's "My Heart Will Go On," and a heartbreaking finale that had many men wiping their eyes, pretending they suddenly had some optic irritation.

This sweeping epic also addressed contemporary themes about economic disparity and gender roles. Cameron was fascinated by "the stoicism and nobility of a bygone age" as most men honorably respected the rescue protocols of "women and children first." But the film mocked the Gilded Age's false innocence, grandiosity, and hypocrisies. And in this age of scientific miracles, *Titanic* offered what Cameron called "a potent reminder of the consequences of arrogance and putting too much faith in technology."

Harry Potter and the Sorcerer's Soul

A book first published in 1997 would become even bigger than *Titanic*, marking the greatest British cultural invasion since the Beatles and James Bond, perhaps since Sherlock Holmes and Queen Victoria. The initiated entered into a crazy, colorful alternate universe, partially insulated from the industrial revolution, hip and modern yet crusty and old-fashioned. It was a world of flying cars and Quidditch tournaments, of invisibility cloaks and sorting hats, of mysterious spells and a villain so evil good people dared not speak his name. At the center of this world was a brave young man with glasses and a lightning-shaped scar on his forehead, aided by his brilliant female friend and his loyal, less-distinguished, yet heroic male sidekick.

In a decade of hyper-realism, when they could access more of the world's wonders and horrors with a click of a mouse, amid post–Cold War patriotism and provincialism, Americans became entranced by an imaginary castle in the Scottish Highlands, near the Forbidden Forest and the Black Lake filled with merpeople and a giant squid. The Hogwarts School of Witchcraft and Wizardry was a secondary boarding school for children aged eleven to eighteen, with magical abilities.

Its creator spent five years mapping out her compelling world. Hogwarts's four houses—Gryffindor, Slytherin, Ravenclaw, and Hufflepuff—were named after the school's founders in 990, all oozing a sense of medieval history and mystery. Yet Hogwarts had no architectural plans. It "would be difficult for the most skilled architect to draw," she explained, "owing to the fact that the staircases and the rooms keep moving." The answer—like the books—reflected her wacky fusion of obsessive-compulsive verisimilitude and childlike innocence.

As if she had swallowed a longer-lasting variety of her magical Felix Felicis or Liquid Luck potions, J. K. Rowling morphed from being an underemployed secretary to a billionaire author who was richer than the Queen and knighted by her. She published her first book, *Harry Potter and the Philosopher's Stone*, in England in June 1997, earning an advance of $3,300, following multiple rejections because the 320-page book was too long for children. The American publishers forced a title change to the more democratic *Harry Potter and the Sorcerer's Stone*. Two decades and seven novels later, nearly half a billion copies had been sold, in seventy-three languages. One Potter neologism, "Muggle," a nonmagical person, had made it into the dictionary.

Many eternal elements in the world of Harry Potter would have made J. K. Rowling's series a blockbuster at any age. Rowling referenced classic myths with her Phoenix and her dragons, her wizards and her goblins, her talking animals and her young heroes. When *Harry Potter* debuted on June 30, 1997, it appealed to young and old living in a new world of wizardry. The talking portraits and live-screen newspapers were as magical to their parents as were the new Windows functions and perpetually updated newspaper websites. In Harry Potter, the magic generated what little technology there was, so the technology had soul and an old-fashioned feel. Light came from torches, heat from fireplaces, and mail from owls like Hedwig, Harry's pet. Technology, *Time* would declare, "is for Muggles, who rely on contraptions because they cannot imagine the conveniences of magic. Who wouldn't choose a wizard's life?"

The obsession with Harry Potter, in Severus Snape's famous first words, "Our new—celebrity," offered children in a celebrity-besotted world an inside look into fame's burdens. Watching this orphan improvise a family reassured children in an age of often disposable families that they, too, could find anchors. The intense Britishness of it all added that sense of aristocratic esotericism Americans still guiltily appreciated in their former mother country, helping them feel more cosmopolitan in this ever-globalizing and shrinking world.

"Books! And cleverness! There are more important things—friendship and bravery," Hermione Granger explains in the debut novel. Albus Dumbledore, recalling Harry's mother's dying to save her son, observes, "If there is one thing [the evil villain] Voldemort cannot understand, it is love." Such noble sentiments shaped the rich, vivid, blood-red, three-dimensional Harry Potter universe, offering an appealing, healing alternative to a technologically dominated world which, the real philosopher Charles Taylor noted, often caused the "narrowing and flattening of our lives."

At his best, when actively arranging jobs for welfare recipients and not merely ending the government's payouts to them, when forging an international Third Way coalition, when trying to merge the best of the left and the right, the political wizard Bill Clinton also sought to tap into a deeper nobility more permanent than the latest Silicon Valley innovation or payout. Clinton not only worried about technology being used for evil, he worried about its unintended consequences on jobs, families, spouses, souls. The American people appreciated his concerns, his grandeur, and his resulting idealism, despite his imperfections, making 1997 his best year as president.

On a Roll?

By Christmas 1997, as the hot seasonal gift the Tamagotchi was challenging its new owners by asking on its package, "what kind of virtual caretaker will you be," depositions in the Paula Jones case were pending. Michael Isikoff was already pursuing leads about Clinton's affair with an intern fed him by a former White House employee, Linda Tripp, and her literary agent, Lucianne Goldberg. President Clinton had enlisted the help of his secretary Betty Currie and his fixer Vernon Jordan to neutralize the threat that the Jones attorneys would discover his affair with Ms. Lewinsky. Yet calm prevailed within the Clinton White House.

Clinton hoped, "in the next four years we would be freer to do the public's business without the turmoil and strife of the first term." When the January 1998 employment figures would report an additional 370,000 jobs gained in December 1997, making 14.3 million new jobs for Americans since 1993, Clinton would exult: "Our nation is on a roll." *The New York Times* said, "1998 will be the year that determines whether he will be remembered for anything more positive than ending the welfare safety net," and anticipated "a spectacular, compassionate finale for the epoch."

At one of the First Couple's endless Christmas parties, the Clintons' battle-weary scandal fighter Lanny Davis had told his boss: "I think it's okay for me to return to my law practice, Mr. President, because all the worst scandal stories are behind us." Little did Davis and the Clintons realize that the president had his own iceberg looming. The year 1998 would teach them what James Cameron identified as the *Titanic's* central lesson: "life is uncertain, the future unknowable . . . the unthinkable possible," and that, as Dumbledore warns, "humans do have a knack of choosing precisely those things that are worst for them," even in the age of Silicon Valley magic.

9

1998: Beverly Hills, 90210
The Great American Moral Panic

Welcome to the age of "un-innocence." No one has breakfast at Tiffany's, and no one has affairs to remember. Instead, we have breakfast at 7:00 a.m. and affairs we try to forget as quickly as possible. Self-protection and closing the deal are paramount. Cupid has flown the co-op. How the hell did we get into this mess?

—Carrie Bradshaw, *Sex and the City*
(Season 1, Episode 1), 1998

O n May 20, 1998, Brandon and Kelly, both looking stunning of course, decided to cancel their wedding. The decision was mutual. Living in TV-land as they did, what normally would be a public humiliation became a great party, with the whole *Beverly Hills, 90210* cast dancing away, all looking equally fabulous.

Eight seasons earlier in 1990, this television show had premiered on Fox, looking doomed. Rupert Murdoch's five-year-old TV network-in-formation, merging Metromedia stations with 20th Century Fox studios, was fragile. The show's thirty-year-old creator, Darren Star, was inexperienced. Jason Priestley only won the role of Brandon Walsh days before shooting commenced.

In the show, the Walsh family, with teenage twins, parachute from the Midwest into Southern California's carnival of consumption. "You didn't wear this much makeup in Minnesota," Mrs. Walsh tells her daughter Brenda. Blurring the line between Hollywood fiction and Beverly Hills facts-as-farce, the producer Aaron Spelling, who had recently completed his $12-million, 123-room, 56,000-square-foot mansion, disliked how his daughter Tori, who starred in the show, dressed on the show. "They always put her in the smallest bikinis in the world," he admitted. "As a producer, I don't mind, but as a father, well . . . the mermaid outfit really freaked me out."

Bill and Hillary Clinton were adaptable and resilient. By 1996, buoyed by a booming economy, many Americans were more accepting of his flaws, and excited about building an America suited for the twenty-first century. The First Lady had also improved her image, avoiding polarizing policy issues and embracing traditional First Lady projects, including her bestselling book *It Takes a Village*. (*William J. Clinton Presidential Library*)

By 1997, Bill Gates, pictured above silhouetted during Microsoft's splashy Windows 95 rollout, was so intent on tapping the transformational power of connecting computers to the Internet that his company was in antitrust litigation on two continents. Clinton and Gore wanted a national fiber-optic infrastructure to make this new world broadly accessible as it changed the way Americans shopped, learned, interacted, and thought. *(Top: AP Photo; Right: William J. Clinton Presidential Library)*

After delivering the first second-term inaugural address by a Democrat since Franklin Roosevelt, Bill Clinton had a great 1997. Prime Minister Tony Blair, the young British centrist, helped Clinton's "Third Way" approach go global. At home, Clinton celebrated substantive policy victories and presided over powerful symbolic moments, including welcoming the "Little Rock Nine" through the infamous schoolhouse door segregationists had blocked forty years earlier. *(William J. Clinton Presidential Library)*

During this Democratic Gilded Age, this age of technological wizardry, anything seemed possible, as Americans joined the world in worshipping a clever, brave wizard Harry Potter, as evidenced by this Chicago crowd stretching around the block for a J. K. Rowling book signing. In this emerging Republic of Everything, society was becoming much more welcoming and pluralistic. Gays became increasingly accepted, as demonstrated by the Clintons' visit to the massive AIDS quilt unfurled on the National Mall. *(Top: AP Photo/Fred Jewell; Right: William J. Clinton Presidential Library)*

Intense journalistic and Republican scrutiny of Clinton's character flaws resulted in the Monica Lewinsky scandal, which Hillary Clinton blamed on a "vast right wing conspiracy," while appearing on *Today*. Her husband tried focusing on his job, especially in his ambitious State of the Union Address as the scandal broke in January, 1998. When the House of Representatives impeached Clinton that December, defiant Democrats rushed to the White House for a partisan rally, denouncing the "politics of personal destruction." *(William J. Clinton Presidential Library)*

After the Senate refused to convict, Bill Clinton had to recover personally and politically. Clinton's apology marathon suited America's therapeutic culture, with Oprah Winfrey serving as its high priestess. Amid the delights of this Republic of Everything, many also feared America was becoming a Republic of Nothing, too violent, too unmoored, and too vulnerable to the kind of violence that occurred at Columbine High School in April, 1999. *(Top: William J. Clinton Presidential Library; Bottom: AP Photo/Kevin Higley, File)*

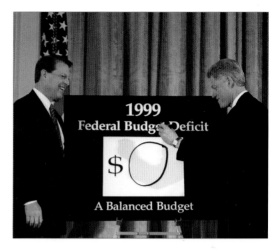

Gradually, the Clintons healed, personally and politically. Hillary Clinton found a popularity as injured spouse while Bill Clinton remained popular, with the budget deficit and crime down and the market up, even though few of his major initiatives advanced during his second term. *(William J. Clinton Presidential Library)*

Hillary Rodham Clinton ended the decade on a high, becoming the first First Lady ever to run for office and eventually winning a Senate seat. Bill Clinton was frustrated that the electoral deadlock that November, 2000, ended with George W. Bush, a Republican, as president. Less than a year after Clinton retired, the terrorist attacks of September 11, 2001, ended the good times abruptly, leaving questions about just what Clinton accomplished, and what ensuing disasters he could or could not have avoided. *(Top: William J. Clinton Presidential Library; Bottom: Eric Draper, Courtesy of the George W. Bush Presidential Library)*

Teenage girls and younger "tweens" first discovered the show during a slow TV summer. In 1991, teen magazine readers called it the show they'd "most like to live in." *The Boston Globe* wondered, "What generation can resist being pandered to?" So many teenage girls in May 1991 mobbed Luke Perry, with his wounded eyes and winsome smile, guards smuggled him out of a Seattle mall in a laundry hamper. By 1998, the show was a decade-defining icon.

Beverly Hills appeared as enchanted and inaccessible to most Americans as Hogwarts. With its rambling homes, landscaped lawns, luxury vehicles, exclusive shops, and showbiz legends, the 32,000-person, mostly white enclave, averaging a mean household income of nearly $150,000, was part Shangri-la, part Sodom and Gomorrah. Supplementing the usual upper-middle-class nannies, tutors, and piano teachers, many children had personal shoppers, trainers, nutritionists, stylists, singing coaches, plastic surgeons, and inevitably, therapists. "Appearance is still everything in Beverly Hills," Carrie Fisher would write. Hollywood royalty as the daughter of Debbie Reynolds and Eddie Fisher, cast as Princess Leia in the first *Star Wars*, Fisher added: "Too many childhoods are missed, too many drugs ingested, too much time is spent in a quest to find your place in a firmament that is already overcrowded."

In 1998, Monica Lewinsky would eclipse that firmament, becoming the most famous Beverly Hillsian for all the wrong reasons. Sex scandals involving twenty-two-year-old women and their powerful or charismatic or simply needy bosses were old news. But like the new viruses mutating exponentially to be compatible with most Internet-linked computers in the 1990s, the spins on this scandal mutated exponentially enough to be compatible with many defining narratives and worries of the 1990s. These included the affluenza epitomized by Beverly Hills, the Clintons' anything-goes morality, and their opponents' suffocating rigidity.

Boomtown Mentality; Consumption Orgy

Even as experts tracked a widening gap between rich and poor, Clinton's Baby Boomer boom fed a boomtown mentality and a consumption orgy. Americans were bombarded with messaging to enjoy, escape, indulge, with no guilt. The brazenness made this an Age of Un-Innocence. Cask & Cream Liqueur lured males and females with a picture of a woman luxuriating in a candlelit bathtub. "Seem a bit indulgent?" the ad asked. "Now you're catching on." "Say good-bye to complexity. Say good-bye to boring. Say hello to iMac," Apple computers preached, promising an endlessly entertaining "user-friendly" world—Mac's ultimate ideal. Now, you could: "Plug it in. Turn it on. Be yourself." Apple's prophets considered technology the path toward self-fulfillment, not a detour. And www.PreciousPlatinum.com declared: "Platinum: A Reflection of You." Indeed, in the Republic of Consumption, you were what you wore.

Jay McInerney, a booster of Eighties' cocaine-fueled hedonism with *Bright Lights, Big City* (1984), published a new manifesto of materialism masquerading as a novel in 1998, *Model Behavior*. McInerney labeled the supermodel, "the representative figure of our times . . . the muse of consumption, the angel of late 20th-century capitalism." The critic James Wolcott dismissed McInerney's work "as an urban safari of superficial people saying superficial things in a superficial culture that is intended to be a Statement of Our Times—a super-superficiality that serves as a funhouse reflection of 90s-boom narcissisms."

Wolcott's schoolmarmish review, nestled amid photos of beautiful models, adoring celebrity photo-shoots, and luxuriant ads, appeared in *Vanity Fair*'s fourth annual issue celebrating the "New Establishment." This 1990s Sears catalog for the rich and trendy had started identifying "The Top 50 Leaders of the Information Age," topped in 1998 by Bill Gates and Rupert Murdoch. Three were women. Supplanting the traditional Wasp establishment of lawyers, bankers, heirs, and industrialists, these media moguls and computer whizzes now controlled much of what Americans saw and felt. Together the 50 owned 14 film studios, 52 magazines, 43 music labels, and 124 daily newspapers, controlling companies with a total market value of $14 billion. The average stock price of the 24 publicly traded companies connected to these information entrepreneurs had appreciated 572.97 percent since August 1994.

These trendsetters were also America's new pashas. Bill Gates's net worth of $60 billion was "more than the gross domestic product of Kuwait and more than the combined wealth of the 106 million Americans who are on the lower rungs of the income scale." Barry Diller, who suggested setting *90210* in Beverly Hills, hoped to dominate electronic retailing, with investments in Ticketmaster and HSN, the Home Shopping Network. Michael Bloomberg actually considered running for mayor of New York. Wags scoffed that it "would be a very expensive ego trip." Three years later, Bloomberg began serving his first of three terms.

These were the leaders of the "New Economy," the Clinton administration economist Martin N. Baily would write, with "globalization, information technology development, and heightened competition" producing "a much more efficient and productive economy." This information-processing, service-oriented America produced ideas and stories more than cars and clothing. Manufacturing now accounted for only 14 percent of America's total output. With finance ascendant, the market as king, the economy globalized, possibilities seemed end-less; recessions passé.

With an average age of fifty, most of these masters of the new universe were Bill Clinton's partners in shaping this Democratic Gilded Age. They had do-nated $2,307,446 to the Democratic National Committee cumulatively since 1993 and only $16,200 to its Republican rival. Eight had slept in the White House. Many boasted of their friendship with the Clintons.

Although only six were among the most hundred charitable Americans, these moguls and their camp followers felt normal and humble by condemn-ing those even more profligate. Readers were fuming about an earlier *Vanity Fair* profile describing "super-polluter" Ira Rennert's "rape" of the Hamptons. This billionaire industrialist was building a 100,000-square-foot-complex of seven buildings on 63 acres of what had been farmland in Sagaponack. The 60,000-square-foot main house would be bigger than the 55,000-square-foot White House. In an aristocratic playground not far from Calvin Klein's $10 million estate and Martha Stewart's two perfectly appointed dream houses, the outrage seemed hypocritical. In this age of shamelessness, Rennert's lawyer, Martin Gilmartin, asked critics, "Why does anybody build a mansion? If some-one has the wealth, is there something wrong with that? Why should it even be a question?"

Moralism with Materialism on *90210*

Despite the allure of Botoxed faces, Lululemon running tights, Porsche con-vertibles, and Gulfstream jets, many in Beverly Hills and beyond, old and young, were suffering. Many Americans increasingly felt inadequate because they were less rich, less famous, less thin, less beautiful, less sexy, less bejeweled, less decked out, than the actors, models, and moguls they were told to worship. Rates of depression, anxiety, alcoholism, drug abuse were unacceptably high. Since 1987, shopping malls outnumbered high schools nationwide. Americans averaged six hours a week shopping with their credit cards and only forty minutes a week playing with their children. Yet the number of happy Americans had peaked back in 1957.

John de Graaf, a social activist, produced a PBS documentary diagnosing American society's affluenza. The documentary team defined the affliction as: "1. The bloated, sluggish and unfulfilled feeling that results from efforts to keep up with the Joneses. 2. An epidemic of stress, overwork, waste and indebtedness caused by dogged pursuit of the American Dream. 3. An unsustainable addiction to economic growth." The documentary proved so successful when aired in September 1997, it inspired a sequel, *Escape from Affluenza,* broadcast in 1998, about those fleeing the materialist life.

Underlying the Nineties' mass social anxiety were guilty feelings stirred in America's still-Spartan soul whenever prosperity hit. Many felt the call of the pinched Puritans, the homespun Framers, the thrifty pioneers, to beware overindulgence. Of course, prosperity was not always perilous, nor was poverty necessarily virtuous.

Even on *Beverly Hills, 90210,* moralism mingled with materialism. Plotlines preached against affluenza's excesses, as viewers delighted in them. "Well, the houses are bigger, the weather is warmer, and the tan lines are outstanding, but it doesn't mean they've cracked the meaning of life," says Brandon Walsh, the show's moral center, about his new neighborhood. In tackling tough issues including premarital sex, teen pregnancy, drinking, drugs, abuse, abortion, accidental death, the show normalized many acts once deemed deviant, while moralizing about them.

The onscreen fantasy world protected the major characters from too much trauma because they had each other, the family-like community anchoring most successful TV shows, including *That '70s Show, Sex and the City,* and *Will & Grace,* all of which premiered in 1998. *90210*'s writers also magically resolved many of the worst problems by the end of the episode, or the arc of episodes, to keep the show fun. Just as Aaron Spelling's *Dynasty* helped define Eighties' glitz, *90210* defined the Nineties as equally ostentatious, and equally vapid, with a veneer of anxiety and complexity. It was the quintessential show of the Democratic Gilded Age, with a soft, left-leaning, open, tolerant, libertine, mildly antimaterialistic spin tolerated as long as the fashion show continued.

The show also helped acclimate teens to their newly wired world. In 1998, the number of cell phone subscribers would pass the 60 million mark, up from 1.6 million in 1988. PC prices had dropped by 40 percent in 1997, encouraging 80 million purchases worldwide. By year's end more than 47 million Americans would be online, up from 28 million. The combined circulation of America's top fifteen newspapers did not match AOL's 15 million subscribers. In 1998, the federal government made its first payment via e-mail, and more United Airlines passengers flew using electronic tickets than paper tickets.

This technological profusion often caused confusion. In one 1998 *90210* episode, Steve discovers his girlfriend is cheating on him when a digital camera connected to the school newspaper's new website broadcasts video of her and

Steve's close friend David "hooking up," as the increasingly popular expression and activity went.

In balancing viewers' sympathy, envy, and contempt, *90210* mimicked the delicate dance in the edgier 1995 movie comedy *Clueless*. The Alicia Silverstone character, Cher Horowitz, acted more flamboyant and harsher than her TV counterparts. The Beverly Hills savant, Cher spit out savvy clothing tips and epoch-defining phrases with her world-weary "whatever," her outraged "As if!," and her willingness to give "snaps," what others called "props," for "courageous fashion efforts" or any worthy initiatives. Before her cinematic redemption, all that attitude captured a girl—and a culture—stricken by affluenza.

Monica of Beverly Hills?

The anxiety and guilt regarding too much hedonism among fictional Beverly Hills types onscreen metastasized into a yearlong, national moral panic when America's president was caught in an adulterous web of lies with a young intern. Monica Lewinsky was no Tori Spelling. Her parents were neither super rich nor famous. Nevertheless, Monica Lewinsky and her family were from the same 90210 neighborhood, making them Beverly Hills enough to typify America's Gilded Age at its worst.

A twisted nature-nurture debate ensued. *The Washington Post* asked: "is *Beverly Hills 90210* a co-conspirator in the White House crisis?" Lewinsky "is completely responding to her upbringing," Arva Holt Rose, a Bel-Air psychotherapist told reporters. "She's a manipulative little girl." One matron sniffed, "I don't believe Monica Lewinsky is a product of Beverly Hills, because her dress came from the Gap. And her little beret? DKNY, not Donna Karan," DKNY being the exclusive label's cheaper, mass-market, youth-oriented brand.

Within weeks of starting her White House internship in July 1995, Monica Lewinsky began what she called "intense flirting" with the president. Some aides regularly arranged for a provocatively dressed woman in the White House to cross paths with the president, while Hillary Clinton's people guarded against inappropriately dressed "clutches" like Monica Lewinsky. All this juvenile commotion reflected what feminists called "a hostile working environment" for women, except when imposed by a pro-choice liberal president, apparently.

The nine "sexual encounters" Monica Lewinsky would catalogue with an Excel spreadsheet were so hurried, furtive, and one-sided, that Clinton would claim they abstained from "sexual relations." Anguished, struggling, Clinton would confess to Dick Morris that he tried to "shut my body down . . . sexually," aware of how scrutinized he was. "But," Clinton admitted, "sometimes I slipped up and with this girl I just slipped up."

Eventually, Hillary Clinton would attribute her husband's affair to all his stress, and her inaccessibility. Bill Clinton would blame the "parallel lives" his childhood traumas induced. He recalled repeatedly trying to end the physical contact. "It was wrong for me, wrong for my family, and wrong for her. . . . I was disgusted with myself for doing it," he would write—unprecedented statements for a president to make about himself in his memoirs.

Washington gossips had been trading rumors about Clinton for years. Bill Clinton's libidinous impulses were central to his identity as the roguish mass seducer. In an age emphasizing the "authenticity" of personal identity, especially sexuality, over a traditional ethic of "responsibility," some feared that shutting down his sex drive may have stopped Clinton from being Clinton.

In the tradition of wandering Southern sinners, be they preacher or pol, Clinton boxed off his compulsive flirtations and assignations from his love for his wife and his belief in family, community, and responsibility. Steve Rabinowitz, a media adviser who spent nearly two years in daily contact with Clinton in 1992 and 1993, recalls the Clintons as "a phenomenal, loving family. Seeing the three of them together, in Little Rock, when they were just being themselves, was very genuine, very moving." Ann Lewis, Clinton's communications director, seeing the fight as a partisan brawl, would dismiss any feminist qualms by asking contemptuously, "Ken Starr? Newt Gingrich? Henry Hyde? Were these the people I should have allied with instead?"

The Double Helix Moral Panic

The Beverly Hills showdown, with people rushing to imbue a twenty-five-year-old's life with so much symbolism, reflected the fact that the United States was in the throes of a moral panic. Academics explain that a moral panic occurs when a "condition, episode, person or group of persons emerges to become defined as a threat to societal values and interests; its nature is presented in a stylized and stereotypical fashion by the mass media; the moral barricades are manned by editors . . . and other right-thinking people." These words, written by the British sociologist Stanley Cohen in 1972, describe what occurred in Washington, D.C., sixteen years later with an eerie accuracy.

Especially in a society eager to type public figures as heroes or anti-heroes, those who trigger moral panics often function as "folk devils," Cohen explained, "visible reminders of what we should not be." In later editions, Cohen would also note the "cultural politics" behind these moments of tremendous "volatility" and "disproportionality" defining them, presciently, "as condensed political struggles to control the means of cultural reproduction."

Like the double helix of the DNA—a popular Nineties metaphor—two mutually reinforcing moral panics ensued. The Republicans cast Bill Clinton as the Folk Devil, threatening the republic's soul, not just its judicial system, with adultery, lies, and cover-ups that became perjury and obstruction of justice. To Democrats, Kenneth Starr was the Folk Devil, threatening the republic's Constitution, not just its elected leader, with overzealousness, leaks, and abuse of power. That both the president and the prosecutor were supposed to be role models not Folk Devils intensified the mass distress.

To Clintonites, Starr's supporters joined with the Republican cabal of co-conspirators, the growing industry aiding and abetting the well-funded, professional Clinton "haters," as Mickey Kantor called them, reporters, lawyers, and activists who never accepted Clinton's legitimacy to govern. To Clinton critics, Clinton's supporters joined his army of enablers, not only facilitating the president's improprieties that escalated into criminality but trying to impose a new cultural and sexual regime after failing to win a majority of the popular vote twice.

Unlike the Watergate scandal, which produced heroes like Judge John Sirica and Senator Sam Ervin, this sordid scandal tarnished everyone involved. Journalists and Republicans looked like bullies. Feminists and Democrats sounded like hypocrites. The people's business suffered. The pornographer Larry Flynt's America too frequently ignored the presidential pantheon of Washington, Lincoln, and Theodore Roosevelt, whose virtues seemed as solid as the granite of Mount Rushmore. Instead came the adulterous trio of FDR, JFK, and LBJ, confirming the Clintonites' "everybody does it" defense.

The Clintons felt victimized by reporters and prosecutors prying into their most personal and painful marital intimacies. In 2014, Monica Lewinsky would define her own sense of victimization from the Internet-enhanced "culture of humiliation." The relationship with Clinton was "consensual," she said. "Any 'abuse' came in the aftermath, when I was made a scapegoat in order to protect his powerful position." Lewinsky considered herself the first victim of cyber bullying.

The Inner Beltway Echo Chamber

Powerful overlapping forces escalated the president's dalliance into a constitutional crisis. Republicans were angry and powerful, mobilized to fight Clinton's

Slick Willie–bad boy persona and the Adversarial counterculture he embodied, despite all his values speak. Kenneth Starr and his special prosecutors were frustrated and powerful, irritated by both Clintons' stonewalling, convinced their petty crimes threatened the Great Republic. Reporters were cynical and powerful, energized by the search for the next Watergate, feeling pressure from 24/7 news on cable and Internet, cycling through stories faster than ever and with fewer filters. And citizens of the republic were skeptical about the powerful, at once fascinated by the scandal's sordid details yet also more cynically forgiving.

Curiously, what Clinton's consultant Frank Greer called the Inner Beltway "echo chamber" convinced reporters Clinton was "dead and gone," even as nationally Clinton's "job performance ratings were at 60 percent." Adversarial reporters wanted to show they were willing to skewer their peer, while right-wing journalists joined in gleefully. Joe Klein speculated that many Adversarials rejected in Clinton the traits "we're most upset with ourselves about." In this "spiritual impeachment" of the quintessential Baby Boomer, Clinton's peers exorcised their own generational indulgences. Klein exclaimed: "and, if there was ever a guy who skated and cut corners and fudged and got off easy, it was Bill Clinton."

Throughout the scandal, the Internet's modern, anarchic, hyper-democratic, tradition-smashing, reputation-trashing, constantly rehashing, immediate, and individualistic abandon trumped the media's traditional, editor-centered, hierarchical, cautious, and consensus-preserving protocols. Matt Drudge, an eccentric thirty-one-year-old gossip who fancied himself the Walter Winchell of the Digital Age, often bullied reporters into rushing stories on air and in print to avoid being outmaneuvered online. Just as the unfiltered blogosphere would increasingly harshen political discourse, a less-filtered media system disseminated all kinds of stories broadly, sloppily.

In television, the intense competition from the all-news-all-the-time cable news networks, combined with the right-wing assault spearheaded by Rupert Murdoch's tendentious Fox News, sullied the broadcast networks' once-august news operations. "Walter Cronkite used to say, we determine what's news," says Lesley Stahl of CBS, recalling how he refused to put his finger to the wind. "Now we were feeling the pressure."

This volatile scandal triggered both long buried and newly placed landmines. The ancient quest for virtuous leaders, the three-centuries-old sense of American exceptionalism, the presidency's unique mix of being prime minister and king, clashed with the Sixties' moral and sexual confusion, the Seventies' political cynicism and sexual frankness, the Eighties' celebrity politics and scandalmongering, and the Nineties' 24/7 everything coverage with nothing being sacred. At the center of this battle stood the charming, idealistic, trashy, roguish president of the United States and his equally baroque wife.

A Cold January in Scandalvania

Clinton and his aides began 1998 exuberantly. America was on a stock market high. Buoyed by that boom and his successful 1997, Bill Clinton was feeling virtuous and enjoying his popularity.

The Paula Jones litigation and the newly expansive scope of sexual harassment depositions weaponized the Monica Lewinsky scandal, making it legal, not just moral and political. On Saturday morning January 17, 1998, Jones's lawyers deposed Clinton for six hours. The lawyers concentrated on the more recent relationship with a government employee, "Jane Doe Number 6," which he denied categorically.

That night, in a defining clash, Matt Drudge's Wild West gossip sensibility overran the media's vetting process. For months, *Newsweek*'s Michael Isikoff had been tracking the story of the Baby Boomer president and the Beverly Hills intern. Despite having the legitimate news hook of Starr expanding his investigation, Isikoff had to watch his scoop get scooped by others. "There are times it's just not worth being first," his editor Ann McDaniel said, preaching an old news sensibility. Drudge emphasized the Internet's freewheeling sensibility slaying the old media's sclerosis, with his post at 2:32 a.m., Sunday, January 18: "*Newsweek* Kills Story on White House Intern."

Clinton gave a series of increasingly clear denials, culminating with his infamous, finger-wagging proclamation: "I did not have sexual relations with that woman, Miss Lewinsky." Few believed him. *The New York Times* columnist Thomas Friedman said: "I knew he was a charming rogue with an appealing agenda, but I didn't think he was a reckless idiot with an appealing agenda." During that first week, the network ratings jumped 6 percent; MSNBC's soared 131 percent.

Hillary Clinton and the Vast Right-Wing Conspiracy

For Hillary Clinton, the frustrations of five years of inquisition reinforced more than a quarter century of enabling. The Clintons slipped into their battle stations. The two never seemed more in sync than when fighting a common enemy. After the first-term role reversal when Hillary not Bill messed up, both Clintons smoothly reverted to their usual roles, as Hillary Clinton spearheaded the counterattack. A few days after Clinton's denial, NBC reporters asked Mrs. Clinton if a president caught lying about committing adultery should resign. "If all that were proven true, I think that would be a very serious offense. That is not going to be proven true," she insisted, although she already knew that the president had given Monica Lewinsky Walt Whitman's *Leaves of Grass,* a gift young Bill had given young Hillary.

The First Lady applied the essential Clintonesque jujitsu honed from years of scandal busting: change the subject, dominate the story line, attack the attacker. Dick Morris warned that an abject apology to the American people would not work—"You can't tell them about it—they'll kill you." Bill Clinton replied: "Well, we just have to win, then."

Using a previously scheduled interview on NBC's *Today* show, Hillary Clinton all but single-handedly saved Clinton's presidency. Six days after the scandal began, she condemned Kenneth Starr and the "vast right wing conspiracy" hounding her husband. Not since Jackie Kennedy rhapsodized about "Camelot" had a First Lady uttered a more potent, epoch-defining, phrase.

Clinton partisans and cynical journalists trashed Monica Lewinsky's reputation. Lewinsky also suffered from Starr's prosecutors and the conservative attack dogs who resented her felonious loyalty to the president. Hillary Clinton privately called her husband's paramour a "narcissistic loony toon." Other Clinton aides and reporters called her a "stalker"; feminists mocked her looks, with the author Katie Roiphe sneering "Monica Lewinsky's not that pretty." The Internet's accelerator mortified her exponentially. "My love life, my sex life, my most private moments, my most sensitive secrets" were "broadcast around the globe," Lewinsky later recalled.

Bill Clinton lost his moral voice. With innuendo in the air, staffers scoured drafts of the State of the Union address to avoid any moralizing that might trigger snickers. Bill Galston had urged the president to celebrate ending "a generation of fiscal irresponsibility at home, build[ing] a democratic peace abroad, and restor[ing] the broad moral center in social policy based on shared American values such as opportunity, responsibility, community, nondiscrimination, and the centrality of faith in our civil society." That would no longer do. Al From had proposed a sweeping speech to secure Clinton's New Democrat legacy and "define what you want to achieve in the rest of your Administration." Ten days later, on January 26, "having witnessed the hysterical, feeding frenzy over the weekend," Al From proposed a speech "to shore up your support—not to try to define history." Speak to the "majority of Americans who believe you are doing a good job as president," directly, clearly, pithily, without "high flying rhetoric" that doesn't "fit" the "circumstances," From advised.

The resulting speech was more subdued, but nevertheless lengthy, substantive, and occasionally preachy. Clinton proposed tools for parents to "protect their children from inappropriate material on the Internet." He spoke about "our shared values" that "we all cherish family and faith, freedom and responsibility." Some legislators tittered when the president said, "We must set a good example." Reporters debated whether Clinton's seventy-one-minute address was "surreal" or "Kabuki theater." An overwhelming majority of viewers polled, however, approved of the speech and the president's focus on the nation's business.

Still, Clinton survived; his grandiose reform plans did not. The bipartisan spirit that culminated in the 1997 budget agreement and had warmed relations between Clinton and Gingrich vanished. Chief of Staff Erskine Bowles had entered 1998 believing the Congress might be ready to tackle Medicare and Social Security reform. However, once the scandal erupted, "It was game over," Bowles would recall; the scandal "was one of the seminal events in American history. . . . Monica changed everything."

Surviving in a 90210 Nation

Clinton survived by lowering expectations of American leaders and followers. America had become, *The St. Louis Post-Dispatch* would headline, the "90210 Nation." The "everybody does it" defense situated Clinton in a march of presidential adulterers, establishing an un-innocent lowest common denominator morality. A master of political jujitsu, Bill Clinton accused his accusers. Michael Isikoff noted that "To prove his lies, Clinton knew, his foes would be forced into the gutter," and end up looking much "worse than he. It was his coldest and most cynical calculation—the mutual assured destruction at the core of his survival." Clinton's defenders dismissed the handwringing as "Sexual McCarthyism." Reducing it all to sex justified deceit, as many accepted the gospel of *Playboy*'s Hugh Hefner that "sex is the only subject in America everyone lies about—to their girlfriends, their wives, themselves." The conservative writer David Frum had identified the "central dogma of the Baby Boomers" at the heart of the scandal as being "that sex, so long as it's consensual, ought never to be subject to moral scrutiny at all." In many ways, so many of the culture wars and moral panics since the 1960s still revolved around this clash between a modernist sexual openness and a more traditional sexual discipline.

The black-and-white approach to truth and morality that Americans traditionally accepted—at least rhetorically—no longer predominated. Historically, Americans have seesawed between collective crusades to purify the body politic and individualistic demands for freedom and privacy. Sixties' libertinism combined with Eighties' libertarianism to tolerate the moral ambiguity that triumphed now in the Nineties. The sex columnist Dan Savage proposed that American couples become "monogamish," approaching monogamy as an ideal achieved frequently like sobriety, rather than an all-or-nothing status like virginity.

Living a more modern, relativistic life, many increasingly-nonjudgmental Americans now agreed with the Protestant theologian Reinhold Niebuhr that "self-righteousness is the inevitable fruit of simple moral judgments, placed in the service of moral complacency." An astounding 84 percent agreed that someone "can be a good president even if you disapprove of his personal life." Two-thirds consistently defined moral leadership in Clinton's terms, as "understanding the problems of people like you." Less than one-third defined moral leadership as having "high personal moral and ethical standards."

Phase 2: Happy Spring (and If True, Irrelevant)

Once Clinton survived phase one of the scandal, the initial exposure, he and his aides argued that the accusations were not true, and besides, his accusers were worse, especially Monica Lewinsky, the emotional stalker, and Kenneth Starr, the legalistic stalker. Clinton vowed "to show the American people that I was on the job and getting results for them." The boom continued. The budget was balanced. By February, Clinton enjoyed 72 percent job approval.

By the spring, Clinton had outlasted the initial impeachment predictions and was thrashing Kenneth Starr in the court of public opinion. On April 1, Judge Susan Webber Wright threw out the Paula Jones case. Clinton decided this made any obfuscations and obstructions irrelevant, a novel legal doctrine. Photographers caught Clinton, in Africa, smoking a cigar and banging happily away on a drum. That summer, *Brill's Content* debuted by eviscerating the leaky independent counsel and the "lapdog-like" press, which bandied about "unconfirmed rumors" and hurled "sleaze ball" stories about "phantom dress" and "a potential DNA trail that would tie Clinton to this young woman." By then, the Lewinsky affair seemed to be ending.

The argument that nothing happened bought enough time for the even-if-it-did-happen-it-did-not-matter defense to solidify. In April, once home, Clinton blocked the importation of 1.6 million assault weapons, announced "the deficit had been completely eliminated for the first time since 1969," and saw the Senate vote to bring Poland, Hungary, and the Czech Republic into NATO. The signing on April 10, 1998, of the Good Friday agreement in Northern Ireland "was one of the happiest days of my presidency," Clinton reported. "No one was even talking about Whitewater anymore." Yet Starr's $40 million investigation continued.

Phase 3: Summer of Scandal

Unfortunately for Clinton, a stained blue Gap dress definitively linked him to Monica Lewinsky and exposed him as a liar. On July 28, Lewinsky signed an immunity deal with Starr's office. On August 17, 1998, Bill Clinton became the first sitting president to appear as a grand jury witness. Finally, he admitted having had "inappropriate contact" with Lewinsky. Still, he defended his Paula Jones deposition. His denials were in the present tense and "it depends upon what the meaning of the word is, is."

That night, Clinton attacked Starr in a nationally televised speech. Clinton continued splitting hairs, saying of his deposition, "While my answers were legally accurate, I did not volunteer information." In four minutes he used the word "private" seven times, insisting: "Even presidents have private lives. It is time to stop the pursuit of personal destruction and the prying into private lives and get on with our national life." *Newsweek* declared the speech an "Utter disaster: Too angry, too lawyerly, and he never apologized." Yet two-thirds of the American people remained supportive.

Hillary Clinton grieved during the Clintons' awkward summer vacation on Martha's Vineyard following the testimony. She soon realized that, as in 1992, she had to forgive her husband to save his presidency. Her friend Diane Blair would note that the two Clintons are "connected in every way imaginable, she feels strongly about him and family and Chelsea and marriage and she's just got to work it through." Mrs. Clinton called the affair a "lapse." She concluded, despite a decade of feminist theorizing, that the relationship "was consensual (was not a power relationship)."

In Washington, D.C., politicos, including many Democrats, abandoned the president more quickly than the people did. More than 140 newspapers demanded his resignation. "Clinton is a cancer on the culture, a cancer of cynicism, narcissism and deceit," Andrew Sullivan thundered in *The New Republic*.

"At some point, not even the most stellar of economic records, not even the most prosperous of decades, is worth the price of such a cancer metastasizing even further. It is time to be rid of it."

Clinton's oldest friend in the Senate, Joseph Lieberman of Connecticut, denounced the president's behavior on September 3. In 1998, "a president's private life is public," Lieberman lectured. The president influences "our collective consciousness" as much "as any Hollywood celebrity or television show," Lieberman noted. As the nation's "role model," he sets "standards of behavior." Lieberman proposed censure rather than impeachment. When asked what he thought about this devastating, measured, scolding, President Clinton bleakly agreed.

That crazy, dispiriting, destabilizing, demonizing summer of 1998, the Clinton-Starr political and cultural brawl echoed broadly. The great conservative William F. Buckley denounced Clinton's "incontinent carnality." The novelist Philip Roth would explain it as "America's oldest communal passion; historically perhaps its most treacherous and subversive pleasure: the ecstasy of sanctimony." In May, the venerable political weekly, *The New Republic,* discovered a rising star, Stephen Glass, had enlivened his articles with fabricated business cards, websites, and business addresses. Glass blamed the pressures he felt to succeed. In July, the Roman Catholic Diocese of Dallas settled with nine victims of one pederast priest for $23.4 million, an early outbreak of a financial and moral contagion that would devastate the church—and undermine respect for all forms of authority nationwide. Summertime surveys showed that 80 percent of leading high school students had cheated in class; two-thirds of American husbands had committed adultery. Statistics regarding this secret activity were unreliable, but the number was more likely in the 20 to 25 percent range.

Baseball was enjoying an epic home run battle between the St. Louis Cardinals' first baseman Mark McGwire and the Chicago Cubs' right fielder Sammy Sosa. Alas, in that un-innocent summer, both brawny bombers were using steroids. Reflecting the anxiety, Robert Coles's book, *The Moral Intelligence of Children: How to Raise a Moral Child,* became a best seller as his Harvard colleague Howard Gardner ramped up "The Good Project" to reestablish basic morality.

Billboard's number one song on the Hot 100 much of that summer described a different love triangle with a girl named Monica. "Brandy & Monica" sang "The Boy Is Mine," inspired by *The Jerry Springer Show*'s love triangles. Another summer hit, "Everybody (Backstreet's Back)," treated sexuality as an inner demon, one of 1998's underlying themes. In the award-winning video, the handsome, hunky Backstreet Boys metamorphosed into monsters.

The movie season featured crass hits such as the adolescent gross-out movie *There's Something About Mary* showing a former nerd now grown up, as Clinton described himself, seeking his old high school sweetheart. In *The Truman Show*, Jim Carrey realizes he lives on an artificial stage set and is starring in his own popular television "reality" show, a glass house feeling Clinton understood.

Wag the Dog, but Protect the Nation

The year's most politically resonant movie, eerily anticipating life, was Barry Levinson's *Wag the Dog*. In it, a libidinous president distracts the nation from a sex scandal by hiring a Hollywood producer to fake a war in Albania. When the con works, the producer rejoices, "This is politics at its finest."

That August, *Wag the Dog* appeared prescient, popularizing a new phrase for politicians artificially exploiting international tensions. On August 6, Monica Lewinsky began testifying to the grand jury. On August 7, bombs detonated within five minutes of each other devastated the American embassies in Kenya and Tanzania. The Nairobi truck bomb killed 224 people including 12 Americans, and wounded more than 4,600. The force ripped open the back of the embassy while leveling a three-story building next door. In Dar es Salaam, a filled water tanker absorbed much of the shock, catapulting over three stories into the air. This bomb murdered 11, injuring 85.

A week later, on Thursday, August 13, Clinton greeted ten flag-draped coffins at Andrews Air Force base. The president looked stricken, with a tear rolling down his face, telegraphing pain, exhaustion, frustration. His wife, watching her shaken husband, looked worried.

Two nights earlier Clinton had been defiant, while fund-raising in Los Angeles. "The truth is that most of you will do all right," he told the Democratic donors. "But the people who are serving food here tonight, the people that are parking cars, the people that work in every place of business that I passed on the way up here tonight, it makes a whole lot of difference to them and their grandchildren." "It" was the Clinton mission.

Mounting evidence implicated the Saudi heir and Islamist ideologue, Osama bin Laden, and his al-Qaeda terrorists in the bombing. Although a special CIA station had been tracking bin Laden since January 1996, and even though he and his henchmen tried to assassinate Clinton in the Philippines in 1996, intelligence officers had only recently identified bin Laden as ringleader not financer. His February 1998 fatwa claimed God wanted every Muslim to kill Americans, because of America's "occupation" of Islam's holy places, meaning the American troops in Saudi Arabia. Al-Qaeda also planned to attack America's Albanian embassy, assuming, Clinton later admitted, that "America was vulnerable because we would be distracted by the controversy over my personal behavior."

Intelligence reports revealed that bin Laden and key aides would be meeting in Afghanistan on August 20. Afghanistan was controlled by the Taliban, Islamist extremists. Clinton's team worried that the president's August 17 grand jury testimony might inhibit him, fearing "Wag the Dog" accusations. Clinton told his National Security Adviser Sandy Berger that they "were going to get crap either way so they should do the right thing."

On Saturday morning August 15, a sheepish Clinton informed his wife and his daughter about his true relationship with Monica Lewinsky. On August 20, three days after Clinton's testy grand jury testimony, the U.S. military fired more than seventy-five Tomahawk cruise missiles at targets in Afghanistan and the Sudan. The barrage missed bin Laden by a few hours, probably due to Pakistani intelligence leaks. Bin Laden survived, and the resulting controversy over the attack on the Al-Shifa pharmaceutical factory in Khartoum constrained Clinton and his team when other opportunities arose. Critics doubted the administration's evidence and motives as "no independent evidence" emerged proving that the factory manufactured chemical weapons, the 9/11 Commission later reported.

Again more cynical than the public, journalists grilled defense secretary William Cohen about the missile strikes' "striking resemblance to *Wag the Dog*." Cohen insisted, "The only motivation driving this action today was our absolute obligation to protect the American people from terrorist activities." Two-thirds of Americans surveyed supported the military attacks. Clinton's approval rating remained at 62 percent. Still, 36 percent in some polls believed the *Wag the Dog* accusation. The commander-in-chief's credibility had suffered. "The world's media right now are giving the filmmakers far too much credit for being clairvoyant," the *Wag the Dog* PR people said.

Americans were not ready to confront the terrorists. Even many intelligence operatives called their CIA colleagues hunting bin Laden "alarmist." The chairman of the Joint Chiefs of Staff, Hugh Shelton, dismissed al-Qaeda's Afghani terrorist training bases as "jungle gym" camps. That fall, *The Siege* portrayed Islamist terrorists bombing New York City buses and Broadway theatres. The movie flopped. It became "the most-rented movie in America after 9/11," according to the movie's screenwriter Lawrence Wright. Hollywood, Wright said, did a "somewhat better job of connecting the dots about terrorism and the threat to America than the intelligence community."

A weakened Clinton would fail to greenlight further attempts on bin Laden's life. "We had opportunities, many opportunities to kill him," according to Michael Scheuer, a twenty-two-year CIA veteran who led "Alec Station," the counterterrorist center's Osama bin Laden unit. "But that's the president's decision." The 9/11 Commission Report would identify "three specific occasions in 1998–1999" when "intelligence was deemed credible enough to warrant planning for possible strikes to kill bin Laden." Each time, "senior policymakers did not regard the intelligence as sufficiently actionable to offset their assessment of the risks."

The hyper-partisan culture of irresponsibility was destructive. Democrats denied how brazenly Clinton had broken the law and how much harm he had done the presidency. Republicans denied how much danger they placed the nation in by fighting so viciously and how much harm they had done the presidency. Containing partisan warfare was essential for democracy's legitimacy and America's safety.

Phase 4: Democrats Heal but Republicans Stew

President Clinton had to restore his credibility. After a direct "intervention" by Erskine Bowles, Clinton finally apologized at the annual Religious Leaders' Prayer Breakfast on September 11, 1998. The president admitted he had not been "contrite enough. I don't think there is a fancy way to say that I have sinned." Clinton vowed to defend himself vigorously with lawyers, try healing humbly with pastors, and "Intensify my efforts to lead our country" effectively.

Clinton's repeated apologies, individually and collectively, always laced with reminders that the country was safe and prosperous, reinforced his message to separate the person from his presidency. At a special Cabinet meeting in his residence, Donna Shalala, the secretary of health and human services, furious that Clinton preyed on an intern, recalls, "I just blew up . . . It was the young person thing. It just hit against every principle I've had in my life and the [academic] world that I come from." Clinton yelled back. The Treasury Secretary, Robert Rubin, provided the framing partisan Democrats needed. "There's no question you screwed up," Rubin said. Still, Rubin believed "the bigger issue is the disproportion of the media coverage and the hypocrisy of some of your critics." Shalala and three other colleagues she refuses to name ultimately concluded, "This is disgusting but we've got to keep going." Washington's polarized politics made the choice binary, Clinton or Starr.

These apologies were necessary so Clinton could lead again, but first he had to survive. After weeks of uncomfortable silence and embarrassing speculation about the state of her marriage, the First Lady started defending her man. "I'm proud of his leadership, I'm proud of his commitment, I'm proud of what he gives our country—and all of us every day—by his commitment," Hillary Clinton proclaimed.

While Clinton played to modern Americans' ambivalence about morality, obsession with sexuality, fierce sense of privacy, and genuine capacity for forgiveness, his critics overdid it. Falling into the trap Clinton's lawyers set, Starr focused on sex, with lurid details, to prove Clinton had lied about sex while arguing that the case, fundamentally, was not about sex. In his zeal to convict the libertine president, Starr, the conservative traditionalist, exposed Americans to surprisingly graphic testimony.

Starr presented his 445-page report to the House Judiciary Committee on September 9. House Republicans rushed it to the public two days later, on September 11, and released the videotape of the president's grand jury testimony on September 21. Both releases, while humiliating Clinton, made the House Republicans look partisan and triggered a mass backlash. The White House accused Starr of exceeding his Whitewater mandate and solely trying "to embarrass the president and titillate the public by producing a document that is little more than an unreliable, one-sided account of sexual behavior." Many people agreed with the Harvard Law professor Alan Dershowitz that "The Starr report poses a far greater danger to the American system of governance than anything charged against President Clinton."

One small three-and-a-half-inch floppy disk in a white envelope, barely noticeable amid vanloads of cartons carrying the copies of the Starr Report the prosecutor delivered to Congress, delivered Starr's words to millions instantly. *The San Francisco Chronicle* would call the report detailing the nine sexual encounters and fifteen phone sex sessions "the most publicized and widely disseminated pornographic text in U.S. history." More Americans turned to the Internet for Starr updates than to their newspapers.

Starr combined Inspector Javert's obsessiveness with Inspector Clouseau's incompetence. Many Americans resented what one Queens labor leader reporting to the Clinton White House called "the damn media . . . Ordinary folks think sex is private and they want the country to move on." By late September, 65 percent surveyed agreed, including 39 percent of Republicans. In November, 53 percent surveyed would agree Starr acted like a "persecutor" not a "prosecutor." Keith Olbermann quit an MSNBC news anchoring job in protest, apologizing to Clinton "for whatever part I may have played in perpetuating this ceaseless coverage." Olbermann mocked his "White House in Crisis" show as "The White

House Isn't in Crisis but We'll Keep Calling It That Because There's a Graphic" show.

One Wall Streeter, who hated Clinton, came home early on September 21. "I prepared a sandwich, and sat in my favorite chair, ready to see Clinton skewered," the financier recalls. "But Clinton was so brilliant, so impressive, and the questioning he endured so unfair, I ended up rooting for him." Half a century earlier, Franklin Roosevelt was equally seductive. "All that man has to do is speak on the radio, the sound of his voice, his sincerity, and manner of delivery just melts me and I change my mind," one Republican admitted.

An Ever-More Explicit Culture

As Clinton's supporters declared sex "private" and Starr's supporters valued sexual discretion, the Starr Report made American culture raunchier than ever. In 1998, the phrase "oral sex" appeared 248 times in *The Washington Post*, and 135 times in *USA Today*. The Oval Office, America's holy of holies, became commercialized and caricatured, a punch line in jokes suggesting that Clinton get "neutered" not impeached, and the setting for suggestive Tommy Hilfiger ads in *Glamour, Elle,* and *Vogue* showing a blonde model in black leather on what seemed to be the president's desk.

The trend, of course, preceded Starr and Clinton. As with an old couch whose worn out stuffing no longer did its job, American popular culture popped a coil. Days after the Starr Report's release, the rock group Marilyn Manson, named after the sex goddess Marilyn Monroe and the serial killer Charles Manson, released an album *Mechanical Animals*. The cover featured Manson as a naked androgynous alien, with fake breasts and androgynous genitalia. A month later, the singer Alanis Morissette wandered nude around Manhattan in her video "Thank U" to show how exposed her new album made her feel. The cultural critic Kurt Andersen lamented the new, brusque explicitness, "If you want to open restaurants where the main attraction is young waitresses with large breasts, you call the restaurants Hooters. . . . We're all Beavis and Butt-head now."

In his essay "Hooking Up," Tom Wolfe catalogued America's increasingly public orgy. "Every magazine stand was a riot of bare flesh . . . Sexual stimuli bombarded the young so incessantly and intensely they were inflamed with a randy itch long before reaching puberty. At puberty the dams, if any were left, burst." Teenagers were no longer romancing each other but "hooking up." Virgin became "a term of contempt," not a social ideal. The term "friends with benefits," decoupling sex from emotional coupling, was popularized in *Jagged Little Pill,* twenty-two-year-old Alanis Morissette's 1996 breakthrough album.

Just as *Time* and *Newsweek* cover stories in the 1970s about the divorce revolution normalized divorce, most experts now blithely normalized adultery, offering exaggerated claims that two-thirds of married men and one-third of married women were unfaithful. In this Age of Indulgence, corporate executives were ditching the wrinkled mothers of their children for "trophy wives." Fifty percent of all Internet "hits" logged onto online sex sites. The seventy-five-year-old former Republican presidential nominee Bob Dole was pitching Viagra, a little blue pill to fight E.D., erectile dysfunction, which sounded less emasculating than "impotence."

The Clinton crisis highlighted feminists' contradictions regarding sex and power. If the Clarence Thomas fight emphasized the movement's prissy side, the Lewinsky episode uncorked feminism's bawdy side. "Nice girls do," Lewinsky's therapist, Irene Kassorla preached, warning: "Guilt is like a traffic jam—it holds everything up." The author of *Fear of Flying,* Erica Jong, wanted a president "alive from the waist down."

Lewinsky would later confess her disappointment that feminists bullied her, too. Women liked Bill Clinton, a pro-choice president with a feminist First Lady, who passed the Family Leave Act. One *Atlanta Constitution* headline charged: "Feminists Abandon Monica Lewinsky for Partisan Agenda." Clinton had not been ensnared by "a right-wing conspiracy," wags noted, but sexual harassment law, championed by his feminist supporters.

The scandal enthralled teenagers as once-taboo subjects were aired, making many parents squirm. Reflecting the Contingency Carnival's I'm-OK-You're-OK ethos, Michael Popkin, a psychologist and parent coach in Atlanta, warned: "Watch for being too judgmental, too moralistic and too authoritarian." One *Washington Post* article about middle-school children in suburban Virginia indulging freely in oral sex, pointing to the president as role model, particularly scandalized readers. One Maryland eighteen-year-old complained: "The '80s defined an era of me, me, me, economically." The Nineties "is defining a world of me, me, me where relationships and love are concerned." The Good Father had triggered a mass conversation about values, but not quite as he planned.

Republicans: Midterm Losses but Impeachment Progresses

During the midterm congressional campaign, the president tried avoiding uncontrolled situations wherein voters might ask him embarrassing questions. He mostly jetted from one fund-raiser to another. With her marriage in crisis, Hillary Clinton clicked with Americans in ways she never had before. This popular Hillary Clinton was more Lady Di than Lady Godiva; her Jackie Kennedy poise not her Eleanor Roosevelt politicking won a 65 percent approval rating. Maureen Dowd called her the "single most degraded wife in the history of the world." The frustrated First Lady told Diane Blair it is "terribly hard to play 'only' the role she's playing now, ie First Wife, First Lady—when she very much wants to be the litigator, the legal defender." Hillary Clinton read the best-selling *Memoirs of a Geisha,* thinking, "What a woman had to do to get power."

A loyal enough wife to use the white glove pulpit, a big enough celebrity to generate star power, and an angry enough Democrat to motivate partisans, the First Lady helped win the 1998 elections. On the campaign trail she insisted: "It matters who is in office in Washington." She described Democrats as delivering on their promises, sponsoring the Family and Medical Leave Act, restoring prosperity, boosting education, fighting crime. She lambasted Republicans for poisoning the atmosphere and being unpatriotically obstructionist.

Defying polls showing Americans more concerned with their president's performance in public, House Republican leaders decided to press forward with an impeachment inquiry. On October 9, every member of the 227-member House Republican majority, along with 31 Democrats, supported impeachment proceedings. One hundred and seventy-six Democrats voted "no."

Cross-Country Hate Crimes

Just as Middle East terrorism shaped the summer, domestic violence intruded in the fall. One Tuesday night in early October, a twenty-one-year-old political science student at the University of Wyoming, Matthew Shepard, went out to the Fireside Bar. He spoke to two locals and may have propositioned one of them. Flirting with him but intending to rob him, they lured Shepard outside. They smashed his skull with the grip of a .357 magnum, stole his wallet and shoes, then lashed him to a secluded ranch fence post, crucifixion style. With one thousand to two thousand gay bashings annually, gays were targeted more than Jews,

Hispanics, or blacks. Like this one, the crimes were often particularly savage, reflecting the perpetrators' revulsion.

A passerby found Shepard in a coma eighteen hours later, after suffering in the frigid night air. The police reported that he looked like a scarecrow, tied to the fence. Members of a fraternity in nearby Fort Collins, Colorado, jokingly prepared a homecoming float, with a scarecrow carrying a sign: "I'm Gay."

Shepard's death five days later traumatized America. His martyrdom coincided with "Coming Out Day," celebrated since 1988 to commemorate "The Great March" in Washington of half a million people on October 11, 1987, for lesbian and gay rights. During Gay Awareness Week at University of Wyoming, many students and professors wore buttons saying "Straight but Not Narrow" in solidarity.

At Shepard's funeral, one evangelical bigot, the Reverend Fred Phelps, waved signs saying, GOD HATES FAGS and MATT IN HELL. "I found it almost impossible to believe that human beings could be so brutal and vicious to a hurting family," said the Reverend Jerry Falwell, a prominent evangelical and Clinton hater. Falwell understood that haters and murderers made all conservatives look evil.

The politics of gay rights was changing. Shepard's death galvanized the gay rights and gay marriage movements. Within a decade, many mainstream Republicans would no longer feel comfortable criticizing homosexuality, just as many Democrats a decade earlier had not felt comfortable defending homosexuality.

Clinton remained cautious about gay rights, preferring to champion hate crime legislation. When preparing his State of the Union address in 1999, speechwriters would propose acknowledging Matthew Shepard's death. Clinton admitted: "Every time I mention gays, my numbers go down in the State of the Union."

Two weeks after Shepard's murder, a sniper shot Dr. Barnett Slepian, a fifty-one-year-old physician standing in his suburban Buffalo kitchen, having just returned home from synagogue on a Friday night. The assassin targeted this father of four sons, aged seven to fifteen, because he performed abortions. Violence against abortionists and abortion clinics, while sporadic, was steady enough that it did not trigger the kind of mass outrage Shepard's death prompted.

Still Democrats nationwide, not just pro-choice forces in Buffalo, were shaken. They noted anti-abortion flyers circulating jokes asking: "What would you do if you were in a room with Hitler, Mussolini and an abortionist, and you had a gun with only two bullets?" The answer: "Shoot the abortionist twice." Jamie Tobias Neely of *The Spokesman-Review* called this affront, "only one of the endless examples of venom which the religious right, radio talk show hosts and cyberworld cranks spew on the topics of abortion and homosexuality." Sitting in Spokane, 963 miles from Laramie and 2,323 miles from Buffalo, Neely denounced "a culture of rhetoric so hateful that it inflames violence."

The nation was still reeling from the brutal murder of a black man, James Byrd Jr., in Jasper, Texas, in June, a town of eight thousand roughly divided between blacks and whites, with about 10 percent Hispanics. Three white supremacists stabbed him, urinated on him, chained him to the back of a truck, and dragged him for more than three miles on country roads, until he was decapitated.

Insisting, "This isn't us," many of Jasper's whites apologized for earlier expressions of racism. A mechanic admitted shortchanging an African American customer on parts; a woman said her daughter confronted her for disrespecting a black man, and vowed never to use "the 'N' word" again. A series of meetings dedicated to "repentance, redemption and economic development," became what *The Wall Street Journal* called "the town's version of South Africa's Truth and Reconciliation Commission."

As in 1995, Clinton exploited these murders to raise concerns about incivility in America, break the conservative monopoly on virtue, and reaffirm many Democrats' faith in themselves and their president. Linking his legal and political troubles with the worst violence coming from the right, Clinton said: "people can too easily be herded into hatred and extremism, often out of a belief that they have absolute truth and, therefore, are entitled to absolute power, that they can ignore any constitution, any laws, override any facts." The hate crimes legislation Clinton proposed following these murders, the Matthew Shepard and James Byrd Crimes Prevention Act, would be signed into law by President Barack Obama in 2009, after epic Democratic persistence and Republican resistance—on the grounds that other laws against violence made this law redundant.

Throughout the campaign, with the president subdued, Hillary Clinton emerged as a political pop star. Democrats would thank her for helping Charles Schumer unseat the three-term Republican senator in New York, Al D'Amato, and for saving Barbara Boxer's California Senate seat.

The November 1998 election results repudiated the Starr Report. Most voters ranked the Lewinsky question the least compelling of seven issues mentioned in exit polls. Sixty-two percent opposed impeachment. Since World War II, the incumbent party had lost on average twenty-eight congressional seats during the midterm elections. In 1994, Clinton's Democrats had lost fifty-two seats. In 1998, for the first time since 1866, a party gained congressional seats during its sixth year in the White House. The Democrats remained stable at forty-five Senate seats while gaining six House seats. An elated Hillary Clinton said of impeachment-oriented Republicans and know-it-all Beltway pundits: "We've rendered them irrelevant."

Impeachment Nevertheless

Despite these Democratic advances, and despite the resignation of Republican Speaker Newt Gingrich, the House impeached President Clinton. Clinton's dishonesty in the January deposition and the August grand jury appearance had made his sins legal and thus constitutional. All hopes of compromise centering on a censure faded when, once again, Clinton overreached and gave dismissive, lawyerly, and slippery responses to eighty-one questions the House Judiciary Committee posed to him. "He mooned the Congress," said one moderate Republican congressman's aide. As a poll-driven politician, Clinton could not fathom his opponents' defiance of the polls. And, as with most presidents, few aides could confront him with the necessary bad news on such a sensitive issue. The result was his great disgrace: impeachment on two counts six weeks after the midterm election triumph.

Just as zealous Republicans from majority Republican districts shaped the politics of Reconstruction in the 1860s, Republican extremists comfortable in gerrymandered districts shaped the politics of the Clinton impeachment. Representative Peter T. King, a New York Republican, estimated that in 180 out of 228 Republican districts, "there's no damage in voting for impeachment. In fact, it would be very popular."

Misled by the election results, the polls, and the changed media tone, the Clintons mobilized too late to stop the impeachment. The First Lady lobbied furiously, articulating legal arguments while embodying a more emotional argument: If she forgave him why shouldn't we?

As the Republicans increased the pressure on Clinton, Clinton increased the pressure on Saddam Hussein. In August, Osama bin Laden had dictated the timetable, attacking the United States, emboldened by Clinton's troubles. With Clinton taking the initiative, worries that he was "wagging the dog" intensified. Since November 1997, Saddam had blocked UN weapons inspectors at least four times. Three times, Clinton authorized attacks then aborted them. On December 16, supported by Tony Blair of Britain, Clinton launched four days of bombing. "Saddam Hussein must not be allowed to threaten his neighbors or the world with nuclear arms, poison gas or biological weapons," Clinton said in a nationally televised address. Former secretary of state Lawrence Eagleburger said the timing "smells to high heaven." *The Washington Post* columnist Charles Krauthammer agreed, while finding it humiliating that Clinton felt compelled "to draw authority from those under him" by listing each member of his national security team. "This is what this wreckage of a presidency is reduced to," Krauthammer mourned: "a man of no credibility desperately trying to borrow some."

On December 19, the House of Representatives debated the president's impeachment. Hillary Clinton again defended her husband, saying, "the vast majority of Americans share my approval and pride in the job that the President's been doing for our country." The pornographer Larry Flynt of *Hustler* offered $1 million to expose any Republican's affairs. Reasoning that "ugly times require ugly tactics," *Salon* magazine outed the seventy-four-year-old chairman of the House Judiciary Committee, Henry Hyde, for an affair three decades earlier. Sanford Ungar, the dean of American University's School of Communication, moaned: "This town has gone nuts."

The Speaker-elect of the House, Robert Livingston, sank in Flynt's cesspool. When Livingston began the debate Saturday morning, he argued for impeachment while urging the president to resign. Knowing that Livingston had committed adultery years earlier, Democrats yelled back "You resign!" Livingston did just that, saying "I must set the example that I hope President Clinton will follow."

This impulsive, honorable move on this topsy-turvy day immediately had Democrats begging the Republican Livingston to reconsider, as Republicans supported his move as a way to pressure Clinton. Near tears, Livingston's Democratic friend, Representative David Obey, asked: "How many more good people are going to be destroyed next by Christmas?" Minority Leader Richard A. Gephardt begged his colleagues to "turn away from the politics of personal destruction and return to the politics of values." He received a bipartisan standing ovation.

The clash was generational, ideological, cultural. Even a *Wall Street Journal* editorial admitted that Kenneth Starr was prosecuting not just Bill Clinton but "the generation that produced him." Republicans invoked traditional values of "honor and decency and integrity and truth," as an emotional Majority Whip Tom DeLay did. Democrats accused the Republicans of partisanship, breach of privacy, and an "attempted coup d'état." Tom Lantos, a European refugee, as unhinged rhetorically as the Republicans, compared the House to "Hitler's parliament" and "Stalin's parliament." Representative Jesse L. Jackson Jr., Democrat of Illinois, was equally inflammatory, claiming Republicans were "impeaching" all the Great Society gains. Then, playing the race card, remembering Andrew Johnson's impeachment in 1868, Jackson charged: "In 1868, it was about Reconstruction. In 1998, it's still about Reconstruction."

The House of Representatives impeached President William Jefferson Clinton on two counts, for lying to the grand jury on August 17 that he never had "sexual relations" with Monica Lewinsky and obstructing justice in the Paula Jones case by encouraging Lewinsky to file a false affidavit. As Henry Hyde led a group of House Republicans to deliver the articles of impeachment to the secretary of the Senate, Democrats walked out of Congress and drove straight to the White House. There, they mounted a strange, post-impeachment, partisan pep rally led by Bill Clinton, Al Gore, and Hillary Clinton. Gore called Clinton "one of our greatest presidents." Clinton echoed Gephardt, saying, "We must stop the politics of personal destruction." The earnest, roll-up-your-sleeves president again emphasized: "We have important work to do."

The Vast Wreckage of the Borderline Presidency

Michael Kelly, the editor of the *National Journal,* resented Clinton's triumphal self-righteousness. With celebrities like Alec Baldwin crying "Stone Henry Hyde to death," the thuggery Clinton attributed to conservatives oozed out of both parties. Kelly concluded: "The vast wreckage about us is one man's work." Clinton's liquid presidency had turned corrosive, eliminating the usual party inhibitions, and poisoning the national well of good feeling a democracy needs.

Bill Clinton survived this near-fatal self-inflicted wound, by going for broke, refusing to concede. In this battle he displayed the discipline, the persistence, the commitment to winning that was missing in the health care battle or the race commission initiative. Clinton's speechwriter Jeff Shesol and other policy aides were impressed by their boss's focus on substance amid the circus. "He would walk in and clap his hands and say 'all right what are we doing,'" Shesol recalls. "He was eager to be at work and really dived in." Critics blamed Clinton's more modest accomplishments on the scandal; but second terms are notorious for growing torpor as presidential power wanes.

In his second term, Clinton proved more adept at defense than at offense, better at bashing enemies and saving programs than at transforming the country. As a result, his policy legacy would lack the grandeur he yearned for or might have been able to achieve with his great skills and America's extraordinary prosperity. Rather than being compared to the greatest presidents, Washington, Lincoln, the Roosevelts, Clinton often found himself compared to the impeached

Andrew Johnson, the slovenly Ulysses S. Grant, the popular but ineffectual William McKinley, the amoral Warren Harding, and the immoral Richard Nixon.

Bill Clinton survived the year, barely. Faced with a choice between Kenneth Starr's relentless, prurient invasion of privacy or Clinton's sloppy, base evasiveness, most Americans stuck with their president. But this Beverly Hills–borne epidemic of affluenza proved debilitating. Clinton's indulgent defense was clever but demoralizing. It was a big drop from "ask what you can do for your country" to "it depends upon what the meaning of the word 'is,' is." Most Americans also yearned for something grander, for yesterday's anchors, which they best identified with the aging World War II veterans who defeated totalitarianism and created modern America's mass middle-class, values-steeped society.

Steven Spielberg's World War II blockbuster, *Saving Private Ryan,* and Tom Brokaw's number one best seller, *The Greatest Generation,* about those D-Day heroes and their peers, celebrated the traditional values Clinton had trampled to save his presidency. "Folks now just don't have an appreciation for what an oath means . . . ," one Marine veteran told Brokaw, appalled by Clinton's slipperiness. "I lost half my squadron. We all knew what an oath was about." Brokaw observed that the retired heroes' "common lament" is "the absence today of personal responsibility" and integrity. The trembling hand of Captain Miller, the schoolteacher turned war hero Tom Hanks portrayed in *Saving Private Ryan,* reflects the bloody battles Spielberg depicted so graphically. The tremor also, perhaps, exposes the worry that this world these veterans are saving will be doomed by their Baby Boomer children. As Miller dies to save Private Ryan, he whispers, "earn this." Brokaw and Spielberg were saying their elders did— but this next generation, the spoiled brats of 90210 nation, had not.

As the torchbearer for the Baby Boomer rebels, Bill Clinton embodied the changes, representing the new sensibility. He lived it and fueled it—gripping onto the presidency after his privacy was so violated by leading a full-fledged "everybody does it" assault on traditional assumptions. Although he survived in office, he, his wife, and his mistress Monica were left stripped of their privacy, with many of their most intimate moments not just exposed but documented, scrutinized, memorialized, mocked.

Even as he became the promiscuous president, the poster child for bad behavior defended with the most cynical defense, he also sincerely championed family, faith, community, responsibility. Supporters did not "get it" when they overlooked his sins; detractors did not "get it" when they dismissed his values. Just like the new video games going 3-D in the 1990s, this presidency must be appreciated from many angles, in many dimensions. And just as in the big 3-D video game of 1998, *The Legend of Zelda: Ocarina of Time,* the female hero Zelda also appears as the Sheik, Bill Clinton's two sides, his parallel lives, invite analysis.

A person suffering from Borderline Personality Disorder has intense, unstable relationships, and alternates between overidealizing and undervaluing people. In this new Republic of Nothing and Everything, Americans often toggled between patriotism and cynicism, as demonstrated by the nostalgia-tinged World War II jubilation and the Lewinsky-Starr-Clinton induced despair. The multiple moral panics revealed a deep discomfort with what America had become, and was becoming.

As the year ended, Clinton was confident of avoiding conviction in the Senate. With another two full years in office, he was already well into his latest self-rehabilitation project. Clinton wanted to make sure that his victory was not pyrrhic; that he could build a legacy to blot out the stain of being only the second president impeached in American history.

10

1999: Chicago
Finding Forgiveness in the
Church of Oprah

Now that the Senate has fulfilled its constitutional responsibility, bringing this process to a conclusion, I want to say again to the American People how profoundly sorry I am for what I said and did to trigger these events.
—BILL CLINTON PRESS BRIEFING IN THE ROSE GARDEN,
TWO HOURS AFTER THE SENATE VOTED AGAINST CONVICTING
HIM ON CHARGES OF PERJURY AND OBSTRUCTION OF JUSTICE,
FEBRUARY 12, 1999

On November 17, 1999, 1,056 people, including 125 reporters, crowded into a ballroom at the Marriott Marquis in New York's Times Square. The tuxedoed and ball-gowned crowd was invited to honor authors such as Ha Jin, Ai, John W. Dower, and Kimberly Willis Holt as the winners of the National Book Awards. "I can't tell you how excited I was when I was told I had been asked to host the awards dinner for the NBA," the comedian Steve Martin joked. "This really isn't the crowd I expected."

In fact, the Fiftieth Anniversary Gold Medal Honoree, Oprah Winfrey, accounted for the unprecedented hoopla. In 1996, Oprah had roused the book world by launching her monthly book club, named, characteristically, after herself. "Oprah Winfrey possesses the magical quality to create bestsellers," the National Book Foundation's executive director, Neil Baldwin, said. As he presented her with a Tiffany crystal sculpture, the audience gave this most unlikely intellectual arbiter the requisite standing ovation.

Winfrey then offered a classic Oprah mix of autobiographical self-puffery and New Age self-empowerment. She described reading the African American poet Maya Angelou's 1969 autobiography, *I Know Why the Caged Bird Sings,* when she was a teenager as "my first recollection of being validated. The fact that someone as poor as I, as Black as I, from the South, from rape, from confusion, could move to hope, to possibility, and to victory, could be written about in a real book that I had chosen in the library was amazing to me." Forever name-dropping, she said, "Books helped me to know, what Maya often says, that we really are more alike than we are different." In celebrating opportunity despite adversity and commonality amid diversity, Oprah reduced books to props in her glorious American uplift project.

Using one of her catchphrases, which millions imitated, the 1990s for Oprah were "three words . . . fa-bu-lous." Her daily talk show shaped America culturally and spiritually. It was lucrative, too, making Winfrey America's first female black billionaire. In 1998, *Time* designated her one of the world's 100 most influential people. At its peak, her show attracted 46 million viewers in 134 countries. Many of the white, middle-class, middle-aged women who formed her core audience were born into homes that only welcomed people like her as domestics to work, certainly not as celebrities to worship.

Mingling self-pity with self-promotion, Winfrey often recalled her Dickensian childhood: "No one ever told me I was loved. Ever, ever, ever"—repetition for emphasis was a signature Oprahism. Raised by her grandmother, sometimes dressed in potato sacks as dresses, sexually abused when young, Oprah suffered Jesus-like agonies before achieving popular salvation. Women at church told her grandmother, "Hattie Mae, this child sure can talk. This is the talkingest child." With the professional entertainer's perfect timing, Oprah would pause, smile and exclaim: "But that talking has paid off."

Oprah Winfrey made the American cult of success about her two favorite subjects, the self and the spirit. Viewers worshipping in the Church of Oprah adored her materialism, her redemptive narratives, her Hallmark Card chestnuts about self-esteem and spirituality, and, most important, Oprah herself. Oprah was as anodyne, accessible, and all-American as Johnny Carson. She was as ideological and judgmental—in her own New Age way—as Rush Limbaugh. She was as cheesy and healing as Phil Donahue. She was as populist and entertaining as Jerry Springer. She was also as smooth as Frank Sinatra, as brassy as Barbra Streisand, as formidable as Katharine Hepburn, and as wired into American sensibilities as Walt Disney. She tapped into the evangelical tradition of the great populist preachers Henry Ward Beecher and Aimee McPherson, selling a gospel of goodness and niceness, laden with Americanism and, in a late-twentieth-century twist, consumerism.

Oprah was to entertainment what Bill Clinton—on his best days—was to politics. These two Baby Boomer scions of the South, both from broken homes, reflected and intensified America's rush toward a more diverse, chaotic, accepting yet somehow anguished and empty horizontal democracy. The two together were the high priest and priestess of America's Republic of Nothing—and Everything.

Clinton and Winfrey were consummate survivors, perpetual comeback kids with tremendous grit. In this twelve-step year, Bill Clinton recovered, his presidency recovered, and America recovered, often by taking a fluid, relativistic, Oprahesque approach. Part of the reason why Clinton recovered, or even survived, was because of a broader renaissance occurring throughout America during his tenure, epitomized by the gentrification and revival of Chicago, which also served as the capital of Oprah-land.

A Chicago Renaissance

At the National Book Awards, Oprah was a New Yorker for a night, but Chicago was her home. She arrived in Chicago after becoming Nashville's first black TV news anchor when she was nineteen. In 1984, at the age of thirty, she anchored *A.M. Chicago,* which she quickly renamed *The Oprah Winfrey Show.* In September 1986, her show went national. In founding Harpo Studios, "Oprah" spelled backward, she became only the third female star to own her own studio— following Mary Pickford and Lucille Ball.

By 1990, Harpo Studios occupied 88,000 square feet of floor space in a former cold storage warehouse in Chicago's Near West Side neighborhood. The Near West Side, once a thriving industrial neighborhood with food wholesalers, flower markets, big insurance offices, and printing companies, was virtually abandoned. The big empty structures had become urban mausoleums.

The Rust Belt's deindustrialization had devastated Chicago. The "Second City" of 2.8 million had become America's third city, behind Los Angeles and New York. Between 1979 and 2000, real manufacturing wages would drop by 17 percent in Illinois, even worse than the 10 percent drop nationwide. Chicago's infrastructure was crumbling, its school system teetering, having been labeled America's worst by secretary of education William Bennett. Downtown was dangerous and depressed.

When Richard M. Daley was elected Chicago's mayor in 1989, few believed in him or his city. He was a cipher, overshadowed by his father, Chicago's legendary "Boss," Mayor Richard J. Daley. Daley junior blossomed as a Midwestern, buttoned-down version of Bill Clinton, similarly pragmatic and centrist. He envisioned an "information-based" city serving as a cultural, intellectual, and economic hub. Chicago became another 1990s boomtown.

Daley's Strategic Neighborhood Action Program developed Oprah's neighborhood, the Near West Side, as part of a $5.3 billion investment in infrastructure. Spending in America's major cities on capital expenditures was increasing 9 percent annually—five times faster than the rate of growth for operating expenses. Open city space surrounded by highways, once developed, often attracted new urban pioneers. More singles were staying single longer. More two-career couples were childless. More empty nesters were carving out long, post-family phases. More gay couples were buying homes.

From 1993 through 1996, the city invested $49 million in the neighborhood, boosted by tax abatements, tax credits, loans, zoning adjustments, tax-exempt bonds, matching funds, and other public-private stratagems. This way, government did what governments did best—widening sidewalks, restoring bridges, fixing potholes, demolishing crumbling structures, even planting flowers and trees.

Harpo Studios became an anchor, joined in 1994 by the United Center. This 960,000 square foot, $175 million new home for the Chicago Bulls and the Chicago Blackhawks, the city's beloved basketball and hockey teams, had the requisite corporate sponsorship and 216 luxury boxes. Nationwide, thirty-one new sports facilities were built between 1989 and 1997.

Within a few years, 5,000 residential lofts budded within the Near West Side's once-abandoned building shells while elegant town houses sprouted on once-vacant lots. Banks, restaurants, and stores followed. Unlike in other gentrifying neighborhoods, there were no poor residents to displace and little residual crime to fight.

Critics noted that, as in most of urban America, an estimated half-million poor Chicagoans were left behind. As the city became more glitzy than gritty, they wondered, "How many Starbucks does a nation need?" The 1996 Democratic National Convention celebrated Chicago's renaissance, healing from the traumas that had made "Chicago" and "1968" two searing words in America's political lexicon.

The Bill Clinton Apology Derby

Bill Clinton found salvation by supplementing some old-time religious repentance with New Age, Oprah-style confessing, amid his brass-knuckle politicking. While fighting the nasty partisan battle in the Senate to survive, he understood that outlasting unpopular enemies was not enough. His presidency needed rebooting, existentially not just politically.

Winfrey preached that "To Love yourself is a never-ending journey" and "once you accept yourself for who you are you become a better person." This conflation of psychological growth with goodness valued modern openness over traditional virtue. Clintonian self-indulgence also found validation in the return of sociobiology, framed in liberal terms by Robert Wright in his popular 1994 book *The Moral Animal*. Reducing human motivation to biological impulses, Wright explained that "Feelings of lust . . . directly aided reproduction." Feminist theorists added a communal dimension to these psychological and biological rationales. In her 1982 classic, *In a Different Voice,* the Harvard psychologist Carol Gilligan said women defined morality as an ethic of responsibility and caring, valuing relationships; while men rooted morality in justice, following rules.

The acceptance of presidential sinfulness had roots in Christian and American thought. The Bible's book of Corinthians describes humans as fragile and flawed vessels, dwarfed by God's power, redeemed by Jesus' sacrifices for their sins. The mid-twentieth-century Protestant theologian Reinhold Niebuhr explained that in the "conflict between spirit and nature," the best to hope for was a "forgiving love" accepting "man's imperfection." Although the Framers cherished individual virtue as the key to national virtue, James Madison wrote realistically in *Federalist* 51, "If men were angels, no government would be necessary." Abraham Lincoln's realism also suited Clinton: "folks who have no vices have generally very few virtues."

Cold War America equated stable families with national strength and embraced a George Washington–like perfectionist commitment to public character as appearing solid, etched in stone. Baby Boomers rejected this traditional posture as hypocrisy. Religious leaders now described Moses as a sinner who killed an Egyptian soldier and Paul as a "blasphemer." With his Christian understanding of leaders as flawed vessels, Father Alan Jurkus of Whitefish Bay, Wisconsin, wondered: "Do I want to be probed into everything I have ever done in my life?"

In modern America's more jaded, more indulgent world, politicians still felt media and political pressure to appear virtuous, but there was growing psychological, ideological, and sociological latitude to roam. Psychologists called adultery "reprehensible" yet "irresistible." *The Tampa Tribune* headlined: "Nation of Hypocrites Had No Right to Cast Its Judgment on Clinton." Philip Roth wanted Christo, the artist who in 1995 wrapped Germany's Reichstag in plastic, to wrap the White House in "a mammoth banner" announcing "A HUMAN BEING LIVES HERE."

Clinton helped lay the groundwork for this new embrace of a messy authenticity over an artificial perfection. In 1992 he said: "The biggest moral challenge is trying to live by what you believe in every day," struggling to avoid being "disappointed" by the inevitable "failures." Clinton viewed life as "a continual search for real integrity." He had to believe in life after death: "I need a second chance." This emphasis on fulfilling his presidential duties and helping the American people, despite his flaws, reflected Gilligan's more fluid, feminine, and feminist conception of morality.

To survive, Clinton made the once-imperial presidency the penitential presidency. He apologized on national television on August 17, 1998. He apologized again three weeks later, on September 10, to 350 Florida Democrats. Then he apologized again the next day, September 11, at a White House prayer breakfast, partially for not being "contrite enough" in August. And after his Senate acquittal in February he would again tell "the American people how profoundly sorry I am."

Beyond the public mea culpas, Clinton relied on ministers as spiritual advisers, in an evangelical-style "accountability circle." He was comfortable with religious idioms. He often incorporated "grace notes" that "fit" his "deep faith" into his speeches, speechwriter Lowell Weiss recalls.

The Clintons also began a yearlong series of marital counseling and prayer sessions, with the president sleeping on the couch for the first two months. One theologian friend helped Mrs. Clinton see her husband's offenses as "sins of weakness" committed by someone whom she still loved and considered "such a fundamentally good person." Republicans, however, were committing "sins of malice" against him, her, and their country.

"Whatever Happened to Gary Cooper?"

A president undergoing religious counseling seemed less threatening to most Americans than his undergoing psychological therapy, the historian Robert Dallek noted. A troubled soul was less disturbing than a troubled mind. The Clintons joined approximately 4.6 million other couples seeking out wisdom from 50,000 licensed family therapists, their clientele having almost quadrupled since 1980. With relationships supposed to fulfill romantic ideals while functioning as practical partnerships, even marriages that weren't in crisis were in trouble. The sociologist Zygmunt Bauman suggested that with so much riding on these "incarnations of ambivalence," many moderns preferred the no-strings-attached hookup, or, increasingly, the online date. As one twentysomething would explain, "you can always press delete."

The marital therapy boom was only one corner of a $69 billion industry in what had become *Prozac Nation,* as Elizabeth Wurtzel's best-selling 1994 memoir dubbed it. By 2000, 80 percent of Americans would have received some form of psychological counseling, up from 14 percent in 1960. Americans were spending $11 billion a year on antidepressants, with 25 million Americans—nearly a tenth of the country—prescribed Prozac. The other most commonly prescribed drugs were ulcer medication and aspirin, proof that the society producing 60 new millionaires daily mass-produced anxiety, too. One survey found that 29 percent of Americans preferred seeing a religious counselor and 13 percent, a family doctor. Beyond that, with far more therapists than librarians, pharmacists, or dentists, clients could choose from among 40,000 psychiatrists, 125,000 psychologists, 10,000 psychoanalysts, and 150,000 social workers. Mark McGwire, the steroid-boosted home-run king, proclaimed: "Hey, everybody needs therapy."

Reflecting their ubiquity, "shrinks" became more prevalent in popular culture, and more likable. At the start of the decade, Dr. Hannibal Lecter in *The Silence of the Lambs* (1991) was diabolical, Dr. Frasier Crane on *Cheers* was juvenile, and Barbra Streisand's character in *The Prince of Tides* (1991) was unethical, sleeping with her patient's brother. In *Good Will Hunting* (1997), Robin Williams plays a therapist who empowers a working-class genius, played by Matt Damon. In *Analyze This* (1999), psychiatrist Ben Sobel, played by Billy Crystal, helps a mob boss, Paul Vitti, played by Robert De Niro. Sobel's fear—"What is my goal here, to make you a happy, well-adjusted gangster?"—and Vitti's homophobic warning—"If I talk to you, and you turn me into a fag . . . I'm gonna kill you"—both imputed nearly magical powers to therapists.

Two months before *Analyze This* premiered, HBO offered a less funny, more complex mobster-therapist relationship when the fictional crime boss Tony Soprano sought help for his panic attacks. "Nowadays everybody's gotta go to shrinks and counselors and go on *Sally Jessy Raphael* and talk about their problems," Tony complains. "Whatever happened to Gary Cooper—the strong, silent type? That was an American. He wasn't in touch with his feelings—he just did what he had to do."

Instead, America's Oprahfied popular culture prized cathartic confessionals, with therapists coaxing troubled clients in offices or with Jenny Jones, Jerry Springer, or Oprah herself lustily baiting distressed guests in studios. In a *New Yorker* cartoon, one prison inmate explains to another: It's OK to plead guilty—but not to *feel* guilty. In a culture that pathologized the normal while normalizing pathologies, Americans were promised cures to "addictions" to shopping, eating, sex, even religion.

By 1999, exhibitionist Americans could court on TV's *Blind Date,* find a home on *House Hunting,* and divorce on a revived *Divorce Court.* Even incest became more openly discussed with Kathryn Harrison's 1997 best-selling memoir, *The Kiss.* Earlier in the decade, Princess Diana had confessed to suffering from eating disorders and the pain of a crowded marriage with her husband still tied to his ex-girlfriend (and eventual second wife). Underlying her bulimia, Di confessed, was low self-esteem, what Oprah would call "the root of all the problems in the world." "I don't know when it became cool to be shameless," said Jill Stein, a UCLA sociologist. "In the mist of difficulty lies opportunity," Oprah insisted.

Clinton Acquitted in the Senate

Beyond Clinton's confessionals, the constitutional conservatism of the American people and the Senate saved him—as it saved Andrew Johnson in 1868. The many ambiguities Clinton's defenders introduced and their counterattack caricaturing the overzealous, often bumbling, special prosecutor made many moderates hesitant to remove the president. The chief House manager, Congressman Henry Hyde, insisted the issue was not "lying about sex" but the "public act" of "lying under oath." He concluded by playing the Greatest Generation card, invoking D-Day's dead, vowing "to make this country the kind of America they were willing to die for. That's an America where the idea of sacred honor still has the power to stir men's souls." Clinton's lead attorney, White House Counsel Charles F. C. Ruff, insisted the charges were baseless and even if true did not meet the standard of "impeachable offenses." Trumping Hyde's World War II card, Ruff honored his own father who "was on the beach 55 years ago," but "didn't fight, no one fought, for one side of this case or the other. He fought, as all those did, for our country and our Constitution."

In this "split-screen presidency," President Clinton delivered his State of the Union speech in the House chamber on January 19, 1999, only hours after Ruff began defending him in the Senate Chamber. The speech showcased Clinton's disciplined focus on his job. In the middle, the president saluted the First Lady and mouthed a very public "I love you" in a tableau of public reconciliation. Shortly thereafter, the Senate acquitted the now badly wounded president. The wrath lingered like a bad smell in the Capitol's halls. Neither party was ready to reach what Oprah defines as "True forgiveness . . . when you can say, 'Thank you for that experience.'"

Clinton took the senatorial failure to convict as redemptive. Increasingly seeing himself as not just victim but hero, he would say that he found "generally in our country's history, that people who are progressive, people who try to change things, people who keep pushing the envelope," suffered. In a March 31 interview with CBS's Dan Rather, Clinton refused to view impeachment "as some great badge of shame." He claimed, absurdly, "I am honored that something that was indefensible was pursued and that I had the opportunity to defend the Constitution."

Within the Beltway, too many Democrats and Republicans now considered their rivals evil. Clinton aides like Sidney Blumenthal, who from the start had schemed to spread negative information about the conservative book agent Lucianne Goldberg and other enemies, put the president's "opponents . . . on a continuum with those firebrands who have pushed the country toward civil war, racial terror and class warfare." Republicans like Senator John Ashcroft continued complaining that "the President's values deficit illustrates that ours is a culture in crisis. Its symptoms include family breakdown, teen pregnancy, violence, and drug abuse."

Sensitive to slights, many Clintonites were vengeful. When ABC Radio's Tom Joyner made a salacious remark about what employment "skills" Monica Lewinsky "learned in the White House," staffers noted: "Please keep this in mind the next time he asks for an interview." However, with 2000 coming up, Robert B. Johnson, the director of domestic policy initiative, warned, "He needs to be kept engaged for our message and for Gore." Johnson added: "Politics Baby!!!!"

On April 12, U.S. District Judge Susan Webber Wright put the case into its proper perspective. She found the president in civil contempt of court for giving "false, misleading, and evasive answers that were designed to obstruct the judicial process," regarding his "intimate contact" with Lewinsky. "The court takes no pleasure whatsoever in holding this nation's president in contempt of court," Judge Wright added, while charging him the $1,202 it cost her to fly to Washington, D.C., to hear his "willful failure" to tell the truth. Subsequently, Wright's contempt finding forced Clinton to reimburse Jones's attorneys $89,484 and led to the president's disbarment by the Arkansas Supreme Court. On January 19, 2001, Clinton's last day in office, he would agree to acknowledge his misconduct publicly, endure a five-year suspension of his Arkansas law license, and pay a $25,000 fine. He would also be disbarred from the U.S. Supreme Court, and resign on November 9, 2001, rather than fight that ruling.

"If Popularity Isn't for This, What's It For?": The Kosovo War

The president had work to do, not just political damage to control. The Yugoslavian mess confounded him again. Mostly Christian ethnic Serbian troops were abusing, raping, and expelling largely Muslim ethnic Albanians in the autonomous province of Kosovo. Simultaneously, the Kosovo Liberation Army (KLA) launched its own violent campaign for independence. Fearing renewed ethnic cleansing, NATO leaders supported the weaker Kosovars against the well-armed Serbs. NATO insisted: "Serbs out, peacekeepers in, refugees back."

President Slobodan Milošević was rabble-rousing about Kosovo, the Serbs' Jerusalem, the focus of their national-religious dreams. Clinton feared it becoming his Vietnam. In July 1998, a Senate resolution urged Hague officials to indict Milošević for "war crimes, crimes against humanity and genocide." On January 15, 1999, Serb troops murdered forty-five Albanian farmers in Racak. By spring 1999, as many as forty thousand Serbian troops and special police forces surrounded Kosovo. More than two hundred thousand Kosovars, mostly Albanians, had fled their homes.

Clinton felt guilty about dithering in the Balkans and Rwanda. With his backing, NATO's ultimatum to Milošević was: accept peacekeepers on the ground or endure a "humanitarian intervention," meaning bombardment. The arrogant Serb denied the ethnic cleansing accusations and insisted foreign troops would never "occupy" the Serbian homeland. Serbs denounced Clinton for fouling "Christian Europe" and trying to distract from his own troubles.

On March 24, NATO attacked a sovereign country for the first time. Yugoslav's capital Belgrade became a primary target, along with the Yugoslavian troops and weapons surrounding Kosovo. "If President Milosevic will not make peace, we will limit his ability to make war," President Clinton pronounced in a four-minute televised address. "Ending this tragedy," he said, was both "a moral imperative" and "important to America's national interests." Two weeks later, Clinton linked this war to his broader mission, this "great battle between the forces of integration and the forces of disintegration, the forces of globalism versus tribalism, of oppression against empowerment."

Clinton faced the liberal interventionist's dilemma. Post–Cold War, many Americans craved isolationism. To Clinton, in "the global village . . . problems that start beyond our borders can quickly become problems within them." His mission was to "match the demands for American leadership to our strategic interests and to our ability to make a difference." While insisting the United States "cannot and must not be the world's policeman" he accepted the responsibility, vowing, if "innocent civilians" are hunted "*en masse* because of their race, their ethnic background or their religion, and it's within our power to stop it, we will stop it."

Americans disagreed about whether to intervene militarily; only 58 percent even recognized the moral challenge. Clinton failed to explain why Kosovo proved more compelling than other hot spots. His director of press advance, Anne Edwards, would articulate the classic American "Innocents Abroad" disdain for these foreign messes. "Everything here is complicated," she wrote White House colleagues from Albania in June 1999, "everything has layers and layers of 'meanings' and histories and vendettas."

Hundreds of civilian deaths, and the accidental bombing of the Chinese embassy in Belgrade in early May, hurt Clinton's popularity ratings. Tony Blair urged the president to commit ground troops. Russian officials opposed the ground invasion, just as they opposed the air campaign. Their impotence would feed a sense of national humiliation Vladimir Putin would still be exploiting a decade and a half later. Clinton held strong, lecturing his skittish advisers: "If popularity isn't for this, what's it for?"

Finally, after 35,000 sorties during 78 days, with 40 Yugoslav bridges, 100 fighter planes and 120 tanks destroyed, 5,000 Yugoslav security forces and 1,200 Serbian civilians killed, and 1 million Kosovars displaced, Milošević broke. On June 10, he agreed to withdraw his troops and accept the peacekeepers in Kosovo he had refused in March. *Time* declared Clinton, "the luckiest president," yet "again." One grateful refugee from Kosovo told reporters: "If Clinton didn't exist, we wouldn't exist as Albanians. He saved our lives." Clinton warned Americans against excessive optimism: "We must never forget: Freedom is not free."

Angry White Males in Columbine: The Middle Children of History

The Kosovo bombings felt distant, especially when violence in American schools hit so close to home. On April 20, in Littleton, Colorado, a town of about thirty thousand 30 miles outside of Denver, two Columbine High School seniors started shooting, killing twelve students and a teacher, wounding twenty-three others. Dylan Klebold and Eric Harris intended to blow up the school cafeteria, to outdo the Oklahoma City bombing, whose anniversary was April 19. Fortunately, most of their explosives were duds. They ended their shooting spree by killing themselves.

Scenes of a suburban school turned killing field shocked America. One defining image showed a bloodied teenager, Patrick Ireland, slowly falling out a second-story window, headfirst, into the arms of two helmeted SWAT-team members, standing on top of their armored truck. From another window, a message scrawled on a white-board announced: "1 Bleeding to Death," as the one teacher shot, Dave Sanders, did just that. The first funeral, of Rachel Scott, a seventeen-year-old who two years earlier had said, "Dad, someday you're going to see me on Oprah," became CNN's most watched funeral ever, including Princess Diana's.

Like another attention-getting Colorado crime, the JonBenét Ramsey killing, Columbine combined true crime mystery with endless morality tales. "Columbine" became shorthand for school shootings—inspiring imitators for years thereafter. Reporters had covered less lethal school shootings since 1997 in Pearl, Mississippi; West Paducah, Kentucky; Jonesboro, Arkansas; and Springfield, Oregon, as idiosyncratic. This white, academic, prosperous, mall-filled, generic Denver suburb was too high tech to be Small Town, U.S.A, with firms like Qwest Communications offering telecommunication services, and Lockheed Martin developing space systems. Littleton became Any Town, U.S.A., jarringly familiar, or Lost Town, U.S.A., the archetypal city of the Republic of Nothing.

Despite a dropping crime rate for seven years, as Clinton frequently boasted, many Americans felt unsafe. *The Boston Globe*'s David Shribman wrote that "Not since 1968," amid assassinations and riots, had "a spate of violent incidents prompted such deep, disquieting introspection." In addition to these kinds of national horrors, local TV news shows devoted one-third of their programming to crime reports.

The Columbine killers' motivations died with them. But reporters quickly imputed social meanings to a story that probably was more about psychopathology than sociology. They seized on the two killers' supposed membership in the "Trench Coat Mafia," along with alleged comments about targeting jocks, to package the Columbine shootings as *Revenge of the Nerds* turned deadly. Reporters depicted the two as Goths, bullied, black-clad, Marilyn Manson–listening islands of alienation oozing an easily detected insanity and lethality. The killers' diaries and websites eventually refuted most of this, making Columbine one of the decade's biggest, most misreported, stories.

It was unfair to blame Columbine on the new America emerging, but it was also unavoidable. Deviants became canvasses on which everyone projected their anxieties and agendas. "I'm thinking if we don't learn from this, we'll see it again," Oprah Winfrey said, blaming school bullying, during the second show on Columbine she did within a month of the massacre. "We exist in a culture that deifies wealth and power and accepts violence, weaponry and poor nutrition. And we wonder why we are sick," a poet and journalist, Sue Anne Morgan, wrote in *The Atlanta Journal-Constitution*. "Horrific tragedies occur because life has become horrific."

That October, *Fight Club,* starring Brad Pitt as a young, angry white male, articulated this New Nihilism. Pitt's character watches "an entire generation pumping gas, waiting tables; slaves with white collars. Advertising has us chasing cars and clothes, working jobs we hate so we can buy shit we don't need. We're the middle children of history, man. No purpose or place." Echoing Clinton's own fears of purposelessness, he continues, "We have no Great War. No Great Depression. Our Great War's a spiritual war . . . our Great Depression is our lives."

Many condemnations linked popular culture and technology, singling out bloody movies like Oliver Stone's *Natural Born Killers* (1994), violent video games like *Doom* and *Quake,* the Internet's fusion of information and entertainment, and the ease of buying weapons and learning bomb recipes online. Denver International Airport's arcade soon pulled its most violent video games.

Eric Harris was adept with computers and voluble online, trashing others, posting pipe bomb recipes, proclaiming: "I destroy what I hate." The Internet's 24/7 mix of anonymity and intensity encouraged "community deviancy," Steven Levy noted in *Newsweek*. In 2000, the Republican candidate George W. Bush would attribute the school shootings to the "dark dungeons of evil on the Internet." Actually, Harris's diatribes were depressingly typical, revealing a nihilistic streak in American teen culture now expressed online as well. The medium had not created his harsh messages, or the mass anguish.

President Clinton blamed easy access to guns along with media violence. He thought most Americans were too complacent. His National Campaign to Prevent Youth Violence, launched in September, hoped to prove "that youth violence is not like the weather, in that it can be predicted, its consequences can be muted." Clinton staffers wanted to get "the message out that America has been training kids to be violent, and that there is something every citizen can do to reduce youth violence." In October, Clinton would say, "6 months after Columbine, no serious person believes that America is as safe as it ought to be."

All these jeremiads ignored the community bonds the tragedy reinforced, the social softness, the all-American sweetness that surged nationwide, as it had after Oklahoma City. A new Healing Fund quickly raised $4.4 million to aid survivors. When the killers' families sank into their guilt-amplified grief, some of the murdered teens' parents embraced them. "Their compassion helped me survive," Dylan's mom, Susan Klebold, later wrote in *O, The Oprah Magazine*. In August 1999, students returning to Columbine High entered via a human chain of loving teachers, parents, alumni, and volunteers who helped restore the school. The media's distorted calculus used two deviants to define a nation, obscuring millions of good people who comforted the victims.

With community standards in flux, and freedom on the rise, old-fashioned, low-tech media could also unnerve millions. Since the 1960s, art had been getting edgier, while becoming more dependent on government subsidies. As a result, controversies over outrageous art often involved politicians and judges, not just artists and patrons. In September, New York's Mayor Rudy Giuliani declared war on the Brooklyn Museum of Art to block its upcoming exhibition, *Sensation*. The most offensive painting, partly made out of elephant dung, depicted the Virgin Mary surrounded by pornographic images of female genitalia. Saying, "You don't have a right to government subsidy for desecrating somebody else's religion," Giuliani cut off the city's $7 million grant and initiated eviction proceedings. A federal district court judge found Giuliani's moves violated the First Amendment. The museum mounted the exhibit with an advisory that the material could be deemed offensive, including warning those with "high blood pressure."

OMG . . . It's the IM Craze

As these controversies raged, online and off, America's teens succumbed to the IM craze. America Online's 40 million users were Instant Messaging, or "IMing" over 430 million messages daily, closing in on the U.S. Postal Service's volume of 500 million pieces of mail daily. Instant Messaging, putting people virtually in touch in "real time," was faster than e-mail and alerted friends as to which friends were online. Launched in 1997, AOL was exclusive to AOL customers. In July 1999, Microsoft's new MSN Messenger service allowed its users to communicate with AOL customers, too.

Suddenly, America's kids were writing LOL—Laugh Out Loud—after a joke or OMG—Oh My God—for emphasis. Kids frustrated parents with telegraphed spelling like "how r u?" Even more mysterious, teens started expressing themselves with standardized emoticons; :) meant smile, ;) meant wink.

By 2001 MSN Messenger would be the most popular IM service, with 230 million unique users using 26 different languages. IMing was the conversational equivalent of a drive-by shooting—fast, scattershot, and occasionally devastating. More than a third of the teens surveyed admitted using IM to "say things they don't want to say in face-to-face conversations with their peers." Seventeen percent asked someone out via IM. Thirteen percent broke up by texting. A quarter pretended to be a different person while using IM, e-mail, or chat rooms.

IM was a most suitable language for an identity-addled, too-frequently violent Borderline nation, often making benign communications edgier. Cruel lists of which girls were "hot" and which boys were "losers" now proved extra devastating when shared virally. Feeling the pressure to respond constantly, immediately, some teens spoke of being "addicted." One teenage told a reporter he had become a "hermit," saying, "I guess there are still kids who go outside and breathe once in a while. But I have no reason to leave. I can just hang out online."

Markets Are Conversations—But Are They Real?

Bill Clinton's unofficial Minister of New Technologies, Al Gore, functioned as the Internet's head cheerleader and chief scold. While celebrating "this stunning technology" and its "incredible world of information," he warned of "some dark corners, some free-fire zones and red light districts in cyberspace from which children must be protected." Beyond pornography, critics feared that individuals living through machines would become individuated and alienated. *The Matrix,* one of 1999's most popular movies, grossed $171 million by warning Americans they were slaves to technology, in "a prison for your mind," and to the Matrix which "is everywhere," yet nowhere, because it is not "real."

"In the era of the one remaining superpower, a single dominant ideology and the spreading advance of the Internet, the Matrix can easily stand for what some have called 'the monoculture,'" the critic Herbert Muschamp wrote. Advanced consumer capitalism, with "its market research standards of normalcy," imposed the smothering uniformity seen in "the network of shopping malls, theme parks," and "suburban subdivisions." Muschamp probably did not realize that Google researchers were learning how to anticipate users' searches, to customize and satisfy consumer desires ever faster.

Internet evangelists rejected these worries. *The Cluetrain Manifesto* predicted that the Web's speed, fluidity, immediacy, and power would restore the "human voice" to markets and revive a sense of "community." *Cluetrain* warned corporations that secrecy, hierarchy, command-and-control were passé on the Wild, Wild Web. "Markets are conversations," declared the four technology bloggers who posted these ninety-five theses à la Martin Luther. Now, everyone could "hyperlink themselves together," making them "smarter" and more "human." Innovators like Apple celebrated the web's openness, yet developed revolutionary technologies like the iPod and the iPhone in secret.

The human voice expressed itself in a noncommercial, idiosyncratic, let-it-all-hang-out way, on a young, exceptionally frank, Swarthmore student's site,

Links.net. Starting in 1994, Justin Hall shared thoughts and links with a growing number of users who enjoyed his candor, as he posted items that would "make my mom blush." With the Generation X's self-involved slogan, "Talking about myself keeps me going," Hall showed how the Internet could build community through self-expression.

In 1997, Jorn Barger coined the term weblog and in 1998, *The Charlotte Observer* updated its coverage of Hurricane Bonnie using one. In 1999, a web designer, Peter Merholz, divided the word into we blog. With only 23 of them around, the word "blog" became the standard term. Within ten years there would be 126 million blogs. By 2015 there more than one billion blogs, with a new one every half second.

The Silicon Valley venture capital firm DFJ takes credit for coining the phrase "viral marketing," in 1997. The idea came from the 1996 launch of Hotmail, which spread as if it were contagious because every e-mail message had an easy-to-click link to the service. In July 1999, a by-now more familiar phenomenon, a simple website—www.blairwitch.com—launched one of the first and most successful viral marketing campaigns. The website of the small, primitive movie, *The Blair Witch Project,* teased out aspects of the film and confused the public as to whether or not three Maryland film students had gone missing in a terrifying occult-tinged episode. The $30,000 movie grossed over $240 million.

The No-Fail Generation?

This dance between techno-optimism and techno-pessimism, between faith and fear in the Internet and the economy, was the theme of the year—and the decade. Many Americans wavered between economic-induced euphoria and culturally triggered anxiety. The boom's numbers invited what the Federal Reserve chairman Alan Greenspan called "irrational exuberance" in 1996. In 1998, the $1.61 trillion merger and acquisition mania included the ten most lucrative mergers ever. In 1999, Pfizer's $87.3 billion acquisition of Warner-Lambert and Vodafone's $185.1 billion purchase of Mannesmann became the two biggest such deals. December 1998, as the 93rd month of economic growth, marked America's "longest peacetime economic expansion." Reagan's 1982 to 1990 stretch lasted 92 months. By January 2000, the expansion would be in its 106th month, having created nearly 20 million new jobs since March 1991. America's production of goods and services increased by 58 percent. Jeff Shesol, a Clinton speechwriter, would recall hearing the latest numbers at senior staff meetings, "and people would laugh at these numbers, this almost incredulous laugh that it was going up."

That March 1999, the Dow Jones would hit 10,000 points. That May, it would break 11,000, the quickest 10 percent jump ever during a boom. This surge would take Bill Gates's net worth to $90 billion. The richest 200 Americans' combined wealth would top $1 trillion for the first time. Three others on the *Forbes* top ten list earned their money from computers. Two of them, Paul Allen and Steven Ballmer, were from Microsoft, as the company became the first corporation worth more than $500 billion. In October, unemployment reached a twenty-nine-year low of 4.1 percent, the eighth straight month of unemployment hovering around 4 percent.

The New Economy's scale and speed rewarded those who could manage and improve it. One superstar, Daniel Lewin, served as an Israeli commando before applying his MIT PhD thesis to solving a major Internet problem—handling spikes in traffic during big news events. Lewin created an algorithm enabling mass video streaming. The company he established with his thesis adviser, Tom Leighton, made the two billionaires the day of Akamai's IPO.

Such stories misled too many Americans into believing the good times would never end. "This generation has never witnessed failure," said Professor Laura D'Andrea Tyson, a former Clinton adviser. "They've never known anyone who's lived through taking a risk and having it not work out." Erich Fertschneider, a thirty-eight-year-old manager at a Toyota dealership, told *Newsweek*: "I'm more buy now, pay later," than his thrifty, Depression-raised, father.

Magical thinking often overrode cautious investing. One "ace money manager" with a "Midas touch" was handling more than 20,000 trades daily, 10 percent of the New York Stock Exchange listed stocks' overall volume. Delivering steady monthly returns, by 1999 his $6 billion hedge fund was the world's largest. A Wall Street statesman, he denounced "day traders" who tried eking out gains with frequent trades generated by daily jumps now easily monitored online. "This is not investing; it's a casino mentality," he lectured, cautioning against amateurish, democratized, Internet trading.

One Boston portfolio manager, Harry Markopolos, tried replicating this Titan's steady success in 1999. The numbers did not add up. No investigators at the Securities and Exchange Commission believed him. After all, he would recall, "This was the legendary Bernie Madoff we were talking about. And I was just the slightly eccentric Harry Markopolos." Only in December 2008, after the financial crash, did Madoff confess it was all "one big lie." Madoff burned through $18 billion in actual investments, which his padded statements artificially ballooned to $65 billion.

The Cup of Life: Partying with a Hispanic Twist

Meanwhile, America partied like it was 1999. Night after night, as many as 29 million people watched *Who Wants to Be a Millionaire,* a dumbed-down TV quiz show that made winners instantly rich, feeding the national fantasy. Weekly, millions watched *Whose Line Is It Anyway?,* a smart series of improvisational sketches. Such wacky, unpredictable "comedy without a net" offered an alternative to what its creator Dan Patterson called all the "safety first television"—and popular culture—around. In February, even normally jaded music industry veterans were jazzed by Ricky Martin's live performance at the Grammy Awards of his song *"La Copa de la Vida"* ("The Cup of Life"). "Do you really want it?" he shouted while gyrating his hips and wearing tight leather pants. "Go, go, go," he cried as drummers marched down the aisle, horns blared, lights flashed, streamers waved, dozens of dancers swayed, and Martin celebrated America's carnival spirit in English and Spanish.

"Thank you, Grammys, for giving Latin music the place that we deserve," Martin proclaimed later that evening when he won the Best Latin Pop Music award. That May, Martin's first all-English language album, with the song "Livin' *La Vida Loca*" ("Living the Crazy Life"), would be the year's hottest selling album. With other Hispanic Americans like Marc Anthony and "J.Lo," Jennifer Lopez, Martin was bringing a Latin sound and sensibility to multicultural America. The video of Marc Anthony's slower, sultry "I Need to Know," released in August, captured the highs and lows of Latino American life. Images of dozens of couples, of all colors, gyrating rhythmically in a sleek club, alternated with Anthony, a Puerto Rican who grew up in Spanish Harlem, pining for his beloved from his shabby tenement window.

"Wealth Is Twice What Your Net Worth Is"

Still, amid all the partying, Prince's 1982 insight from his song about 1999 that "life is just a party / And parties weren't meant to last," resonated. Woodstock 1999, celebrating the thirtieth anniversary of the famous generational love-in, imploded. With its own embossed MasterCard, charging $150 for tickets plus a steep service charge, and selling water for $4 a bottle, this carnival of commercialism ended violently. Fans torched twelve tractor trailers, looting overpriced soda cans, overpriced snacks, and overpriced Woodstock merchandise.

The generation gap had closed; now everyone felt alienated. A depressingly familiar take on suburban emptiness, *American Beauty,* would win five Academy

Awards, including Best Picture. When the harsh, two-timing Carolyn asks her alienated, defeated husband Lester Burnham, played by Kevin Spacey, to beware spilling beer on their $4,000 sofa, she warns: "This is not just a couch." He snaps: "It's just a couch! This isn't life. This is just stuff, and it's become more important to you than living."

This addiction to stuff, what the economist Robert H. Frank called America's *Luxury Fever,* was spiking. "Keeping up with the Joneses" now meant competing with fictional characters on television or the new American royalty, celebrities. In a land with a run on $17,000 watches, where a Victoria's Secret bra with 2,000 diamonds sold for $10 million and Bill Gates paid $6.5 million for a swimming pool, nothing was ever enough. *USA Today* found millionaires who would only feel rich if they had $1 million in cash; someone with $1 million in cash yearned for $2 million. At $5 million, one analyst noted, "You start to see the level of insecurity decrease." A thirty-two-year-old mutual fund manager admitted, "Wealth is twice what your net worth is, whatever that is."

Sixty years earlier, in John Steinbeck's *The Grapes of Wrath,* the preacher Jim Casy observes an unhappy land owner: "If he needs a million acres to make him feel rich, seems to me he needs it 'cause he feels awful poor inside hisself, and if he's poor in hisself, there ain't no million acres gonna make him feel rich." Psychologists reported seeing clients unhappy because they could not earn enough to keep up and those with "sudden wealth syndrome" stricken by an empty feeling once they made it. Dr. Jessie O'Neill, an heiress whose grandfather Charles E. Wilson led General Motors, had clients speak to a "money chair," as they healed their "money wounds."

Experts feared the impact of all this excess, pressure, and misery on the next generation. Merrill Lynch's wealth management services started offering parental coaching. Some wealthy parents with "bratlash," a backlash against spoiled children, started limiting their children's consumption. Some experts encouraged personal revolutions, including "downshifting," simplifications in lifestyles and returns to core values; others considered collective solutions, such as progressive taxes on luxury spending.

The tragic death of the country's most celebrated heir added a note of futility to the debate. While trying to earn a reputation for seriousness with his political magazine *George,* John F. Kennedy Jr. died of a rich man's conceit—flying his private plane before he was fully qualified. "John-John" was thirty-eight years old. His death came two years after his cousin Michael LeMoyne Kennedy, Robert Kennedy's son, died skiing in Aspen.

Anti-Microsoft Antitrust

This ambivalence about personal wealth shaped the monumental Microsoft antitrust case. Microsoft, whose $507 billion stock value in 1999 was said to rival Spain's GDP, was the Standard Oil of this Gilded Age. Bill Gates and his colleagues wanted to seem like modern philosopher-kings, technological geniuses whose smarts triumphed—just as the Clintons advanced thanks to their brains. They hid their bullying tactics behind Ivy League and Ivy League dropout geekspeak.

Gates's desire to bundle the Windows operating system with Microsoft's Internet Exlorer (IE) browser triggered the Browser Wars, angering state attorneys general and the U.S. Justice Department. It was as if NBC in the 1950s only broadcast programming on RCA televisions, or if Standard Oil produced gasoline exclusive to Fords. Gates publicized his ferocity on December 7, 1995, when he declared war on Netscape, vowing to dominate the Internet-related software market. Within a year of this "Pearl Harbor Speech," Microsoft's browser market share jumped from 20 to 50 percent. Netscape's share dropped from 70 to 50 percent. Two years later, Microsoft dominated three-quarters of the browser market.

Microsoft's belligerence violated an existing 1995 Department of Justice consent decree from an earlier antitrust investigation. By 1997 the DOJ wanted to fine the company $1 million a day for forcing computer manufacturers to install Microsoft's Internet Explorer Web browser to get a Windows 95 license. The Department of Justice filed an antitrust suit in May 1998, joined by twenty states, accusing Microsoft of "illegal, anticompetitive practices . . . to destroy its rivals." The states also accused Microsoft of imposing Microsoft Office and Outlook Express on manufacturers.

Judge Thomas Penfield Jackson's 207-page fact-finding in November 1999, followed by his court decision in April 2000, concluded that Microsoft abused its power to secure "a dominant, persistent and increasing share of the worldwide market for Intel-compatible operating systems." Jackson wanted Microsoft divided. One business would sell its Windows operating system, another would develop computer programs and Internet businesses. Eventually, in November 2002, a new presiding judge would approve a settlement ending Microsoft's restrictions and retaliations against PC makers who added non-Microsoft software. The acrimonious battle affirmed the government's role in fighting antitrust actions in the Internet age, even as experts mocked the sanctions for being too soft.

Ending Glass-Steagall, Pleasing Wall Street

Occasional antitrust squabbles could not keep the Clinton administration off the boom-time bandwagon. On November 4, a day before Judge Jackson tried breaking up Microsoft, Congress approved what Clinton would call "historic" banking reform legislation. The "Financial Services Modernization Act" repealed parts of the Depression-era Glass-Steagall Act and the 1956 Bank Holding Company Act limiting commercial banks, brokerage houses, and insurers from entering each other's businesses. The director of the National Economic Council, Gene Sperling, explained that establishing "fair competition" with fewer regulations, "will drive firms to achieve and pass savings on to consumers," who would enjoy one-stop shopping for financial services. "We have done right by the American people," Clinton rejoiced at the November bill signing.

Only eight senators and fifty-seven representatives resisted the popular sentiment, the president's enthusiasm, and lobbyists' lucre to vote no on the final version. Senator Paul Wellstone, a Minnesota Democrat, leading progressive, and trained political scientist, warned: "We seem determined to unlearn the lessons of history. Scores of banks failed in the Great Depression as a result of unsound banking practices, and their failure only deepened the crisis." When the inevitable financial crisis would come, institutions would need insulation not integration. Nearly a decade before the phrase became commonplace, these critics worried about concentrating too much power in too few firms, creating financial institutions that politicians would consider "too big to fail."

Indeed, following the 2008 crash, the banking reform would epitomize the Clinton administration's overreach. The Nobel Prize–winning economist Joseph Stiglitz would claim the Glass-Steagall repeal fostered a "high-risk gambling mentality" in the financial field as "the culture of investment banks" infected commercial banks. Other experts blamed the subprime mortgage crisis on the too-easy credit resulting from the "folly" of Clinton's indulgent banking deregulation.

The Glass-Steagall repeal also reflected Wall Street's power in Washington. The growing complexity of financial markets made a revolving door between Wall Street and the Treasury Department on Pennsylvania Avenue necessary. The flood of campaign contributions, the blizzard of lobbyists, and the deification of financial and political power in an age besotted with success and celebrity, spread this exhilarating faith that this Baby Boomers' boom would never end.

In retirement, ex-president Clinton would resist blaming the reforms, noting the "heavy regulation," which remained in the banking field. He claimed the bill eased the purchase of Merrill Lynch by Bank of America, which stabilized the system. Also, investment banks like Bear Stearns and Lehman Brothers and the insurance giant AIG collapsed first, not the financial supermarkets the legislation created.

Clinton valued this repeal as further proof of his political vindication. Gene Sperling and other aides had long seen this Glass-Steagall repeal as an opportunity for "the Administration to exert positive leadership—helping to guide legislation in a direction that promotes competition, innovation, and consumer choice, keeps the financial system safe and sound," and showed Congress "how to reconcile competing policy interests in a manner consistent with the Administration's objectives." Buoyed by the stock market and his irrepressible nature, Clinton viewed every new initiative, every new idea, every new event, every new speech, every new meeting, as one more back-in-business building block of his legacy.

Battle in Seattle Against Globalization . . . and Clinton

In December, 45,000 protesters denouncing the World Trade Organization (WTO) Summit in Seattle repudiated Clintonomics from the left. Clinton was hosting delegates from 135 countries, to celebrate the New Economy globally. Instead, Seattle officials had to mobilize the National Guard, postpone the summit temporarily, and impose a curfew. Protesters donning ski masks and handkerchiefs smashed storefront windows and ignited garbage cans. Armored cars rumbled about, helicopters whirred above, concussion grenades boomed sporadically, tear gas canisters popped then whizzed, and rubber bullets pinged as protesters made human chains, shouting, "OUR STREETS, OUR STREETS," and, echoing the 1960s, "The Whole World Is Watching." They waved placards demanding SYSTEM CHANGE NOT CLIMATE CHANGE; PEOPLE AND NATURE BEFORE PROFITS; STOP WTO.

"We've got to beat back the corporate attack," an Earth First activist who called herself "Shazzam" yelled. When activists harassed the Estonian trade ambassador, he barked: "I'm a socialist . . . you people are nuts." As Seattle's political sensibility clashed with its latte culture, activists even vandalized a Starbucks coffee shop.

The protesters combined reedy environmentalists, bearded anarchists, pimple-faced college activists, tattooed street people, and beefy union members, who held an orderly rally for 25,000 in Seattle's Memorial Stadium. "The citizens are revolting" against "corporate greed," Teamsters president Jimmy Hoffa Jr. said, at what organizers called the largest rally in modern labor history. Locals compared the moment to Seattle's general strike in 1919. Wildcat strikes in Seattle, Tacoma, Oakland, Los Angeles, and Long Beach reinforced Hoffa's message.

After a placid decade, many activists celebrated this renewed Sixties' spirit, with a more fluid, democratized twist. "This is the first movement born of the anarchic pathways of the Internet," the critic of consumerism Naomi Klein wrote. The mob was so democratic its messaging was chaotic. The protesters lashed out wildly against trade, trade rules, and globalization.

Protest leaders offered more nuance. They condemned corporate-dominated trade insensitive to environmental concerns and human exploitation. They feared the WTO's trade rules favored wealthy countries and profiteering businesses that exported American jobs and exploited workers abroad. They proposed harnessing globalization to spread prosperity and quality of life more equitably around the planet.

Protesting against globalization in 1999 was as futile as protesting against clouds in Seattle. Francis Fukuyama thought the post–Berlin Wall hard left, desperately seeking a cause, had stumbled onto the wrong target. Thomas Friedman insisted that the WTO was not the problem but the potential solution. James Pinkerton, a former Bush adviser, doubted "the politics of radical nostalgia will prevail in a country where the most popular TV show is *Who Wants to Be a Millionaire.*"

Both Big Bills of the 1990s suffered black eyes. Bill Gates co-chaired Seattle's welcoming committee only to see downtown trashed and Christmas sales threatened. Bill Clinton faced chaos on the streets, deadlocks at the negotiating table, and dashed hopes of ending this difficult year with a big global win.

When he first became president in 1993, Clinton listed steps "to create the kind of world that I wanted our children to live in, in the new century," so they could live "in peace and stability; in democracy and prosperity." Six years later, he saw progress. The United States supported European unity and the EU's expansion. The Euro debuted as an accounting currency on January 1, 1999, with Euro coins and banknotes planned for 2002. In March 1999, the former Warsaw Pact countries of Hungary, Poland, and the Czech Republic joined NATO. America was defusing regional and tribal conflicts, making peace in Ireland, Bosnia, Kosovo, and, it seemed at the time, Israel.

Clinton also wanted to support "the integration of China, Russia, and the Indian subcontinent," politically and economically. Both the United States and the new Russia were now cooperating to maintain international stability. Reciprocal visits had cemented ties with China, although the goodwill dissipated when America bombed China's Belgrade embassy in May, and the Cox Report shortly thereafter accused China of stealing American nuclear technology. Similarly, relations in India teetered when Clinton sanctioned India for its 1998 nuclear test, but improved when Clinton mediated after Pakistan invaded Kashmir in 1999.

Clinton was realizing his liberal interventionist vision of America as a force for good in a "cruel" world in which "the Internet tells us everything," and "we are solving all the problems of the human gene." The "biggest problems of human society" remained the "oldest ones" of racial, religious, and tribal clashes. He believed the free trade elixir could extinguish atavistic enmities with peace, prosperity, and progressive practices. The WTO could perfect this "interdependent global economy that runs alongside our interdependent international information society."

In 1994, when the Uruguay Round talks established the World Trade Organization to facilitate international trade, Clinton was pursuing George Washington's Farewell Address prescription of free trade enriching America and the world. The Cold War victory allowed everyone to benefit from the world's "interconnections," understanding that when "our neighbors . . . do better, we will do better." Recognizing "trade as more of an opportunity than a threat," the American people backed him.

Five years later, Clinton maintained his free trade gospel despite the riots. While condemning the violence, he graciously welcomed the protesters into the conversation, saying "their voices now count in this debate." His "interconnected global economy" had to increase "prosperity and genuine opportunity for people everywhere."

Yet that week, "Everyone just went home angry," *The New York Times* reported. Seattle was remembered "not for the new ground broken, but for the windows shattered." Clinton officials resented the protesters for rioting, the police for overreacting, and the delegates from emerging countries for refusing to protect workers. Many developing country delegates bashed the United States for protecting its powerful corporations and the status quo. And Democratic Party officials, recoiling from the anger, feared Bill Clinton's free trade and pro-prosperity legacy would hurt their 2000 nominee with these angry unionists and activists.

Squashing the Y2K Bug

As the bad blood from the Battle in Seattle lingered, Americans experienced one of their periodic mass bouts of media-induced anxiety from some abstract danger with catastrophic potential. The globalized world was filled with such threats as terrorism, pollution, and climate change, that Clouded the Commons, turning benign communal acts, thoroughly modern moments broadly shared, into looming disasters, be they natural or man-made.

Scholars quibbled over whether the new millennium would begin on January 1, 2000, or January 1, 2001, but apocalyptic worries centered on New Year's 2000. Survivalists checked supplies, preparing for "The End of the World as We Know It" or TEOTWAWKI, according to the Internet's compulsive acronym makers. Starting in 1995, a retired minister, Tim LaHaye, collaborated with a former sportswriter, Jerry Jenkins, to write a series of *Left Behind* novels, meshing new techno-fears with more traditional militia-inflected millennial nonsense imagining global chaos, systems failing, financial meltdowns, and "the Antichrist" establishing "a one-world economic system." Together, thirteen books published over twelve years would sell 65 million copies.

Millions more feared the Y2K bug causing mass computer crashes at midnight, when 12 31 99 became 01 01 00, if computers decided it was 1900. America's messianic liberal nationalism, rooted in a Christian-infused sense of the nation's special destiny, had long sensitized many Americans to millennial hopes and fears. Now, in a world addicted to computers but still conscious of their novelty, this nightmare possibility seemed plausible. The Federal Reserve distributed $80 billion in currency, four times the usual amount, to absorb any panic surges in cash withdrawals. One poll found 59 percent of Americans concerned about the Y2K bug problem, with 47 percent withdrawing more cash than usual from their accounts, 33 percent stockpiling water and food, and 26 percent refusing to fly on an airplane New Year's Day.

The government's Y2K czar worked fifteen-hour days in a $50 million command center out of the Executive Office Building for almost two years. John A. Koskinen coordinated twenty-five task forces with a staff that mushroomed to two hundred as the deadline approached. The government set up a consumer hotline (1-888-USA-4-Y2K) and a website (www.y2k.gov). The transportation, financial, energy, pharmaceuticals, and telecommunications sectors had their own command centers.

On the big day, little happened. One South Korean returning a video received an 8 million won—or $7,000—fine for being a century overdue. Nevertheless, feats of technological and scientific mastery evoked more pessimism than optimism. In 1978, the nuclear disaster averted at Three Mile Island left more unnerved than reassured. In the 1990s, fears of an AIDS epidemic lingered despite scientific breakthroughs managing the disease. Similarly, in 2000, the pride many Americans should have had in their government and their new technologies paled in comparison to the persisting "what ifs" so many reporters had stoked.

The fear, along with fears of a spectacular terrorist attack by a shady Saudi Arabian named Osama bin Laden, did not stop parties or optimistic rhetoric greeting the New Year, the new century, and the new millennium. Martha Stewart advised millions of her followers to try throwing a party lavish enough that people would remember it a thousand years later. Oprah Winfrey used the millennium to issue another invitation to each viewer to find "your authentic self," before 2000, balanced by materialist marketing with broadcasts highlighting a Millennium Fashion Show, and Millennium Makeovers. Inspired by Oprah's New Age proposal to "light a candle for the new millennium," an elderly woman mistakenly set fire to her twelve-story Chicagoland apartment building, hospitalizing thirteen people.

A Presidential Oprah?

During one presidential press conference in late 1997, ABC's John Donvan asked if one of Clinton's race-initiative town meetings "was little more than Presidential *Oprah*." Clinton bristled. But in 1999, during Clinton's personal and national healing, various "Presidential *Oprahs*" actually helped. When he sought to understand his impulsivity and neediness, when he connected with Americans' needs and dreams, Clinton demonstrated why he and Oprah Winfrey were so darned successful. Clinton and Oprah each operated on a central fault line in 1990s' culture, able to access America at its best by also engaging America at its most self-involved, which also sometimes ended up being its silliest.

The White House's three-day millennium celebration illustrated that duality, too. The MC of a dusk-to-dawn White House party, Will Smith, was now a movie star. Guests included the "American Pie" folksinger Don McLean and the anti–Vietnam War boxer Muhammad Ali. Now, blacks were treated as honored White House guests while radical outsiders became celebrated insiders. A black man presiding over the White House might soon be possible. Yet the unbearable lightness of so many celebrity guests, including actors Mary Tyler Moore and Jack Nicholson, and the absence of serious thinkers, leaders, inventors, or entrepreneurs, suggested a shift in Washington's and America's gravitational center. While celebrating its triumph over totalitarianism and its festival of freedom in the twentieth century, the Great Republic had become the world's greatest playground, its biggest shopping mall, more starstruck than contemplative, more indulgent than productive.

Launching the millennium festivities, congratulating himself while spurring his fellow citizens ahead, President Clinton toasted this "unique moment for our country. Our economy is strong; our social fabric is on the mend. We're moving forward on America's remarkable journey of creating a more unified nation, a more just society, a more perfect Union." Clinton felt optimistic. He had saved his presidency. Now, he intended to shape his legacy and extend his administration in the best way possible—by installing his vice president, Al Gore, in the Oval Office.

11

2000: Miami
"The Purpose of Prosperity"

*Dilemmas of Multiculturalism and Hedonism
in America's Pleasure Capital*

> *We are today more tolerant, more decent, more humane, and more
> united. Now, that's the purpose of prosperity.*
> —BILL CLINTON, FAREWELL TO THE DEMOCRATIC NATIONAL
> CONVENTION, AUGUST 14, 2000

November 7, 2000, began, like most Miami days, with sunshine, the first of thirty-six rain-free days in a row on the way. With glistening malls and beautiful beaches, overrun by models and tourists, Miami competed with Las Vegas for the title of Fun Town, U.S.A. In the 1970s, Miami and Miami Beach had started decaying. South Beach's pastel-colored, curved, Art Deco buildings from the 1920s and 1930s crumbled. Crime spread. So many old people flocked to its decrepit third-rate hotels with first-class views that this once-exclusive area had become "God's Waiting Room."

By the 1990s, a newly gentrified and carefully preserved South Beach was booming, along with Miami itself, despite jolts of danger thanks to the occasional, sensational, local-kills-lost-tourist headline horror. Most people marveled at Miami's colorful mix of ages and cultures; the billions of dollars flooding in, especially from South America; the expanded power structure welcoming Hispanics, especially Cubans, as well as Haitians and African Americans; all amid a happy, peppy, party atmosphere.

One of hedonistic America's most decadent fleshpots, South Beach boasted a Venetian sense of style, a Herculean appetite for excess, and a Dionysian zest for fun. Sipping piña coladas at the Clevelander Hotel's bar-by-the-pool just off Ocean Drive now offered first-class, deliciously stereotypical, people-watching. Elderly Jews in plaid golf caps, Hawaiian-shirt-and-cargo-shorts-clad tourists,

Euro-trash poseurs in silk, newly arrived Haitian immigrants, slickly attired Cuban couples, hunky gay men, and thinny-thin, bikini-clad supermodels paraded by regularly. With 1,500 cover girls living on South Beach, *Playboy* toasted this greatest "concentration of female beauty . . . in the history of the planet."

Amid all this fun, America's twelfth largest metropolitan area in America's fourth largest state, with nearly 16 million people, was also a critical social, cultural, and political battleground. Miami's mass of insular, Spanish-speaking Cubans threatened the American assimilationist assumption that integration into a changing, ever-more liquid America was preferable to segregation as a subgroup to preserve particular values and identities. This Diversity Dilemma in turn affected the contest for Florida's twenty-five electoral votes in presidential elections, even without the slapdash amateurish procedures that made November 7 the day Florida deadlocked democracy.

The Rainbow Rebellion:
The Browning of America

The capital of Hispanic America, America's gateway to Latin America and South America, and America's most foreign big city, Miami in 2000 foreshadowed the blacker, browner, more diverse majority of minorities expected to predominate by 2050. The trend started earlier, but the president's 1997 race-relations initiative recognized and validated this trajectory. Sixty percent of the residents of this two-thirds majority Hispanic city of 362,470 were foreign-born. Three-quarters of the residents over five spoke a language other than English at home, mostly Spanish. America's Hispanic population of 35.3 million was growing by 1 million people a year—ten times faster than the white population. From 1990 to 2000, America's percentage of Hispanics grew from 9 percent to 12.5 percent, as the percentage of whites dropped from 80 percent to 75 percent. The estimated number of illegal immigrants doubled to 7 million, perhaps 8.5 million—yet another mess for Bill Clinton's successors.

Miami was a leading multiculti laboratory, mixing different languages, cultures, business styles, leavened with healthy doses of profit, goodwill, and sunshine. With so many subgroups bumping and grinding together, interracial coupling became mainstreamed. The governor of Florida, Jeb Bush, elected in 1998 and a forceful backer of his brother George W. Bush in 2000, was married to a Mexican-born Catholic, Columba Garnica Gall. During the 1988 presidential campaign, George H.W. Bush had called his three Mexican American grandchildren, "the little brown ones." He claimed he was being affectionate; others suggested America's most prominent Wasp was still adjusting to his son's life choices. Such white-Hispanic marriages were the most likely intermarriages, three to four times more prevalent than white-Asian or white-black unions.

The number of American interracial marriages multiplied sevenfold from 1960 to 1992. What was taboo in the 1970s was occasionally unexceptional in the 1990s, such as the interracial dimension of Kevin Costner's relationship with Whitney Houston in *The Bodyguard* (1992). In other movies, like *Jungle Fever* (1991) and *A Bronx Tale* (1993)—set in the racist 1960s—the forbidden black-white love provided dramatic tension. In 2000, when the U.S. Census invited respondents to select "one or more race categories" for the first time, 2.4 percent of the population, over 6.8 million Americans, checked that box.

The star golfer Tiger Woods was multiracial America's poster child. He bought his first home in Windermere, Florida, outside Orlando, in 1996. A year later, the twenty-one-year-old became the youngest Masters Tournament winner ever. Woods told Oprah Winfrey it "bothered" him when people praised him as the first African American winner, golf's Jackie Robinson. He called himself "Cablinasian," his own word blending Caucasian, black, Indian, and Asian. Many blacks saw this distancing as delusional. The olive-skinned Colin Powell said, "In America, which I love from the depths of my heart and soul, when you look like me, you're black."

Affirmative Action and Destructive Resignation

As the wealthy, heavily taxed downtown prospered, with annual growth spurts in international trade as high as 20 percent some years, the rest of Miami earned its ranking as America's fourth poorest city. Race riots protesting police shootings of civilians in 1980 and 1989 made Liberty City and Overtown two of America's most notorious ghettos. Liberty City was 95 percent African American, with 33 percent single-mother households. Nationally, 48 percent of all African American families in 2000 consisted of married couples with children—down from 68 percent in 1970. Forty-four percent of African American families now had single mothers at the helm, reflecting the crisis of the black male—and the abandonment of the black woman, especially in urban ghettos. Blacks were more likely to die in childbirth, suffer from cancer, live fewer years than whites, and earn less. The most inflammatory statistic to emerge from the 2000 census claimed that the 791,600 imprisoned African American men outnumbered the 603,032 African American men studying in universities. Eventually, Howard

University professor Ivory Toldson noticed an initial undercount of black students, although the underlying problem remained.

Conservatives still blamed cultural and moral problems within the African American community for this growing gap. Liberals still blamed institutionalized racism. Blacks still lived in the country that had enslaved them, symbolized by the Confederate flag flying over South Carolina's state legislature—which became controversial during the 2000 Republican presidential primary.

While most underclass blacks were trapped in a negative cycle, abandoning society, paralyzed by destructive resignation, affirmative action programs helped many middle-class blacks soar. From 1990 to 2000, the number of black officeholders grew by 22 percent to 9001, including the mayor of once-segregationist Selma, Alabama. Breaking what women were calling "the glass ceiling," black men headed the National Science Foundation and the American Medical Association. Black women presided over the American Association of Retired Persons, the National Parent Teacher Association, Brown University, and, in a patriotic touch, the National League of Women Voters. In 1970, barely a third of African Americans had completed high school. By 2000, nearly three-quarters had. Similarly, median black income in 1999 was the highest ever recorded.

With the ever-growing gap between glittery Miami and gritty Miami, with multiple, crisscrossing tensions along its rainbow spectrum of groups, Miami's politics was combustible. African Americans often resented the rise of immigrant blacks from Haiti and elsewhere, along with the growing power of Hispanics, particularly the domineering, prospering, and right-leaning Cuban-exile community. Whites tried maintaining their power in one of America's most transient states, whose population had grown by 23.53 percent in a decade. "The Hispanization of Miami is without precedent in the history of major American cities," the Harvard political scientist Samuel Huntington would note.

The fight over Elián González, the six-year-old Cuban boy rescued at sea while fleeing to America, exemplified Miami Cubans' segregationist impulse. After the boy's mother drowned in the Atlantic, his father demanded Elián's return to Cuba. His American relatives—with mass Cuban American support—tried keeping him in Miami. Two-thirds of Americans supported the father's custodial rights, including most non-Hispanic Floridians. Some feared Miami-Dade's "independent foreign policy" reflected its "virtual secession" from America.

Vice President Al Gore, courting Cuban Americans, initially opposed the administration's plan to return Elián. After six months, Gore—in an unhappy indicator of his doomed 2000 race—hedged, alienating both sides. On April 22, 2000, federal agents in full combat gear raided González's relatives' house and seized the scared child. Cuban American media outlets ran terrifying photos of the SWAT team invading the home; others ran heartwarming photos of Elián reuniting with his father.

Cuban American anger persisted. The 1993 Whitney Biennial and the edgy identity politics on campus showed the fury bubbling up as once-marginal voices tried becoming mainstream. The Elián González case indicated that twenty-first-century America would be challenged by some autonomous subgroups uninterested in joining the American mainstream, no matter how rainbow-colored they claimed to be.

That November, Gore would regret his waffling and the administration's actions. In 1996, Clinton won 35 percent of Florida's Cuban vote; in 2000 Gore only won 19 percent. Cuban American revenge cost Gore the presidency.

Gender Bender: Hillary As Pol Not "Wife Of"

On February 6, Hillary Clinton made history again by becoming the first First Lady to throw her headband into the electoral ring. Running to become one of New York's senators liberated her from the First Lady's crystal cage. Spending more time in their new house in Chappaqua, New York, she made Bill Clinton the first president since Woodrow Wilson was widowed in 1914 to lack a full-time First Lady in residence. The misogynist attacks on Hillary Clinton as Lady Macbeth, as a radical mole, waned. Substantive questions about her plans for New York State replaced gossipy inquiries about the state of her marriage. Controversy about her evolving political positions and her shifting loyalties from Illinois to Arkansas to New York now upstaged controversy about her changing hairstyles.

Having tried the co-presidency and failed, having played a more traditional couple and been humiliated, the Clintons were now testing a more egalitarian, commuter marriage model whereby both spouses seek fulfillment independently. Despite Bill Clinton's enthusiastic endorsement of his wife's candidacy, he missed the loss of intimacy, the absence of—as he described her in October 1991—"my wife, my friend, and my partner." For the White House correspondents' dinner in April, Bill Clinton recorded a satirical video of his "Final Days" at the White House, as abandoned spouse and has-been. Bored, he golfs, answers the phone, discovers e-mail and eBay, washes the presidential limo, and plays battleship with the chairman of the Joint Chiefs of Staff. The First Lady appears briefly, impatiently sitting in a limousine in the White House driveway, confident "that Bill has everything under control." As she drives off, enacting a role reversal millions of American men now experienced daily, Clinton comes running out shouting, "Wait, wait!," holding the brown bag lunch he prepared and she forgot.

Hillary Clinton's Senate campaign symbolized women's many gains in the 1990s, despite the "backlash" predictions. Bill Clinton appointed the first women to serve as attorney general, secretary of energy, secretary of the air force—or any military branch—and secretary of state. Lt. Kendra Williams became the first female fighter pilot to bomb the enemy during Operation Desert Fox against Iraq in 1998. A year later Lieutenant Colonel Eileen Collins commanded a space shuttle mission. Women now constituted 13 percent of all police forces, and 4 percent of firefighters, as the words "policeman" and "fireman" became too restrictive. The number of women lawyers and doctors doubled. Women now accounted for 46.74 percent of the workforce. There were slightly more women than men in "Management, professional and related occupations," as well as "Service occupations." Women were now paid 80 cents for every dollar men earned hourly, up from 63 cents in 1979.

If in the 1980s women were first entering executive office suites, the 1990s focused on breaking the "glass ceiling," the barriers to women becoming CEO. Discrimination remained—and was fought more effectively, thanks to George Bush's 1991 civil rights law. Law firms operating on contingency could enjoy handsome payouts. In March 2000, the federal government offered a record $508 million to compensate 1,100 women denied jobs and promotion at the U.S. Information Agency from 1974 to 1984. That same spring, the army's highest-ranking woman, Lieutenant General Claudia J. Kennedy, helped scuttle Major General Larry G. Smith's promotion by charging sexual harassment.

Feminizing the American Family

The working mother's dilemmas persisted, with ongoing debate about the "Mommy Track"—as new mothers debated taking time off from work, reducing hours, or simply diminishing burdens as the primary caretakers, in most two-career couples. Machines, helpers, and altered attitudes reduced the average amount of time both partners in traditional couples spent doing housework. Still, women usually did twice as much as men, although twenty years earlier they had done triple the amount.

The burdens on working mothers, combined with the technological revolution, encouraged creativity in workplaces. More flexibility, creativity, productivity often entailed more pressure and hours. Flextime risked becoming all work all the time, as PalmPilots and cell phones tethered workers to their bosses and e-mail encouraged expectations of immediate results.

With women working more, the number of married couples dropped. Americans married older and still divorced in great numbers. The number of nonfamily households continued rising steadily, hitting 31.94 percent in 2000, up from 29.8 percent in 1990. The mainstreaming of nontraditional arrangements reduced pressure on single women to marry quickly. Just over 12 percent of households were women-led, but these female householders with children under eighteen constituted 34.3 percent of the people living below the poverty line. Only 6.6 of impoverished households had the traditional married couple-with-children arrangement. More dramatically, married couples with families had median incomes of $57,345, more than twice the average income of single female householders at $25,458.

This proliferation of lifestyle choices stemmed from ideological change facilitated by medical breakthroughs, especially the birth control pill. In September 2000, the FDA finally approved the RU-486 "abortion pill," twelve years after France approved it. Known in the United States as Mifeprex, it could end pregnancies as advanced as seven weeks with a few pills. The relative ease and accessibility would help fulfill the Clintons' vision of making abortions "safe, legal and rare." In the ensuing decade and a half, more than 2 million American women would use Mifeprex. Contrary to opponents' fears, the ease of pill popping did not encourage abortions. From 1.6 million abortions in 1990, there were 1.3 million in 2000, and 1.1 million in 2010.

Normalizing Gay Life

With the feminizing of the American family opening up alternatives, and the technological conquest of nature making everything seem mutable, the revolution in attitudes toward gays advanced. The growing openness toward homosexuality paralleled a great openness toward sex in general. Forty percent of those surveyed no longer criticized premarital sex. Regardless of the taboos, 33.2 percent of births were to unmarried mothers in 2000, up from 26.6 percent when the decade began.

Regarding gays, Americans were experiencing the most dramatic attitudinal transformation since the civil rights movement made racism illegitimate—and at a faster pace. In 1990, three-quarters of Americans condemned homosexuality. A decade later, that number had dropped to 54 percent. The percentage who approved of homosexuality doubled from 12.3 percent to 26.4 percent. In 2000, for the first time, 50 percent of Americans said society should approve homosexuality, including supporting basic civil rights—although only a third supported gay marriage.

The modern argument for gay rights resonated in a society that was increasingly liquid, tolerant, nonjudgmental. Treating homosexuality as inherent made the civil rights issue one of acknowledging rights "endowed by the creator," rebutting claims it was an immoral lifestyle preference. The growing numbers of gays coming out of the closet generated an exaggerated multiplier effect, thanks to the pseudo-scientific claim that 10 percent of Americans were homosexual. The more gays "came out," the more they were accepted.

By the late 1990s, television shows like *Will & Grace* were normalizing the lifestyle and propagandizing against homophobia. In *My Best Friend's Wedding* (1997), Julia Roberts's clearly gay friend pretends to be her fiancé—and charms everyone with a showstopping fantasy describing their allegedly heterosexual love, sung to "I Say a Little Prayer for You." This delightful scene recruited viewers as collaborators in a modern identity hall of mirrors. So, too, in *The Birdcage* (1996), with Robin Williams and Nathan Lane as the good guys with a stable, long-term marriage, and Gene Hackman as the conservative heterosexual prig.

Even as Hollywood affirmed gays' rights to marry rather than just party, millions still resisted. Senate Majority Leader Trent Lott compared homosexuality to sex addiction or kleptomania. Reverend Pat Robertson declared "the acceptance of homosexuality . . . the last step in the decline of Gentile civilization." More moderately, Roy Schmidt, the city commissioner of Grand Rapids, Michigan, opposed extending civil rights protections to gays, because he felt his own lifestyle under attack: "The core family unit already has enough problems. I don't want my three sons to think that the gay life-style is acceptable." Schmidt also sensed, correctly, that expanding hate-bias legislation would eventually threaten to ban his views.

The law lagged behind the changing attitudes. On July 1, 2000, Vermont became the first state to allow civil unions, which paralleled marriage's rights and responsibilities. Hawaii and California already offered same-sex couples legal status. This "everything that is marriage but the name" law countered the thirty states that passed variations on Clinton's Defense of Marriage Act. Vermont's governor Howard Dean paralleled Clinton's caution in 1996, and signed the controversial civil union law privately.

The Liquefying of American Culture

Being so free in the land of the broken compass was stressful. The self was not enough of an anchor; it was an unreliable GPS for life. David Samuels, writing for *The New York Times Magazine* in 1999, captured the emptiness, the weightlessness, afflicting Generation X, following the Rainbow Rebellion and the sexual revolution, deprived of the Cold War's collective discipline and mission. He and his fellow Ivy League graduates, he wrote, were "free to be white or black, gay or straight, to grow our hair long, shave our heads, meditate for days on end, have children or not, drink bottled water, work out at the gym, watch television until 3 in the morning." But "this freedom from the gravity of age-old constraints was accompanied by a weightless feeling that attached itself to even the most fundamental decisions. Why bother? Why get married?" In the Republic of Everything, the answers "were so multiple and contingent and arbitrary that they never really felt like answers at all."

Popular culture fed this sense of vertigo. By 2000, *Sex and the City* became a defining show for the Age of Clinton, what Candace Bushnell's Carrie Bradshaw labeled the Age of Un-Innocence. These brash, crass but alluring characters, dedicated to "the two L's, labels and love," worshipping at the altar of the $400 Manolo Blahnik shoe and the quick hookup, reflected a culture that Clinton's solvents helped make so voyeuristic and exhibitionist. They, along with candid AIDS reporting, the Starr Report, and the decline of the Cold War's gelling power, turned the once unspeakable into broadcast-worthy language. These four post-feminist powerhouses were the result of America's decades-long Gender Bender, having liberated themselves from traditional female constraints and delighting in a world where gays and straights mingled and swingled together, ever fashionably, ever obsessively. They would be joined in TV-land in 2000 by *Queer as Folk,* an equally explicit show, this time about sex-obsessed homosexuals.

These four lily-white women lived in a world made by the Rainbow Revolution, easily interacting with people of color—as long as they were arch and well-dressed, too. In 2000, *In Living Color*'s Keenen Ivory Wayans with his younger brothers, Shawn and Marlon Wayans, would make *Scary Movie* for $19 million, launching a five-part, $800-million franchise, epitomizing successful African Americans' ascent into the entertainment and financial stratospheres.

Carrie, Miranda, Samantha, and Charlotte, the four vixens of Oprah Winfrey's Contingency Carnival, lived the if-it-feels-good-do-it philosophy without Oprah's goody-two-shoes uplift. In this sullied environment, the Family Friendly Programming Forum somehow championed as wholesome the new comedy

Gilmore Girls, featuring a sixteen-year-old teenager who seemed wiser and more mature than her thirty-two-year-old single mother. "Sixty-three percent of American families are now considered dysfunctional," the comedian Christopher Titus boasted on *Titus,* his new Fox comedy. "That means we're the majority. We're normal."

The *Sex and the City* cast members were Digital Revolution pioneers, early adapters casually incorporating each technological change emerging from 1998 through 2004. They were scouts presaging the Millennials' persistent, public self-purging in the Facebook Age, with Carrie Bradshaw publicizing her most personal secrets. In 2000 alone the number of websites doubled to 20 million from February to September, while 40 million customers had already purchased a product online.

Carrie and her friends were the spoiled brats of the Information Age Reset, denizens of a booming, high-tech, ever more ritzy New York, with seemingly endless bank accounts—or at least unlimited food, clothing, and entertaining budgets. Their jobs rearranged the way people looked at sex (Carrie the columnist), brands (Samantha the PR person), art (Charlotte the dealer), or reality (Miranda the attorney). It takes lots of money and lots of attitude to snicker and say: "I like my money right where I can see it . . . hanging in my closet."

The show appeared apolitical—not believing in the Republican Party or the Democratic Party, but "just . . . in parties." Nevertheless, the show throbbed with a "Blue State" sensibility. Christian groups denounced what one fundamentalist called "sluts in the city." Such celebrations of selfishness, feeding the cult of immediate gratification, and such demonizing responses, feeding political polarization, doomed good government in the Age of Indulgence.

Digitizing the American Mind, Body, and Soul

The pace of producing space-age innovations intensified in 2000. Geneticists deciphered the human genome. Astronomers mapped the universe with a robotic telescope. Neurologists taught the brain to reorganize circuitry after strokes paralyzed patients' limbs. Biologists cloned five little piglets, anticipating xenotransplantation, using pig organs to replace human ones. More practically, the Segway Human Transporter used computers and gyroscopes to move people upright while Toyota introduced the fuel-efficient hybrid Prius to drive green in America. As cell phones became ubiquitous, with 1990's 5.2 million pioneers, 1995's 34 million elites, now approaching 100 million regular users, AT&T offered instant text messaging for those mobile phones. Resulting afflictions included loud, rude talking, distracted driving, and brain cancer fears. In 2000, the Pentagon stopped imposing inaccurate timing on commercial Global Positioning Systems for security purposes, making the GPS more popular. Dick Tracy's personal communication device from the 1930s, and the talking map from Dora the Explorer, the Spanish-speaking Latina who debuted on Nickelodeon in 2000, had jumped from cartoonists' imaginations to store shelves.

The Great American Hook-Up intensified. In 1996, less than a quarter of North Americans aged sixteen and older had "access online"; in 2000, half the population surfed regularly. Betting on this Internet-dominated future, asserting digital media's dominance, America Online bought a content provider, Time Warner, for $165 billion, the biggest merger ever. This social media pioneer would own 55 percent of the quintessential old media company combining Time and Warner Bros. Studios, both founded in 1923.

"There were 50 sites on the World Wide Web when I became president," Clinton boasted. "There are over 20 million now." Clinton also echoed many of the Internet manifestos hailing the coming revolution. "I believe the computer and the Internet give us a chance to move more people out of poverty more quickly than at any time in all of human history," he said.

The Internet was digitizing Americans' body, mind, and soul. Pornography moved from sleazy sex shops into America's bedrooms—and offices. By 2000, online pornography was a $1.4 billion business, accounting for 69 percent of all e-commerce. Porn merchants improved e-commerce immeasurably. They familiarized millions with the "Shopping Cart" and perfected online credit card payments. They pioneered streaming and other vehicles to transmit huge graphics files. The first-glance-at-*Playboy*-centerfold rite of passage became digitized and popularized. The Internet offered deep immersion in mass perversion at younger and younger ages.

By 2000, the search for the ultimate search engine was intensifying. Yahoo!, founded in 1994, began with the now-anachronistic assumption that Internet users were trolling around, exploring, rather than consciously seeking out information. Google, founded four years later by Stanford computer buddies Larry Page and Sergey Brin, began with Page's quest to "download the whole Web, and just keep the links," to best customize each user's search for information. By 2000, Google engineers were pursuing their quest "To organize the world's information, making it universally accessible and useful." Google algorithms soon analyzed a user's history so effectively, consumers often sensed that the search engine anticipated their desires. The human-computer mind meld was being achieved. In October 2000, with the self-service, user-friendly, pay-through-click Google AdWords, Google's engineers found their commercial Holy Grail, a way to "monetize" their services.

Growing Internet use meant growing worries about what the administration's white paper on Critical Infrastructure Protection of May 22, 1998, called "cyber/information warfare." Cybersecurity had to combat criminal and foreign threats. In January, a hacker named "Maxus" admitted to stealing three hundred thousand credit card numbers from CD Universe, an online record store, hoping to extort $100,000. Anxiety was also growing about lost privacy from "cookies," which tracked users' browsing habits. In May, a computer "virus" crashed e-mail systems worldwide with its "I love you" message invading software systems.

In 2000, the recording industry declared war on Napster, an online music file sharing service. Just as a VCR copied one TV program legally, Napster assumed it could copy one recording legally, then share it online. Seeing revenues vanish as millions "file-shared" from that one copy, the music industry disagreed. "Napster happened at the worst possible time for the music business," says Steve Greenberg, the record producer who would win a 2000 Grammy Award for the exuberant Baha Men hit "Who Let the Dogs Out?" With the music business booming, "no one had any incentive to adapt." The rapper Dr. Dre and the heavy metal members of Metallica started targeting fans—users who had downloaded songs—as well as universities, whose computer systems crashed with so many students copying, er, file sharing. Ultimately, Napster closed in 2001 after losing its legal battle. But, Greenberg would lament, industry arrogance precluded any attempts "to try to work with Napster to create a legal, monetizable service." Apple imposed much harsher terms regarding iTunes sales on record companies when record executives panicked in 2003.

The Gilding of America: Gold or Gold-plated?

Digitization and the Internet lowered barriers, allowing consumers to bypass stockbrokers and trade stocks online. Sitting at home, amateurs picked up stock tips by watching CNBC, scanning the Internet, reading e-mails. Clicking some buttons, they started buying, confident the New Economy's market would always rise. With deregulation rampant, finance was king, the markets seemed to rule. Over half of American households owned stock by now. When the technology-heavy NASDAQ, after doubling its value in half a year, peaked in March 2000, at 5,132, one e-commerce site, Ameritrade, was processing 173,000 stock trades daily and welcomed 279,000 new customers. This democratization of the once exclusive stock market lured capital into the market but made many vulnerable. President Clinton warned high-tech executives, "The silicon chip has [not] repealed all the economic laws that govern nations."

No boom lasts forever. In 1999 venture capitalists had invested nearly $20 billion in 1,800 new Internet companies, with 300 IPOs then raising another $22 billion. Too many spiraling IPOs overvalued too many dot-coms now failing to monetize their business. Many offered such steep discounts to encourage traffic that each sale cost them money. Amazon's sales grew from $16 million in 1996 to $1.6 billion in 1999 to $2.8 billion in 2000. But $2.1 billion in debt was crushing. Amazon was big enough yet lithe enough to survive. Most others weren't and didn't.

As Greenspan inched interest rates up, some economists warned that households carried too much debt. With stock prices soaring, more people bought on margin. Paper profits in the market also encouraged overspending, further overheating the economy.

On January 14 the Dow Jones peaked at 11,722.98. The number of American billionaires had now tripled in a decade, from 99 to 298. The average earnings of the top 5 percent of householders jumped from $94,700 in 1990 to $145,500 in 2000. Economists, sociologists, philosophers, and politicians debated whether the gold was distributed broadly enough in this new Gilded Age or Americans were living a gold-plated illusion of mass prosperity enjoyed mostly by a few.

Clinton acknowledged the inequality challenge but insisted that this boom was more democratic. Ronald Reagan's proverbial economic pie was growing enough to enlarge everyone's slice. With 8 million jobs created from 1997 to 2000, April's unemployment rate would dip below 4 percent. Clinton's disgruntled former Labor Secretary Robert Reich nevertheless admitted that "The Fed's interest-rate policies" encouraging economic growth kept "the labor market reasonably tight," thus boosting "wages from the bottom." Additionally, Clinton's prized Earned Income Tax Credit "proved to be a much larger and more significant antipoverty program than anyone had envisioned."

When the St. Louis Rams beat the Tennessee Titans in the 2000 Super Bowl, the fourteen high-tech start-ups paying $1.1 million to $3 million for commercial time made it famous as the "Dot-Com Bowl." Eight of these companies did not exist a decade later. Pets.com, an online pet supply store advertised by a lovably obnoxious canine sock puppet, dropped from an IPO price of $11 a share in February 2000 to $0.22 that November.

On February 25, the Dow Jones dropped below 10,000 as investors, fearing higher interest rates, began abandoning stocks, especially those underperforming, overvalued, dot-coms. That spring, even as the unemployment rate hit its lowest rate since 1970, employers started panicking, cutting 116,000 jobs in May, the first employment dip since the boom began.

As the bubble burst, rookie stock buyers panicked. The loss of nearly $3 trillion from April to December and $8.5 trillion over the next two years wiped out many day traders. Ameritrade's stock trading slowed by a third.

The New Economy mostly held through the end of Clinton's term. In October the administration announced its third surplus, at $237 billion. Clinton anticipated a future surplus as high as $5 trillion. Real wages grew by 8.3 percent from 1995 to 2001. Household indebtedness fell. The end of the 1990s would mark the most lush and equitable economic years in two decades, before what the economist Edward N. Wolff calls the "middle-class squeeze" began after 2001. With Greenspan warning about economic "speed limits," Clinton continued hailing America's economic miracle.

Boosted and Diminished by a Fantasy President

With his infectious exuberance, Bill Clinton fit the political scientist James David Barber's character typology as an "active positive" leader. Martin Sheen's President Josiah "Jed" Bartlet on the hit TV series *The West Wing* amplified Clinton's most appealing traits and proactive outlook. At the 2000 Emmys, Aaron Sorkin's show, inspired by his own 1995 movie *The American President,* won a record nine awards for its 1999 rookie season. The show originally focused on White House staffers. President Bartlet proved so popular, he overshadowed the others, just as the president dominates modern politics despite the Framers' intentions.

Mocked by conservatives as "the Left Wing," the show offered a Hollywood liberal's fantasy president, wise and witty, tough yet humane. "You look well, Mr. President," the Indian ambassador oozes. Bartlet snaps: "I was looking a lot better before your country breached about 14 ceasefire conditions without so much as a phone call." Balancing imperiousness and self-deprecation, this president, with a formidable wife safely working as a doctor rather than a co-president, wears his liberalism easily, naturally. When his young aide Charlie asks to date his daughter, the president agrees. Unruffled that Charlie is black, but still a father, Bartlet quips: "Just remember these two things: she's nineteen years old, and the 82nd Airborne works for me."

The West Wing depicted the president's idealized version of himself, while facilitating one of those mystical transfers of affection from the saintly, Nobel Prize–winning, brilliant, magnanimous, upstanding, television president to the actual chief executive—who also appeared to most Americans as a disembodied TV image. In boosting Clinton, *The West Wing* also diminished him, offering Americans a taste of the kind of fortitude and rectitude many craved yet never received. Clinton joked at the White House correspondents' dinner that *The West Wing*'s "first season got a lot better ratings than mine did . . . not to mention the reviews."

The West Wing further blurred the line between fiction and reality by echoing contemporary politics and American history. Bartlet's campaign slogan was "It's the economy, stupid." When the National Security Adviser speculates about foreign suspects after the president is shot, one name she mentions is "bin Laden," eleven months *before* the 9/11 attacks. Americans were watching a fake president often work through real issues on NBC, as millions were starting to watch Jon Stewart, a comedian, crack jokes about real news during his "fake news" show on Comedy Central.

With fiction upstaging reality, TV producers also turned to reality to raise the stakes in ways fiction never could. The result was 2000's mass crowd pleaser, the reality show *Survivor*. More than 125 million people watched at least part of the first season's August 23 finale. Part color war, part group therapy, part Outward Bound, this entrancing show taught Americans to say "the tribe has spoken" to imply consensus and "you have been voted off the island" to reject someone.

Sixteen normal-looking Americans, not the sculpted Greek gods and goddesses usually starring on TV, ate larvae, raced to collect firewood, confronted inner demons, and schemed against one another when necessary, in their thirty-nine-day quest to avoid having their tiki lamp extinguished and win $1 million. The winner, Richard Hatch, was an openly gay man who liked competing in the buff. As with *Jerry Springer* and *Oprah,* the contestants' exhibitionism fed Americans' growing voyeurism. In this age of shamelessness, a third of Americans said they would appear on a reality TV show wearing pajamas or kissing, but only a quarter would allow filming of crying or arguing. At the 2000 Emmy Awards, host Garry Shandling convened his own "tribal council" with other late night hosts to defend their turf, complaining: "real people should not be on television. It's for special people like us, people who have trained and studied to appear to be real."

The 2000 Campaign: Clintonism Without Bill Clinton

After nearly eight years of a president who was too real in his larger-than-life flaws, the two nominees battling to be his successor lacked Clinton's compelling if confounding authenticity. The Democratic nominee, Vice President Al Gore, was so stiff he joked that his version of the Macarena was standing ramrod straight. The Republican nominee, Texas governor George W. Bush, was so guarded that few Americans saw the warmth or intelligence his aides said they saw, away from those TV cameras, which frequently elicited his deer-in-the-headlights look.

Al Gore should have won the election easily. The economy was booming. The nation was at peace. His boss, Bill Clinton, remained popular. Almost every political science model forecast a Gore victory. One Bush relative, off the record, wondered why, during the debates, Gore never asked Bush: "Could you remind me, governor, just what is it about peace and prosperity you don't like?"

Bill Clinton thought Gore should run for a third Clinton term. In his ninety-minute 2000 State of the Union address Clinton proclaimed: "We are fortunate to be alive at this moment in history. Never before has our nation enjoyed, at once, so much prosperity and social progress with so little internal crisis or so few external threats."

Clinton quantified his economic accomplishments. "We begin the new century with over 20 million new jobs; the fastest economic growth in more than 30 years; the lowest unemployment rates in 30 years; the lowest poverty rates in 20 years; the lowest African American and Hispanic unemployment rates on record; the first back-to-back surpluses in 42 years; and next month, America will achieve the longest period of economic growth in our entire history."

Evoking his 1993 Memphis address, Clinton celebrated America's moral revival: "crime down by 20 percent, to its lowest level in 25 years; teen births down 7 years in a row; adoptions up by 30 percent; welfare rolls cut in half, to their lowest levels in 30 years." He insisted: "My fellow Americans, the state of our Union is the strongest it has *ever* been."

To compete, George W. Bush marketed himself as a "Compassionate Conservative," a phrase echoing his father's "kinder, gentler" passive-aggressive distancing from Reaganism. Bush advocated helping the poor through faith-based initiatives, using local charities, inculcating values not just transferring money. His education policies included subsidizing parents who sent their children to private schools, a conservative concern, along with accepting the Democratic demand for statewide math and reading tests. Bush's rhetoric about "an optimistic, governing conservatism" had Rush Limbaugh "troubled," with other conservatives fearing Bush Jr. sounded like "Clinton Jr."

Like most vice presidents, Gore wanted to win independently even though his political identity stemmed from the president's. Gore also wanted distance from Clinton's immoral behavior while benefiting from Clinton's economic legacy. A visionary legislator and leader but a stilted politician, Gore felt diminished by the constant comparisons with Clinton's virtuosity. Clinton was glandular, instinctive, effervescently fluid, and cerebral; Gore, while also smart, was deliberate, square, and offputtingly awkward. Clinton's roguishness compelled; Gore's priggishness—exacerbated by his post-Lewinsky indignation—repelled. The Secret Service's code name for the smooth, soaring, majestic president was Eagle; Gore's code name was the wooden, workabee, and most definitely earthbound Sawhorse.

"Al just needs to be himself," Clinton often told friends, as he watched the stiff, slick version of the hipper behind-closed-doors vice president stumble on the campaign trail. Gore's zeal in running away from the president and his record offended Clinton loyalists. "You would have thought he wasn't even part of the administration," Secretary of Commerce Mickey Kantor later marveled. "I think it was a major political mistake." When Gore selected the moralistic Senator Joe Lieberman as a running mate, the White House press secretary Joe Lockhart bristled at the Lewinsky-inspired scolding Gore was implicitly giving Clinton.

Gore noted Clinton's low personal approval ratings of 27 percent, not just Clinton's high job approval ratings. Reporters were particularly, unfairly, tough on Gore, pummeling him for white lies after years of enabling Clinton's whoppers. "Somewhere along the line, the dominant political reporters for most dominant news organizations decided they didn't like him, and they thought the story line on any given day was about his being a phony or a liar or a waffler," ABC's political director Mark Halperin later admitted. Having been seduced by Clinton, reporters sought liberation from those Clintonite wiles while skewering Clinton's successor for lacking them.

Gore tried softening his image. He smooched his wife, Tipper, passionately when accepting the Democratic nomination. People loved it. On September 11, 2000, Al Gore appeared on *Oprah Winfrey* to reveal that he liked Wheaties, Chinese food, the Beatles, and sleeping naked. When Winfrey asked him to identify the country's greatest problem, he replied, earnestly, vapidly: "We need more meaning in our national life." Oprah, who had previously avoided hosting politicians, but had donated $12,000 to Democrats since 1992, gushed that Gore was a "fun, funny guy." He joked back, "Hard to believe, isn't it?"

A week later, fairness dictated that George W. Bush appear. Once again, fluff trumped substance, as Oprah exposed Bush's love for peanut butter and jelly on white bread, tacos—for some diversity, no doubt—and the song "Wake Up

Little Susie." Oprah's body language conveyed discomfort with the Republican nominee.

Many feared these appearances represented one more descent toward America's "Oprahfication." The conservative columnist George Will was relieved to see that Bush was "fluent in the emotive language of today's therapeutic ethos." Gore was considered the Baby Boomer candidate, not Bush, even though Bush was born the same year as Clinton, 1946. George W. Bush—and millions of Republican Baby Boomers—shared many generational sensibilities even while dissenting from the Adversarials' culture and politics.

Pursuing a Clintonized electorate while fleeing Clinton, Al Gore triangulated. He echoed Clinton's neo-Reaganite language of downsizing, reinventing government, and budget surpluses. Most Americans surveyed, 58 percent, preferred "smaller government with fewer services." Still, wooing women, minorities, and union members, Gore vowed to have an "iron-clad lockbox" for entitlements, while promising to "invest in our country and our families, and I mean investing in education, health care, the environment." "Investing" was now preferable to "spending."

Both nominees' Clintonism without Bill Clinton charted a Third Way between Reaganite hostility to government and McGovernite big-government-is better approach. The reigning American ideology now combined 1960s-style middle-class welfarism with 1980s-style moralistic posturing. Bush the Republican supported "'affirmative access'—not quotas, not double standards," a patient's bill of rights, and variations on Ronald Reagan's "safety net" of basic government goodies. Gore the Democrat supported the death penalty, morality crusades to curb Hollywood, and tax cuts. Both often sounded in the debates as if they were running for the local school board not commander-in-chief, promising to fix the schools, encourage good parenting, and improve the American moral climate. With each nominee mocked for preferring Band-Aids to big reforms, both campaigns proved that, thanks to Bill Clinton, America's revolutionaries had rediscovered Edmund Burke's teaching: "But what is liberty without wisdom, and without virtue? It is the greatest of all possible evils; for it is folly, vice, and madness, without tuition or restraint."

Gore confused voters by intermittently emitting a populist growl. At the Democratic convention, he compared Republicans and Democrats, saying "They're for the powerful, we're for the people." Gore railed against "big tobacco, big oil, the big polluters, the pharmaceutical companies, the H.M.O.'s," many of whom were sponsoring his nominating convention. Senator Russell Feingold was the rare Democrat willing to challenge his own party's Clintonite hypocrisy.

In the three minutes during a slow afternoon that party bosses allocated him to address the convention, Feingold charged: "This convention is all about money, and especially corporate money."

A presidential election decided by the right kiss, the wrong word, a too-tall tale might seem trivialized. Americans long wanted a president to be king and prime minister, both a political and cultural icon. To fill George Washington's mythic shoes, to be effective, to mobilize millions in a diverse democracy, presidents needed charisma, leadership skills, the right stuff. The blurring of the line between information and entertainment on television made both Ronald Reagan and Bill Clinton function as celebrity-in-chief. And Clinton's supernatural political abilities confirmed the importance of likability, accessibility.

It was an equally long-standing American tradition to bellyache about this focus on personalities, to fear democracy's degeneration. Americans wanted a slugfest and a seminar, candidates who were both aggressive and honorable. Nominees gave the people what they wanted by acting like fighting schoolboys and Olympian statesmen, just as publishers ran editorials bemoaning the focus on personalities expressed in their own front pages. Clinton at once further addicted many Americans—and most reporters—to his politics of seduction and embarrassed them with their own susceptibility to his charms.

Still, Gore's stiffness, his missing likability gene, hurt him. The linguist Steven Pinker explained that voters listened through Bush's warm verbal mush—"We ought to make the pie higher"—but were alienated by Al Gore's elegant, literate but "condescending . . . motherese." Many Americans showed during the Clinton sex scandal they no longer had to venerate a president, but they still wanted to like him. As Clinton left office, he enjoyed record public approval ratings of 66 percent to 29 percent, higher than Dwight Eisenhower and Ronald Reagan as they retired. But only one in ten gave Clinton high marks for ethics, serving as a role model for children, or honesty. Americans were learning to compartmentalize and judge the president most on job-related skills, not personality.

Deadlock: The "Reddening," "Blueing," and Blackening of American Politics

"Thank you. Thank you. Thank you. Thank you so much. I mean, wow, this is amazing. Thank you all. Thank you," New York's senator-elect gushed. On America's wild, wacky Election Night, when Al Gore won the nationwide popular vote by half-a-million ballots but failed to secure an Electoral College majority, the First Lady's big victory was big news. Hillary!—her campaign literature preferred the exclamation point to her last name—trounced her boyish opponent, Congressman Rick Lazio. Through sixteen months of county fairs and rubber chicken dinners, visiting New York's sixty-two counties, Mrs. Clinton had earned her new, independent power base. The First Lady's reincarnation as Senator Hillary! was a modern tale of celebrity and scandal, of feminism and empowerment, of humiliation and redemption, powered by old-fashioned grit and guts.

Nationally, the great thirty-four-day electoral deadlock of 2000 began. With Gore at 255 electoral votes and Bush at 246, both candidates needed Florida's 25 electoral votes to surpass the 270 electoral votes and win the presidency. In a Florida race so tight it triggered an automatic statewide machine recount of the election's 5,963,100 popular votes, Cuban revenge over Elián González was one of many factors that hurt Gore. Others included the 97,421 votes Ralph Nader's insurgent candidacy attracted, and the thousands of votes nearsighted elderly Jewish voters who misread the infamous butterfly ballot mistakenly cast for their least favorite candidate, Pat Buchanan, rather than Al Gore.

The divided electorate reflected a divided America. Despite Bill Clinton's bridge building and triangulating, America in the 1990s became more polarized. Using the television electoral vote map, commentators identified George Bush's "Red America" and Al Gore's "Blue America." Red America was centered in the South, the Rocky Mountain States, and the Plains States. It was more male than female, more white than black, more churchgoing than secular, more married than single, more rural and small town than urban. Gore, leading Blue America, won 90 percent of the African American vote, 71 percent of big city residents, 70 percent of gays, 62 percent of Hispanics, 62 percent of union members, 61 percent of non-churchgoers, 58 percent of women who worked outside the home, 58 percent of those who did not own guns, 57 percent of the unmarried, 55 percent of Asians, 54 percent of women, and only 42 percent of whites.

The state-oriented electoral map made the divide look regional but the phenomenon was more sociological and ideological. "Blue" sensibilities could be found in most cities. Although Red America was "religious" and Blue America "tolerant," both were stubborn about their respective beliefs.

For all the Red-Blue talk, Clinton's America remained Reaganized and indulgent. Conservatives still outnumbered liberals by 29 percent to 20 percent. Fifty percent of voters called themselves "moderate." Fifty-three percent preferred smaller government to big government. Culturally, rates of modern, nontraditional behavior such as abortion, divorce, drug use, and Hollywood movie watching were distributed broadly throughout the fifty states. Attitudes toward the behaviors varied more than the popularity of the behaviors themselves.

Throughout the deadlock, Miami mayor Alex Penelas's hostility continued to hurt Gore. Penelas somehow failed to provide sufficient security to protect Miami-Dade County officials counting ballots on November 22. That oversight emboldened young Republicans, many of whom were blue-blazered-khaki-pants-wearing party operatives or white-pearled, power-suit-wearing congressional staffers suddenly seized with a desire to visit the Sunshine State, to bully county officials during the recount. "Shut it down," Republican congressman John Sweeney shouted, as dozens of Republican activists tried swarming into a smaller room the officials had moved into for the recount.

In the waning days of the Clinton administration, the American people had one of their last Rashomon moments in a tenure rife with polarized impressions and relativist justifications. Democrats labeled the protest a violent riot, giving the impression that masses of hired hands had undermined the democratic process, preventing the necessary vote count. This exaggeration fed a broader Democratic impression of right-wing Republican thuggery, clumping together Newt Gingrich, Rush Limbaugh, the Contract with America, evangelical Christians, the militias, the Oklahoma City bombing, and America's sad legacy of gun violence and racism. Shortly after the election, Jesse Jackson framed the issue as Redneck America's assault on "one-person, one-vote," attempting to suppress the black voice, thundering, "They still keep these chains."

Republicans insisted they were merely exercising their democratic rights, monitoring against attempted vote fraud. This overly innocent spin reinforced a broader Republican impression of left-wing Democratic corruption, linking Bill Clinton's win-at-all-costs, play-by-my-own rules Whitewater, Travelgate, Fostergate, and Lewinsky finagles to an overall drop in traditional standards, heralding this Anything Goes Republic's decline.

This "Brooks Brothers Riot" compelled Miami-Dade officials to resubmit their original counts, leading Florida secretary of state Katherine Harris to certify Bush as winner by 537 votes four days later. This shift cast Gore as the potential spoiler. The Florida Supreme Court issued a court order favorable to Gore to review more than 45,000 uncounted ballots in the state's 67 counties by hand. Instead, a divided U.S. Supreme Court decided on December 12 to halt any recounts, immediately certifying the election, and handing the White House to George W. Bush. "While I strongly disagree with the court's decision, I accept it," Gore said, elegantly. "For the sake of our unity . . . and the strength of our democracy, I offer my concession."

Watching Republican and Democratic talking heads invade TV studios daily, each charging the other with "stealing the election," America looked fractious, polarized, and quarrelsome. Yet amid the media and political hysteria, the American people were remarkably cool, tracking the story without becoming inflamed. During Thanksgiving most Americans seemed far more focused on the turkeys gracing their tables than the elephants and donkeys clashing in Florida. Most Americans easily accepted the new president as legitimate.

Couch Potato Nation

America was more Couch Potato Nation, or even Mouse Potato Nation, than the Crossfire Nation caricatured on CNN. As with Clinton's impeachment, the gap between the partisans' intensity and the people's detachment partly testified to an enlightened, patient, body politic. Even more, it suggested the truth of sociologist Robert Putnam's warnings that Americans were "Bowling Alone," becoming spectators not participants in democracy. Many sociologists diagnosed that disengagement as another malaise of modern life. The problems the Florida fiasco uncovered ran deeper than a hanging chad here, and a dimpled chad there.

As George W. Bush rushed ahead with his compressed transition, Bill Clinton prepared his own transition to civilian life. At the White House correspondents' dinner, he had joked about writing his resume, using "the active voice . . . You know, things like 'commanded U.S. Armed Forces'; . . . 'served three terms as President'—everybody embellishes a little—'designed, built, and painted bridge to 21st century'; 'supervised Vice President's invention of the Internet'; 'generated, attracted, heightened, and maintained controversy.'"

Unfortunately, Clinton's presidency ended with new storms, even as he tried floating out of the Oval Office, Ronald Reagan style, as the wise, calm statesman. Clinton's farewell tour started strong, including a nostalgic visit to New Hampshire to thank voters for making him the "Comeback Kid," a celebratory visit to Ireland to emphasize his peacemaking legacy, and a White House bash for the Clintons' extended political family.

Clinton toasted the new senator from New York, graciously remarking that he could now be freed of the "guilt" that when "Hillary came to Arkansas and married me . . . I kept her out of a career in politics that she should have had." He flew to Little Rock. While detailing all of the jobs created, debts paid, minority businesses launched, homes purchased, colleges attended, and welfare rolls cut, he graciously said that, of all presidents, "I'm the only one that I can honestly say got to be president because he had personal friends who stood up, traveled the country, fought, spoke up, and determined to make the campaign go." And he distributed twenty-eight Citizens Medals, including to the former antiwar radical and nimble boxer Muhammad Ali, the Holocaust survivor Marion Wiesel, the home run king Hank Aaron, and the living legend Elizabeth Taylor. The cast of honorees, dominated by people of color and civil rights activists, testified to the more diverse, more democratic America that elected Clinton and which he nurtured.

In his Farewell Address, revisiting the themes he articulated a decade earlier, Clinton said, "I have steered my course by our enduring values: opportunity for all, responsibility from all, a community of all Americans." He urged Americans to continue his legacies of cultivating "fiscal responsibility," of fighting the forces of "global destruction," and of weaving together a "fabric" of one America. In his final whirl of activities, he showed yet again, "I had loved being President, even on the bad days."

That winter, however, brought bad days. Clinton hated the Supreme Court decision awarding Bush the presidency, describing Gore's campaign as "the first Presidential campaign in history that was so clearly winning, a court had to stop the vote in order to change the outcome." That comment triggered fears that the outgoing president was trying to undermine the incoming president's legitimacy.

Tragically, Clinton's high-pressure, high-minded, marathon Middle East peacemaking initiative sputtered as his presidential power dwindled. When the Palestinian leader Yasser Arafat made his unprecedented twenty-fourth White House visit, *Time* said Arafat already held the "title of the administration's Most Frequent Visitor." Clinton was frustrated. Israel's Prime Minister Ehud Barak had agreed to a sweeping deal withdrawing from most of the 1967 territories and compensating the Palestinians with land swaps. But Arafat was dithering— and Palestinian violence was mounting.

Arafat tried flattering the president, calling him a "great man," while refusing to compromise. "I am not a great man," Clinton would recall replying, "I am a failure. And you have made me one." Clinton later said, "Arafat never said no; he just couldn't bring himself to say yes." Trying to explain Arafat's "error of historic proportions," Clinton would speculate, "Perhaps he simply couldn't make the final jump from revolutionary to statesman." Frank Greer, Clinton's media consultant, confirmed that "It fell apart because of Yasser Arafat at the last minute." Ambassador Nancy Soderberg realized belatedly that Arafat was "never" going to "compromise." Greer was not even sure Clinton "was dealing with a rational person in that situation." This failure, followed by waves of Palestinian terrorism, resulted in thousands of deaths—often in gruesome suicide bombings that even killed three generations of one Israeli family sharing a meal—and perpetuated the Israeli-Palestinian stalemate for at least another decade and a half.

Pardon Me: A Tawdry Exit

A more embarrassing incident again showed both Clintons' pettiness despite their grand achievements. As he retired, Clinton issued 176 pardons and sentence commutations. He pardoned his brother, Roger Clinton, as well as Marc Rich, the fugitive financier living in Switzerland charged with 51 counts of tax evasion.

Many of those pardoned enjoyed special access and gave special favors to the administration. Rich's ex-wife Denise Rich donated more than $1 million to the Clinton presidential library and the Democratic Party. *The New York Times* called pardoning a fugitive "indefensible." Mickey Kantor, a close friend, would call the Rich pardon "the single most inexplicable, devastating thing" Clinton did, particularly because it was "the one thing that has bothered" his core constituents. Equally frustrating, Clinton "was at the top of his game . . . and just like he's always done," sabotaged himself.

The Clintons also accepted $190,027 worth of gifts to help fill their two new houses, in Chappaqua and Georgetown, while taking some furniture donors had deeded to the White House not to its temporary occupants. Clinton's blurred boundaries between himself and his office, along with an odd match between the Clintons' neediness and their supporters' fawning, fed what the conservative Barbara Olson called this "final frenzy." Despite his pending $10 million book deal and her $8 million advance, despite six-figure post-presidential speaking fees looming, the Clintons felt "broke." As much as $10 million in legal bills, for a couple who never had any significant assets, was daunting but for them manageable.

In March, Hillary Clinton had filled out a password-protected gift registry at Borsheims, a luxurious department store in Omaha. A Beverly Hills friend, Rita Pynoos, encouraged other donors to send what ended up being $38,617 in china and sterling silver gifts, along with $68,770 worth of furniture. Steven Spielberg gave nine 5-piece place settings, and eight soup bowls worth $4,920. Iris Cantor, who in 1996 fought a nasty succession battle with her late husband B. Gerald Cantor's protégé Howard Lutnick over controlling Cantor Fitzgerald, gave $4,992 in china. Walter Kaye, the donor who recommended Monica Lewinsky, gave gifts worth $9,683 including a cigar humidor.

In damage-control mode, the Clintons would write checks totaling $85,966 to purchase the gifts, while returning $28,000 worth of furniture to the White House. Still, the last-minute pardons, the gift grabbing, and word that George W. Bush's people moved into White House offices with obscene messages and computer keyboards missing the "W" key, fed one final moral panic. Republicans overreacted with their usual Clintipathy, calling what many Democrats called Clinton's "bad judgment" "corruption." Most Americans opposed another inquisition as a new presidency began.

Clinton resented being "mugged one more time on the way out the door." He wrote a *New York Times* op-ed in February invoking tax experts to justify Marc Rich's pardon. Mamie Eisenhower had furnished the Eisenhowers' Gettysburg farm with gifts from wealthy supporters. John Kennedy had failed to convince his wife not to accept two gorgeous stallions from Saudi Arabia, because the president feared dwarfing some Israeli gift of $12 Bibles. Still, times had changed, and the Clintons knew it.

The gap between the president's behavior and his lofty self-presentation remained wide. The liberal columnist Richard Cohen wrote an open letter, complaining: "You let me down—Yes, me and everyone else who has ever defended you." Cohen called the Marc Rich pardon "a pie in the face of anyone who ever defended you. You may look bad, Bill, but we look just plain stupid."

"I love liberals," George Will remarked dryly on ABC. "They put up with this guy through perjury, suborning perjury, obstruction of justice and use of the military to cloud discussion of his problems. Then he steals the toaster and they say, 'That's it, we've had it.'" Will said Clinton was "not the worst president we ever had, just the worst person who was ever president." *The Washington Post* editorialized: "It's the Clinton administration in miniature. They do something wrong and force the country to stoop to their level to make them get it right."

In M. Night Shyamalan's movie *The Sixth Sense* (1999), millions felt chills when the psychologist played by Bruce Willis was revealed to be a ghost administering to a child who told viewers all along, "I see dead people." Many Americans experienced a similar revelation, the Greeks call it "anagnorisis," as the star reveals his true self. Bill Clinton, a talented politician, clearly was more morally tone deaf and personally hollow than many admitted; while his wife was often co-conspirator, not just victim or enabler. In 2002, when *Newsweek* asked him if he had second thoughts about pardoning Rich, Clinton answered obtusely, acknowledging: "It was terrible politics." Deeply amoral, obsessively tactical, Clinton kept saying he had done his job. His approval ratings remained high.

Clinton left a new and improved America to George W. Bush, but this woulda, shoulda president coulda done better. In December 1997, feeling strong, Clinton predicted, "Nineteen ninety-eight will be a year of vigorous action on vital issues that will shape the century to come." He talked about climate change, health care, child care, "setting up excellence and lifetime learning" initiatives, addressing "the entitlements challenge, because we have to honor the good that has been done by Social Security and Medicare for retirees," and finding "a security framework in the world that enables us to both pursue our interests and our values." Within weeks, Lewinsky-mania, then lame-duck status, shelved much of this long-term agenda.

Clinton also neglected a more pressing item. In October, al-Qaeda terrorists off Yemen's coast had detonated a bomb against the hull of the USS *Cole*, murdering seventeen sailors and injuring thirty-nine more. Although FBI agents confirmed Osama bin Laden's guilt within three weeks, Clinton and other parts of the security establishment awaited more definitive confirmation and proposed responses. Too many attacks on America by bin Laden had now been unavenged. The master terrorist was feeling too confident.

12

2001
"Let's Roll"

America the Functional Under Attack

What we owe the Little Rock Nine is to do our part in this time to deal with the new problems of this time and the unresolved problems of their time, so that when our time is done, at least our kids have something else to worry about.

—BILL CLINTON, REMARKS AT A CANDLELIGHT VIGIL HONORING THE LITTLE ROCK NINE IN LITTLE ROCK, ARKANSAS, SEPTEMBER 27, 1997

On the morning of September 11, 2001, George W. Bush's America was looking as strong, prosperous, distracted, and fun as Bill Clinton's America. The United States was a remarkably functional country that late summer morning. The world's first mass middle-class civilization—and the world's post–Cold War hyper-power—was thriving. Three-quarters of American adults had jobs. A record two-thirds of Americans owned their own homes. Sixty percent of Americans were married. Reflecting a society that could afford to invest in the future, America's school year was starting with 73,124,000 students.

Year by year, Americans produced the most magical medicines, the most wondrous medical procedures, the most marvelous computer programs, the most entertaining shows, the most impressive healing initiatives for body and soul, and the niftiest technological devices, to prolong life—and make living more fun and more meaningful. Despite culture wars and political battles, momentary traumas and persistent worries, day to day, most of America's 285 million inhabitants led orderly, good, healthy, moral, ever-improving lives. The biggest headline of the times should have been that America worked: it was both productive and functional.

Living in the Ireland of North America, 90 percent of Americans believed in God. Even as growing numbers "disaffiliated," 41 percent recently had attended church. That Sunday in Minneapolis, the Calvinistic Baptist, John Piper, a "Christian Hedonist" seeking happiness through faith, preached against moderns' justifying Christianity as socially and politically "useful." It's not useful, it's true, he bellowed. In Odessa, Texas, the Reverend Ernest L. Easley fought the Contingency Carnival by labeling John's Gospel "required reading," not optional.

Such sermons, frequently fought modernity while echoing it. America's indulgent culture forced religions to adapt, like successful businesses. Many churches renew their theology while expanding their missions to include do-gooding, skill-building, healing, and self-help. "The church is people," said one hip reverend, as the modernizing "Emerging Church" wooed young Protestants, while free "Birthright Israel" heritage trips to Israel wooed young Jews.

Religious and secular Americans worshiped together, en masse, in America's secular, open-air cathedrals—the sports stadiums dotting the country, housing 118 teams in the four major sports of baseball, football, basketball, hockey. Sports generated over $200 billion in economic activity annually. In New York, Giants fans were mourning their football team's opening loss, 31 to 20, to the Denver Broncos. New York Yankees fans were thrilled. Their team had won ten of eleven baseball games, putting them thirty games over a .500 winning percentage. Sports partially replaced the Cold War's sense of mission, functioning as the great solidarity maker, water-cooler conversation agenda setter, aggressive male emotions channeler, and noble war substitute.

On Monday, September 10, as Americans returned to work from a leisure-filled weekend, most held very different jobs than their ancestors had. Few made things or worked with their hands. Most now worked white-collar and service jobs, managing information, ideas, or people. Typical commuters, after standing on what seemed like a permaline at Starbucks, now performed many activities routinely, which seemed alien the first time they tried them during the Nineties: checking for messages on a Nokia cell phone; dialing up for Internet access to get news updates on the Web after booting up Microsoft Windows 98; Googling for information; ordering online at eBay or Amazon.

Americans were the world's most charitable people. The nonprofit sector constituted 8 percent of gross domestic product, with more than 1.5 million registered, tax-exempt nonprofits—up from 13,000 in 1940. Close to 75 percent of households donated charitably annually. Computer titans started making mega-donations, including $11 billion from Bill Gates in 1999 and $5 billion from Gordon Moore of Intel to their respective foundations.

America's 4.1 million professional, scientific, and technical workers were inventing the future. In January, Apple had introduced iTunes, the digital jukebox, anticipating an October release date for the iPod, promising "1,000 songs in your pocket." Now everyone could make their own radio station—even as XM Satellite Radio offering a hundred channels nationwide debuted in September 2001.

America's $45 billion medical research community helped extend American life expectancy from forty-seven years in 1900 to seventy-six in 2000. "If you think research is expensive, try disease," said Mary Lasker, the medical philanthropist who died in 1994. On July 2, 2001, surgeons in Louisville, Kentucky, implanted a battery-operated artificial heart, AbioCor, in fifty-nine-year-old Robert Tools. Tools bravely lived with a *whir* instead of a heartbeat for 151 days.

The National Institutes of Health funded more than 2,000 research centers. These medical miracle makers reduced fatality rates in heart attacks and strokes, extended the five-year-cancer rate of survival from 35 percent in the 1950s to 60 percent, and fed the conceptual pipeline to 1,300 biotechnology firms and the $87 billion pharmaceutical industry. At the Boston University Medical Center, Susan Kim Hanson, a Korean immigrant, was preparing her microbiology immunology dissertation defense. First, she and her husband, Peter, a Grateful Dead Deadhead turned software marketing vice president, decided to visit Disneyland with their toddler, Christine.

When Hell Landed from the Skies

Tuesday morning, September 11, 2001, as New York's Democratic mayoral candidates prepared for a primary showdown, tens of millions followed their weekday routines. As many as 1 million people would be flying that day into or out of North America. By 9:00 a.m. nearly four thousand commercial jets would be aloft in American airspace, part of a sophisticated global aviation system that worked so smoothly most took for granted the marvel of flying. Todd Beamer, the PalmPilot-addicted ORACLE salesman, preferred staying home with his pregnant wife, Lisa, and their two young sons overnight, then flying out for his business meetings Tuesday morning. He left for Newark airport at 6:15 a.m. to catch United Airlines Flight 93 for San Francisco. In Virginia, the Clinton critic Barbara Olson also took an early morning flight, American Airlines Flight 77 to Los Angeles, to film Bill Maher's contentious talk show *Politically Incorrect,* having stayed home the night before to celebrate her husband's birthday. Before she left, she tucked a card into his bed wishing him a happy sixty-first. In Boston, the Hanson family boarded their cross-country United Flight 175. At Logan Airport, Daniel Lewin, the American-Israeli former commando turned whiz kid, David Angell, the creator of *Wings* and *Frasier*, and his wife, Lynn Angell, all caught American Airlines Flight 11 to Los Angeles. Seth MacFarlane, the creator of *Family Guy*, another arch, zeitgeist-shaping *Simpsons*-like animated show, missed the flight by half an hour, misinformed by an incompetent travel agent.

Bill Clinton was in Australia earning $150,000 to address a private equity firm. Clinton was already outdoing other ex-presidents in the crassness of his money-making and the flamboyance of his do-gooding. Asked a day earlier about terrorism, Clinton said, "I nearly got him," meaning Osama bin Laden. "And I could have killed him, but I would have to destroy a little town called Kandahar in Afghanistan and kill 300 innocent women and children, and then I would have been no better than him. And so I didn't do it." Most Americans opposed causing what Pentagon spinmeisters called "collateral damage," especially because few feared al-Qaeda. As the 9/11 Commission Report would later confirm, "The nation was unprepared." Americans' charmingly naïve feelings of innocence and invulnerability prevented them from taking the al-Qaeda threat seriously, despite the Saudi Arabia, Tanzania, Kenya, and Yemen massacres.

That morning of September 11, Osama bin Laden's al-Qaeda terrorists exploited what Clinton called "the forces of interdependence—open borders, easy immigration and travel, easy access to information and technology." By 7:40 a.m. nineteen terrorists had boarded four different cross-country jets. Within fifteen minutes of takeoff, the hijackers controlled Flight 11 and had murdered their first victim, Daniel Lewin. Given his anti-terrorist training, Lewin probably tried intervening, unaware that another hijacker sat behind him. These attacks caused the spikes in Internet traffic Lewin's mathematical model anticipated, saving his company financially on the day he died.

Hell landed from the skies in lower Manhattan. At 8:46 a.m. American Airlines Flight 11 slammed into the World Trade Center North. Flying on the second Boston jet, Peter Hanson called his father telling him: "I think they're going to try to crash this plane into a building." At 9:05 Peter said, "Oh, my God," softly, three times. Then United Airlines Flight 175 hit the World Trade Center South and exploded. Christine Hanson would be the youngest victim that day. She was two and a half years old. Eventually, rescuers found one 6-inch piece of Peter Hanson's bone.

By 10:30 a.m., Barbara Olson's jet had crashed into the Pentagon and Todd Beamer, calling "Let's Roll," had led a passenger's revolt that crashed Flight 93 into a Pennsylvania field. Both Twin Towers had collapsed, five other buildings were destroyed, the Pentagon was burning, and millions were coping with an incomprehensible crime that killed 2,996 people.

Suddenly, people who moments ago had been thinking of the upcoming day's trades, or the end of the night shift, or the weekend ahead, were wondering how to say good-bye to their loved ones in a phone call—amid blazing heat, thickening dust, piercing screams, growing panic. One person first told his wife about his death benefits and other financial plans. A second thanked his father-in-law, detailing his welcoming moves made over the years. A third simply said "I love you." Others died immediately, reduced to a dust authorities brought to each grieving family whose loved one's remains were not found. Some 9/11 widows recoiled at the package, disgusted that the terrorists' ashes might be mixed with the victims.

Hundreds of firefighters and police officers poured into the burning buildings, evacuating thousands. That day, 421 first responders died, 2,000 were wounded. Fortunately, the buildings were half full so early in the day, and, since the 1993 bombings, the Port Authority had updated emergency procedures.

Responsibility and Community As a Nation Mourns

Most 9/11 heroes fit comfortably in the American pantheon: Todd Beamer the pious family man, Daniel Lewin the start-up commando. Victim 0001, the fire department's chaplain Father Mychal Judge, became an American hero with a modern twist. Judge was a beloved priest, seemingly omnipresent whenever disaster struck, never afraid to hug the burned, the scarred, the homeless, the AIDS-infected. As jumper after jumper crashed onto the plaza outside the North Tower lobby, where he was ministering, Father Mike cried, "Jesus, please end this right now! God, please end this." Some witnesses say that as he shouted, a piece of concrete from the collapsing South Tower killed him.

Four days later, Bill Clinton, whisked back from Australia by military jet, eulogized Father Judge's life as "an example of what has to prevail." By then, Father Mychal Judge had become the "gay saint of 9/11." Although celibate, he identified as gay, sharing the information selectively.

Mychal Judge's secular canonization was an early step in a national catharsis. The World Trade Center, with its globalized name, its majestic intrusion into the heavens, its shopping mall below, and its financiers above, symbolized all that Islamists hated about America.

But Osama bin Laden miscalculated. He aimed at America the soft, the innocent, the decadent, the distracted; America the strong, the determined, the democratic, the good, hit back. It was not a white-bread America: although the World Trade Center casualties were disproportionately white males working in white-collar jobs, the missing posters papering the city after the tragedy testified to the new, diverse America of many colors, religions, languages emerging. It was not a fearful America: Americans were thrilled by the heroism of the first responders, of the Flight 93 rebels, of Abe Zelmanowitz who perished because he stayed with a disabled coworker on the twenty-seventh floor, of Michael Benfante and John Cerqueira who carried a wheelchair-bound woman down sixty-eight flights of steps to safety. It was not a selfish America: volunteers, donations, torrents of love poured into New York and Washington. And it was not a divided America: 150 members of Congress gathered on the Capitol steps and starting singing "God Bless America." David Gelernter, the Unabomber's victim, explained in his memoir of recovery, "If you insert into this weird slot machine of modern life one evil act, a thousand acts of kindness tumble out."

"They failed in terrorizing us. We were calm," one refugee from the North Tower's eighty-seventh floor posted online. "If you want to make us stronger, attack and we unite. This is the ultimate failure of terrorism against the United States." Liquid America could be quite solid.

Two national memorial services illustrated two sides of modern America, united in common pain and love. On September 14, President George W. Bush led a prayer service at the National Cathedral in Washington, D.C., accompanied by national leaders including the four living former presidents, George H. W. Bush, Jimmy Carter, Bill Clinton, and Gerald Ford. Reverend Billy Graham, born in 1918, a confidante to presidents since Dwight Eisenhower, the symbol of America the Square and the Beautiful, emphasized that "we're more united than ever." Bush unapologetically declared: "Our responsibility to history is already clear, to answer these attacks and rid the world of evil."

New York City's ceremony, "A Prayer for America," held in Yankee Stadium, was multicultural, New Age, and celebrity oriented. Oprah Winfrey officiated. With no talk of evil, Oprah shared "that when you lose a loved one you gain an angel whose name you know." The Harlem Boys and Girls Choir sang "We Shall Overcome." The brassy singer Bette Midler sang "Wind Beneath My Wings." A parade of preachers prayed. They were black and white, male and female, Catholic, Protestant, Jewish, Sikh, Armenian, Greek Orthodox, Hindu, and Muslim.

The emotional contagion of terrorism in the age of mass media mass-produced communal trauma. Terrorists Clouded the Commons, darkening shared public spaces with fear, suspicion, and anguish, making routine activities feel threatening. But Americans responded by taking responsibility and affirming a broad sense of community, two of Clinton's favorite themes.

The Day the Nineties Died

On this day, the Nineties died, ending the good times as abruptly as the Great Crash had ended the 1920s' bacchanal. "The '90s surely goes down as the decade of waste and lost opportunity," a Democratic radio commentator from New Hampshire, Arnie Arnesen, lamented. Rudy Giuliani's chief speechwriter, John Avlon, would note that having "been distracted by flash and wit and cash for too long," on 9/11 New Yorkers rediscovered enduring values such as grace, grit, and courage, while defending America valiantly, unquestioningly, as a "beacon of freedom, diversity, and equal opportunity."

Frustrations about frittering away the 1990s' potential, while letting Osama bin Laden get away, triggered new rounds of the post-Clinton legacy wars. Since 1999, President Clinton had tried freeing his legacy from the shadow of scandal, while trying to hide how concerned he was about doing it. To avoid looking self-conscious, the White House banned talk of the "L word," legacy, even as staffers catalogued Clinton's accomplishments. When pressed, Clinton proposed an epitaph for himself: "He had to make America work in a new world." Clinton said scholars would ask: "Did I help America transform itself so that we would still be the greatest nation in the world in a global economy" while uniting "the most . . . diverse population in our history."

Clinton resented Al Gore's distancing during the 2000 campaign. Gore rarely rebutted George W. Bush's barbs against Clinton. Accepting the Republican nomination, Bush dismissed Clinton's legacy, saying: "Our current president embodied the potential of a generation. So many talents. So much charm. Such great skill. But in the end, to what end? So much promise, to no great purpose." Charging that prosperity had been a drug "dulling our sense of urgency," Bush led thousands in shouting: "They had their chance. They have not led. We will."

At the Democratic National Convention, Clinton defended his legacy, after a suitably showy entrance. Handheld cameras followed him rock star style as he walked onto the stage to thrill his adoring fans and upstage Gore at Gore's own coronation. Clinton quoted Harry Truman, that "If you want to live like a Republican, you should vote for the Democrats." Clinton claimed, by Ronald Reagan's 1980 "are you better off" standard, "we're not just better off; we're also a better country . . . . more decent, more humane, and more united. Now, that's the purpose of prosperity."

As Clinton took his final bows, his cheerleaders listed family leave, welfare reform, NAFTA, budget surpluses, the booming economy, the renewed values conversation, the progress toward peace in Ireland. They echoed his pointillist picture of America the thriving: 22 million jobs, home ownership at 67 percent, 100,000 more police, and a job approval rating of 66 percent.

Most pundits and historians offered mixed reviews, agreeing that Mount Rushmore did not need rechiseling. After acknowledging improved numbers economically, socially, culturally, many complained that Clinton's flawed character prevented him from doing more, and made his governing process so messy. Progressive naysayers particularly irked Clinton. The journalist Christopher Hitchens snarled in *The Nation*: "He gutted welfare, bombed Sudan, and rented out the White House. If he were a Republican, liberals would have been appalled." Hitchens added that the Clinton years "locked-in the Reagan revolution." Richard Goodwin, a John Kennedy staffer, excoriated Clinton for the failing health care system, the worsening educational system, the intractable poverty, the "hard problems of race, and especially the squalor of the inner city." Amid so much bounty, Goodwin charged: "That lost opportunity is at the heart of the Clinton legacy."

The Great Clinton Disconnect

September 11 renewed this sense of missed opportunity. Clinton's fiscal policy helped nurture the boom. His welfare reform was a triple play. It expressed core beliefs, synthesized Great Society ideals with Reaganite realities, and worked, despite liberal predictions of mass misery. Clinton also tried jump-starting a values-based conversation, but his own foibles made him symbolize the problem rather than solve it.

Here, then, was the Great Clinton Disconnect. Bill Clinton was a magnificent politician who had many items to list in his White House stealth-legacy memos. These presidential successes resulted from his natural abilities, his near-perfect political pitch when he was focused, his policy mastery, his substantive Third Way vision, his love of politicking, his delight in governing, his passion for people, and his towering ambition. But as with an earnest student who memorizes facts for tests but cannot write analytic essays, Clinton's accomplishments did not add up to the historic, nation-building, society-transforming achievements he sought—or America needed.

The failure to capture Osama bin Laden was characteristic. Clinton made enough moves to be able to argue he tried. But his half-hearted approach, with critical lapses and a mystifying refusal to blame bin Laden for the USS *Cole* bombing, failed. Ali Soufan of the FBI recalls captured terrorists at Guantánamo saying: "You're responsible for 9/11. You didn't retaliate after the *Cole* and it emboldened bin Laden so he felt that we are untouchables." The 9/11 Commission confirmed that the political environment resisted such action—although Clinton demonstrated more courage with Kosovo. When the Cabinet opposed a massive attack to retaliate for the *Cole* bombing, the state department coordinator for counterterrorism, Michael Sheehan, asked: "What's it going to take to get them to hit al-Qaeda in Afghanistan? Does al-Qaeda have to attack the Pentagon?"

Many observers blame Clinton's failings on "Saturday Night Bill's" promiscuous, distracted, indulgent approach. His trashy pardon-gift-and-furniture-grab when leaving the White House reinforced theories blaming his professional shortcomings on his personal failings. Rather than focusing on the biographical, zooming out instead of zeroing in, solves this Clinton conundrum.

Viewing Clinton in the context of the 1990s makes it clear how daunting a task he faced. Clinton loved demonstrating his foresight by warning that this New Economy would force workers to "recareer" repeatedly; until pollsters warned that this prediction upset voters, even as it impressed them. Similarly, often, the more effective Clinton was in preparing America for the open, fully wired, twenty-first century, the less successful he was in defending tradition. The more he helped make America liquid, and the more he facilitated the rise of the Republic of Nothing and of Everything, the more the Republic of Something he sought to reform and preserve vanished.

This overwhelming task was too big for any president, especially in the post–Cold War age of polarized politics and divided government. Powerful social, cultural, and technological forces were creating a different society. These new realities unnerved many Americans, with no clear moral or social script, cheap, short-term jobs replacing stable employment, diversity in so many aspects of life, and the computer-boosted Internet revolutionizing everything. Clinton's behaviors did not make America modern or profane, although his lapses as his day's model American made things worse.

True, Clinton failed to solve the systemic problems of racial tensions, inequality, health care dysfunction, looming breakdowns in Social Security and Medicare, partisan polarization, epidemic personal distress, and family dysfunction, just as Ronald Reagan only slowed the growth rate of government. This list of "failures" actually demonstrates Clinton's audacity. Calling his inability to complete such tasks "failures" penalizes him for trying. Presidents are not magicians. In America the cranky, suspicious reporters, hostile rivals, and distracted constituents limit presidential power. Politicians—and historians—need more realistic expectations regarding what any leader can accomplish.

Clinton Defends His Legacy Aggressively

Over the years, Clinton defended his legacy ever more aggressively. In 2004, ABC's Peter Jennings interviewed him about a comparative poll among historians ranking him high on persuasiveness and economics, but low on morality. Clinton charged that historians underestimated the harm Kenneth Starr's $100 million unconstitutional "apparatus" caused, failing to find one "example of where I ever disgraced this country publicly." He admitted to having "made a terrible personal mistake—but I paid for it many times over." Clinton also asked why Jennings and his cronies "repeated every little sleazy thing" Starr "leaked."

Two years later, Clinton was even more belligerent. On the fifth anniversary of 9/11, ABC had broadcast a two-part "docudrama," *The Path to 9/11.* Downplaying the ambiguous intelligence and public skepticism, the $40 million show portrayed Clinton officials as vetoing an easy shot at bin Laden. Despite a Clinton-coordinated assault that forced some last-minute tweaks, Clinton was still fuming two weeks later. He pummeled Chris Wallace during a Fox News interview saying, "You did your nice little conservative hit job on me." Clinton acknowledged his failure to kill bin Laden but insisted, "I tried."

During Hillary Clinton's 2008 Democratic nomination battle, Bill Clinton attacked Barack Obama so aggressively even some friends accused him of race-baiting. Once again, as Clinton's standing cratered, his comeback began. Both Clintons' ultimately graceful acceptance of Obama's victory dissipated the bad feelings. Although Toni Morrison's labeling during the Lewinsky scandal of Clinton as the first black president was foolish, Clinton's warm relations with African Americans helped pave the way for America's actual first black president. The 2008 economic crash fed nostalgia for Clinton's good times, as Democrats blamed Republicans, obscuring Clinton's role.

A Bill Clinton Balance Sheet: Peace, Prosperity, Pluralism, and Progress

President Clinton was like that iconic Baby Boomer cartoon character Bugs Bunny, dodging disasters—many of his own making—outsmarting enemies, scoring victories, large and small. Clinton only won the presidency with 43 percent of the popular vote. He abandoned his signature health care reform months before Democrats lost the Congress for the first time since Dwight Eisenhower. He failed to break the 50 percent mark two years later in 1996. In 1998, he became the first elected president ever impeached. He left the country politically deadlocked.

Nevertheless, this indomitable, brilliant, raffish, never-say-die enchanter became the first Democratic president since Franklin Roosevelt to earn re-election. If Ronald Reagan's presidency could be summarized by three Ps of peace, prosperity, and patriotism, Clinton's presidency entailed four Ps of peace, prosperity, pluralism, and progress. Clinton benefited from governing after the Cold War ended and during America's longest peacetime economic expansion, with 116 months of growth in a row, generating 22 million new jobs. He presided over the Democratic Gilded Age, the twentieth century's only peace-and-prosperity decade without a Republican in charge—and without Democrats in opposition tempering the excess.

Clinton forged a Third Way, continuing Reagan's project of ending "the era of big government" with a leaner government, without abandoning the middle class, minorities, and the poor. Just as the Republican Dwight Eisenhower legitimized Franklin Roosevelt's Democratic revolution, at times Clinton legitimized Reagan's anti-Great-Society counterrevolution—while denying it, of course. Clinton's communications director Don Baer says that "If the FDR project was about using government as a leveraging force on the market to make the market system ready for progress after World War II, Clinton offered the mirror image. He used market forces to temper government so it could become a more effective force for progress going into the twenty-first century."

While demonizing Newt Gingrich as an "extremist," Clinton would seize the new, Reaganized center as a deficit-cutting, crime-busting Good Father: a Reaganite with a bigger heart and more fiscal self-control. Clinton injected a Democratic twist with his Family Leave Act, support for abortion rights, and push for diversity. While worrying about the materialistic excess this Baby Boomer boom triggered, he saw a broadly distributed prosperity as mass-producing the dignity and middle-class values that would unite a multicultural America as the exemplary mass middle-class nation.

Clinton's presidency was not as scandal-scarred as Richard Nixon's, as star-crossed as Jimmy Carter's, or as celebrated as John Kennedy's. It was not as tumultuous as George W. Bush's, as sobering as Barack Obama's, or as transformational as Ronald Reagan's. But it was unduly chaotic. Clinton's manic-depressive presidency often operated in the awkward intersection between

American politics at its most serious and American culture at its most absurd. As he sought to restructure the economy, reform health care, reinvent government, and reimagine America's future, as he coped with foreign messes in Bosnia, China, Kosovo, Somalia, Israel, and Rwanda, he also had to protect himself from American popular culture's gossip and his own moral failings.

Ultimately, Clinton shared responsibility for four disasters. Politically, many began speaking of two Americas, what would be George W. Bush's provincial, conservative, traditionalist Red America and Al Gore's more cosmopolitan, liberal, modernist Blue America. Culturally, Clinton's behavior validated the immorality he denounced, feeding a growing moral panic. Internationally, his admitted "failure" to neutralize the arch terrorist Osama bin Laden was part of a progression of blunders that failed to prevent the mass murders of September 11, 2001. And economically, just as the good times of the 1980s and 1990s were a bipartisan achievement, the crash of 2008 would be a bipartisan failure, rooted in Clinton's populist easy credit push to democratize home ownership by lowering mortgage standards and his elitist deregulatory rush to let Wall Street police itself. Clinton's potholed presidency fed and reflected the Nineties' querulous mood.

If in the 1980s Americans under Ronald Reagan looked back and, ultimately, reconciled with the Sixties' revolutions, the 1990s involved looking forward and pioneering the new world all these technological transformations would generate. Although he spoke about it so often it became the stuff of caricature, Clinton was correct: America was building its bridge to the twenty-first century. In the final decade of this brutal, magical, centrifugal century, this brave, new, bewildered America was more alienating yet more welcoming. How Americans navigated those contradictions would shape those years, and still shapes our times today.

Hillary Clinton's Bumpy Ride

Hillary Clinton had her own bumpy ride as First Lady. Act I was as Co-President and Health Care Czarina. In Act II, after the health care failure, she became Hillary the Celebrity, peddling her best-selling book *It Takes a Village*. Act III was most humiliating, as the Wronged Wife, although playing this more traditional role made her more popular. Finally, Act IV for the First Lady was the Independent Woman, as she fought to save her husband's presidency, starred in the 1998 congressional race, then ran successfully for the Senate.

Popular presidents often need a lightning rod, a close associate to play the enforcer and attract criticism away from them. For Ronald Reagan, it was Nancy Reagan. For George H. W. Bush, it was John Sununu. For Bill Clinton, it was Hillary Clinton. The role came naturally to Hillary Clinton. She was pricklier than her husband, especially when younger. Hillary Clinton became Hillary! by maturing, becoming wiser, less insecure, and less brittle privately, as well as independent publicly.

During the 1990s, Hillary Clinton emerged as a more pungent phrasemaker than her husband, who was more the quicksilver seducer than the Churchillian orator. During the 1992 campaign, her "I'm not sitting here [like] some little woman" and "I could have stayed home and baked cookies" quips stoked the gender wars, as her call for a "zone of privacy" anticipated the Clinton wars. Her 1995 statement in China that "human rights are women's rights and women's rights are human rights" reflected her modernist sensibility, even as her popularization of the African phrase "It takes a village to raise a child" reflected her traditionalism. And her January 1998 counterattack against the "vast right wing conspiracy" shaped the debate about presidential character in an age of hyperpartisanship and super-scandals.

Hillary Clinton's turbulent 1990s helped her find her voice and forge her own path as leader. The frustrated 45-year-old of 1992 turned 53—with a celebrity-heavy, $2 million-dollar birthday fundraiser—shortly before winning her Senate seat in 2000. It seems she tasted what *The Atlantic*'s Jonathan Rauch has popularized as the U-Turn. Neurological changes help explain the often abrupt reversal many experience from dashed expectations in the forties to the return of gratitude in the fifties, from obsessing about what you lack to appreciating all you have. In the twenty-first century, Hillary became the history-making, policy-generating Clinton as senator, secretary of state, and two-time presidential candidate. Reporters now speculated about what a voluble, irrepressible, male ex-president could do as First Spouse.

The Democratic Gilded Age

One of the many 1990s manifestos celebrating the newly wired world declared: Technology=Culture and Culture=Technology. This synthesis applies to politics, too. In a 1995 speech at Georgetown University, Clinton defined "our problems" as "personal and cultural and economic, political, and social," with the response requiring "public and private decision-making."

Clinton's America in the 1990s was like Reagan's in the 1980s with Democrats in charge, without the Soviets as a politically defining and culturally clarifying enemy, and with technological change on turbo speed. Without the Democrats in opposition, the 1990s became what many feared the 1980s would be—a time of aggressive capitalism and rampant selfishness, a Democratic Gilded Age, with a liberal leader implicitly approving, or at least rationalizing, the excess. "The Nineties are the Eighties without the moral disgust," Maureen Dowd sneered in *The New York Times*. Yet, at the same time, this lower case "d" democratic Gilded Age, this explosion of mass prosperity, allowed tens of millions to enjoy, indulge, feel safe, and dream as America became more diverse, inclusive, and happier.

Clinton's unique mix of vice and virtue, of cynicism and idealism, of craftiness and innocence, of frankness and falseness, worked in the 1990s. The Age of Clinton was an Age of Giddiness because so many of the social niceties that choreographed and constrained American public life had disappeared. The son of the man in the gray flannel suit now might be traipsing around in a sweat suit; young left-wing activists were not what one author called "rebels in white gloves"—and blue blazers—or even long-haired, unwashed hippies. In this syncretic age a conservative woman might sport a tattoo, a dot-com millionaire could very well have an earring or nose ring.

Beyond appearances, the Age of Clinton was an Age of Indulgence because fewer and fewer Americans followed the detailed road maps their parents and grandparents had followed—or at least pretended to publicly—emphasizing devotion to family, church, community, nation, and God, along with precepts such as fidelity, honor, grace, patriotism, self-control, and faith. The nation no longer had the Cold War's social and ideological corset, which reinforced values, even after the Sixties challenged them. The days of what the Reaganite social conservative William Bennett appreciated as "constructive hypocrisy" had become the time of "everybody does it." Fewer even pretended to stretch beyond indulging their immediate impulses and perceived "needs," meaning desires.

On a deeper level, the Age of Clinton was an Age of Skepticism because more and more Americans doubted the wisdom of having such a cultural and social consensus; they no longer knew what to believe and often doubted their own goodness. Rather than picking out whatever virtues there were in having a national script, many could only see the sexism, racism, narrowness, and provincialism that had buttressed America's traditional consensus.

For all he did to spawn this more cynical America, Clinton feared many of these changes. He knew a healthy America needed boundaries, anchors, uniting values, shared responsibilities, common dreams. He understood freedom's costs and complexities, not just its blessings. An America that rejected any kind of consensus would drift, like a hiker with no compass.

Clinton's Age was un-innocent but not un-idealistic. "America is an idea," Clinton believed, with diversity central to that idea. The prince of pluralism, he wondered how to "weave the threads of our coat of many colors into the fabric of one America," as he put it in his Farewell Address.

For Independence Day 2000, *The New York Times's* "op-art" feature "What is America" illustrated Clinton's America of many colors. Thirty-five different people were photographed, each waving an American flag and saying a word or two: "freedom . . . money . . . power . . . hot dogs . . . Chevrolet . . . sacrifice . . . sex . . . imperialism . . . diversity . . . star power . . . religious freedom . . . plastics . . . possibility . . . ignorance . . . my adopted country . . . contradiction . . . choice . . . E-Z Pass . . . needs healing . . . hope . . . open-minded . . . jazz . . . ketchup . . . corny . . . original ideas . . . business . . . consumerism . . . fun . . . relentless comedy . . . exhaustion . . . lost opportunities . . . Sundar (beautiful) from India . . . excess . . . everything," and, finally, two black twins from New York City just said "Ahhhhhhhh!" Not one was a white male dressed in jacket and tie. This prose poem captured the Clinton Nineties' sensibility in its fluidity, diversity, self-criticism, and irreverence, mixed with pride, creativity, and love.

Historians tend to overlook these good feelings and grimace at epochs that made most people smile. In packaging decades as morality tales, historians treat eras of great prosperity—the Twenties, the Fifties, the Eighties, and the Nineties—as times of great selfishness that end with the proper punishment. By contrast, the years of the Depression in the 1930s are "great"; the generation that fought in World War II was "the greatest." The 1990s were both awesome—an overused word then and now—and awful, an era of impressive expansiveness and sobering shoddiness, in Americans and their leaders.

Clinton wondered how to "widen the circle of opportunity, deepen the meaning of freedom, and strengthen the bonds of our community." He was struggling with the meaning of freedom, in a culture that often sought freedom from any kind of meaning. Both "opportunity" and "freedom" served as solvents in the modern world, undermining "community," promoting irresponsibility. He wanted pluralism with some internal cohesion and without balkanization. He wanted to protect American freedom, individualism, and opportunity, now accelerating at warp speed on the information superhighway, from spinning off into libertinism, hedonism, and a corrosive selfishness. And, most practically, he believed that without a stable, well-distributed, more equitable economic foundation, without meaningful work as well as living wages for as many Americans as possible, America's mass middle-class civilization would be embattled. Essentially, Clinton was struggling to see what he could define as solid and shared in an America that was often changing and increasingly individualistic, for better and worse.

In *Tuesdays with Morrie* by Mitch Albom, the Oprah-boosted mega-best seller and 1999 made-for-TV movie, the wise, dying sociology professor, Morrie Schwartz, objects to the all-American 24/7 "brainwashing" that insists: "Owning things is good. More money is good. More property is good. More commercialism is good. More is good." In his 1998 novel, *A Man in Full*, Tom Wolfe observed that this "endless quest" for more was supposed to provide tranquility "and instead you become a bigger and bigger slave to how you think others are judging you."

These afflictions were the natural side effects of American capitalism, consumerism, and individualism. Alexis de Tocqueville called individualism the democratic ailment, which first "saps the virtues of public life," then metastasizes into untrammeled "egotism." A century later, in 1944 Morrie Schwartz's favorite poet, W. H. Auden, predicted that "Idealism will be replaced by Materialism" and "Knowledge will degenerate into a riot of subjective visions"—a fair description of modern American popular culture. These processes were so powerful in addicting individuals to materialism while melting basic bonds that the Orwellian fear of a *1984* dystopia had become moot. Anarchy not autocracy, aimless anomie not Big Brother, now threatened the American community—and psyche.

Following the Cold War, Americans traded demons. Fears of a totalitarian Big Brother and of superpower nuclear war were replaced by Everywhere Evils that Clouded the Commons, ubiquitous everyday forces that could turn suddenly deadly or deadly forces that made the humdrum lethal. Clinton's Farewell Address warned that "the forces of integration that have created these good opportunities also make us more subject to global forces of destruction, to terrorism, organized crime and narco-trafficking, the spread of deadly weapons and disease, the degradation of the global environment." Dr. Tevi Troy, George W. Bush's deputy secretary of health and human services, notes that "The first decade of the twenty-first century brought numerous unpredictable crises to American life, including terror attacks, destructive hurricanes, massive snowstorms, raging wildfires, and near global economic collapses originating in both the United States and Europe. This unprecedented series of natural and man-made catastrophes has generated concerns about our ability to respond to future emergencies."

Clinton's occasional wistful jokes about missing the Cold War's clarity were on point. The Cold War identified clear enemies and united America. John Updike, in *Rabbit at Rest* (1990), would have his emblematic character Harry

Angstrom wonder "Without the Cold War, what's the point of being an American?" The Cold War gave regular Joes like Harry "a reason to get up in the morning," and patriotic politicians incentive to cooperate. Instead, Harry "eats too much lunch, consuming the last French fry that came with his tasteless hamburger, mopping up salt with it in his fingers."

At their worst, as in the gift-grabbing-and-pardon-granting episodes of January 2001, Bill and Hillary Clinton reflected this modern American decadence. Their behavior frequently revealed them to be small, tawdry, arrogant, presumptuous, yet always self-righteous. They did not raise the behavioral bar, as they promised, they demolished it—becoming one more solvent, bringing about this Age of Un-Innocence, where many Americans did not even try to stretch, did not aspire morally high enough to be hypocritical.

Although a sentimental patriot who could shed tears at a stirring July fourth ceremony, Clinton was no sap. One of his favorite books was Reinhold Niebuhr's *Moral Man and Immoral Society*. In that 1932 masterpiece, Niebuhr preached that "Collective man . . . must content himself with a more modest goal . . . not the creation of an ideal society . . . but a society in which there will be enough justice, and in which coercion will be sufficiently non-violent to prevent his common enterprise from issuing into complete disaster." In embracing so many different, even contradictory, positions, Clinton accepted this subtle, sober vision for America—and for his own behavior. He was OK with paradox, with complexity. He also had such a powerful life force he wrapped this realism, like Whitman's Mystic Trumpeter, in his "exulting, culminating song," with "Joy! joy! in freedom, worship, love! joy in the ecstasy of life!"

Bill Clinton brought joy, exhilaration, exaltation, inspiration to the American people; but he also brought shame, anger, frustration, disappointment, confusion, and despair. What should have been a euphoric time with an incredibly popular president, a new Era of Good Feelings, was instead an Era of Mixed Feelings with a polarizing president, laced with fears of economic decline, moral collapse, individual drift, and political gridlock. After the 1990s and Clinton's tenure, America was more inclusive, thanks to the Rainbow Rebellion; more horizontal, thanks to the Digital Revolution; more prosperous thanks to the Information Age Reset; more forgiving, thanks to all the Gender Bending; more fun thanks to the Contingency Carnival, and more wary of excess thanks to the Republican Resistance. But it was also a lonelier and angrier country that was more confused, more self-indulgent, more nihilistic, and more balkanized. Seeing how these phenomena played out in the 1990s explains many of today's contradictions, tensions, limitations, and blessings.

Bill Clinton was the poet laureate of the Republic of Everything, the first rainbow president. He genuinely celebrated the new diverse America that was emerging. He appreciated the power of the Internet as the Ultimate Everything Machine, this information superhighway going in numerous directions simultaneously, with a googol on-ramps and off-ramps, starting points and destinations. Clinton's exuberant expansiveness, powered by the Internet's capacity, would inspire the next generation, the Millennials, to see everythingness as its own reward. Mark Zuckerberg, sixteen years old when Clinton left the White House and three years away from launching Facebook, would devote himself to his "mission" of "making the world open."

Although Clinton feared that too much openness would create a people adrift, a Republic of Nothing, the propulsive power of America's new technologies and constantly renewing popular culture proved too formidable for him. Although he was smart enough to understand the need for enduring values and traditional anchors in a Republic of Something, his own character flaws made matters worse. His "everybody does it defense" hastened the rise of the Republic of Nothing.

Bill Clinton understood that coping with snakes permanently in the garden should never preclude hoping for a garden free of snakes, individually and collectively. This appealing American character trait, seeking "a more perfect union"—and president—in an imperfect world, created glorious hypocrites and noble game changers like Bill and Hillary Clinton. Modern Americans lived in a world with change as the only constant even as the Constitution endured. The tumult would continue in the twenty-first century, with terrorism, hyperindividualism, economic distress, cultural drift. But remarkably, and thanks to the communal glues and ingenious catalysts both Clintons updated and strengthened, America's new Republic of Everything and Nothing not just survived, it thrived.

Author's Note on Method and Sources

Having written about the Clintons as both a real-time commentator during the 1990s and as an historian in both books and articles, writing this book has been a particularly interesting intellectual experience, charting my own evolution. With the passage of time, learning about the administration from the inside out and not just through the headlines, and, benefiting from my technique, which is seeing the Clintons in the context of the 1990s, I have become more appreciative of what Bill Clinton tried to do, what he might have been able to do, and what he actually did. I recently assigned my 2008 book *Why Moderates Make the Best Presidents* to a class studying the "History of the American Presidency." One student found my interpretation there of Clinton particularly tough. My disappointment with Clinton reminded her of her generation's disappointment with Barack Obama.

Herein, of course, lies the excitement of interpretive history. As we learn more, as we uncover more evidence, as we place the information in a broader context, and as we assess from a longer chronological perspective rather than in the moment, our understandings evolve, becoming richer, more lasting. My big "aha moment" with Clinton came from reading the memos, writings, and, most particularly, the oral histories of moderate, Third Way, New Democrat advisers like Al From and Bruce Reed, supplemented by interviews with aides such as Michael Waldman, Don Baer, Jeff Shesol, and Al From himself. Starting to see what Waldman called the "connective tissue" in the Clinton story, I concluded that Clinton was as ideological a president as Ronald Reagan, with a take, an approach, he kept to surprisingly consistently while governing, although not always of course. I have tried not to be too affected by the false nostalgia for Clinton in the Age of Obama, or seduced by his infectious exuberance. Still, it is important to appreciate Clinton's love of people, politics, policy-making, and the job of being president, in all it frustrations and glories, especially given the contrast with a tired, dispirited Barack Obama.

Seeing the initiatives the administration launched that lasted, and what issues the press harped on that disappeared, as well as pulling back the camera lens and understanding the Clinton administration in the context of the 1990s' sweeping transformations, I can now appreciate both Clintons' insight and far-sight more than I did before. Al From and Bruce Reed emphasized welfare reform as the defining issue, the proof that Bill Clinton was no Great Society, big government Democrat. Moreover, Clinton's welfare reform worked, defying liberals' doomsday predictions, showing that the Third Way could be the Way to Go. To me, the fight against crime is as important, if not more so. It proved that Bill Clinton refused to be a "Bleeding Heart Liberal" or a "Limousine Liberal." He could feel the pain of millions, both black and white, traumatized and held hostage by America's appalling post-1960s crime wave.

At the same time, in this reading, both Hillary and Bill Clinton's moral blind spots, although clearly exaggerated by their enemies, nevertheless become even more appalling. Undermining a presidency that truly could have been great is a greater sin than undermining a presidency destined to be mediocre.

That consciousness of the gap between the potential and the achievement, and the often petty reasons why the hopes about the man from Hope went unfulfilled, explains my deep disappointment with Clinton when he governed. Broadening my perspective in retrospect, absorbing and trying to make sense of the Clintons in the context of the 1990s, made me more forgiving. The intensity of the change in the 1990s generated an anxiety about change in the 1990s that few leaders could change. And as the Change-Agent-in-Chief, Clinton often attracted the anxiety toward him. Bill and Hillary Clinton's very boldness and vision in facing change often made them defined and burdened by those changes.

This book rests on four research pillars. The first pillar is the real-time voices of Bill Clinton, Hillary Clinton, and their aides, captured in the documents now available in the William Jefferson Clinton Presidential Library, many of which were released in the last year. These memoranda, e-mails, and position papers were supplemented by the American Presidency Project's online collection of every formal presidential statement ever made. Together, these help the researcher listen in to history as it was being shaped.

The second pillar is many of these history-makers' recollections, captured most vividly in the Miller Center of the University of Virginia's extraordinary Oral History Program stemming from its William J. Clinton Presidential Project. Fortunately, the first batch of more than one hundred interviews was released on November 14, 2014, making this book one of the first to use them, along with these newly released Clinton papers. I supplemented these testimonies with some interviews, and thank Julian Adams, Don Baer, Richard Behar, John Dickerson, Thomas Dunne, Al From, David Greenberg, Steve Greenberg, Stephen Hess, Ann Lewis, Thomas McLarty, Norm Orenstein, Dan Patterson, Steve Rabinowitz, Jonathan Rauch, David Samuels, Jeff Shesol, Lesley Stahl, Michael Waldman, and two businessmen and one journalist who requested anonymity. I also scrutinized various memoirs from the time. Most helpful were Bill Clinton's memoir, Hillary Clinton's memoir, and the detailed presidential memories recorded so effectively by Taylor Branch in *The Clinton Tapes*.

The third pillar, moving beyond the White House and Washington, is rooted in extensive research in the newspapers, magazines, books, movies, television shows, songs, and videos from the 1990s. In this Internet age, historians can bathe in the popular culture of the period, absorbing the moving images and sounds, as well as the ideas of the time.

Finally, more conventional secondary sources round out a rich and illuminating base for discussing the 1990s as the Age of Clinton. The Notes section details my intellectual debt to so many thoughtful writers about the period. Still, I am particularly indebted to the sociologist Zygmunt Bauman, whose work builds on *The Communist Manifesto*'s enduring insight about capitalism and modernity turning the solid liquid and the sacred profane. Works by the philosopher Charles Taylor, the sociologist Robert Putnam, and the late historian Christopher Lasch rounded out my understanding of the 1990s as modern times, aided in particular by Walter Isaacson's magnificent book *The Innovators*, analyzing what I came to call the Great American Hook-Up, when computers went online. The journalists Joe Klein, John Harris, and Haynes Johnson, did admirable work in providing the first draft of history, with rich reporting and insights about Clinton and the 1990s. The historians Steven M. Gillon in *The Pact*, James T. Patterson in *Restless Giant*, and Daniel T. Rodgers in *The Age of Fracture*, among many, many others, helped me put it all in historical perspective.

Thanks to the ease of finding all presidential statements online in the easily searchable American Presidency Project database, www.presidency.ucsb.edu /index.php, none are specially cited below. Similarly, most statistics, unless cited, are from census data or other easily searchable sources.

More broadly, just as Hillary Clinton taught that it takes a village to raise a child, it takes a network of goodwill and great helpers to produce a book. I thank: McGill University colleagues, especially Elizabeth Elbourne and Chris Manfredi for their remarkable support; various archivists at the William Jefferson Clinton Presidential Library, the George H.W. Bush Presidential Library, and the George W. Bush Presidential Library, with special praise for Herbert Ragan, who spent two days feeding me amazing photographs; Washington friends Barry Jackson, Andrew Selee, and especially Steven Bennett and Darrell West, who invited me to the Brookings Institution this fall.

Every page in this book benefited from the amazing research and partnership of Adam Culligan, along with the always reliable Sébastien Alexander and Zemira Zahava Wolfe.

I also appreciate Chris Allbritton's thoroughness, John Avlon's vision, Ephraim Gerber's erudition, Donniel Hartman's wisdom, Carolyn Hessel's extraordinary support, Amy Sheon's perception, Suzanne Last Stone's challenges, Peter Wyetzner's classical background, and Thea Wieseltier's flair.

Very special thanks to Noam Zion, Steve Greenberg, and my two brothers, Tevi Troy and Dan Troy, for reading the manuscript so carefully; the tremendous time and sagacity each invested reflects a broader gift from them individually of enduring friendship.

Among his many contributions and kindnesses, my agent Don Fehr signed me with the legendary Thomas Dunne, whose American history training, love of politics, and extensive publishing experience made him the ideal editor. I thank Thomas and his impressive team, especially Peter Joseph—whose edits were only the first of many contributions to this project—Melanie Fried, Heather G. Florence and Will Anderson.

Finally, remembering Bob Dole's rejoinder to Hillary Clinton—"it does not take a village to raise a child; it takes a family to raise a child"–I thank my parents, Elaine and Bernard Dov Troy, my father-in-law Marcel Adams, and, most important, my wife and four children, who, like the dove of peace, have blessed me with golden beauty and spring-like hope since the 1990s.

A Guide to Abbreviations in Notes

AAS	*Austin American Statesman*
BosG	*Boston Globe*
BC	Bill Clinton
BC Lib	William J. Clinton Presidential Center and Park, Little Rock, Arkansas
BC Mem	William J. Clinton, *My Life* (New York, 2004)
Blair MSS	Series 1-3 Diane D. Blair Papers (MC 1632), Special Collections, University of Arkansas Libraries, Fayetteville, Arkansas
CSM	*Christian Science Monitor*
HRC	Hillary Rodham Clinton
LAT	*Los Angeles Times*
OH MilC	Oral History from the William J. Clinton Presidential History Project, Miller Center of Public Affairs, University of Virginia, Charlottesville, Virginia, millercenter.org /president/clinton/oralhistory
Nwswk	*Newsweek*
NYT	*New York Times*
NYTM	*New York Times Magazine*
PInq	*Philadelphia Inquirer*
PR	Previously Restricted Document
TNR	*The New Republic*
USNWR	*U.S. News & World Report*
WasPo	*Washington Post*
WSJ	*Wall Street Journal*

Notes

Prologue

p. 2 Mourning the 18,300 . . . : Kevin J. Strom and Marianne W. Zawitz, "Firearm Injury and Death from Crime, 1993–97," National Criminal Justice Reference Service, U.S. Department of Justice (2000), 1.

p. 2 "just welled up. . . .": Taylor Branch, *The Clinton Tapes* (New York, 2009), 82, 83.

p. 3 "government has . . .": *WasPo*, November 16, 1993, A21.

p. 3 "premier civil rights issue . . .": *BosG*, November 6, 1993.

p. 4 "Saint Hillary": *NYTM*, May 23, 1993, 6:22.

p. 4 "white glove pulpit": Nancy Reagan, "Remarks for Associated Press Publishers' Luncheon," May 4, 1987, 6, F95–109, White House Office of Records Management, Ronald Reagan Library, Simi Valley, CA.

p. 5 "Government did not . . ." Interview with Jeff Shesol, February 4, 2015, Washington, DC.

p. 5 "saved progressive . . .": Interview with Al From, February 3, 2015, Washington, DC.

p. 7 "Hyperlinks . . .": Frederick Levine et al., *The Cluetrain Manifesto* (New York, 2000), xxii.

1. 1990

p. 11 Charging $12,500 . . . "if he'd . . .": *Inc.*, April 2, 1982. See also *BosG*, November 26, 1987, 39.

p. 11 quick flight: *AAS*, December 31, 1989, B2. See also *LAT*, January 2, 1990, A20.

p. 11 Houstonians were . . . : See *Houston Chronicle*, December 29, 1989, 6. See also *Houston Post*, January 1, 1990, A21, A22.

p. 12 "New Year's Eve Party . . .": *Houston Chronicle*, December 29, 1989, 1.

p. 12 "the greatest . . .": *NYT*, January 17, 1990, A25.

p. 12 "When people are . . .": Interview with Al From, February 3, 2015, Washington, D.C.

p. 13 "recivilization": Steven Pinker, The Better Angels of Our Nature (New York, 2011), 116.

p. 13 "an entire Venezuela's . . ." Robert Lang in *USA Today*, August 10, 2011, A1.

p. 13 at least 438,000 . . . more than double . . . : "Estimates of the Unauthorized Immigrant

Population Residing in the United States: 1990 to 2000," Office of Policy and Planning, U.S. Immigration and Naturalization Service (Washington, D.C., 2003), 8.

p. 14 "We were the earliest . . . give up . . .": *LAT,* January 2, 1990, A20.

p. 14 "The Cold War is not . . .": Frances Fitzgerald, *Way Out There in the Blue* (New York, 2000), 467.

p. 15 "the most difficult . . .": Michael R. Beschloss and Strobe Talbott, *At the Highest Levels* (Boston, MA, 1993), 172.

p. 16 "losing favor" . . . : *Nwswk,* January 4, 1988, 46.

p. 16 "the movie . . .": Charles Kolb, *White House Daze* (New York, 1994), 3.

p. 16 "Ronald Reagan left . . .": *WSJ,* January 5, 1990, A8.

p. 16 rating of 76 percent: *LAT,* February 19, 1990, 27.

p. 16 "He actually . . .": *WSJ,* January 5, 1990, A8.

p. 17 "defining deviancy down": Daniel P. Moynihan, "Defining Deviancy Down: How We've Become Accustomed to Alarming Levels of Crime and Destructive Behavior," *American Scholar* 62 (1993), 17–30.

p. 17 "The true winner . . .": *USA Today,* March 14, 1990, 6A.

p. 18 Peter Bloch sarcastically . . . : *NYT,* April 11, 1990, A25.

p. 18 "women wearing . . . : *WasPo,* July 15, 1990, G1.

p. 18 "age of escapist . . .": *Time,* June 25, 1990, 16.

p. 18 "make a good . . . Values are . . .": *USNWR,* June 25, 1990, 22.

p. 19 "two Achilles' . . .": *Time,* October 22, 1990, 26.

p. 19 "By breaking . . .": *TNR,* May 22, 2000, 25.

p. 19 "Remember, George . . .": Margaret Thatcher, *Downing Street Years* (New York, 1993), 824.

p. 19 "the two George . . .": *Time,* January 7, 1991, 18.

p. 19 "I'll prevail . . .": Colin L. Powell with Joseph E. Persico, *My American Journey* (New York, 1995), 486.

p. 20 Ninety percent . . . : *WSJ,* January 15, 1990, A10.

p. 20 "We're not . . . There won't . . .": *WasPo,* January 21, 1990, A1.

p. 20 18.7 million . . . $30 trillion . . . : *NYT,* January 17, 1990, A25.

p. 20 7,370 blacks: Joint Center for Political and Economic Studies, *Black Elected Officials 1990* (Lanham, MD, 1991), 1.

p. 20 "when there were . . .": *NYT,* January 1, 1990, L27.

p. 20 "Know what . . .": *LAT,* January 7, 1990, 1.

p. 21 "We love . . .": *WasPo,* January 24, 1990, A22.

p. 22 Howard Schultz . . . : *WSJ,* November 6, 1989, B1.

p. 22 "Thank you . . .": Steven Levy, *In The Plex* (New York, 2011), 275.

p. 22 "nice kid . . .": *CNN All Politics,* August 6, 1998.

p. 23 "We revealed . . .": BC Mem, 314.

p. 25 "opportunity quotient . . . anxiety . . .": Ted Morgan, *On Becoming American* (Boston, MA, 1978), 4.

p. 25 liquidity: Zygmunt Bauman, *Liquid Modernity* (Cambridge, UK, 2003), viii.

p. 25 "An era in . . .": Interview with Michael Waldman, February 2, 2015, New York, NY.

p. 26 "universalization . . .": Francis Fukuyama, "The End of History," *The National Interest,* Summer, 1989: 3–18.

2. 1991

p. 28 "what can happen . . .": Charles Jennings, J. Gordon Routley, and Mark Chubb, "High Rise Office Building Fire, One Meridian Plaza, Philadelphia, Pennsylvania," USFA Fire Investigation Technical Report Series Report 049, FEMA (Washington, D.C., 1991), 2, 1, 13, 16.

p. 28 "squirted like . . .": *Philadelphia Daily News,* October 21, 2009, 7.

p. 28 lawsuits drained . . . : *WSJ,* October 16, 1992, A1.

p. 28 "tort taxes": *USNWR,* May 22, 1995, 24.

p. 28 Richard Overton sued . . . : *Overton v. Anheuser-Busch Co.* 205 Mich. App. 259 (1994).

p. 29 McDonald's: NYT, October 28, 2013.

p. 29 After Aetna . . . : *PInq,* November 23, 1999, A1.

p. 29 lost thirteen. . . . : *American Forces Press Service,* February 27, 2001.

p. 29 "What happens . . .": *Time,* January 7, 1991, 24.

p. 30 "as a father . . .": "President George Bush Self Typed Letter to Family," December 31, 1990," Selected Documents from the Archives, George Bush Presidential Library and Museum, College Station, Texas.

p. 30 "the mother . . .": *WSJ,* January 21, 1991, A9.

p. 30 "scheduled to die . . .": *WasPo,* February 28, 1991, D1.

p. 30 "You cannot have . . .": Colin L. Powell with Joseph E. Persico, *My American Journey* (New York, 1995), 168.

p. 31 Only John F. Kennedy's . . . : *NYT,* January 18, 1991, A14.

p. 31 "I learn more . . .": *Time,* January 6, 1992, 24.

p. 31 "help the enemy": Peter Petre and H. Norman Schwarzkopf, *It Doesn't Take a Hero* (New York, 1992), 399.

p. 31 Eighty percent . . . : *WasPo,* February 21, 1991, D1.

p. 31 "I knew . . .": Powell, *My American Journey,* 529.

p. 32 "some wars . . .": *TNR,* February 18, 1991, 8.

p. 32 "This may be . . .": *WSJ,* March 1, 1991, A1.

p. 32 "something basic . . .": Schwarzkopf, *It Doesn't Take a Hero,* 441, 442.

p. 32 Bush's poll . . . : *WasPo,* March 6, 1991, A1.

p. 33 "These days . . .": *Sun Sentinel,* December 31, 1991, 1E.

p. 33 "Bush has shown . . .": *LAT,* March 2, 1991, 29.

p. 33 70 percent: *WasPo,* March 6, 1991, A1.

p. 33 He subsequently lost . . . : New York *Daily News,* June 19, 2012.

p. 33 "Every black . . .": *LAT,* December 16, 1991, 1.

p. 34 "Marriage among . . .": *LAT,* July 17, 1990, 14.

p. 34 The child poverty rate . . : *NYT,* January 5, 1990, A31.

p. 34 "ghetto poor": *NYT,* August 26, 1990, A4.

p. 35 "cultural tourism . . .": *TNR,* November 11, 1991, 24.

p. 35 "up to the Jew . . .": Henry Goldschmidt, *Race and Religion Among the Chosen People of Crown Heights* (Piscataway, NJ, 2006), 45.

p. 36 "frame . . . never saw. . . .": Goldman, Breslin in *Jewish Week,* August 9, 2011.

p. 36 rioters injured: Edward S. Shapiro, "Interpretations of the Crown Heights Riot," *American Jewish History* 90 (2002): 97.

p. 36 "bitch, bitch . . .": *NYT,* July 2, 1991, A1.

p. 37 "Who would I . . .": *WasPo,* October 6, 1991, A10.

p. 37 "the ultimate . . .": *Chicago Tribune,* December 29, 1991, 1.

p. 37 "The times . . .": *NYT,* October 8, 1991, A1.

p. 37 "spoken of . . .": "Nomination of Judge Clarence thomas to Be Associate Justice of the Supreme Court of the United States: Hearings Before the Committee on the Judiciary," United States Senate, 102d Congress, 1st Session, October 11–13, 1991 (Washington, D.C., 1993), 37, 64, 124, 38.

p. 37 "The lateness . . .": *NYT,* October 8, 1991, A1.

p. 38 "We have never . . .": *NYT,* October 12, 1991, L10.

p. 38 "They are trying . . .": George H. W. Bush letter to Robert W. Black of Lubbock, Texas, October 10, 1991, in George Bush, *All The Best, George Bush* (New York, 2013), 537, 538.

p. 38 "their daily lives . . .": *WasPo,* October 17, 1991, A1.

p. 38 "They are men . . ." *NYT,* October 8, 1991, A1.

p. 38 "I died . . .": Jane Mayer, *Strange Justice* (New York, 1994), 257, 299.

p. 38 "still have . . .": *NYT,* October 13, 1991, A1.

p. 38 "in excruciating . . .": Ellis Cose, *The Rage of a Privileged Class* (New York, 1993), 1.

p. 38 "Being black . . .": Shelby Steele, *The Content of Our Character* (New York, 1991), 37, 4.

p. 38 secretly filmed . . . : "True Colors," *ABC Primetime Live,* September 26, 1991.

p. 39 "Graduate of Thelma . . .": *NYT,* April 26, 1992, A31.

p. 39 "We must never . . .": *PInq,* June 6, 1997, A3.

p. 40 "being called unethical . . .": "Another Judge Thomas Digest," rec.humor.funny, www .netfunny.com/rhf/jokes/91q4/jud.html.

p. 40 "the faults . . .": *Orlando Sentinel,* November 1, 1991, A23.

p. 40 "articulate, well-spoken . . .": *Newsday,* December 20, 1991, 133.

p. 40 "all rapists . . .": *Vanity Fair,* March 1992.

p. 40 "I'm not a blue. . . .": *BosG,* December 20, 1991, 3.

p. 41 "In David Duke . . .": *Time,* November 25, 1991, 110.

p. 41 "the promoter . . ." *WasPo,* October 26, 1991, A6.

p. 41 "soft male. . . .": Robert Bly, *Iron John* (Cambridge, MA, 1990), 2, 6.

p. 42 "reading and. . . .": Dinesh D'Souza, *Illiberal Education* (New York, 1991), 6–9.

p. 42 "attack on . . .": Arthur M. Schlesinger Jr., *The Disuniting of America* (New York, 1991), 125, 17.

p. 42 "a singular citizenship . . .": Michael Walzer, *What It Means to Be an American* (New York, 1996), 17.

p. 42 "threatened . . .": Richard Bernstein, *Dictatorship of Virtue* (New York, 1994), 23.

p. 42 "the inequality. . . .": Todd Gitlin, *The Twilight of Common Dreams* (New York, 1995), 234, 126.

p. 43 less than half . . . Seventy percent . . . : *WasPo,* October 23, 1991, A1.

p. 43 Forty percent. . . . If we raised . . . : *NYT,* June 21, 1990, A16.

p. 44 "smelling if not . . .": *PInq,* March 17, 1992.

p. 44 "George Bush Went . . .": *LAT,* November 6, 1991, 1.

p. 44 "They have an . . .": *WasPo,* October 17, 1991, A1.

p. 45 "Democrats for the . . . Southern white . . .": Kenneth S. Baer, *Reinventing Democrats* (Lawrence, KS, 2000), 81, 82, 126.

p. 45 "offer a progressive. . . .": William A. Galston, "Putting a Democrat in the White House," *The Brookings Review* 7 (1989): 21–25.

p. 45 "a national . . .": Baer, *Reinventing Democrats,* 164.

p. 45 "the Democratic Party's. . . .": Democratic Leadership Council, "The New Orleans Declaration: A Democratic Agenda for the 1990s," National Conference, March 22–25, 1990.

p. 45 "equal opportunity . . . : Al From OH 2006, MilC.

p. 45 "out of touch . . .": Bill Clinton in Al From, *The New Democrats* (New York, 2013, 2014), pp. ix, 1–2.

p. 46 "When someone . . . ": Bruce Reed OH 2004, MilC.

p. 46 "leaner, activist . . .": *TNR,* February 3, 1992, 24.

p. 47 Jock Young would observe . . . : Jock Young, *The Exclusive Society* (London, UK, 1999), 164.

p. 47 "culture of narcissism": Christopher Lasch, *The Culture of Narcissism* (New York, 1979).

p. 47 "emotional hemophilia": Jerold J. Kreisman and Hal Straus. *I Hate You—Don't Leave Me* (New York, 1991), 11, 12.

p. 48 "Are you living . . .": *WasPo,* March 16, 1990, B1.

3. 1992

p. 50 "The best thing . . .": *WasPo,* November 4, 1992, C1.

p. 50 "the most successful . . .": *NYT,* April 6, 1992, A1.

p. 51 "We've got . . .": Karen Blumenthal, *Mr. Sam* (New York, 2011), 47.

p. 51 Multiple studies . . . : Stephen Ciccarella, David Neumark, and Junfu Zhang, "The Effects of Wal-Mart on Local Labor Markets," *Journal of Urban Economics* 63 (2008): 405–30.

p. 52 "If it is possible . . .": Interview with Thomas Dunne, February 27, 2014, New York, NY.

p. 52 "to maintain . . .": *WSJ,* February 13, 1992, A3.

p. 53 "If you're . . .": HRC, *Living History* (New York, 2003), 52.

p. 53 "this subject . . .": Stan Greenberg OH 2005, MilC.

p. 53 "Hillary loves . . .": Gail Sheehy, *Hillary's Choice* (New York, 2000), 171.

p. 53 "adversary culture . . . . legitimization": Lionel Trilling, *Beyond Culture* (New York, 1965, 1978), xv, 23.

p. 53 "that the system . . . .": HRC, *Living History,* 38, 41.

p. 54 "another Bobby . . .": Al From OH 2006, MilC.

p. 54 "by at least . . .": *PInq,* February 29, 1992, D1.

p. 55 "We're voting for . . .": *Nwswk,* February 3, 1992, 23.

p. 55 "What do you . . .": "In 1992, Clinton Conceded Marital 'Wrongdoing,'" *WasPo,* Special Report, 1998.

p. 55 "at odds with him . . .": Stan Greenberg OH 2005, MilC.

p. 56 "We entered . . .": Interview with Richard Behar, February 27, 2014, New York, NY.

p. 57 "maturing Baby Boom . . . .": *Orlando Sentinel,* February 3, 1992, C1.

p. 57 "To be a modernist . . .": Marshall Berman, *All That Is Solid Melts into Air* (New York, 2009), 345–46.

p. 57 "I suppose . . .": *WasPo,* March 17, 1992, A1.

p. 58 "whether a governor . . . :" *NYT,* March 8, 1992, A1.

p. 58 She and her cronies . . . : Sally Bedell Smith, *For the Love of Politics* (New York, 2007), 19.

p. 58 "electability problem . . . .": *Buffalo News,* March 16, 1992, A1.

p. 58 "The Hillary Problem": *NYT,* March 26, 1992, A23.

p. 58 "the overbearing . . .": *NYT,* May 18, 1992, A15.

p. 58 "We may not . . .": David Maraniss, *First in His Class* (New York, 1995), 375.

p. 59 "feminine identity": Dana Crowley Jack, *Silencing the Self* (Cambridge, 1991), 72.

p. 59 "You know . . .": Stan Greenberg OH 2005, MilC.

p. 59 "I have compromised . . .": "Thanksgiving Day, 1996," Blair MSS.

p. 59 "reorganization of . . .": Saul Hillel Benjamin to BC, HRC, et al., March 17, 1992, Blair MSS.

p. 59 "Sex always sells . . .": *NYT,* January 26, 1992, C1.

p. 60 "You're stupid . . .": Susan Thomases OH 2006, MilC.

p. 60 Forty-two percent . . . : *LAT,* February 19, 1992, 1.

p. 61 Half of Americans . . . : *NYT,* March 30, 1992, A15.

p. 61 twenty-two overdrawn: *NYT,* August 23, 1992, A41.

p. 61 "a reactionary . . .": *NYT,* March 17, 1992, A18.

p. 61 "Folks, you've . . .": *Buffalo News,* May 23, 1992, A4.

p. 62 "this remarkable tale . . . .": Robert James Waller, *The Bridges of Madison County* (New York, 1992), ix.

p. 62 In 1991 . . . country proved . . . : *Rolling Stone,* April 16, 1992, 16.

p. 62 "And I didn't . . .": *LAT,* April 27, 1992, 1.

p. 62 "Don't do it . . . BLACK . . .": *TNR,* May 25, 1992, 23.

p. 63 "LAPD ARE . . . BLACK POWER . . .": *LAT,* April 30, 1992, 1.

p. 63 "war whoops . . .": *LAT,* May 1, 1992, 1.

p. 63 "I'm ashamed . . .": *NYT,* May 3, 1992, A17.

p. 63 "Even on . . .": *TNR,* May 25, 1992, 24.

p. 64 13,000 military . . . : *LAT,* May 10, 1992, 1.

p. 64 "An uneasy . . . I always assumed . . .": *TNR,* May 25, 1992, 24.

p. 64 "Black people . . . justice is . . . I especially": *LAT,* May 2, 1992, 7, 1.

p. 64 "looked like Beirut . . .": *Hollywood Reporter,* April 27, 2012.

p. 64 "as much as . . .": Phyllis Johnson, *KJLH-FM and the Los Angeles Riots of 1992* (Jefferson, NC, 2009), 10.

p. 65 "Government in . . .": *WasPo,* November 6, 1992, D5.

p. 65 "George Herbert . . .": Russell Leslie Peterson, *Strange Bedfellows* (New Brunswick, NJ, 2008), 115.

p. 65 "race-specific . . .": *NYT,* March 17, 1992, A25.

p. 65 40 percent . . . : *NYT,* November 14, 1992, L1.

p. 66 "Manhattan project . . .": Smith, *For the Love of Politics,* 21.

p. 66 "coarsened . . . anything that . . .": *Baltimore Sun,* December 27, 1992, 1E.

p. 66 "If you break . . .": John M. Orman and Darrell M. West, *Celebrity Politics* (Upper
     Saddle River, NJ, 2003), p. 25.

p. 67 "vigil . . .": Stan Greenberg OH 2005, MilC.

p. 67 "Democrat talking . . .": Eli Jay Segal OH 2006, MilC.

p. 67 "most important . . .": Al From OH 2005, MilC.

p. 67 Unemployment hit . . . : *BosG,* December 27, 1992, 61.

p. 68 "Murphy Has . . .": *Philadelphia Daily News,* May 20, 1992, 3.

p. 68 "the media elite . . .": *LAT,* May 22, 1992, 23.

p. 68 "I don't know . . .": *NYT,* July 20, 1992, C14.

p. 68 "the most anti-choice . . .": *LAT,* April 6, 1992, 1.

p. 68 "the imperial . . .": *NYT,* June 30, 1992, A1. See also Ronald Dworkin, *Taking Rights
     Seriously* (London, 1977). See also Mary Ann Glendon, *Rights Talk* (New York, 1991).

p. 69 "an amazing . . .": *LAT,* June 30, 1992, 10.

p. 69 "two nations . . .": *WSJ,* July 2, 1992, A8.

p. 69 "Can I quote . . .": *BosG,* June 5, 1992, 28.

p. 70 "revitalized": *NYT,* July 17, 1992, A1.

p. 70 "a religious . . .": *NYT,* August 18, 1992, A8.

p. 70 "Saying that . . .": *LAT,* January 2, 1992, 3.

p. 71 a sign in . . . : George Stephanopoulos, *All Too Human* (New York, 1999), 88.

p. 71 "Take your vitamins . . . .": *WasPo,* November 4, 1992, C1.

p. 72 Half of . . . : *Sun Sentinel,* November 22, 1992, 4G.

p. 72 "No one cares!": *LAT,* January 27, 1992, 1.

p. 73 "a tremendous advocacy . . ." *LAT,* March 31, 1993, 1.

p. 73 "messianic consciousness": Reinhold Niebuhr, *The Irony of American History* (Chicago,
     IL, 1952, 2010), 69.

p. 73 "first in his class": David Maraniss, *First in His Class* (New York, 1995).

p. 73 "natural": Joe Klein, *The Natural* (New York, 2002).

p. 73 "an affair": Benjamin Barber, *The Truth of Power* (New York, 2001), 291.

p. 73 "survivor . . . I'm the . . .": John F. Harris, *The Survivor* (New York, 2005), 334.

p. 74 "If you don't . . .": *Atlantic Monthly,* September 2004, 80.

p. 74 "I'm almost . . .": *Globe and Mail,* November 4, 1992, A1.

p. 74 "a cultural . . .": David Brock, *Blinded by the Right* (New York, 2002), 148.

p. 75 "What has . . .": *Buffalo News,* December 27, 1992, A7.

4. 1993

p. 76 "You know . . .": *WasPo,* January 21, 1993, A1.

p. 76 "finally . . .": Ibid., D1.

p. 76 "Not with . . . Menopause . . .": *WasPo,* January 31, 1993, W11.

p. 77 "we must . . . flaky": Taylor Branch, *The Clinton Tapes* (New York, 2009), 25.

p. 78 "the first window . . . first . . .": Alasdair Nairn, *Engines That Move Markets* (Hoboken, NJ, 2002), 414.

p. 78 "It was almost . . .": *LAT,* February 27, 1993, 1.

p. 79 "I CAN'T . . .": *Commentary,* July 1993, 51.

p. 79 "in your . . .": *New York,* March 22, 1993, 71.

p. 79 "Fiesta . . .": *Time,* March 22, 1993, 68.

p. 79 "I hate . . .": *NYT,* April 25, 1993, A1.

p. 79 "the ongoing . . .": Thelma Golden, John Hanhardt, Lisa Philips, and Elisabeth Sussmann, *1993 Biennial Exhibition* (New York, 1993), 13.

p. 80 "At the end . . .": *NYT,* January 23, 1993, L1.

p. 81 "Kitschification . . . .": Daniel Harris, *The Rise and Fall of Gay Culture* (New York, 1997), 236.

p. 81 "the cultural . . .": John F. Harris, *The Survivor* (New York, 2005), xxvii.

p. 81 "experts and . . .": Bob Woodward, *The Agenda* (New York, 1994), 100.

p. 81 "the most impressive . . .": *NYT,* December 25, 1992, A30.

p. 81 "Baird's Hiring . . .": *WasPo,* January 15, 1993, A14.

p. 82 "This is something . . . .": *WasPo,* January 23, 1993, B1.

p. 82 "Bernie . . .": Bernard Nussbaum OH 2002, MilC.

p. 82 "Give him , , ,": *NYT,* January 21, 1993, A1.

p. 82 "the courageous . . .": Matt Miller to Bob Boorstin, "The Political Case for Greater Boldness on the Deficit," February 6, 1993, Robert (Bob) Boorstin, PR, BC Lib.

p. 83 "how much . . . .": Alice Rivlin OH 2002, MilC.

p. 83 "we're all . . .": Woodward, *The Agenda,* 165.

p. 83 "weave the . . .": Raymond Moley, *After Seven Years* (New York, 1939), 48, 51. And David Stockman, *The Triumph of Politics* (New York, 1986), 109.

p. 83 Thirty-seven million . . . : *WasPo,* January 26, 1993, A1.

p. 83 "Chief of . . . .": Leon Panetta OH 2003, MilC.

p. 84 "Please don't . . .": Joan N. Baggett OH 2005, MilC.

p. 84 "more honest . . . .": *NYT,* January 27, 1993, A22.

p. 84 "is not just . . .": *Nwswk,* December 28, 1992, 23–25.

p. 84 "Saint Hillary . . . .": *NYTM,* May 23, 1993, 622.

p. 84 "I loved . . .": BC Mem, 501.

p. 85 "After Waco . . .": Ibid., 499.

p. 85 "As a Jew . . .": "Elie Wiesel's Remarks at the Dedication Ceremonies for the United States Holocaust Memorial Museum, April 22, 1993," United States Holocaust Memorial Museum, Washington, D.C..

p. 85 "vacuity over . . .": David Rieff, *Slaughterhouse* (New York, 1995), 27.

p. 85 "We were adjusting . . .": HRC, *Living History* (New York, 2003), 170.

p. 85 "Season of . . .": "The First 100 Days—Accomplishments of Vice President Al Gore," April 25, 1993, Virtual Library Publications, Clinton Presidential Materials Project.

p. 85 "On the Wrong . . .": *NYT,* April 29, 1993, A22.

p. 85 "a better . . .": *LAT,* April 28, 1993, 1.

p. 85 "was too big . . .": Rivlin OH 2002. See also Nussbaum OH 2002.

p. 86 "confuse motion . . .": *NYT,* April 29, 1993, A22.

p. 86 "We saw ourselves . . .": George Stephanopoulos, *All Too Human* (New York, 1999), 122.

p. 86 Reporters described . . . : Thomas E. Patterson, *Out of Order* (New York, 1993), 20.

p. 86 "microscope . . .": *Time*, April 16, 1984, 24.

p. 87 "culture clash": BC Mem, 520.

p. 87 "Being responsible . . . bad publicity . . .": Branch, *The Clinton Tapes*, 64, 71.

p. 87 FAA records . . . : *Newsday*, June 30, 1993, 19.

p. 87 "that the American . . .": BC Mem, 520.

p. 88 "I'll be the . . .": Branch, *The Clinton Tapes*, 70.

p. 88 "When these . . .": *Sun Sentinel*, June 4, 1993, 1A.

p. 88 A birthday card . . . : *NYT*, June 6, 1993, A1.

p. 88 "Mr. President . . . this was . . .": Nussbaum OH 2002. See also Virginia Clinton Kelley with James Morgan, *Leading with My Heart* (New York, 1994), 26.

p. 89 47 percent . . . : *Newsday*, July 20, 1993, 16.

p. 89 "stand up . . .": *Rolling Stone*, December 9, 1993, 40–45.

p. 89 "A can of . . .": William H. Chafe, *Bill and Hillary* (New York, 2012), 193, 253.

p. 89 "communicate a . . . overcrowded agenda . . .": Bob Boorstin et al. to George Stephanopoulos, David Gergen, and Mark Gearan, "Draft Communications Memo for Monday Meeting," July 23, 1993, Robert "Bob" Boorstin, PR, BC Lib. See also Mark Gearan et al. to David Gergen et al., "Fall Calendar," July 19, 1993, Robert "Bob" Boorstin, PR, BC Lib.

p. 90 "Bye, bye . . .": Branch, *The Clinton Tapes*, 68.

p. 91 "I could not . . .": *WasPo*, August 7, 1993, A1.

p. 91 "Democrats believe . . .": *NYT*, August 6, 1993, A1.

p. 91 "neither sensational . . .": BC Mem, 648.

p. 91 ideas synthesized . . . : Ted Gaebler and David Osborne, *Reinventing Government* (Boston, MA, 1992).

p. 91 "Surveys . . .": Michael Waldman et al. to George Stephanopoulos, David Gergen, and Mark Gearan, "Draft Communications Memo for Monday Meeting," July 23, 1993, Robert (Bob) Boorstin, PR, BC Lib.

p. 92 "a significant . . .": White House memo, "Health Care Reform and the Congress," Health Care Task Force [Seg. 3], PR, BC Lib.

p. 92 "the emotionless . . . She is not . . .": *NYT*, September 22, 1993, A24.

p. 92 200 million guns . . . 640,000 crimes . . . : *Time*, December 20, 1993, 18.

p. 92 Gun sales . . . : *WasPo*, July 5, 1992, A3.

p. 92 "Last Chance . . .": *Time*, December 20, 1993, 18.

p. 93 "the twentieth . . .": David H. Gelernter, *Drawing Life* (New York, 1997), 3.

p. 94 "social immune . . .": James G. Banks and Peter S. Banks, *The Unintended Consequences* (Lanham, MD, 2004), ix, x.

p. 94 "brain-dead . . .": Frederick F. Siegel, *The Prince of the City* (New York, 2005), 67. See also *New York*, November 18, 2002, 18.

p. 95 Two-thirds of . . . : *NYT*, October 5, 1993, A1.

p. 95 "the age of . . .": *TNR*, October 31, 2013.

p. 95 "Uncle Tom . . . .": *WasPo*, December 9, 1993, A1.

p. 96 "SHAFTA": *WSJ*, September 9, 1993, A20.

p. 96 "a giant . . .": *AAS*, August 29, 1993, C8.

p. 96 "the politics of . . .": *WasPo*, November 10, 1993, A1.

p. 96 "a textbook . . .": David Gergen, *Eyewitness to Power* (New York, 2000), 285.

p. 96 "Now I . . .": *LAT*, September 20, 1993, 5.

p. 96 "It's not like . . . .": Branch, *The Clinton Tapes*, 84.

p. 97 "It was Thugs . . .": *Orlando Sentinel*, December 26, 1993, G1.

p. 97 His 58 percent . . . : *WasPo*, December 21, 1993, A10, and *NYT*, May 29, 1993, L7. *Chicago Tribune*, September 21, 1993, 15.

p. 97 The freewheeling . . . Walter Isaacson, *The Innovators* (New York, 2014).

p. 97 In 1981 . . . : *Network World*, August 15, 2013.

p. 98 11,000 interlocking . . . 102 countries . . . : Gary Chapman and Marc Rotenberg, "The National Information Infrastructure: A Public Interest Opportunity," *Computer Professionals for Social Responsibility Newsletter* 11 (1993): 1–5, 16–17. *NYT*, December 12, 1993, A7.

p. 98 "new, interactive . . . : *NYT*, July 26, 1993, D6.

p. 98 "A couch . . . : *NYT*, January 24, 1993, A1.

p. 98 "telecast . . .": *TNR*, May 24, 1993, 18.

p. 98 "Imagine . . .": Information Infrastructure Task Force, "National Information Infrastructure: Agenda for Action," Telecommunications and Information Administration (Washington, 1993), 5.

p. 98 "The Internot": *NYTM*, December 19, 1993, 18.

p. 98 "Who has time . . .": *Nwswk*, December 20, 1993, 111.

p. 99 Phone companies . . . : *WasPo*, December 16, 1993, A25.

p. 99 "One of the biggest . . .": "Remarks by Vice President Al Gore at National Press Club," December 21, 1993, Office of the Vice President.

p. 99 "the godfather . . .": David Haward Bain, "The Transcontinental Railroad," in Brian Lamb and Susan Swain, eds., *Abraham Lincoln: Great American Historians on Our Sixteenth President* (New York, 2008), 111. See also Richard Nixon, "Statement on Signing a Highway and Mass Transit Bill," August 13, 1973, The American Presidency Project.

p. 99 November's *Congressional* . . . : *CQ Almanac 1993* (Washington, D.C., 1994): 30–36.

p. 100 "more a business . . .": *American Spectator*, December 20, 1993, 30.

p. 100 "I think . . .": Elizabeth Drew, *On the Edge* (New York, 1994), 384.

p. 100 "the incredible . . . .": *NYT*, December 23, 1993, A12.

p. 101 "era of politics . . .": Darrell M. West and John Orman, *Celebrity Politics* (Upper Saddle River, NJ, 2003), x.

p. 101 Louis Sass . . . : Louis A. Sass, *Madness and Modernism* (Cambridge, MA, 1998).

p. 102 "to foam at . . .": HRC, *It Takes a Village* (New York, 1996), 69.

p. 102 Excel graphs: Jeffrey Toobin, *A Vast Conspiracy* (New York, 1999), 112.

p. 102 "politics of preemption" . . . : Stephen Skowronek, *The Politics Presidents Make* (Cambridge, MA, 1993, 1997), 459–60. See also interview with Al From, February 3, 2015.

5. 1994

p. 104 "The worst . . .": *Spin,* April 2004, 67.

p. 104 While suicide . . . : Donna Gaines, *Teenage Wasteland* (Chicago, IL, 1998), 7.

p. 105 "He was . . .": *USA Today,* April 11, 1994, 1D.

p. 105 "the New . . .": *Rolling Stone,* April 16, 1992, Cover.

p. 105 "I know . . . .": *Rolling Stone,* May 13, 1999, 46–48.

p. 106 "to try . . .": Everett True, *Nirvana* (Cambridge, MA, 2007), 43.

p. 106 "identity bracelets": *Nwswk,* February 6, 1995, 46.

p. 106 "bridge between . . . I'm adorning . . . We're not . . .": *Patriot,* July 8, 1995, 1.

p. 106 As America . . . : *Hartford Courant,* November 19, 1996, E2.

p. 106 "modern primitives . . .": *USNWR,* July 31, 1995, 16.

p. 107 "Boomer Envy . . . .:" Douglas Coupland, *Generation X* (New York, 1991), 21, 5, 27.

p. 108 "self-pitying . . .": *Orlando Sentinel,* March 30, 1994, E4.

p. 108 "a movie about . . .": *NYT,* February 13, 1994, H11.

p. 108 "There's room . . .": *WasPo,* March 18, 1990, Y8.

p. 108 "one of the . . . : *Time,* June 8, 1998, 144–45.

p. 109 "Compared with . . .": *Montreal Gazette,* August 4, 1993, B5.

p. 109 "Buffcoat and . . .": *BosG,* October 22, 1993, 49.

p. 109 "no hugging . . .": *Rolling Stone,* September 22, 1994, 46.

p. 109 "because I'm . . .": *Cincinnati Post,* May 13, 1998, 1B.

p. 109 "my favorite city . . .": *Seattle Post-Intelligencer,* October 3, 2007.

p. 110 "latte town": David Brooks, *Bobos in Paradise* (New York, 2000), 104.

p. 110 "the Starbucks . . .": Howard Schultz, *Onward* (New York, 2011), 13.

p. 111 "biggest river . . .": Brad Stone, *The Everything Store* (New York, 2013), 34.

p. 111 With 15 percent . . . : Ken Conca, Michael Maniates, and Thomas Pinrcen, eds., *Confronting Consumption* (Cambridge, MA, 2002), 201.

p. 112 "seemed like . . . condo by condo . . . they wanted . . .": *Seattle Times,* May 13, 2004, A1.

p. 113 "Go OJ . . . terrible to . . .": *Time,* June 27, 1994, 28.

p. 113 "false intimacy . . .": *Nwswk,* June 27, 1994, 25.

p. 113 "It can't be . . .": *NYT,* June 20, 1994, A17.

p. 113 Rates of spousal . . . : Lawrence A. Greenfield et al. "Bureau of Justice Statistics Factbook: Violence by Intimates," U.S. Department of Justice (Washington, D.C., 1998). See also Callie M. Rennison, "Bureau of Justice Statistics: Crime Data Brief: Intimate Partner Violence, 1993–2001," U.S. Department of Justice (Washington, D.C., 2003).

p. 114 "reckless . . . tabloid trash . . .": *WasPo,* May 7, 1994, A1.

p. 114 "this year's bimbo . . .": *Time,* December 26, 1994, 157.

p. 114 "It's not . . .": *LAT,* December 6, 1992, 1.

p. 114 "credible evidence . . .": HRC, *Living History* (New York, 2003), 215.

p. 114 "clueless . . .": Bernard Nussbaum OH 2002, MilC.

p. 115 "the worst . . .": BC Mem, 542.

p. 115 "furious . . .": "Memo re BC's Supreme Court appointment," May 11, 1994, Blair MSS.

p. 115 "a golden . . .": John F. Harris, *The Survivor* (New York, 2005), 115.

p. 116 "If you like . . . .": *National Review,* February 7, 1994, 53–56.

p. 116 "inspired . . .": *AAS,* September 9, 1993, B6.

p. 116 59 percent approved . . . only 17 . . . : *WasPo,* October 12, 1993, A1. See also interview with Al From, February 3, 2015, Washington, D.C.

p. 116 "impossibly . . . .": Joe Klein, *The Natural* (New York, 2002), 121.

p. 117 "lack of . . . .": Mike Lux to Harold Ickes and Greg Lawler, "Follow-Up to Our Meeting," 27 Jan. 1994, Health Care Task Force [Seg. 3], PR, BC Lib.

p. 117 "drive down . . . .": *Pittsburgh Post-Gazette,* 10 Aug. 1994, A6.

p. 117 "Health care . . .": *Nwswk,* February 14, 1994, 26–28.

p. 117 "What the fuck . . .": Harris, *The Survivor,* 118.

p. 117 only 41 percent . . . : *Nwswk,* February 14, 1994, 26–28.

p. 117 "America's ready . . .": *CBS News Special Report,* September 22, 1993.

p. 117 "was in big . . .": Tom Daschle OH 2007, MilC.

p. 117 "breakdown . . .": Stan Greenberg OH 2007, MilC.

p. 118 During his . . . : *NYT,* January 16, 1994, A20.

p. 118 "Billary's . . .": Rush H. Limbaugh, *See, I Told You So* (New York, 1993), 25.

p. 118 By 1996 . . . : Roger Chapman, *Culture Wars* (New York, 2010), 323.

p. 118 "historians . . . New Democrat . . .": Limbaugh, *See, I Told You So,* xvi, 27.

p. 119 "the leader . . .": *National Review,* September 6, 1993, 44.

p. 119 From February . . . : *WasPo,* March 25, 1994, A1.

p. 120 "quit doin' , , ,"; *St. Petersburg Times,* June 14, 1994, 6B.

p. 120 "disingenuous . . .": *New York,* April 11, 1994, 10.

p. 120 "overdone . . . journalistic . . . .": *NYT,* April 10, 1994, A4.

p. 120 "Defend HRC . . . No distance between . . .": "Key Points on Whitewater for Press Conference," March 24, 1994, Whitewater [Part 7], PR, BC Lib.

p. 120 "work through . . . Why . . .": "Untitled," Blair MSS.

p. 121 "we were . . .": Robert S. McNamara, *In Retrospect* (New York, 1995), xix.

p. 122 "contains . . .": *WasPo,* August 22, 1994, A1.

p. 122 "The price . . .": BC Mem, 612.

p. 123 Vin Weber and Joe Klein in *Nwswk,* April 25, 1994, 31.

p. 123 "affecting the . . .": David Dreyer and Michael Waldman to Leon Panetta et al., "Memo to Leon, Harold, Joan, George, Pat G., Mark, T," August 22, 1994, Michael Waldman, Speechwriter, PR, BC Lib.

p. 123 "stature . . .": David Dreyer to Leon Panetta et al., "Now to November, Objectives for Scheduling/Presentation," August 9, 1994, Don Baer, PR, BC Lib.

p. 123 "only knew . . .": Joan N. Baggett OH 2005, MilC.

p. 123 "mistook . . .": *Nwswk,* December 26, 1994, 18.

p. 124 "Republican storm troopers": *Buffalo News,* November 17, 1994, A1.

p. 124 "trickle-down . . .": *WasPo,* December 15, 1994, A26.

p. 124 "shellshocked": Baggett OH.

p. 124 "scabrous . . .": *NYT,* October 26, 1994, A27.

p. 124 "manifesto . . .": *New Yorker,* November 28, 1994, 139.

p. 124 "cognitive . . .": *National Review,* December 5, 1994, 58–61.

p. 125 "Segregated . . .": *Nwswk,* December 26, 1994, 18.

p. 125 cultural dimension . . . "It took . . .": *Nwswk,* November 21, 1994, 44.

p. 126 only 22 percent . . . : *Nwswk,* December 26, 1994, 18.

p. 126 Exit polls . . . : *WSJ, Europe,* November 17, 1994, 12.

p. 126 "the Reagan . . .": *Seattle Times,* November 18, 1994, A1.

p. 126 "The excitement . . .": *Harrisburg Evening News,* February 9, 1995, A11.

p. 127 "acts of genocide": David Halberstam, *War in a Time of Peace* (New York, 2001), 276, 277.

6. 1995

p. 129 "the worst terrorist . . . .": *NYT,* April 21, 1995, A26.

p. 129 "This is . . .": *NYT,* April 20, 1995, B11.

p. 129 "Sure we . . .": *Ottawa Citizen,* 21 April 21, 1995, A3.

p. 129 Three-quarters . . . : *NYT,* April 30, 1995, L1.

p. 130 Throughout . . . "I'm at ORU . . .": *Memphis Commercial Appeal,* September 9, 2000, A11.

p. 130 In 1950 . . . : W. David Baird and Danney Goble, *Oklahoma* (Norman, OK, 2008), 252.

p. 131 "interlocking . . .": David E. Campbell and Robert D. Putnam, *American Grace* (New York, 2010), 550.

p. 131 "the largest . . .": *Orange County* (CA) *Register,* April 23, 1995, A27.

p. 131 "You can't . . .": *Guardian,* March 30, 2001, L13.

p. 132 an estimated 858 . . . .: Mark Potok, "The Year in Hate and Extremism," *Intelligence Report* 149 (2013), Southern Poverty Law Center, Montgomery, AL.

p. 133 "enemies of normal . . .": *LAT,* November 17, 1994, 13.

p. 133 "the self-righteous . . .": BC Mem, 633.

p. 133 "Does that . . .": Allen Ginsberg, *Collected Poems, 1947–1997* (New York, 2006), 1082.

p. 133 "muzzle . . .": *Baltimore Sun,* December 6, 1994, 2A.

p. 133 "the busiest . . . He is . . .": *USA Today,* January 5, 1995, 1A.

p. 134 "The Lost . . .": *NYT,* February 6, 1995, A17.

p. 134 "The Problem . . .": *BosG,* February 8, 1995, 13.

p. 134 "Barney Fag . . . climate of . . .": *NYT,* January 28, 1995, A1.

p. 134 "age of . . .": *NYT,* December 31, 1994, L1.

p. 134 "big lie . . . . More children . . .": *Atlanta Journal,* October 2, 1995, A8.

p. 134 "We both . . . my grandfather . . .": *Nwswk,* April 10, 1995, 20.

p. 135 "no civilization . . .": *WasPo,* April 8, 1995, A12.

p. 135 only 38 percent . . . : James G. Gimpel, *Fulfilling the Contract* (Boston, 1996), 126.

p. 135 Gingrich's job . . . : Elizabeth Drew, *Showdown* (New York, 1996), 184.

p. 136 "the first crisis . . .": Nigel Hamilton, *Bill Clinton* (New York, 2007), 400.

p. 136 "least popular . . .": *NYT,* May 24, 1995, A21.

p. 136 "pander bear . . .": Michael Waldman to Don Baer and Bruce Reed, "Speech," December 14, 1994, Don Baer, PR, BC Lib.

p. 136 "to enlarge the President . . .": Bill Galston to Don Baer and Mark Gearan, "Draft 6," December 15, 1994, Don Baer, PR, BC Lib.

p. 136 "like being . . .": Michael Waldman to Don Baer and Bruce Reed, "Speech," December 14, 1994, Don Baer, PR, BC Lib.

p. 136 "Charlie . . . . by compromise . . . .": Dick Morris, *Behind the Oval Office* (New York, 1997), 83, 40.

p. 136 "I had always . . .": BC Mem, 660.

p. 136 "to eliminate . . .": Morris, *Behind the Oval Office,* 93.

p. 137 "Gingrich lite": *Philadelphia Daily News,* December 19, 1994, 60.

p. 137 "triangulation . . .": George Stephanopoulos, *All Too Human* (New York, 1999), 336.

p. 137 "all I detest . . .": Robert Reich, *Locked in the Cabinet* (New York, 1997), 273.

p. 137 "McBOR": *LAT,* February 2, 1995, 5.

p. 137 "quietly filed . . .": BC Mem, 650.

p. 138 "Every once . . . .": Al From OH 2007, MilC.

p. 138 "second violent . . .": Allan J. Lichtman, *White Protestant Nation* (New York, 2008), 427.

p. 138 "irresponsible and . . .": *NYT,* April 25, 1995, A19.

p. 138 "to disarm . . .": Randy Bobbitt, *Us Against Them* (Lanham, MA, 2010), 68.

p. 138 "the harsh . . .": *WasPo,* April 25, 1995, A1.

p. 139 "promotes . . .": *WasPo,* May 10, 1995, A24.

p. 139 "It is grotesque . . .": *WasPo,* April 25, 1995, A17.

p. 139 frowned on anger: Carol Z. Stearns and Peter N. Stearns, *Anger* (Chicago, IL, 1986), 211.

p. 139 "America is angry . . .": *NYT,* October 22, 1994, L23.

p. 139 median wealth . . . : Edward N. Wolff, ed., *International Perspectives on Household Wealth* (Northampton, MA, 2006), 110.

p. 139 "The locus . . .": Jacqueline Jones, *The Dispossessed* (New York, 1992), 269.

p. 140 "are like me . . .": *NYT,* February 27, 1996, A16.

p. 140 Generation Xers . . . : *Bergen County* (NJ) *Record,* June 27, 1999, B1.

p. 140 "We knew . . .": Joseph E. Stiglitz, *The Roaring Nineties* (New York, 2003), 184.

p. 140 "Good news . . .": *CSM,* June 19, 1995, 16.

p. 140 "I hold . . .": William Finnegan, *Cold New World* (New York, 1999), xvii.

p. 141 "Evil and . . .": Gregory Maguire, *Wicked* (New York, 1995), 21.

p. 141 "we must . . .": *Catholic New Times,* May 26, 1996, 8–9.

p. 141 13 percent of . . . : James A. Morone, *Hellfire Nation* (New Haven, CT, 2003), 468.

p. 141 Experts debated . . . : See Clifton D. Bryant and Dennis L. Peck, eds., *21st Century Sociology* (Thousand Oaks, CA, 2011), 415–24.

p. 142 approval ratings jumping . . . : *NYT,* April 27, 1995, A1.

p. 142 "had a two . . .": Morris, *Behind the Oval Office,* 34.

p. 142 "to show . . . he ain't . . . one hundred . . .": BC Mem, 657, 658.

p. 143 "people came . . .": *NYT,* October 19, 2008, A1.

p. 143 "Welcome . . .": *Baltimore Sun,* June 12, 1995.

p. 143 One Secret Service . . . : BC Mem, 658.

p. 143 "What is Internet . . .": YouTube, "1994: "Today": "What Is the Internet Anyway?"

p. 143 "the most . . .": *Guardian,* August 17, 1995, 7.

p. 144 Frenzied bidding . . . : *WasPo,* August 10, 1995, D9.

p. 144 "Golden . . .": *Time,* February 19, 1996, Cover, 42. See also Walter Isaacson, *The Innovators* (New York, 2014).

p. 144 By October . . . .: *WSJ,* October 30, 1995, B3.

p. 144 "frantic scramble . . .": *Las Vegas Review-Journal,* January 1, 1997, 15B.

p. 144 "the computer . . .": Sherry Turkle, *Alone Together* (New York, 2011), xi.

p. 145 "vision for . . . Windows . . . : *Seattle Times,* August 24, 1995, A1.

p. 145 "the world's first . . .": *Newsday,* August 8, 1995, B25.

p. 145 a $21 billion . . . : *Newsday,* October 11, 1996, B27.

p. 146 "opportunity society": Newt Gingrich, *To Renew America* (New York, 1995), 14.

p. 146 "the digital . . .": *Wired,* October 1996, 42–47.

p. 146 "cocooned . . .": *Weekly Standard,* September 18, 1995, 53.

p. 146 "are we . . .": Stephanopoulos, *All Too Human,* 392.

p. 146 150 million . . . : *Nwswk,* October 16, 1995, 28.

p. 147 "Shit": Stephanopoulos, *All Too Human,* 393.

p. 147 "Were we watching . . .": *Nwswk,* October 16, 1995, 28.

p. 147 Eighty percent . . . : Jennifer Lynn Eberhardt and Susan T. Fiske, *Confronting Racism* (Thousand Oaks, CA, 1998), 286.

p. 147 "How could . . .": *USA Today,* 3 Nov. 1994, 2B. See also Patricia A. Turner, *I Heard It Through the Grapevine* (Berkeley, CA, 1993).

p. 147 "Why is the problem . . .": *Nwswk,* October 16, 1995, 28.

p. 147 "great white . . . We have . . .": *NYT Book Review,* September 17, 1995, 7.

p. 148 "isolated from . . .": Cornel West, *Race Matters* (New York, 1993), 56.

p. 148 "the new . . .": *Nwswk,* November 29, 1993, 65.

p. 148 "stereotypes . . .": *San Francisco Chronicle,* February 27, 1995, A19.

p. 148 More than . . . : *Nwswk,* November 29, 1993, 65.

p. 148 "America is . . .": John J. Dilulio Jr., "White Lies About Black Crime," *Public Interest* 118 (1995): 3.

p. 148 "oppositional . . .": Elijah Anderson, *Code of the Street* (New York, 1999), 107.

p. 148 "criminal occupation . . .": *Nwswk,* November 29, 1993, 65.

p. 148 "the black . . .": Stanley Crouch, *The All-American Skin Game* (New York, 1995), 30, 250.

p. 148 "criminals and . . . every time . . .": *CNN.com,* October 17, 1995.

p. 151 "an affront . . .": *TNR,* January 8, 1996, 21.

p. 151 "We're somewhat . . . Just when . . .": *WasPo,* September 9, 1995, D1.

p. 151 "exhaustive advice . . .": *Weekly Standard,* September 18, 1995, 61.

p. 151 "reassert and renew . . .": Gingrich, *To Renew America,* 7.

p. 152 "Bill already . . .": Reich, *Locked in the Cabinet,* 283.

p. 152 "I just can't . . . He *does* . . . : Nigel Hamilton, *Bill Clinton* (New York, 2007), 519–21.

p. 153 "This is petty . . .": *NYT,* November 17, 1995, A1.

p. 153 "Cry Baby . . .": New York *Daily News,* November 16, 1995.

p. 153 By the end . . . : *NYT,* December 14, 1995, A1.

p. 153 "my policy . . . enormous . . .": David H. Donald, *Lincoln* (New York, 1995), 15, 14.

p. 154 "future preference . . .": BC Mem, 78.

7. 1996

p. 155 "Thank you . . .": Anthony Rapp, *Without You* (New York, 2006), 136.

p. 155 "*Rent* . . .": *Irish Times,* June 3, 2000, 65.

p. 156 "Lower East . . .": *Time,* March 4, 1996, 71.

p. 157 "The police . . .": *LAT,* December 24, 1995, 1.

p. 157 inquiries to . . . : *Time,* January 15, 1996, 54.

p. 157 a third of . . . : John A. Eterno and Eli B. Silverman, "The New York City Policy Department's Compstat: Dream or Nightmare?," *International Journal of Police Science and Management* 8 (2006): 219.

p. 158 Harvard's . . . : Juliet Schor, *The Overworked American* (New York, 1993).

p. 158 many American workers . . . : Jerald Hage and Charles Powers, *Post-Industrial Lives* (Newbury Park, CA, 1992), 40.

p. 159 "V-chips . . .": *CNN/Time All Politics,* October 14, 1996.

p. 159 "with each . . .": Dick Morris, *Behind the Oval Office* (New York, 1997), 230.

p. 159 Nearly 1 million . . . : *USA Today,* January 24, 1996, 11A.

p. 159 "parents matter . . .": Urie Bronfenbrenner, "Ecology of the Family as a Context for Human Development: Research Perspectives," *Developmental Psychology* 22 (1986): 726.

p. 159 "love for . . .": *TNR,* October 16, 1995.

p. 160 before the company . . . : *Daily Mail,* October 26, 2009, 9.

p. 160 "attachment . . . welcoming your . . .": William Sears, *Nighttime Parenting* (Franklin Park, IL, 1999), 6.

p. 160 "Bill Clinton . . .": *Time,* December 29, 1997, 63–64.

p. 160 "electronic . . .": Terri LeMoyne and Tom Buchanan, "Does "Hovering" Matter? Helicopter Parenting and Its Effect on Well-Being," *Sociological Spectrum* 31 (2011): 400.

p. 161 divorce rate for college . . . : *NYT,* April 19, 2005, F7.

p. 161 22 percent . . . two-thirds . . . : Christine A. Bachrach and Stephanie J. Ventura, "Nonmarital Childbearing in the United States, 1940–99," CDC: National Vital Statistics Reports 48 (2000), 6. See also Elizabeth A. Mulroy, *The New Uprooted* (Westport, CT, 1995), 85.

p. 161 "Unless . . .": William J. Bennett, *Index of Leading Cultural Indicators* (New York, 1999), 12.

p. 161 "Generative . . . .": David C. Dollahite and Alan J. Hawkins, *Generative Fathering* (Thousand Oaks, CA, 1997), xii, 5.

p. 162 "the great . . .": Tom Wolfe, "The Great Relearning," *American Spectator,* December 1987, 14.

p. 162 "girl-poisoning . . . courage, competency . . .": Mary Pipher, *Reviving Ophelia* (New York, 1994), 12, 18.

p. 162 "enmeshing . . .": Michael Gurian, *The Wonder of Boys* (New York, 1996), xx.

p. 162 "romance . . .": Helen Fielding, *Bridget Jones's Diary* (New York, 1996), 43.

p. 163 "I'm the projection . . .": Richard Lowry, *Legacy* (Washington, D.C., 2003), 111.

p. 163 "nagging . . .": "Marc Rudov: 'Clinton's Nagging Voice Lost Her the Male Vote,'" Fox News, January 4, 2008, www.youtube.com/watch?v=OFeCXHuNoP4.

p. 163 "It's the . . . .": "Thanksgiving Day, 1996," Blair MSS.

p. 163 "hell to pay . . .": *NYT,* January 5, 1996, D20.

p. 163 By August . . . : *CBS News,* March 31, 2009.

p. 164 "fear of . . .": *LAT,* May 12, 2008, A8.

p. 164 "full-time . . .": HRC, *Living History* (New York, 2003), 265.

p. 164 "mass culture . . .": HRC, *Living History,* 333.

p. 165 "nation that . . . intact . . . .": HRC, *It Takes a Village* (New York, 1996), 7, 41, 50.

p. 166 "Don't ever . . . I know . . .": "Thanksgiving Day, 1996," Blair MSS.

p. 165 "Saint . . .": *Nwswk,* January 15, 1996, Cover.

p. 165 "a congenital . . . The President . . .": *NYTM,* February 4, 1996, 18.

p. 166 "not a diet . . .": HRC, *Living History,* 335.

p. 166 "reacts violently . . .": Mickey Kantor OH 2002, MilC.

p. 166 "I'm tired . . . .": Taylor Branch, *The Clinton Tapes* (New York, 2009), 338, 339.

p. 166 "defend . . .": Paul Begala to Don Baer, "The S.O.T.U. and the First Lady," January 23, 1996, Don Baer, PR, BC Lib.

p. 166 "the drag . . .": *TNR,* March 4, 1996, 24.

p. 166 When asked . . . : *Star Tribune,* August 9, 1996, 18A.

p. 166 In 1996 exit . . . : *CNN/Time All Politics,* August 29, 1996.

p. 167 "his blueprint . . .": Bruce Reed OH 2004, MilC.

p. 167 "At times . . .": *LAT,* June 13, 1996, 1.

p. 167 "Terrific . . .": *Bergen County* (NJ) *Record,* January 26, 1996, N7.

p. 167 "This is not . . .": *LAT,* February 11, 1996, 10.

p. 168 "Don't wait . . . .": Bruce Reed and Gene Sperling to BC, "Ideas for Speech to NGA Education Summit," March 21, 1996, Box 16, Folder 2, "Domestic Policy Council," Clinton Administration History Project, BC Lib.

p. 168 "He's a much . . .": *BosG,* January 24 1996, 1.

p. 168 "internal mantra . . .": George Stephanopoulos, *All Too Human* (New York, 1999), 415.

p. 168 the best aspect . . . : *USNWR,* June 24, 1996, 35.

p. 168 A Pew . . . : *USA Today,* August 26, 1996, 6A.

p. 169 "thirst for . . .": "Investigation on Illegal or Improper Activities in Connection with the 1996 Federal Election Campaigns: Final Report," Volume 5, United States Senate, 105th Congress, 2d Session (Washington, D.C., 1998), 51.

p. 169 The director . . . : Jason DeParle, *American Dream* (New York, 2005), 3.

p. 169 "boob bait . . .": John F. Harris, *The Survivor* (New York, 2005), 234.

p. 169 One in seven . . . : *Time,* July 29, 1996, 53.

p. 169 Republican backbenchers . . . : *Time,* August 12, 1996, 18.

p. 170 "if he . . .": Stephanopoulos, *All Too Human,* 419.

p. 170 "welfare repeal": *Newsday,* August 2, 1996, A7.

p. 170 "Shirk . . .": *TNR,* August 12, 1996, 20.

p. 170 "whole purpose . . .": Robert Reich, *Locked in the Cabinet* (New York, 1997), 320, 321.

p. 170 "the president's decision . . . What good . . .": Morris, *Behind the Oval Office,* 300.

p. 170 "This is a . . .": *Time,* August 12, 1996, 18.

p. 170 "I want to . . .": Joe Klein, *The Natural* (New York, 2002), 153.

p. 170 "That's it . . .": *Nwswk,* August 12, 1996, 42.

p. 170 "most important . . .": BC Mem, 721.

p. 171 "If there are people . . .": Morris, *Behind the Oval Office,* 230.

p. 172 "almost a whole . . .": Interview with Dr. Julian Adams, August 3, 2014, Montreal, Canada.

p. 172 "For helping lift . . .": *Time,* December 30, 1996, 54.

p. 172 "innate . . . .": Bruce Bawer, *A Place at the Table* (New York, 1994), 29.

p. 172 "A need to rebel . . .": *TNR,* August 28, 1989, 20.

p. 172 "legitimation": Urvashi Vaid, *Virtual Equality* (New York, 1996), 36.

p. 172 "proverbial . . .": Daniel Harris, *The Rise and Fall of Gay Culture* (New York, 1999), 61.

p. 173 "love, commitment . . .": Evan Wolfson, *Why Marriage Matters* (New York, 2007), 90.

p. 173 "Clinton could . . .": Stephanopoulos, *All Too Human,* 416.

p. 173 "Why? What . . .": Morris, *Behind the Oval Office,* 333.

p. 174 Two hundred . . . reached . . . : *Atlanta Constitution,* July 29, 1996, S36.

p. 175 "Jewell Syndrome": See *Vanity Fair,* February 1997.

p. 176 "on the wrong . . .": *NYT,* June 19, 1996, A19.

p. 176 Ultimately . . . : John H. McWhorter, *Losing the Race* (New York, 2000), 11.

p. 176 "The Internet . . .": *Computer Reseller News,* September 9, 1996, 216.

p. 176 "too cranky . . .": *BosG,* September 20, 1996, A27.

p. 176 "largely negative . . .": Morris, *Behind the Oval Office,* 208.

p. 176 Bob Dole, Joe Klein in: *Nwswk,* March 18, 1996, 22.

p. 177 "both social virtues . . . .": Amitai Etzioni, *The New Golden Rule* (New York, 1996), xviii.

p. 177 "I'm sick . . .": *Time,* September 9, 1996, 42.

p. 177 "the economic . . .": Reich, *Locked in the Cabinet,* 311, 312.

p. 177 "adjustable ethics . . .": Gary Aldrich, *Unlimited Access* (Washington, D.C., 1996), ix.

p. 178 "Hillary has gotten . . .": David Brock, *The Seduction of Hillary Rodham* (New York, 1996), xi.

p. 178 "With all due . . .": *NYT,* August 28, 1996, A1.

p. 179 "most of the news . . .": David Brock, *The Republican Noise Machine* (New York, 2004), 313.

p. 179 "this era's . . . arguably . . .": *Atlantic Monthly,* September 2003, 81.

p. 180 "We're the ones . . .": *BosG,* January 24, 1996, 1.

p. 180 "character-starved culture": Don Eberly, *The Content of America's Character* (Lanham, MD, 1995), 6.

p. 180 only 41 . . . : Everett C. Ladd, "The Status-Quo Election: Introduction," *Public Perspective* 8 (1997): 4–5.

p. 180 "a sober reminder . . .": BC Mem, 734.

8. 1997

p. 182 "Apple lives . . .": *LAT,* August 7, 1997, A1.

p. 182 the tomorrow-shapers . . . : Thomas Mahon, *Charged Bodies* (New York, 1985), 4. See also "Silicon Valley—What Is That?" www.silicon-valley-story.de/sv/sv_whatIsThat.html.

p. 183 $6.7 million . . . : Gary Rivlin, *The Godfather of Silicon Valley* (New York, 2001), 47.

p. 183 "proven . . .": Adam Cohen, *The Perfect Store* (New York, 2002), 142.

p. 183 Average salaries . . . : Martin Kenney, ed., *Understanding Silicon Valley* (Stanford, CA, 2000), 192.

p. 183 A four-bedroom . . . : *USA Today,* November 22, 1999, B, 3:2.

p. 183 "creative spirits . . .": *Financial Times,* August 7, 1997, 24.

p. 184 the innovative thinking . . . : Interview with Don Baer, February 4, 2015.

p. 184 "Any sufficiently . . .": Arthur C. Clarke Jr., *Profiles of the Future* (New York, 1973), 14.

p. 184 the buzz involved . . . : See Alex Bracetti, "The 90 Best Gadgets of the '90s," Complex .com, www.complex.com/pop-culture/2012/04/the-90-best-gadgets-of-the-90s/34.

p. 185 "the birth heard . . .": *Nwswk,* October 3, 1997, 52.

p. 186 "We just don't . . .": *NYT,* March 3, 1997, A1.

p. 186 "Second Term . . . .": Greg Simon to Don Baer, "Second Term Legacy Projects," December 10, 1996, Box 126, "Second Term Strategy," Bruce Reed Papers, BC Lib.

p. 186 "wherever the lamb . . .": *Nwswk,* March 10, 1997, 52.

p. 186 "important genetic . . . .": Tim Newell to BC, "Cloning Meeting and Statement," March 4, 1997, Box 114, "Human Cloning," Bruce Reed Papers, BC Lib.

p. 186 "I am not . . .": *NYT,* March 3, 1997, A1.

p. 186 "Ethically, we . . .": *Montreal Gazette,* March 2, 1997, B9.

p. 186 "It's the ultimate . . .": *Time,* January 11, 1999, 48.

p. 187 "security blankets": Lisa Beamer, *Let's Roll!* (Carol Stream, IL, 2002), 125.

p. 188 "Diana—you'll . . .": *WasPo,* September 1, 1997, A1.

p. 188 "people's princess": *International Herald Tribune,* September 1, 1997, 1.

p. 188 "Even in a world . . ." *Time,* December 29, 1997, 137.

p. 189 By 1990 . . . : *NYT,* May 4, 1990, D1. And *NYT,* October 2, 1996, L23.

p. 189 Phase two . . . : *WasPo,* August 1, 1995, A1.

p. 189 "a place . . .": *NYT,* January 16, 2004, A10.

p. 189 "not just . . .": *NYTM,* December 14, 1997, 56.

p. 189 "small complicated . . .": Alexis de Tocqueville, *Democracy in America* (New York, 1840), 339.

p. 190 "creepy . . . developed a new . . . I used . . . This is no . . .": *NYTM,* December 14, 1997, 56.

p. 190 "We have so little . . .": *Chicago Tribune,* May 12, 1994, 3.

p. 190 Disney recorded . . . : *Sacramento Bee,* November 19, 1997, G1.

p. 191 "is the one street . . .": *NYTM,* April 2, 1984, 31.

p. 191 "I would like . . .": Joseph W. Sorra, *Corporate Power in the United States* (Portland, OR, 1998), 115.

p. 191 "mall sensibility . . . .": *NYT,* October 2, 1996, A23.

p. 191 "There is a tendency . . .": *Smithsonian,* February 1998, 34.

p. 192 Fast food was . . . : Eric Schlosser, *Fast Food Nation* (Boston, MA, 2012), 3, 4.

p. 192 Dieting was . . . : "Diet Wars," PBS, April 8, 2004.

p. 192 Health club memberships . . . : *Businesswire,* September 8, 2000.

p. 192 By 1990, the typical . . . : Katherine Presnell and Eric Stice, *The Body Project* (Oxford, UK, 2007), 125.

p. 192 "Now boys can . . .": *NYTM,* August 22, 1999, 6.

p. 193 Three-quarters of . . . : Schlosser, *Fast Food Nation,* 4.

p. 194 "anti-tobacco . . . Yes, but . . .": *NYT,* April 15, 1994, A1.

p. 194 "safe haven for . . . most corrupt . . . Tobacco kills . . . Nobody had. . . .": PBS Frontline, "Inside the Tobacco Deal: Interviews Michael Moore" (1998).

p. 195 "Smoking ain't going . . .": *WasPo,* June 22, 1997, A1.

p. 195 "the most productive . . .": Michael Waldman and Terry Edmonds to BC, "Major Speeches . . . ," August 21, 1997, Michael Waldman, Speechwriter, PR, BC Lib.

p. 196 "The percentage . . .": "A History of the White House Domestic Policy Council,"

Box 16, Folder 2, "Domestic Policy Council [1]," Clinton Administration History Project, BC Lib.

p. 197 "media's limited . . ." BC Mem, 744.

p. 197 "taking real . . .": Don Baer to Erskine Bowles et al., March 2, 1997, Don Baer, PR, BC Lib.

p. 197 "President has . . . .": Don Baer et al. to Harold Ickes and Evelyn Lieberman, "Memorandum for Leon E. Panetta," October 30, 1996, Don Baer, PR, BC Lib.

p. 198 "No day . . .": Howard Kurtz, *Spin Cycle* (New York, 1998), xiii.

p. 198 "antidiscrimination" . . . : Christopher Edley Jr., *Not All Black and White* (New York, 1996), 37.

p. 198 Faith in a . . . : Sylvia Mathews and Maria Echaveste to BC, "Reconciliation Outreach Efforts," May 21, 1997, Box 11, Folder 2, "NLWJC—Kagan Emails Received [05/22/1997]," Elena Kagan, BC Lib.

p. 199 In drafting . . . : Bruce Reed to Michael Waldman, "Comments on the Latest Draft," June 13, 1997, Box 125, Bruce Reed Subject File Series, BC Lib.

p. 200 "suffocating in its . . .": Michael Waldman, *POTUS Speaks* (New York, 2000), 172.

p. 200 "the least racist . . .": *Las Vegas Review-Journal,* June 30, 1997, 7b.

p. 200 "diversity in age . . .": *Today @Colorado State,* February 22, 2010.

p. 200 "valuing differences. . . .": Caleb Rosado, "What Do We Mean by 'Managing Diversity?'" in Sumati Reddy, ed., *Workforce Diversity,* Vol 3: *Concepts and Cases* (1997, 2006), 6, 2, 11, rosado.net/pdf/Managing_Diversity_3.pdf

p. 200 "employee population . . . .": "Diversity as an Engine of Innovation," January 1, 2011, updated, Deloitte University Press, demographics245.rssing.com/browser.php?indx =14167085&last=1&item=4

p. 201 "This historic investment . . .": *LAT,* August 3, 1997, 26.

p. 201 "cosmopolitan nationalism . . . .": Anthony Giddens. *The Third Way* (Cambridge, UK, 2013), 95.

p. 202 "Yes to the market . . .": *Independent,* November 21, 1999, 23.

p. 202 "elitist . . . .: Ralf Dahrendorf, "The Third Way and Liberty: An Authoritarian Streak in Europe's New Center," *Foreign Affairs*, 78 (5):13–17.

p. 202 "appeared no . . . .": Sidney Blumenthal, *The Clinton Wars* (New York, 2003), 299.

p. 202 In April . . . : *Baltimore Sun,* April 3, 1997, A1.

p. 202 One hundred and three . . . One discovered . . . : "Investigation on Illegal or Improper Activities in Connection with the 1996 Federal Election Campaigns: Final Report," Executive Summary, United States Senate, 105th Congress, 2d Session (Washington, D.C., 1998).

p. 203 "During his first . . .": *Hartford Courant,* February 27, 1997, A18.

p. 203 Two-thirds . . . : *WSJ,* February 28, 1997, 14.

p. 203 Clinton's approval . . . : *Time,* March 10, 1997.

p. 203 "True, I had . . .": *WasPo,* October 9, 1997.

p. 203 The Democratic National . . . : "Investigation on Illegal or Improper Activities in Connection with the 1996 Federal Election Campaigns," Executive Summary.

p. 204 "The White House is . . .": *Chicago Tribune,* July 30, 1997, 11.

p. 204 "high-level . . .": *WasPo,* July 9, 1997, A1.

p. 204 an estimated . . . : "Reeducation Through Labor in China," *Human Rights Watch,* June 1998.

p. 204 "horrendous . . .": *Sun Sentinel,* March 30, 1993, 1A.

p. 205 "We are facing . . . lip synching . . .": Rahm Emanuel et al. to BC, "Options List for Campaign Finance Reform," February 19, 1997, Don Baer, Communications Office, PR, BC Lib.

p. 205 "a credible . . .": Lanny J. Davis, *Truth to Tell* (New York, 1999), 165.

p. 205 "Every day . . .": *NYT,* March 4, 1997, A18.

p. 205 "with one hand . . .": *LAT,* June 23, 1998, 7.

p. 206 "class bias . . .": *St. Petersburg Times,* December 15, 1996, 1D.

p. 206 "Drag a . . . magnet for . . . the Constitution . . .": *Nwswk,* January 13, 1997, 26.

p. 206 "pattern of . . .": *Nwswk,* August 11, 1997, 30.

p. 206 "put her . . .": *WasPo,* June 5, 1997, A1.

p. 206 "felt ambivalent . . . .": Michael Isikoff, *Uncovering Clinton* (New York, 1999), 167, 168.

p. 207 55 percent approval . . . : *USA Today,* December 29, 1997, 5A.

p. 207 "He had learned . . .": Philip Roth, *American Pastoral* (Boston, MA, 1997), 81.

p. 207 "Marian and I . . . .": Don DeLillo, *Underworld* (New York, 1997), 121, 120.

p. 208 "This country is . . .": Roth, *American Pastoral,* 276, 277.

p. 208 "the stoicism . . .": *Pittsburgh Post-Gazette,* April 4, 2012, C1.

p. 208 "a potent reminder . . .": *NYT,* November 4, 1997, E2.

p. 209 "would be difficult . . .": *Scholastic,* February 3, 2000.

p. 210 "is for Muggles . . ." *Time* (Canadian edition), September 20, 1999, 46.

p. 210 "Our new . . . Books and . . . If there is . . .": J. K. Rowling, *Harry Potter and the Sorcerer's Stone* (New York, 1999), 136, 287, 299.

p. 210 "narrowing and . . .": Charles Taylor, *The Ethics of Authenticity* (Cambridge, MA, 1991), 6.

p. 211 "in the next . . .": BC Mem, 735.

p. 211 "1998 will . . .": *NYT,* January 1, 1998, A20.

p. 211 "I think it's . . .": Davis, *Truth to Tell,* 12.

p. 211 "life is uncertain . . ." *Pittsburgh Post-Gazette,* April 4, 2012, C1.

p. 211 "humans do have . . ." Rowling, *Harry Potter and the Sorcerer's Stone,* 297.

9. 1998

p. 212 "They always . . .": *Rolling Stone,* February 20, 1992, 22.

p. 213 "most like to live in": *NYT,* August 4, 1991, A29.

p. 213 "What generation . . .": *BosG,* August 16, 1992, B25.

p. 213 "Appearance is . . . .": *WasPo,* September 23, 1998, D1.

p. 213 "Seem a . . . :": *Vanity Fair,* October 1998, 163, insert between 59–60, 209.

p. 214 "the representative . . .": *Guardian,* July 25, 1998, 1.

p. 214 "as an urban . . .": *Vanity Fair,* October 1998, 154.

p. 214 "New Establishment . . . .: Ibid.,* 176, 206, 214.

p. 214 "New Economy . . .": Martin N. Baily, "Comments," in Jeffrey A. Frankel and Peter R. Orszag, eds., *American Economic Policy in the 1990s* (Cambridge, 2002), 415. See also Joseph Stiglitz, *The Roaring Nineties* (New York, 2003), 4.

p. 215 donated $2,307,446 . . . : *Vanity Fair,* October 1998, 214.

p. 215 "super polluter . . . .": *Vanity Fair,* August 1998.

p. 215 "Why does anybody . . .": *PInq,* July 31, 1998, A1.

p. 215 Since 1987 . . . happy Americans . . . : John de Graaf, "The Overspent American," *Amicus Journal* 21 (1999): 41–43.

p. 215 "1. The bloated . . .": PBS, September 15, 1997.

p. 215 number of cell . . . : *Orlando Sentinel,* June 4, 1999, E5.

p. 216 "is Beverly Hills . . . is completely . . . I don't believe . . .": *WasPo,* September 23, 1998, D1.

p. 217 Excel spreadsheet . . . : Jeffrey Toobin, *A Vast Conspiracy* (New York, 1999), 112.

p. 218 "shut my body . . .": John F. Harris, *The Survivor* (New York, 2005), 307.

p. 218 "parallel lives . . . .": BC Mem, 811, 773, 775.

p. 218 "phenomenal, loving . . . .": Interview with Steve Rabinowitz, February 4, 2015, Washington, D.C.

p. 218 "Ken Starr? . . .": Interview with Ann Lewis, March 2, 2014, Washington, D.C.

p. 218 "condition, episode . . . .": Stanley Cohen, *Folk Devils and Moral Panics* (London, UK, 1972), 1, 2, xiiv, xxxiv, xliv.

p. 219 "haters . . .": Mickey Kantor OH 2002, MilC.

p. 219 "culture of humiliation . . . .": *Vanity Fair,* June 2014.

p. 220 "echo chamber . . . .": Frank Greer OH 2005, MilC.

p. 220 "we're most . . . .": *Washington Monthly,* December 1998, 13.

p. 220 "Walter Cronkite. . . .": Interview with Lesley Stahl, November 7, 2014, New York, NY.

p. 221 "There are times . . .": *WSJ,* April 1, 1999, A20.

p. 221 "*Newsweek* . . . : *Nwswk,* February 2, 1998, 30.

p. 221 "I knew he . . .": *NYT,* January 27, 1998, L19.

p. 221 network ratings . . . : Marvin Kalb, "The Rise of the 'New News': A Case Study of Two Root Causes of the Modern Scandal Coverage," Discussion Paper D-34, Joan Shorenstein Center, Harvard University (Cambridge, MA, 1998), 23.

p. 222 "If all that . . .": *Buffalo News,* September 12, 1998, C3.

p. 222 "You can't tell them . . . Well . . .": *NYT,* November 21, 1999, L1.

p. 222 "vast right wing . . .": *WasPo,* December 18, 1998, A1.

p. 222 "narcissistic loony toon": Untitled, August 9, 1998, Blair MSS.

p. 222 "My love life . . .": *Vanity Fair,* June 2014.

p. 222 "a generation . . .": Bill Galston to BC, "1998 State of the Union," October 23, 1997, Michael Waldman, Speechwriter, PR, BC Lib.

p. 222 "define what . . .": Al From to BC, "1998 Politics and the State of the Union," January 16, 1998, Michael Waldman, Speechwriter, PR, BC Lib.

p. 222 "having witnessed . . .": Al From to BC, "The State of the Union," January 26, 1998, Michael Waldman, Speechwriter, PR, BC Lib.

p. 223 "surreal . . . .": *USA Today,* January 28, 1998, 3A.

p. 223 "It was game . . .": Steve Gillon, *The Pact* (New York, 2008), 224.

p. 223 "90210 Nation": *St. Louis Post-Dispatch,* February 19, 1998, B6.

p. 223 "To prove . . . .": Michael Isikoff, *Uncovering Clinton* (New York, 1999), 352.

p. 223 "Sexual McCarthyism": Alan M. Dershowitz, *Sexual McCarthyism* (New York, 1998).

p. 223 "central dogma . . . .": *NYTM,* October 11, 1998, 46.

p. 224 "monogamish": *NYTM,* July 3, 2011, 22–27, 46.

p. 224 "self-righteousness is . . .": Reinhold Niebuhr, *TNR,* December 1, 1958, 8.

p. 224 An astounding 84 . . . : *WasPo,* March 22, 1998, C1.

p. 224 "to show . . .": BC Mem, 778.

p. 224 Clinton enjoyed . . . : *Chicago Tribune,* February 1, 1998, 1.

p. 224 "lapdog . . . a potential DNA . . .": *Brill's Content,* November 1998.

p. 225 "was one of the happiest . . . .": BC Mem, 784.

p. 225 "Utter disaster . . .": *Nwswk,* August 31, 1998, 4.

p. 225 "connected in every . . .": Untitled, September 9, 1998, Blair MSS.

p. 225 More than 140 . . . : *Florida Times Union,* December 18, 1998, A13.

p. 225 "Clinton is a cancer . . .": *TNR,* September 14, 1998, 22.

p. 226 "a president's private life . . .": *WasPo,* September 5, 1998, D1.

p. 226 "incontinent carnality": *National Review,* September 14, 1998, 74.

p. 226 "America's oldest . . .": Philip Roth, *The Human Stain* (New York, 2000), 2.

p. 226 20 to 25 percent: See Michael W. Wiederman, "Extramarital Sex: Prevalence and Correlates in a National Survey," *Journal of Sex Research* 34 (1997): 167–174.

p. 228 "America was vulnerable . . .": BC Mem, 798.

p. 228 "were going to . . .": *The 9/11 Commission Report,* National Commission on Terrorist Attacks (New York, 2004), 118.

p. 228 "striking resemblance . . .": *USA Today,* August 21, 1998, 6A.

p. 228 Two-thirds . . . : *Hartford Courant,* August 23, 1998, A1.

p. 228 "The world's . . .": *Las Vegas Review-Journal,* August 23, 1998, 22A.

p. 228 "jungle gym": Hugh Shelton, Ronald Levinson, and Malcolm McConnell, *Without Hesitation* (New York, 2010), 440.

p. 228 "the most-rented . . .": *Voice of America News,* April 20, 2007.

p. 228 "somewhat better . . .": *Deadline Hollywood,* May 4, 2011.

p. 229 "We had opportunities . . .": Fox News Sunday with Chris Wallace, October 1, 2006.

p. 229 "three specific . . . .": *The 9/11 Commission Report,* 12.

p. 229 "I just blew . . .": Donna Shalala OH 2007, MilC.

p. 229 "There's no question . . .": BC Mem, 810.

p. 229 "This is disgusting . . .": Shalala, OH.

p. 230 "I'm proud . . .": *WSJ,* September 11, 1998, A16.

p. 230 "to embarrass . . .": *WasPo,* September 12, 1998, A48.

p. 230 "the most publicized . . .": *San Francisco Chronicle,* December 27, 1998, 25.

p. 230 65 percent . . . including . . . : *NYT,* September 25, 1998, L1.

p. 230 53 percent . . . : George Gallup, *The Gallup Poll* (Wilmington, DE, 2000), 93.

p. 230 "for whatever . . .": Keith Olbermann to BC, Oct. 1998, Monica Lewinsky [Seg. 1], PR, BC Lib.

p. 231 "I prepared . . .": Anonymous source, New York, NY, November 5, 2014.

p. 231 "If you want . . . :" *New Yorker,* March 20, 1998, 13.

p. 231 "Every magazine . . .": Tom Wolfe, *Hooking Up* (New York, 2000), 5.

p. 232 claims that two-thirds . . . : *NYTM,* October 4, 1998, 6, 59:1.

p. 232 Fifty percent . . . : Wolfe, *Hooking Up,* 5.

p. 232 "Nice girls . . .": *NYTM,* October 4, 1998, 6, 59:1.

p. 232 "Guilt is like . . .": *People,* March 16, 1981.

p. 232 "alive from . . . ." : *New York Observer,* September 2, 1998.

p. 232 "Feminists Abandon . . .": *Atlanta Constitution,* August 23, 1998, G5.

p. 232 "Watch for being . . .": *St. Louis Post-Dispatch,* January 28, 1998, A8.

p. 232 "The '80s defined . . .": *WasPo,* February 12, 1999, A24.

p. 233 "single most . . .": *NYT,* December 9, 1998. L29.

p. 233 "terribly hard to . . . What a woman . . .": Untitled, Blair MSS.

p. 233 With one thousand . . . : *Time,* June 27, 1994, 54.

p. 234 "Straight but . . .": *LAT,* October 13, 1998, 1.

p. 234 "God Hates . . . I found it . . .": *Sun Sentinel,* October 25, 1998, 3H.

p. 234 "Every time I mention . . .": "Complete transcript of meeting tapes," January 11, 1999, Michael Waldman, Speechwriter [Seg. 1]," PR, BC Lib.

p. 234 "What would . . . only one . . . .": *Spokesman-Review,* November 6, 1998, B6.

p. 235 "This isn't us . . . the town's . . .": *WSJ,* October 1, 1998, A1.

p. 236 "We've rendered . . .": Untitled, December 27, 28, 1998, Blair MSS.

p. 236 "He mooned . . .": *Nwswk,* December 14, 1998, 32–35.

p. 236 Just as zealous . . . : David Donald, *The Politics of Reconstruction, 1863–1867* (Baton Rogue, LA, 1965).

p. 236 "there's no damage . . .": *NYT,* December 20, 1998, L1.

p. 237 "smells to high . . .": *LAT,* December 18, 1998, 44.

p. 237 "to draw authority . . .": *WasPo,* December 18, 1998, A29.

p. 237 "the vast majority . . .": *NYT,* December 19, 1998, L1.

p. 237 "ugly times . . .": *WasPo,* December 20, 1998, F1.

p. 237 "This town . . .": *WasPo,* January 13, 1999, A22.

p. 237 "You resign . . . I must . . .": *WasPo,* December 20, 1998, A1.

p. 237 "How many . . . turn away . . .": Ibid.

p. 237 "the generation . . .": *Nwswk,* December 28, 1998, 58.

p. 237 "honor and decency . . .": *WasPo,* December 20, 1998, A1.

p. 237 "Hitler's parliament . . .": *WasPo,* December 23, 1998, A23.

p. 238 "impeaching . . . .": *NYT,* December 19, 1998, 1.

p. 238 "one of our . . .": Gore, Baldwin, Kelly in *WasPo,* December 23, 1998, A23.

p. 238 "He would walk . . .": Interview with Jeff Shesol, February 5, 2015, Washington, D.C.

p. 239 "Folks now . . . .": Tom Brokaw, *The Greatest Generation* (New York, 2000), 123, 37, 24.

10. 1999

p. 241 "I can't tell . . .": *CNN.com,* November 18, 1999.

p. 241 "Oprah Winfrey . . .": "Introduction of Oprah Winfrey, 50th Anniversary Gold Medal Recipient," National Book Awards Acceptance Speeches, National Book Foundation.

p. 241 "my first . . .": "Oprah Winfrey, 50th Anniversary Gold Medal Recipient Presented at the 1999 National Book Awards," National Book Awards Acceptance Speeches, National Book Foundation.

p. 242 46 million . . . : Janice Peck, *The Age of Oprah* (Boulder, CO, 2008), 3.

p. 242 "No one . . . Hattie Mae . . .": Trystan T. Cotton and Kimberly Springer, *Stories of Oprah* (Jackson, MS, 2010), 6, 7.

p. 243 real manufacturing . . . "information-based": Dominic A. Pacyga, *Chicago* (Chicago, IL, 2009), 386.

p. 244 From 1993 . . . : *NYT,* April 20, 1997, L5.

p. 244 the United Center . . . : *Chicago Tribune,* December 30, 1999, 4.

p. 244 Critics noted . . . : *Chicago Tribune,* December 27, 1999, 1.

p. 244 "How many . . .": *LAT,* January 24, 1999, 4.

p. 244 "To Love . . .": *People,* January 12, 2009, 49.

p. 245 "Feelings of . . .": Robert Wright, *The Moral Animal* (New York, 1994), 86.

p. 245 "conflict between . . .": Robert M. Brown, eds., *Reinhold Niebuhr* (New Haven, CT, 1986), 66–67.

p. 245 "Do I want . . .": *Milwaukee Journal Sentinel,* September 14, 1998, 4.

p. 245 "Nation of . . .": *Tampa Tribune,* March 21, 1998, 19.

p. 245 "a mammoth . . .": Philip Roth, *The Human Stain* (New York, 2000), 3.

p. 245 "The biggest . . .": *WasPo,* June 29, 1992, A1.

p. 246 "grace notes . . .": Lowell Weiss to Mara Silver, October 26, 2000, Clinton Presidential Records, Email, WHO ([Lewinsky]), Folder [09/06/2000–01/18/2001], OA/Box Number 500000.

p. 246 "sins . . .": *ABC News,* June 6, 2003.

p. 246 A president undergoing . . . : *NYT,* September 17, 1998, 27.

p. 246 The Clintons joined . . . : *Time,* February 27, 1995, 48.

p. 246 "incarnations . . . you can always . . .": Zygmunt Bauman, *Liquid Love* (Cambridge, UK, 2003), viii, 65.

p. 246 $69 billion industry . . . 80 percent . . . $11 billion . . . : Eva S. Moskowitz, *In Therapy We Trust* (Baltimore, MD, 2001), 5, 6. See also Frank Furedi, *Therapy Culture* (New York, 2004), 9.

p. 247 29 percent . . . : *Time,* February 27, 1995, 48.

p. 247 40,000 psychiatrists . . . : Moskowitz, *In Therapy We Trust,* 6.

p. 247 "Hey, everybody . . .": *NYT,* September 17, 1998, A27.

p. 248 "the root . . .": Furedi, *Therapy Culture,* 153.

p. 248 "I don't know . . .": *Orange County Register,* October 16, 2000, E1.

p. 248 "lying about sex . . .": *WasPo,* January 16, 1999.

p. 248 "impeachable . . .": *NYT,* January 20, 1999, A26.

p. 249 schemed to spread : see Sidney Blumenthal to Dacor@aol.com 1998 in WHO (Lewinsky))A/Box Number 500,000, July 6, BC Lib.

p. 249 "opponents . . .": Sidney Blumenthal to BC et al., "The State of the Union 1999," December 29, 1998, Michael Waldman, Speechwriter, PR, BC Lib.

p. 249 "the President's values . . .": *American Politics Journal,* January 1999.

p. 249 "skills . . . Please keep . . .": Megan C. Moloney to Robert B. Johnson, et al., "Excerpt from Joyner's show today," March 2, 1999, Monica Lewinsky [Seg. 1], PR, BC Lib.

p. 249 "He needs . . .": Robert B. Johnson to Megan C. Moloney et al., "Re: Excerpt from Joyner's show today," March 2, 1999, Monica Lewinsky [Seg. 1], PR, BC Lib.

p. 251 58 percent . . . : *LAT,* March 25, 1999, 17.

p. 251 "Everything here . . .": Anne Edwards to Megan C. Moloney and Jennifer M. Palmieri, "To Meg and Jen," June 6, 1999, Wesley Clark, PR, BC Lib.

p. 251 "If popularity . . .": Sidney Blumenthal, *The Clinton Wars* (New York, 2004), 639.

p. 251 "the luckiest . . .": *Time,* June 14, 1999, 42.

p. 251 "If Clinton . . .": *Chicago Tribune,* June 23, 1999, 1.

p. 252 "1 Bleeding . . .": Dave Cullen, *Columbine* (New York, 2009), 56.

p. 252 "Not since . . .": *BosG,* August 12, 1999, A1.

p. 252 "I'm thinking . . .": Brooks Brown and Rob Merritt, *No Easy Answers* (New York, 2002), 180.

p. 252 "We exist . . .": *Atlanta Journal,* August 26, 1999, A19.

p. 253 "I destroy . . .": *LAT,* April 22, 1999, 15.

p. 253 "dark dungeons . . .": *BosG,* March 14, 2000, A12.

p. 253 "Their compassion . . .": *O, The Oprah Magazine,* November 2009, 161–62, 232–33.

p. 254 "You don't have . . .": *NYT,* September 23, 1999, A1.

p. 254 40 million . . . : *WasPo,* July 22, 1999, E3.

p. 254 More than a third . . . .: "The Rise of the Instant-Message Generation," Pew Research Internet Project, June 20, 2000.

p. 255 "I guess there . . .": *Orlando Sentinel,* June 21, 2001, A1.

p. 255 "this stunning technology . . .": *Chicago Tribune,* May 6, 1999, 4.

p. 255 "In the era . . .": *NYT,* May 2, 1999, AR25.

p. 255 "Markets are . . .": Frederick Levine et al., *The Cluetrain Manifesto* (New York, 2000), xiv, xxix.

p. 256 "make my mom . . . .": Walter Isaacson, *The Innovators* (New York, 2014), 426.

p. 256 The Silicon . . . : *Irish Times,* November 20, 2009, 9.

p. 256 "irrational exuberance": *NYT,* December 7, 1996, A1.

p. 256 $1.61 trillion . . . : *Salt Lake Tribune,* January 1, 1999, E1.

p. 256 Pfizer's . . . : *WSJ* (Europe), February 4, 2000, 1.

p. 256 nearly 20 million . . . America's . . . : *Nwswk,* February 7, 2000, 26.

p. 257 "and people would laugh . . .": Interview with Jeff Shesol, Washington, D.C., February 5, 2015.

p. 257 The richest 200 . . . : *AAS,* June 21, 1999, A3.

p. 257 first corporation . . . : *NYT,* July 17, 1999, A1.

p. 257 "This generation . . . I'm more . . .": *Nwswk,* February 7, 2000, 26.

p. 257 "ace money . . .": *WSJ,* December 16, 1992, C1.

p. 257 handling more . . . : *BosG,* November 8, 1992, 75.

p. 257 "day traders . . .": *NYT,* February 1, 1999, C1.

p. 257 "This was the . . .": Harry Markopolos, *No One Would Listen* (Hoboken, NJ, 2010), 38.

p. 258 "comedy without . . .": *Tulsa World,* August 5, 1998, 5. Interview with Dan Patterson, October 26, 2014, Tel Aviv.

p. 259 "You start . . .": *USA Today,* June 20, 1997, 1A.

p. 259 "If he needs . . .": John Steinbeck, *The Grapes of Wrath* (New York, 2006), 207.

p. 259 "sudden wealth . . . money chair . . .": *NYTM,* October 15, 2000, 42.

p. 259 "bratlash": *New York,* January 31, 2000, 13.

p. 260 browser market share . . . : Haynes Johnson, *The Best of Times* (New York, 2001), 57, 60.

p. 260 "illegal, anticompetitive . . .": *WSJ,* May 19, 1998, A3.

p. 260 "a dominant . . .": *Nwswk,* November 15, 1999, 52.

p. 261 "fair competition . . .": Gene Sperling to BC, "Treasury's Proposed Financial Services Modernization Legislation," March 1997, Financial Services Modernization Act & Community Reinvestment Act, PR, BC Lib.

p. 261 "We seem . . .": *NYT,* October 24, 1999, WK14.

p. 261 "high-risk . . .": *ABCNEWS.go.com,* September 19, 2008.

p. 261 "heavy regulations": *WSJ,* October 2, 2008, A24.

p. 262 "the Administration . . .": Gene Sperling to BC, "Treasury's Proposed Financial Services Modernization Legislation," March 1997, PR, BC Lib.

p. 262 "OUR STREETS . . . .": *LAT,* December 1, 1999, A, 1:4.

p. 263 "This is the first . . .": *NYT,* December 2, 1999, A35.

p. 263 Francis Fukuyama . . . : *WSJ,* December 1, 1999, A26.

p. 263 Thomas Friedman . . . : *NYT,* December 1, 1999, A23.

p. 263 "the politics of radical . . .": *LAT,* December 7, 1999, 9.

p. 264 "Everyone just . . .": *NYT,* December 5, 1999, L26.

p. 265 "a one-world . . .": *Nwswk,* January 18, 1999, 60.

p. 265 One South Korean . . . : *WSJ,* January 3, 2000, A5.

p. 266 "your authentic . . .": *St. Louis Post-Dispatch,* December 19, 1999, F3.

p. 266 an elderly . . . : *Chicago Tribune,* December 23, 1999, 3.

11. 2000

p. 268 "God's . . .": *BosG,* November 14, 1999, M, 1:2.

p. 269 "concentration . . .": *Playboy* quoted in *Atlanta Constitution,* July 16, 1997, A, 6:2.

p. 270 interracial marriages . . . : *Nwswk,* January 1, 2000, 28–30.

p. 270 "bothered . . . Cablinasian": *Detroit News,* August 7, 1997, A14.

p. 270 "In America . . .": *BosG,* February 18, 2001, D8.

p. 270 with annual growth . . . : *Time,* Fall 1993 Special Issue, 82.

p. 270 Eventually, Howard . . . : *Root,* February 28, 2013.

p. 271 "The Hispanization . . .": Samuel P. Huntington, *Who Are We?* (New York, 2004), 247.

p. 271 Two-thirds . . . : *NYT,* April 17, 2000, A14.

p. 271 "independent . . . .": *NYT,* April 1, 2000, A1.

p. 273 Women now constituted . . . : *WasPo,* December 30, 2003, A1.

p. 273 paid 80 cents . . . .: *Atlanta Journal-Constitution,* April 7, 2003, A1.

p. 273 a record $508 million . . . : *WasPo,* March 23, 2000, A1.

p. 274 In the ensuing . . . : Heather D. Boonstra, "Medication Abortion Restrictions Burden Women and Providers—and Threaten U.S. Trend Toward Very Early Abortion," *Guttmacher Policy Review* 16 (2013).

p. 274 three-quarters . . . .: Tom W. Smith, "Public Attitudes Toward Homosexuality," National Opinion Research Center, University of Chicago (2011), 2.

p. 275 Senate Majority Leader . . . "the acceptance . . .": *Time,* October 26, 1998, 32.

p. 275 "The core family . . .": *Time,* May 2, 1994, 57.

p. 276 "free to be . . .": *NYTM,* October 17, 1999, 6, 120:1.

p. 277 40 million . . . : Pew Internet Project, December 29, 2002.

p. 278 In 1996 . . . in 2000 . . . : *NYT*, August 14, 1996, D2. See also *WasPo*, August 24, 2000, E8.

p. 278 online pornography . . . .: *BosG*, June 2, 2000, C1.

p. 278 "download . . .": Ken Auletta, *Googled* (New York, 2009), 43, 31.

p. 279 "cyber/information . . .": Presidential Decision Directive 63, Critical Infrastructure Protection (1998).

p. 279 "Napster happened . . .": Interview with Steve Greenberg, November 7, 2014, New York, NY.

p. 280 "The Fed's interest-rate . . .": Robert Reich, "Comments," in Jeffrey A. Frankel and Peter R. Orszag, eds., *American Economic Policy in the 1990s* (Cambridge, 2002), 743.

p. 280 fourteen high-tech . . . : *San Francisco Chronicle*, September 13, 2000, D1.

p. 282 a third of Americans . . . . : *Time*, June 26, 2000, 9.

p. 282 "real people . . .": *New York Post*, September 11, 2000, 95

p. 283 "Could you remind . . .": Joe Klein, *The Natural* (New York, 2002), 201.

p. 283 "troubled": *LAT*, October 8, 1999, 1.

p. 284 "Al just . . .": John F. Harris, *The Survivor* (New York, 2005), 388.

p. 284 "You would . . .": Mickey Kantor OH 2002, MilC.

p. 284 "Somewhere along . . .": Sidney Blumenthal, *The Clinton Wars* (New York, 2004), 708.

p. 284 "We need . . . .": *NYT*, September 12, 2000, A22. And *Atlanta Constitution*, September 12, 2000, A10.

p. 285 "fluent in . . .": *AAS*, February 7, 1999, H3.

p. 285 Most Americans . . . "iron-clad . . . .": *WSJ*, October 5, 2000, A26.

p. 285 "'affirmative access' . . .": *Seattle Post-Intelligencer*, October 25, 2000, A8.

p. 285 "They're for the powerful . . .": *USA Today*, August 18, 2000, 5A.

p. 286 "This convention . . .": *In These Times*, September 18, 2000, 10.

p. 286 "condescending . . .": *Seattle Post-Intelligencer*, November 2, 2000, B6.

p. 288 "Shut it down . . .": *WSJ*, November 24, 2000, A16.

p. 288 "one-person . . . .": *BosG*, December 10, 2000, H4.

p. 288 "While I strongly . . . .": *BosG*, December 14, 2000, A36.

p. 289 becoming spectators . . . : Robert Putnam, *Bowling Alone* (New York, 2000).

p. 290 "title of . . .": *Time*, January 2, 2001.

p. 290 "I am not . . .": BC Mem, 944.

p. 290 "It fell apart . . .": Frank Greer OH 2005, MilC.

p. 290 "never . . . .": Nancy Soderberg OH 2007, MilC.

p. 290 "was dealing . . .": Frank Greer OH 2005, MilC.

p. 291 "indefensible": *NYT*, January 24, 2001, A18.

p. 291 "the single . . . .": Mickey Kantor OH 2002, MilC.

p. 291 $190,027 . . . : New York *Daily News*, January 25, 2001, 5. See "Problems with the Presidential Gifts System," Seventh Report by the Committee on Government Reform, House of Representatives, 107th Congress, 2d Session, Report 107–768. See also abcnews .go.com/sections/pdf/finalclintongift.pdf

p. 292 In damage-control . . . : *NYT*, February 4, 2001, L29. See also Barbara Olson, *The Final Days* (Washington, D.C., 2001), 1.

p. 292 "mugged . . .": *Nwswk,* April 8, 2002, 42–45.

p. 292 a *New York Times . . .* : *NYT,* February 18, 2001, WK13.

p. 292 "You let . . .": *WasPo,* February 1, 2001, A21.

p. 292 "I love . . .": *National Post,* February 19, 2001, A14.

p. 292 "It's the Clinton . . .": *WasPo,* February 6, 2001, A16.

12. 2001

p. 294 90 percent . . . : Forty-one . . . : Gallup, May 10–14, 2001. See also Arthur C. Brooks, *Who Really Cares* (New York, 2007), 3.

p. 296 "If you think . . .": *LAT,* December 26, 2010, A38.

p. 297 "I nearly . . . And I could . . .": *New York Post,* August 1, 2014, 10.

p. 297 "The nation was . . .": "The 9/11 *Commiss*ion Report: Final Report," National Commission on Terrorist Attacks (New York, 2004), xv.

p. 297 "the forces . . .": BC Mem, 955.

p. 297 "I think they're . . .": *CNN.com,* April 11, 2006.

p. 297 "Let's Roll": *Pittsburgh Post-Gazette,* September 11, 2002, F2.

p. 298 "Jesus, please . . .": Michael Daly, *The Book of Mychal* (New York, 2008), 336.

p. 298 "an example . . ." *BosG,* September 16, 2001. A23.

p. 299 "If you insert . . .": David Gelernter, *Drawing Life* (New York, 1997), 4.

p. 299 "They failed . . .": *LAT,* September 11, 1009, A35.

p. 299 "we're more . . . .": *Chicago Tribune,* September 15, 2001, 12.

p. 299 "that when you . . .": *Christianity Today,* April 1, 2002.

p. 300 "The '90s surely . . .": *BosG,* November 11, 2001, 16.

p. 300 "been distracted . . . .": John Avlon, "Resilient City," in Kenneth T. Jackson, David S. Dunbar, eds., *Empire and City* (New York, 2002), 966, 975.

p. 300 "Our current . . . .": *WasPo,* August 4, 2000, A20.

p. 300 They echoed . . . : *BosG,* January 19, 2001 A23. See also *Chicago Tribune,* December 14, 2000, 1.26.

p. 301 "He gutted . . . .": *Nation,* September/October 2000, 55.

p. 301 "hard problems . . . .": *LAT,* July 2, 1999, 7.

p. 302 "you're responsible . . .": Peter L. Bergen, *The Longest War* (New York, 2011), 47.

p. 302 "What's it going . . .": *American Spectator,* October 2003, 51–53.

p. 303 "example of where . . . .": Kate Darnton, Kayce Freed Jennings, and Lynn Sherr, eds, *A Reporter's Life: Peter Jennings* (Philadelphia, PA, 2007), 128,129.

p. 303 "You did your . . .": *WasPo,* September 25, 2006, C1.

p. 304 "If the FDR . . .": Interview with Don Baer, February 4, 2015, Washington, D.C.

p. 306 U-Turn: Jonathan Rauch, "The Real Roots of Midlife Crisis," *Atlantic,* December, 2014.

p. 306 Technology=Culture: . . . *Wired,* October 1996, 42–47.

p. 307 "The Nineties are the Eighties . . ." *NYT,* December 31, 1997, A15.

p. 307 "rebels in white gloves": Miriam Horn, *Rebels in White Gloves* (New York, 1999).

p. 307 "constructive hypocrisy": *Chicago Tribune,* October 30, 1995, 11.

p. 308 "What is America . . .": *NYT,* July 4, 2000.

p. 309 "brainwashing . . . .": Mitch Albom, *Tuesdays with Morrie* (New York, 1997), 124.

p. 309 "endless . . . .": Tom Wolfe, *A Man in Full* (New York, 1998), 672.

p. 309 "saps the virtues . . .": Alexis de Tocqueville, *Democracy in America Volume 2* (New York, 1840), 104.

p. 309 "Idealism will . . .": Edward Mendelson, ed., *W.H. Auden Collected Poems* (New York, 2007), 393.

p. 309 "The first decade . . .": Tevi Troy, *"Shall We Wake the President?"* (New York, 2015).

p. 310 "Without the . . .": John Updike, *Rabbit at Rest* (New York, 1990), 442, 443, 353.

p. 310 "Collective man . . .": Reinhold Niebuhr, *Moral Man and Immoral Society* (New York, 1932), 22.

p. 311 "mission . . . .": Mark Zuckerberg interview, *Wired,* May 28, 2010.

p. 311 The tumult: See Michael G. Kammen, *People of Paradox* (New York, 1980), 298.

Index